D1565684

Henry Miller:
Years of Trial & Triumph,
1962-1964

THE CORRESPONDENCE OF HENRY MILLER AND ELMER GERTZ
EDITED BY ELMER GERTZ AND FELICE FLANERY LEWIS

Southern Illinois University Press
CARBONDALE AND EDWARDSVILLE

Feffer & Simons, Inc.
LONDON AND AMSTERDAM

Copyright © 1978 by Southern Illinois University Press

All rights reserved

Printed in the United States of America

Designed by George Lenox

Library of Congress Cataloging in Publication Data

Miller, Henry, 1891–
    Henry Miller : years of trial and triumph, 1962–1964.

    Includes bibliographical references and index.
    1. Miller, Henry, 1891–   —Correspondence.
2. Gertz, Elmer, 1906–   3. Authors, American—
20th century—Correspondence. 4. Lawyers—United
States—Correspondence. 5. Censorship—United States.
6. Miller, Henry, 1891–   Tropic of Cancer.
I. Gertz, Elmer, 1906–   joint author. II. Lewis,
Felice Flanery.
PS3525.I5454Z552   818'.5'209 [B]   78-3547
ISBN 0-8093-0860-6

Contents

List of Illustrations

(*between pages 102 and 103*)

Introduction

Henry Miller became a septuagenarian on December 26, 1961, just eight days before his correspondence with Elmer Gertz began, but neither age nor intermittent health problems had slowed his pace or dampened his ebullience. His 163 letters, postcards, and telegrams to Gertz between January 1962 and July 1964 reveal him as still hyperactive: writing, painting, travelling—experimenting with artistic mediums new to him—contracting for works in progress, for film and theatrical rights, for the republication of his books throughout the world—attending to family matters—even falling in love; and all of this in a period of crescendoing public pressure, when he found himself suddenly and for the first time widely celebrated, and just as widely castigated, in his native land.

It was of course *Tropic of Cancer* that catapulted Miller into the limelight, the book that had started him on the road to international acclaim when it was published in 1934 by Obelisk Press of Paris in an English-language paperbound edition. And it was one of the sixty or more obscenity cases that sprang up nation-wide, after Grove Press issued the first American edition of *Cancer* in June, 1961, in defiance of a twenty-seven-year Customs ban, that brought Miller and the Chicago attorney Elmer Gertz together. This set of circumstances alone, leading as it did to a record of what was transpiring at each stage of several *Cancer* cases and the involvement of Miller and Gertz in them, justifies publication of their correspondence. In addition, nearly all of Miller's previously published letters are from earlier periods, and the biographical sketches of him that extend to the 1960s barely touch on his pursuits in those years. Moreover, because the exchanges between

Miller and Gertz were so open, unstudied, and discursive, we gain from them a sense of having known, intimately, two men who have played a significant role in the history of our times.

Reading the letters that introduced each to the other, we immediately understand why from the beginning theirs was much more than an author-lawyer relationship and why the bond between them, so quickly established, became a lasting one. Dissimilar as their professional and personal lives had been, Miller and Gertz clearly shared a number of fundamental personality traits. Both were driven from youth by their aspirations to learn and to attain. Both were insatiable, eclectic readers, excited by the worlds that opened to them as they read, yet independent thinkers whose value judgments were based on strongly-held convictions. And despite their preoccupation with demanding careers, both were generous in extending themselves, not only in attention to friends from every walk of life but in offering encouragement and aid to individuals who had no personal claim on them. At the same time, neither was short on ego, a characteristic that undoubtedly accounted in large measure for each man's prodigious fecundity.

Gertz, in spite of being unusually well read and by avocation a literary critic and historian, was unfamiliar with Miller's writing when he was asked to defend *Cancer* in Illinois. This is one of many indications that before the 1960s Miller was seldom regarded as a preeminent author in the Anglo-American world, although in France and other countries he had long since been accorded that status. Needless to say, he was not entirely unappreciated in England and the United States. A select roster of critics and writers had saluted him as outstanding from the earliest years of his career. For example, in 1940 George Orwell, in the title essay of his book *Inside the Whale*, wrote that T. S. Eliot, Herbert Read, Aldous Huxley, John dos Passos, and Ezra Pound were among the admirers of *Cancer*. He added: "From a mere account of the subject-matter of *Tropic of Cancer* most people would probably assume it to be no more than a bit of naughty-naughty left over from the 'twenties. Actually, nearly everyone who read it saw at once that it was nothing of the kind, but a very remarkable book."[1] This essay, which is credited with having been the first of consequence by a major writer to deal with Miller's work, was far from being an unmitigated panegyric. Nevertheless, Orwell said that in his opinion Miller was "the only imaginative prose-writer of the slightest value who has appeared among the English-speaking races for some years past."[2] Edmund Wilson, in one of the few early reviews of *Cancer* in an American journal, said much the same of Miller: "He has written the most interesting book which, as far as my reading goes, has come out of [the left Bank] in many years."[3] However, the supercilious comments about *Cancer* in the November 21, 1938, issue of *Time* magazine were more typical of the way Miller's autobiographical novels would be regarded in America for nearly three decades. "This strange book," *Time* implied, was noteworthy chiefly because Miller "deals primarily with matters which, while not exactly left out of modern books, are usually slurred over, and in his pages four-letter words are as common as the things they stand for." The article conceded that *Cancer* was not "ordinary pornography," but dismissed it as a "mess."

By 1939, Obelisk Press had not only published five editions of *Cancer* but *Aller Retour New York*, two editions of *Black Spring*, *Max and the White Phagocytes* and *Tropic of Capricorn*, as well as two shorter works (*Un Être Étoilique* and *Scenario*); a Czech edition of *Cancer* had appeared in Prague; *What Are You Going to Do About Alf?*, a long letter published in Paris at Miller's expense, had gone into a second edition; *Booster Publications* of Paris had brought out the brochure *Money and How It Gets That Way*; Michael Fraenkel had sponsored the first volume of his and Miller's *Hamlet* correspondence; and Miller's essays were being accepted regularly by avant-garde journals here and abroad. Yet it was only in 1939, when New Directions became the first American firm

---

1.   London: V. Gollancz Ltd., 1940, p. 133.
2.   Ibid., p. 187.
3.   "Twilight of the Expatriates," *New Republic*, March 9, 1938, p. 140.

to publish a Miller book (*The Cosmological Eye*, a potpourri from earlier works), that he began to be noticed to any extent by this country's periodicals. For a while it seemed the tide had turned—nearly every literary magazine and big daily newspaper rushed to offer an opinion about *The Cosmological Eye*, and some reviewed *Hamlet* into the bargain. Miller's next book, *The Wisdom of the Heart*, slipped by with little comment, but his account of the months he had spent in Greece, *The Colossus of Maroussi* (1942), received a good press.

After that, however, the interest of American critics waned, though Miller's reputation was growing steadily in other parts of the world. Only inveterate readers of the *New Republic*, the *Nation*, or the *New Yorker* were apt to have seen a review of *Sunday After the War* (1944). *The Air-Conditioned Nightmare* (1945) and *Remember to Remember* (1947) did not fare a great deal better. Miller's suppressed novels, which by 1945 included the first volume of *Sexus*, were mentioned occasionally in passing, but seldom did the critics bother to take a fresh look at them or attempt a thoughtful retrospective of his work as a whole, although articles about Miller the man and his fabled life at Big Sur appeared every now and then. Incredible as it seems today, the December 24, 1945, issue of *Time* described *The Happy Rock* as a tribute to an author whose books most people had never read; a decade later Kenneth Rexroth was writing of "The Neglected Henry Miller" for the *Nation*;[4] and as late as 1957 John Haverstick, in a *Saturday Review* article,[5] asserted that Miller's name was better known than his works—this in the face of his having published in America during the preceding eight years, in addition to a variety of shorter items, *The Books in My Life* (1952), *Big Sur and the Oranges of Hieronymus Bosch* (1955), *Nights of Love and Laughter* (1955), *A Devil in Paradise* (1956), and *The Time of the Assassins* (1956); and in Paris the second volume of *Sexus* (1949), *Plexus* (1953), and *Quiet*

---

4.   November 5, 1955, pp. 385–87.
5.   "Henry Miller: Man in Quest of Life," Part I, "His Turbulent Career," *Saturday Review*, August 3, 1957, p. 8.

Days in Clichy (1956). Meanwhile, about twenty of Miller's titles, including the novels banned in the United States, had been published abroad in one or more foreign languages: French, Italian, German, Danish, Swedish, Dutch, Czech, Japanese, and Hebrew. "Though most of our own literary reviews wouldn't let you know about it," Walker Winslow said in 1951, "he is one of the American writers who is taken most seriously in Europe."[6]

For more proof that Miller's writing was little known here in the 1940s and 50s, we need only recall how hard pressed he was financially. In 1942, the fourth year in which American firms had published his uncensored books, Miller wrote Lawrence Durrell from Hollywood: "I earn no money. $450 last year, for royalties and magazine articles and everything."[7] Fourteen months later the *New Republic* printed excerpts from an open letter in which Miller asked that his water colors be bought at whatever price a purchaser would offer, adding: "I would also be grateful for old clothes, shirts, socks, etc. I am 5 feet 8 inches tall, weigh 150 pounds, 15½ neck, 38 chest, 32 waist, hat and shoes both size 7 to 7½. Love corduroys." Incidentally, the anonymous *New Republic* staffer who introduced that request knew scarcely more about Miller than the average citizen did: "He is the author of four books, 'Tropic of Cancer,' 'The Cosmological Eye,' 'The Wisdom of the Heart,' and 'The Colossus of Maroussi.' His frankness about sex makes it necessary for one of his books to be published abroad, and has presumably restricted the circulation of other work of his."[8]

When the war ended Miller began receiving royalties from Europe, enough to pay off his very substantial debts and to buy a miniscule house on a Big Sur hillside, a house "almost Japanese in its austerity," he wrote Durrell.[9] Yet as simply as he lived, money

6.   Harold Maine [pseud. Walker Winslow], "Henry Miller: Bigotry's Whipping Boy," Arizona Quarterly, Autumn 1951, p. 198.
7.   George Wickes, ed., Lawrence Durrell and Henry Miller: A Private Correspondence (New York: E. P. Dutton & Co., Inc., 1963), p. 175.
8.   "From The New Republic Mail Bag," New Republic, November 8, 1943, p. 656.
9.   Wickes, Lawrence Durrell and Henry Miller, p. 234.

remained a problem—in 1947: "Always without a sou. And pressed
on all sides"; in 1948, word from James Laughlin of New Directions, who had published six Miller titles, that his books were
hardly selling at all; in 1949: "Financially, things are at their worst
now. I am bartering for the necessities of life."[10] And though his
income improved considerably through the 50s, he was still strapped
in December 1957: "I do want to travel, yes. But it's a great problem. Right now, for example, I am a thousand dollars in debt, and
begging my publisher in New York (New Directions) to advance
me 500 dollars to tide over." In that letter to Durrell, Miller provided a bemusing footnote to literary history. He had asked T. S.
Eliot for a thousand-dollar loan and received "a no, polite, to be
sure."[11]

Part of Miller's difficulty was that in the absence on the open
market of major works like *Cancer*, his reputation as the apotheosis
of the rebellious subculture that came to be known as "Beat" made
better copy than his accomplishments, a circumstance that was
perhaps inevitable in soap-opera-minded America but was abetted
by the suppression of his novels. In 1941, Philip Rahv helped to
establish this approach by placing Miller in the school of writers
who exemplified "The Artist as Desperado."[12] Mildred Edie Brady
dated "The New Cult of Sex and Anarchy," in a 1947 *Harper's*
article, from "the arrival of Henry Miller in the Big Sur sometime
late in 1943."[13]

The raw material of drama was certainly there—in his early
thirties abandoning his first wife and a daughter for June Edith
Smith, a Broadway dance hall hostess whom he married in 1924;
quitting a responsible position with Western Union and leading a
hand-to-mouth existence while he tried to write; in 1928 touring
Europe with June on money provided by one of her admirers; two
years later, with ten dollars in his pocket, returning to France alone;
surviving four penniless "expatriate" bohemian years largely on the

10.   Ibid., pp. 243, 254–55, 259.
11.   Ibid., pp. 321–22.
12.   *New Republic*, April 21, 1941, pp. 557–59.
13.   April 1947, p. 318.

bounty of fellow artists while distilling his Paris experiences into *Tropic of Cancer*; hitting the literary bull's eye with that first published novel and succeeding ones, only to have them outlawed in England and America; with the outbreak of World War II, beginning again in the United States on a shoestring; marrying for the third time, at the age of fifty-three, a young woman in her twenties whom he met on a lecture tour; and nine Big Sur years, two children and numerous books later marrying a fourth young woman (and a fifth, when he was nearing seventy-six). Since Miller himself has never hesitated to draw on this material, we can scarcely blame others for following suit. However the result was that, with journalists tut-tutting about "the philosopher on a binge" and "the gadabout of the avant-garde,"[14] Miller was reduced to being thought of as little more than the progenitor of a sexually-permissive, anti-social cult.

A great deal of the neglect Miller suffered may be explained by the mere fact of his having written books considered too obscene for publication in this country, which caused some critics to dismiss him, a priori, as a sensation-monger undeserving of serious notice; this, and his polemics, his hyperbole, his criticism of things American, his anarchistic philosophy, his eccentric style. More damaging in the long run, however, were the procrustean efforts of those who did undertake an objective analysis of his work to fit it into a literary tradition, such as the Lawrence school of anti-intellectualism, which resulted in certain aspects of his writing being overemphasized while others were slighted.

If critics were unable to see the forest for the trees, or seeing the forest did not quite grasp its essence, this is excusable on the grounds that Miller was a forest one would never expect to happen across in the ordinary course of events, of American redwoods next to China-grass nettles and Scotch pines and Japanese cherries. But as the literarti began to realize that Miller was undeniably a phenomenon, whether or not one that appealed to their particular tastes, there should have dawned concommitantly an understanding

---

14.   Rahv, "The Artist as Desperado," p. 557.

that he could not be evaluated fairly by a resort to established standards of criticism alone; rather, that an effort was required to judge whether his defiance of longstanding conventions served a legitimate artistic purpose and whether that purpose had been realized. In general, only with respect to Miller's sexual material and forthright language was such an attempt made. Orwell, for instance, in discussing Miller's departure from "the Geneva language of the ordinary novel," in *Cancer*, pointed out why this was defensible: "The truth is that many ordinary people, perhaps an actual majority, do speak and behave in just the way that is recorded here."[15] Yet, like nearly everyone else he complained about the unevenness of Miller's style without considering whether that too was consonant with Miller's purpose.

Along these same lines, only a few critics appear to have searched Miller's works for what Durrell called "a connecting line of development" (and which Durrell speculated would not become clear until the last of Miller's planned series of autobiographical novels had been published).[16] Those who posited a unifying thread usually saw it as being either Miller's search for self-realization and growth through his art, or the documentation of his emergence as an artist. A more inclusive thesis, which is borne out by much that Miller himself has said, is that he decided early on, in his first Paris years, to reveal everything that had made Henry Miller the man he was, without the slightest dissembling. Thackery wrote in an introduction to the first edition of *Pendennis*: "Since the author of *Tom Jones* was buried, no writer of fiction among us has been permitted to depict to his utmost power a MAN. We must drape him, and give him a certain conventional simper. Society will not tolerate the Natural in our Art." If we accept the premise that Miller saw his path to becoming a writer as being the presentation of a MAN, the one he knew best, in toto (though impressionistically rather than realistically), and that this became his overriding resolve, then

15. *Inside the Whale*, pp. 137–38.
16. "Studies in Genius: VIII—Henry Miller," *Horizon* (London), July 1949, p. 50.

many of the criticisms levelled at his work become of questionable
astuteness at the very least. His obsessive exploration of the mi-
nutest details of his life, even to the writing of a volume on the
books he had read, was labeled self-indulgent and egotistical, but
how else could he transmogrify that life, whole, into literature? And
as Miller has pointed out, an egotistical man would scarcely have
presented himself in as unsympathetic a light as he often did. Again,
that his philosophizing was so unstructured as to seem chaotic at
times, and dealt with every speculation that crossed his mind, was
termed a serious flaw; yet if Miller was intent on depicting how his
mind worked, rather than on formulating a systematic ontology,
this criticism too had little relevance. William A. Gordon, for one,
has found that Miller's various philosophic positions are related to,
and consistent with, the Romantic tradition.[17] But whether or not
Miller consciously adopted and succeeded in conveying a single
point of view, to have avoided revealing the reflections that made
him vulnerable to ridicule, as most of us try to do, would have been
to give an incomplete and thus distorted picture of his thought
processes. And why did he seem at times insensitive to stylistics,
to have no critical sense, when in other instances his writing approached blank verse? Perhaps because, having determined that he
would tear down the curtain of artifice between the writer and the
reader, he rejected ingratiating literary conventions when he thought
they would undermine the pristineness of the "truth" he wanted to
depict. This kind of an approach to Miller, while it would not
necessarily have led to his being judged a greater writer, might have
provided a more apt starting point from which to have evaluated
his work.

   Many of us would not agree with Miller's apparent conclusion
that artistic form must be sacrificed on the altar of Truth. One
thinks immediately of Whitman, to whom Miller is most often
compared and whose influence he has acknowledged. Yet in gaining
the control that artistry requires something is usually lost, a modi-

17. *The Mind and Art of Henry Miller* ([Baton Rouge, La.]: Louisiana
     State University Press, [1967]), Introduction, pp. xxiii, xxiv.

cum of unselfconsciousness, or spontaneity, or honesty, or openness. It was what we might call the embodiment of the naked soul that Miller valued above all else, in the writing of others as well as his own. As is evidenced time and again in his letters to Gertz, if he found this quality in a book he was unstinting in his praise, however alien its author's premises were to his own. For example, he wrote Gertz on January 23, 1964: "Last night I went to bed with Marie Corelli's 'Life Everlasting,' written in 1911. When I started the Prologue I knew I had something: it was like taking a draught of crystal clear water. What wisdom she had, what radiance, what supreme faith and courage. Nobody would believe, I suppose, that yours truly could find a writer like Marie Corelli instructive and inspiring. But she is."

It seems reasonable, as Miller has claimed, that this was why he gave free rein to his subconscious, however shocking or disaffecting the material that came to mind. No words could better encapsulate his method than the distinction he drew between writing and "writing about" in his January 19, 1962 letter to Gertz: "To write (punkt!) is another matter. You then become involved—and responsible in a different way. Responsible, perhaps, to God, let us say. You invite defeat, humiliation, rejection, misunderstanding. You speak solely as the 'unique' being you are, not as a member of society. . . . Once seriously engaged, the ego falls away. You are happy—and blessed—just to be an 'instrument.' "

Insights like this into the organizing principles of Miller's life, which are found throughout the correspondence with Gertz, do much to illuminate his work and the qualities that make it unique. Various critics have noted that in certain respects his writing is like that of Petronius, Rabelais, Restif de la Bretonne, Casanova, Blake, Rousseau, Wordsworth, Whitman, Céline, Joyce, Lawrence, and Wolfe, among others. In the progression of his career, and in his fictionalization of highly personal incidents, he resembles another American who was eventually recognized as a master in spite of his style, Theodore Dreiser. Yet indebted as Miller undoubtedly was to many of his predecessors, it is difficult to think of anyone who equals him in having at once revealed so

openly every facet of his sensibility, so much about the character
of his times, with so much moral concern, in so many diverse ways,
and so evocatively.

The "connecting line of development" in the correspondence
selected for this volume is the historic struggle to free *Cancer* of
obscenity charges. That campaign began in 1959, when Barney
Rosset of Grove Press first contacted Miller about an American
edition of the novel. For two years, Miller demurred. Unlike Upton
Sinclair and H. L. Mencken, who in the late 1920s challenged the
Boston censors by courting arrest, Miller was reluctant to expose
himself to notoriety.[18] Also, he thought there was little chance that
the ban against his novels would be lifted, and with good reason.
Only a few years earlier the Director of the American Civil Liberties Union of Northern California had forced a test case by openly
importing copies of *Tropic of Cancer* and *Tropic of Capricorn*,
the result of which was that the two books were declared obscene
in 1950 by the United States District Court, Northern District of
California, and by a Federal Court of Appeals in 1953. However
Rosset, who as an undergraduate at Swarthmore had been intrigued
by Miller's writing, felt that Grove's success in defending publication of *Lady Chatterley's Lover* was proof that the time was ripe
for *Cancer*. Rosset's judgment was vindicated eventually, but the
unprecedented furor that broke out after Grove issued its hard-
cover edition in June of 1961 and followed it with a paperback in
October was much worse than either Miller or Rosset had antici-
pated.

Oddly enough, part of Grove's trouble stemmed from a lifting
of the Customs ban before a pending importation action could be
decided (*Upham v. Dill*). Due to this, and the Post Office's withdrawal from the fray after seizing a few copies of the book, there
was no immediate test in a federal court as there had been in the
case of *Lady Chatterley's Lover*. With a rash of litigation developing in state after state, Rosset encouraged booksellers by letting it

18. E. R. Hutchison, *Tropic of Cancer on Trial* (New York: Grove Press,
     1968), pp. 42–50.

be known that Grove would defend those who were prosecuted, regardless of whether there was a legal obligation to do so. Through Charles Rembar, Grove's chief counsel, Elmer Gertz was selected to handle any difficulties that might arise in Illinois.

In the Fall of 1961, police officials in Chicago and adjacent villages were systematically intimidating paperback dealers who stocked *Cancer* and in some instances arresting clerks. Gertz took action when a suit was filed, on behalf of prospective purchasers but under the auspices of the American Civil Liberties Union, to restrain those officials from interfering with sale of the novel. As he said later in A Handful of Clients, "I thought it would be better if the publisher and author intervened in the proceeding and sought not only a restraining order on the police but a finding that the book was not obscene."[19]

In preparation for the trial, Gertz read everything by and about Miller that he could locate. Noticing a brief reference in Alfred Perlès' *My Friend Henry Miller* to an ancient Yemenite amulet that Miller wore,[20] Gertz asked Edward Schwartz of Minneapolis, founder of the Henry Miller Literary Society, whether he could supply more information about the talisman. On January 3, 1962, Miller initiated the correspondence with Gertz by replying personally to this inquiry. The rest of the *Cancer* story is told, as it unfolded, in the letters of Miller and Gertz.

The correspondence reproduced here is from the Elmer Gertz collection, which is on loan to the Morris Library, Special Collections, Southern Illinois University at Carbondale. In the collection are 259 original Miller letters, postcards, notes, and telegrams to Gertz dating from January 1962 through July 1975; carbon copies of Gertz's responses (293) dating to August 1975; and related miscellaneous items, such as envelopes on which Miller wrote, numerous letters to and from other individuals, a few articles by both men in draft or published form, and clippings. Approximately two-

---

19.   Chicago: Follett Publishing Company, 1965, p. 231.
20.   New York: John Day Company, 1956, p. 213.

thirds of Miller's communications (163) were transmitted during the period covered by this volume, and about half of Gertz's (141). Of these, 265 have been set forth in full. Due to publication limitations, the remaining 39 have been summarized briefly.

More often than not the letters exceed a page in length, and many are several pages long. The correspondence was heaviest during its first three months, when both Miller and Gertz wrote, on the average, a letter every two or three days. Thereafter, except when Miller was abroad, they seldom wrote less than one or two letters a week. Rather than awaiting a reply, both tended to write whenever they had something to convey—occasionally twice in one day. Thus, several communications might intervene between the time a subject was raised and the time it was addressed by the respondent.

Most of the originals of Gertz's letters through the year 1969 are among the papers that Mr. Miller has given to the University of California, Los Angeles.[21] The donated Gertz documents, which include supplementary material forwarded to Miller by Gertz— primarily copies of his letters to persons involved in *Tropic of Cancer* cases, and to various other individuals on Miller's behalf— are filed chronologically in UCLA's University Research Library, Department of Special Collections. Miller's incoming mail since 1969 has merely been deposited at intervals with UCLA, and is unsorted.

In order to keep the text of the communications transcribed as uncluttered as the demands of completeness and clarity would allow, the number of special symbols has been held to a minimum.

---

21.   The UCLA Miller-Gertz collection contains a Gertz original, dated September 17, 1962, for which there is no carbon copy in the Gertz collection at Southern Illinois University. Of the Gertz communications transcribed or referred to in this volume, those dated as follows are missing from the UCLA collection: for 1962—1/5; 2/21 (telegram); 4/6; 5/15; 5/28; 6/8; 7/16; 8/6; 10/12; 10/23; 10/29; 11/7; 11/8; 12/3; 12/19; for 1963—4/10; 7/2; 7/17; 10/9; 10/21; 10/30; 12/2 (the one-page letter of this date); 12/10 (both letters of this date); 12/11; 12/12; 12/23; for 1964—4/24; 5/8.

However, every effort has been made to preserve the essential character of the correspondence without overburdening the non-specialist reader. Punctuation has not been changed even when it is clearly wrong.

Recovered cancelled readings are enclosed in angle brackets. When a word or fragment has been cancelled by writing something else over it, the original reading is enclosed in angle brackets and the new reading follows the closing angle bracket with the customary intervening space: thus "⟨parole⟩ clemency." Unrecovered cancelled readings are indicated by the word "obliterated" in angle brackets.

Editorial insertions are enclosed in square brackets and are italicized: "Edith [*Hamilton*]"; discretionary suppressions, such as private telephone numbers, are indicated likewise: "His home telephone is [*omitted*]."

Obvious errors which the writer failed to correct, such as transpositions, double commas, missing halves of pairs of parentheses or quotation marks, have been silently corrected when there is no doubt about the intended reading, when the error is of an excessively disconcerting or distracting nature, and when the emendation makes no appreciable change in the meaning of the text.

Interlineations and other readings added by the writer after completion of the initial inscription appear in the text unaccompanied by special symbols.

Marginal postscripts of more than a word or two, and holograph postscripts added to a typewritten letter, have been identified by footnotes.

Departures from customary usage, such as superscript letters, have been regularized; thus 18th has been rendered 18th.

Underlinings in the letters have been reprinted by means of normal typographical conventions: letters underlined once have been set in italic type; letters underlined twice in small capitals; and letters underlined three or more times in full capitals.

In order to avoid needless repetition, an inside address has been included only when it varied from that of the preceding letter to the recipient.

The symbols employed at the head of each letter or postcard indicate the following: "TLS"—typed letter, signed; "ALS"—holograph letter, signed; "TL(cc)"—carbon copy of typed letter; "APS"—holograph postcard, signed.

The copy-text for the Gertz correspondence was his collection of carbon copies. However, these were compared with the available originals, and variant readings are described in the footnotes.

Elmer Gertz's letters, unlike Henry Miller's, were typed by a secretary. The secretary's initials have been omitted.

THE EDITORS ARE DEEPLY INDEBTED TO Elliott S. M. Gatner, Director of Libraries, and his colleagues in the Salena Library Learning Center, The Brooklyn Center, Long Island University; to Kenneth W. Duckett, Curator, Special Collections, the Morris Library, Southern Illinois University at Carbondale; to Brooke Whiting, Curator of Rare Books, Department of Special Collections, the University Research Library, University of California, Los Angeles; to Francis O. Mattson, Rare Books Division, New York Public Library; and to the staffs of the Chicago Public Library, the Illinois State Historical Library, and South Illinois University Press. A special note of thanks is due Mrs. Mamie Gertz, who contributed the index for this volume.

Felice Flanery Lewis

Glen Cove, New York
September 3, 1977

Henry Miller: Years of Trial and Triumph, 1962–1964

THE CORRESPONDENCE OF HENRY MILLER AND ELMER GERTZ

1962:

January 3–December 31

January   Gertz represents Miller and Grove Press in *Cancer* trial before Judge Epstein (10th to 31st). Miller works on "Nexus, Vol. II" (unpublished).

February   Miller writes preface to *Stand Still Like the Hummingbird*, and article "Joseph Delteil" for *Aylesford Review*. *Tropic of Cancer* published in Hebrew.

21 February   Judge Epstein declares *Cancer* not obscene.

March   Chicago Police Superintendent files appeal from the Epstein *Cancer* decision.

April–May   Miller in London, Paris, Mallorca (for the Formentor Conference), Berlin.

June   Miller and Gertz meet for the first time, in Minneapolis. Eve McClure and Miller receive final divorce decree.

July   Hoke Norris's " 'Cancer' in Chicago" published in *Evergreen Review*, together with "Statement in Support of Freedom to Read" signed by 200 authors and publishers. *Cancer* cleared by Supreme Judicial Court of Massachusetts.

August   Miller attends Edinburgh International Writers Conference. Miller and Lawrence Durrell make a tape for BBC Radio and, in Paris, recordings for "La Voix de l'Auteur."

September–October   Miller in Denmark and Germany. Grove Press publishes *Tropic of Capricorn*.

November   Miller visits the Gertzes, and appears before Parole Board in Missouri on behalf of Roger Bloom. Illinois Supreme Court hears the *Cancer* appeal. Criminal charges filed against Miller and Grove Press in a Brooklyn *Cancer* case.

December   Miller negotiates *Cancer* film with Joseph Levine.

TLS, 2PP.
661 Las Lomas, Pacific Palisades, California
January 3, 1962

Mr. Elmer Gertz,
120 Lasalle Street,
Chicago, Ill.,

Dear Mr. Gertz,   I have just this instant received Eddie
Schwartz's[1] special delivery letter regarding the Yemenite amulet
I used to wear about my neck but now carry in my pocket because
I am tired of answering the foolish questions people put to me. I
am indeed perplexed. Can't possibly imagine what relevancy this
talisman has to the court proceedings against "Tropic of Cancer."[2]
But I shall do my best to tell you about it. Yes, as described by my
friend Perlès,[3] it is in the shape of a thin, rectangular silver tablet,
and the characters are in Hebrew, archaic style, I believe. The talisman itself is supposedly about 500 years old and came from Yemen.
The text is from a well known prayer which the rabbi recites on
special occasion in the synagogue. I shall give you now my understanding of its meaning, but mine will be somewhat inaccurate, as
I never bothered to write it down. I believe you could get the
exact rendition (in Hebrew, or English) from my good friend
Ephraim Doner, who is a scholar and whose grandfather was a
very famous rabbi in the old country.*

"God bless you and protect you. May the radiance of His
vision illumine your countenance. And may He instruct you in his
ways." Various people have translated it for me, always with slightly
different shades of meaning. Doner could give you accurate information whence it derives, and so forth.

As for the Hebrew characters he inserted on the tile mosaic
of my home at Big Sur (the studio) I no longer remember the
exact significance. But he can tell you.

I could have a photo made of the talisman, if you desire. But
I am unable to go out at present, having been confined to bed for
two weeks with the grippe. That is why I type so poorly. My first
attempt at the machine.

Of course I don't see (yet) what the Lutheran minister[4] hopes
to find—of significance—in these things. There are thousands of

these talismen floating about in Israel and elsewhere. Certainly there is nothing "cabalistic" about the words. Though this brother-in-law[5] who sent it to me has frequently sent me cabalistic documents—two just recently—one of which he said I must put on the east wall only. Which I did.

As for what my friend Perlès wrote about it, that must be taken with a grain of salt. It happens to be true that I received this gift at a very low ebb in my life and that from the moment I received it my "luck," so to speak, turned. I attribute this good fortune more to the spirit in which my friend sent it than to any magic inherent in the words. If I had consulted my horoscope then I might have discovered that it was also written there that the bad period had come to an end. All these things are coincidental and not the cause but the proof rather of what takes place without our knowledge. So I think.

The fact that I am no Jew has nothing to do with it either. In a way, I am more of a Jew than the Jew. My favorite thinker is Erich Gutkind, author of "The Absolute Collective" and "Choose Life: the Biblical call to ⟨obliterated⟩ Revolt."[6] But I have never met another Jew like him. Everything he writes is clear to me, whereas with the exception of Doner, none of my Jewish friends can make anything of Gutkind's work. But then neither do my Christian friends understand anything of the true spirit of Christianity.

I do not regard myself as a mystic. And I am not above being superstitious. I am a truth seeker and at home in all waters. The men I revere include such diverse types as Laotse, Milarepa the Tibetan, Ramakrishna, Vivekananda, Krishnamurti, St. Francis of Assisi, and dear Erich Gutkind, who I trust is still alive[7] but certainly the least known of all who deserve to be known in this day and generation.

Well, I trust this may be of some help to you, my dear Elmer Gertz. Let me take this occasion to pay my humble respect to you. You are one of the unique ones in your profession.

If you wish a photo of the talisman, please wire my friend (also Jewish) Dr. Robert Fink, 18418 Hiawatha, Northridge, California. His home telephone is—[*omitted*]. Ask him to come and get the talisman from me. Be sure you make clear who you are, as some of my friends receive strange messages concerning me and are sometimes skeptical.

*Here is Ephraim Doner's address: Route 1, Box 98, Carmel, California. He has a phone but I don't have the number now. He lives in Carmel *Highlands*—mail says Carmel, simply. If you could get him on the phone I think he could recite this prayer (on the talisman) off hand. If you know Hebrew, let him do it in Hebrew first—it is such a wonderful thing to hear in the original. He is a wonderful man, this Ephraim. You should get to know him some time. Incidentally, there is quite a full length portrait (in words) of him in my book "Big Sur and the Oranges of Hieronymus Bosch."[8]   Sincerely yours, Henry Miller

P.S. I ought to ask—how goes the case for—or against—the Tropic of Cancer? Any hope of success? You know, one way or the other, the book will eventually win out. That too is written in the stars. One has to have infinite patience, especially in dealing with imbeciles, eh what?

---

1.   Edward P. Schwartz, Minneapolis printer and publisher. A founder of the Henry Miller Literary Society, Schwartz served as its President, and published the Society's *Newsletter* (1959–63).

2.   *Tropic of Cancer* was Miller's first published book (Paris: Obelisk Press, 1934, with preface by Anaïs Nin). This and other *Cancer* cases mentioned in the letters stemmed from the first American edition (Grove Press, 1961).

3.   Alfred Perlès, *My Friend Henry Miller*, with a preface by Henry Miller (New York: The John Day Company, 1956), pp. 211, 213. (London: Neville Spearman, 1955).

4.   Prospective witness in *Tropic of Cancer* case. See Gertz letter of 1/4/62.

5.   Bezalel Schatz, Palestinian artist who designed and illustrated *Into the Night Life*, with text from *Black Spring* in Miller's handwriting (Berkeley, Cal.: Privately printed, Henry Miller and Bezalel Schatz, 1947).

6.   Born in Berlin in 1877, Gutkind fled Germany in 1933 and settled in the United States. Miller listed *The Absolute Collective* among the hundred books that had most influenced him (*The Books In My*

Life, [New York]: New Directions, [1952], Appendix 1). For Miller's comments on Gutkind's philosophy see "The Absolute Collective" in his *The Wisdom of the Heart* (Norfolk, Conn.: New Directions, 1941, pp. 78–93).

7.   Gutkind died three years later (1965).
8.   New York: New Directions, 1957, pp. 192–204. Miller met the artist Ephraim Doner in Paris in the early 1930s, but only came to know him well after both settled in California.

TL(CC), 2PP. AIR MAIL   January 4, 1962

Mr. Henry Miller
661 Las Lomas
Pacific Palisades, California
Dear Mr. Miller: I was pleased, almost beyond words, to receive your letter of January 3. (An attorney, like a clergyman, is never really at a loss for words. Albert Einstein once told us that he inherited his brevity from his young son; but my not-too-young son is as verbose as I am.)

Eddie Schwartz asked the question with respect to the talisman in these circumstances. I was interviewing a very interesting young Lutheran minister, who is a great admirer of your writing. I intend to use him as a witness in the case which is to be tried before Judge Samuel B. Epstein of our Superior Court, commencing January 10. This clergyman found certain definite religious aspects to your work, almost in the spirit of what you have said in your book "The World of Sex."[1] I was intrigued by what he had to say and explored the ins and outs of the subject, sometimes dwelling upon the important and sometimes upon the unimportant. At the moment, the talisman with the Hebrew text seemed of great interest and possibly of significance. Having read your letter, I now see it in the proper light. I assure you that the minister's testimony will be on a high and persuasive level.

I once heard Supreme Court Justice Cardozo[2] say that the purpose of the law is to preserve the ancestral smell. Certainly, there is something ritualistic about it, particularly trial work. Still, it is a good way of arriving at the truth on occasion; and I think that we are going to be able to persuade the court to enter a decree in our favor. My feeling is that we are putting more into the evidence than is usual; this for the purpose of ⸺ng an atmosphere in which the judge will find it irresistible to ⸺ in your favor.

Incidentally, Judge Epstein is the son ⸺ Dean of Orthodox rabbis in Chicago³ and the brother ⸺ ⸺ston.⁴ He is far better than most judges. That is one reason ⸺ a great amount of optimism.

Our Chicago situation is rather complicated. There are three prosecutions brought against booksellers, as well as one in a neighboring village.⁵ In addition, we have the suit pending in the Superior Court which is going to trial on January 10, in which we seek what is called a declaratory judgment that the book is not obscene and a restraining order and damages as to various police chiefs for interfering with the sale of the book. Finally, we have a case pending in the United States District Court pursuant to the Federal Civil Rights Act. The significant thing about our situation is that, for the first time, we have taken the initiative. Usually, all that a publisher or author can do is to sit back and await the outcome of prosecutions brought by the police. Through the two proceedings that I have mentioned, we are making the police chiefs understand that book censorship can be dangerous to them. If we should prevail, then it will be extremely unlikely in the future that they will act with such haste and unlawfulness, as in the present situation.

I was much interested to read in one of your books that Frank Harris was the first great writer you ever met. One of the sins of my youth is that I wrote a book about him over thirty years ago.⁶ I wrote it while supposedly taking notes in some of my law school classes. Have you ever seen the book? You might even survive the reading of it.

I hope that the New Year brings you and yours good health, victories over the blue-noses and abundant joy.

Sincerely yours, [*Elmer Gertz*]⁷   ELMER GERTZ

BC: Edw. P. Schwartz
    Sidney Z. Karasik⁸

1. Printed by J[ohn] H[enry] N[ash], For Friends of Henry Miller, [1940].
2. Benjamin N. Cardozo, Associate Justice, United States Supreme Court, 1932–38.
3. Rabbi Ezriel Epstein.
4. Rabbi Louis M. Epstein.
5. Maywood, Illinois.
6. A. I. Tobin and Elmer Gertz, *Frank Harris: A Study in Black and White* (Chicago: Madelaine Mendelsohn, 1931).
7. Inasmuch as all of the original Gertz letters on file at UCLA through July 24, 1964, were signed "Elmer Gertz," with two exceptions, no further editorial insertion of this signature is included. The exceptions are noted in Gertz's letters of 7/10/62 and 3/17/64.
8. Attorney Sidney Z. Karasik was Gertz's associate in the *Cancer* cases mentioned in this letter.

TL(CC), 1P.   January 5, 1962

Dear Mr. Miller: I notice from a brochure loaned to me by Eddie Schwartz that you are selling certain Henry Miller items that I would like to own. For the enclosed remittance, please send them to me, inscribed, if it is not too much trouble:

1) Big Sur and the Oranges of Hieronymus Bosch $ 6.50
2) My Friend, Henry Miller, by Perles   3.75
3) The Smile at the Foot of the Ladder[1]   2.50
4) Brochure explaining Into the Night Life[2] 1.00
5) Of, By and About Henry Miller[3]   2.00
6) Maurizius Forever[4]   1.00
7) Reprint of Appendix from French Edition
   of "Books in My Life"[5]   5.00
                                            _____
                                             $21.75

Warmest regards.   Sincerely yours, ELMER GERTZ

Enc.

---

1. Henry Miller, *The Smile at the Foot of the Ladder* (New York: Duell, Sloan and Pearce, 1948).
2. Henry Miller and Bezalel Schatz, publicity brochure for *Into the Night Life* (Los Angeles: publisher not determined; date probably 1947).

3.   Henry Miller, et al, *Of, By and About Henry Miller* (Yonkers, N.Y.: The Alicat Bookshop, 1947).
4.   Henry Miller, *Maurizius Forever* (San Francisco: The Colt Press, 1946).
5.   Henry Miller, *Les Livres dans ma vie* (Paris: Gallimard, 1955). The extensive list of books read by Miller which was included in this appendix was omitted in English and American editions.

ALS, 2PP.   Jan. 6th 1962

Dear Mr. Gertz—   I am sending you from here these—
   1.) My Friend H.M.
   2.) The Smile
   3.) Night Life Brochure
   4.) Reprint of appendix—Books in My Life
The others will come from Big Sur. It's possible I may not have any more of "Of, By & About."

Funny, but I was about to send you the Appendix from "Books in My Life"—thought it might interest you.

Was delighted to see your text on Frank Harris. He had invited me to come and stay at his place in Nice but I was too shy to take him up on it. How wonderful he looks in that photo! So vigorous. I loved him. He once took a text of mine for the magazine he took over—from McClure, I think. But I can't trace it down. Forget title and every thing.[1]

I think it's wonderful that you can introduce so much "evidence"—usually the judge rules it out, no? I never could picture myself in court answering yes or no, or answering anything to any one's satisfaction. I go to Mallorca end of April to act as member of the jury for the Formentor Prize. Hard put to think of any American writers I can nominate—must be fiction writers. I'm going to fight hard to give it to John Cowper Powys.[2] Remember him?

If you win in this fight you will have accomplished a very big thing—for writers *and* readers. I think the time is ripe—and I have a hunch you are the man to do it.

I often wonder about Leopold or Loeb—what he is doing with himself now that he is free.[3]

Should I ever pass through Chicago I would like to see you and have a good talk with you.

Meanwhile all the best.   Sincerely, Henry Miller

P.S. I feel a bit ashamed to take your check, but I don't want to embarrass you by returning it. If you don't have the "Monographie" by Rowohlt Verlag,[4] let me send you one. It's a documentary book, full of interesting photos. The text is dull—written by the President of the German Pen Club.

P.S. I wonder too if Judge Epstein knows Erich Gutkind's book![5]

---

1. From Miller's letter of 11/18/62, it appears that he was referring here to *Pearson's Magazine*, which Frank Harris edited from 1916 to 1922 and for which he was a contributing editor until April 1925 (Tobin and Gertz, *Frank Harris*, p. 369). In the February 1925 edition of *Pearson's* (page 58), one of Miller's "Mezzotints" was located —"A Bowery Phoenix"—attributed to June E. Mansfield, a pseudonym used by Miller's second wife. The Mezzotints, short prose poems, were sold door to door by June, each printed on a sheet of colored paper bearing the Mansfield name and the Millers' address, 91 Remsen Street, Brooklyn. See Bern Porter's *Henry Miller Miscellanea*, pp. 11–12, for "A Bowery Phoenix." (Porter's version differs in minor but interesting ways from the one in *Pearson's*. He appeared to be unaware that the article had been published, and this plus the nature of the dissimilarities leads to the conclusion that Porter reproduced Miller's original, but edited it. In *Pearson's* we find: Michael Angelo's . . . bon-fire . . . "de luxe" . . . Mishapen . . . bowlegged; in Porter: Michelangelo's . . . bonfire . . . "deluxe" . . . Misshapen . . . bow-legged.)
2. Miller's admiration for Powys dated from his youth, when he had heard the Welsh author lecture in the United States. Later the two corresponded, and Powys defended Miller's works. (See Perlès, *My Friend Henry Miller*, pp. 196, 223–24; William A. Gordon, *Writer and Critic* [Baton Rouge, La.: Louisiana State University Press, 1968], pp. 15–16.) Miller saw Powys, then an octogenarian, in the summer of 1953 at Corwen, Wales (George Wickes, ed., *Lawrence Durrell and Henry Miller: A Private Correspondence* [New York: E. P. Dutton & Co., Inc., 1963], p. 297).
3. The sensational Leopold-Loeb murder case made headlines in 1924.

For an account of Gertz's association with Nathan Leopold, and the plea that finally secured Leopold's release after 34 years of incarceration, see Elmer Gertz, *A Handful of Clients* (Chicago: Follett Publishing Company, 1965), pp 3–192.

4. Reference is apparently to Walter Schmiele, *Henry Miller in Selbstzengnissen und Bildokumenten*, ([Reinbek bei Hamburg]: Rowohlt, [1961]).

5. Written vertically in left margin of first page.

ALS, 2PP. Jan 7th 1962

Dear Mr. Gertz— The books and brochures are coming to you in instalments.

Enclosed is something I wrote in 1953 for the lawyer—Maître Sev, Paris—who defended *Sexus*.[1] I had appeared, with him, before the Juge d'Instruction (for which we have no equivalent here). Then he (Sev) asked me to write something which he could use in the forthcoming trial. But there never was a trial. The case was dropped. I was given a wonderful hearing by that Judge—almost as if I were another Baudelaire, Balzac, Zola.

In any case, a friend of mine recently showed me this script. I had forgotten about it completely. And, so far as I know, it was never published any where, which is rather mysterious, as every thing I write usually finds its way into print.

Now then, this friend had copies made and asked my permission to place it for me in some magazine. (He wants nothing for his services—just thinks it ought to be known.)

Meanwhile it occurred to me that it might be of use to you now, or parts of it. I don't know, but I felt you ought to see it. Naturally, I wouldn't want it to be given to the newspapers or a magazine—not yet anyway. I leave it to your discretion.[2]

In one of the packages you will receive you will find the Rowohlt "Monographie" I mentioned. I feel sure you don't own a copy.

Enough. I am holding that Frank Harris text, unless you wish it back. Must get back to work soon on Nexus—Vol. II.[3]

By the way, I assume you have Plexus and Nexus (Vol. 1.)[4] If not, I'll have my French publisher send you copies—in English.

One of the books I like—and which is almost impossible to find now—is Hamlet (in 2 Vols.—almost 1,000 pages) written with Michael Fraenkel.[5] Do you know it? You would enjoy it, I'm sure.   Sincerely, Henry Miller

---

1.   Sexus (2 vols.; Paris: Obelisk Press, [1949]), the first part of Miller's trilogy The Rosy Crucifixion, was published in two French editions, one expurgated, the other not. References to the Sexus litigation in France may be found in Richard Clement Wood, ed., Collector's Quest: The Correspondence of Henry Miller and J. Rives Childs, 1947–1965 (Charlottesville, Va.: University Press of Virginia, 1968), pp. 80, 81, 82, 87; and in Lawrence Durrell and Henry Miller: A Private Correspondence, p. 280.

2.   The manuscript sent to Gertz was entitled "Morality in Literature." Miller had evidently forgotten that this article had been published as "Obscenity in Literature" in New Directions 16 in Prose and Poetry ([New York]: New Directions [1957], pp. 232–46). Under the latter title it was reprinted in Thomas H. Moore, ed., Henry Miller on Writing ([New York]: New Directions [1964], pp. 189–203).

3.   Volume II of Nexus has not been published (1977).

4.   Plexus (2 vols.; Paris: Obelisk Press, [1953]) and Nexus [Vol. I] (Paris: Obelisk Press, [1960]) are the second and third parts of The Rosy Crucifixion.

5.   Hamlet [Vol. I] (Santurce, Puerto Rico: Carrefour, [1939]), not complete; [Vol. 2] (New York: Carrefour, 1941); [Vol. 1] (New York: Carrefour, 1943), complete.

TL(CC), 2PP., AIR MAIL   January 9, 1962

Dear Mr. Miller: I, too, look forward to a good talk with you. I hope that it will be a sort of victory celebration, but, in any event, some sort of meeting. Our lives have touched at so many points that it will be good to exchange notes.

While these various trials are going on, my style, such as it is, is decidedly impaired. When I hear myself dictating this letter, I feel as if I were reading off a list of items to the Chinese laundry-man around the corner.

Another side of me can be observed, if you care to observe it, in my various writings. Under separate cover, I am sending you a group of articles that I wrote for a little publication that would have interested you. It was called "The Paper" with becoming modesty. Nominally, I was the publisher, but the copy girl, Lois Solomon,[1] really ran it. She is a young woman, in her mid-thirties, who discovered your writings when she was at college and wrote about them. My contribution to "The Paper" covered a good many of the individuals and events in my life and it is possible that some of them will interest you and that others will even be of value. In addition to the issues containing my writings, two will be of particular pleasure to you, I think. One issue is devoted to Kenneth Patchen,[2] and the other deals with a Japanese artist, Setsu. "The Paper," incidentally, has gone to sleep because of lack of funds. One day we hope to revive it. Perhaps, we will salute its rebirth by my writing an article about you, and your writing to tell us how bad the piece is.

Of course, I have written for many other publications, including "The Nation"; "The Progressive"; and "American Mercury."

I am looking forward to the receipt of the books that you refer to in your letter. No, I do not have the monograph to which you refer and I hope that you will send it to me. I would like to have as complete a collection of material about you as possible. That is the reward of working on new legal matters. I find myself adventuring everywhere.

Nobody would ever dream that you could have been too shy to visit with Frank Harris. I was much more brash, I suppose, because we addressed each other by first names when I was scarcely out of high school.

You make amusing observations with respect to the trial. I may be too optimistic in my expectations, about what I will get in evidence, but I shall make heroic efforts. I agree with you that it will be a real achievement to win the pending cases. The opposition knows that, if we succeed, the walls will come tumbling down, so far as the censorship of literary works is concerned.

Have you seen the book on Federal Censorship by Professors Paul and Schwartz?[3] They acknowledge your assistance; and at page 128 there is an extremely interesting footnote which I am going to try to get into our case. The authors asked the heads of the English Departments of the leading universities about you, and the opinion of all was that your works should be studied in courses dealing with contemporary literature.

Of course, I was pleased by your knowledge that I was the attorney in the Leopold case. I somehow assumed that I knew much about you, but that you knew little about me. The Leopold case was one of the most rewarding in which I was ever involved. And each day I am more pleased about it. He is doing extremely well in a special research project in Puerto Rico and is happily married. Nobody would ever have dreamed such things in 1924, or even in 1958, when I obtained his release for him. I hear from him ⟨sometimes⟩ as much as several times a week. I am pressing a suit now against Meyer Levin, Simon & Schuster, and various moving picture outfits, because of the novel "Compulsion,"[4] which was published not only minus Leopold's consent, but over his objection.

I shall get hold of Gutkind's books and see if they are usable in connection with the case.

Now I must get to work, as tomorrow is the great day.

Always yours, ELMER GERTZ

1.   Lois Solomon married the well-known civil liberties lawyer Bernard Weisberg.
2.   Kenneth Patchen, Ohio-born poet who died in 1972, was according to Miller "the living symbol of protest," but rebelled "out of love, not out of hate." (See "Patchen: Man of Anger and Light," in Henry Miller, *Stand Still Like the Hummingbird* ([New York]: New Directions, [1962], pp. 27–37), first published by Max Padell in 1946 together with Patchen's "Letter to God."
3.   James C. N. Paul, and Murray L. Schwartz, *Federal Censorship: Obscenity in the Mail* (New York: Free Press of Glencoe, Inc., 1961).
4.   Meyer Levin, *Compulsion* (New York: Simon and Schuster, 1956).

TL(CC), 1P., AIR MAIL   January 10, 1962

Dear Mr. Miller: What a very moving essay you sent to me—
the one you have entitled "Morality in Literature." I shall bear in
mind your request about not releasing it to the press. I think that,
having absorbed its contents, I am in a better position to conduct
the case. At an appropriate moment, however, I may read a portion
of the statement.

Trial work is an art, rather than a science, and one cannot
always be sure what is best. Very often I decide, by an intuitive
process, what question to ask, what not to ask, what move to make,
what move not to make. You may be sure that everything about
this case grips me. I know of no matter that has received more continuous attention from me, unless it be the Leopold case.

Of course, you may keep my Harris article. I am flattered that
you request it.

No, I do not have "Plexus" and "Nexus"; nor do I have your
"Hamlet." I am grateful that you are offering to send them to me.
I find myself reading your books constantly, not simply for the insight they give me in the conduct of this case, but because they
are worth reading in themselves. I am fortunate that my wife, a
very warm woman whom you would love, shares my interest in
your writings. We have much fun discussing you, the case and,
indeed, everything else.

Do you know that the Philadelphia Bar Association has intervened in your behalf in the legal situation in the City of Brotherly
Love? I wish our Bar group had that much guts.

In a few moments I will be interviewing my first witness, so
back to work.   Always yours, ELMER GERTZ

ALS, 1P.   Jan. 11th 1962

Dear Mr. Gertz—   Good of you to write me these fulsome
letters in the midst of all this activity. I've just written my (2) Paris

publishers to send you Plexus and Nexus, and am scouting about for *Hamlet* too.

You mentioned Kenneth Patchen. I am trying once again to do something for him. Needs help in a big way. He seems to think that if he can get a publisher to bring out (all) his collected work he may then be able to get a grant of aid from some foundation. He has no idea how difficult it is to find such a publisher. Thinks I have the magic touch. I enclose a letter just received from him. He has been in this horrible condition going on 20 years now. I don't quite know where to turn—no one seems the least interested.

This in haste, Henry Miller

ALS, 2PP.   Jan. 14th 1962

Dear Mr. Gertz—   Here is another text of mine, which just appeared in "Elle" (Paris)[1] but in mutilated form and in a weak translation. Again, please do not give any part of it to an editor of a newspaper or magazine. (I am trying to decide where to place it in America.) But I thought it would interest you, because of the subject.

I am slowly going through the issues of "The Paper" you sent me. Can't take all that jazz at one gulp! Liked very much your review of "Le Balcon" (Genet). He's a writer I can't seem to read. I was also much impressed by Wm Packard's article on Patchen in the Dec. 31, 1960 issue.[2]

I am wondering how effective might be an open letter from me—along Packard's lines—to the editors of such mags as "The New Republic," The Nation, The Saturday Review, Esquire, Playboy—and others. And if I dare write them all at once. The few lines I addressed to the New Republic in 1942 or '43, on my own behalf, worked wonders.[3]

But don't bother your head about such matters now. Just put it aside until after the trials. You need all your powers of concentration, I imagine, to win the battle. And I feel certain you will! It's so unusual (in this country, at least) to find a lawyer who is also a literary man. More, *who can write.*

Do let me know the outcome of the trial(s) soon as possible, or even a little word as to which way the wind is blowing.

Sincerely, Henry Miller

1.   Probably "Les Amours, n'est pas l'amour," *Elle*, Dec. 15, 1961. "Love and How It Gets that Way" (mentioned in Gertz, 1/19/62) was published in *Mademoiselle*, January 1964, pp. 49–51, 118, 119.
2.   This edition of *The Paper* is in the Miller-Gertz files at UCLA. Packard's letter to the editor requested assistance for Kenneth Patchen.
3.   "From The New Republic Mail Bag," *New Republic*, Nov. 8, 1943, p. 656; "Another Open Letter," *New Republic*, Dec. 6, 1943, pp. 813–14.

TL(CC), 2PP., AIR MAIL   January 17, 1962

Dear Mr. Miller: Of course, I am working day and night on the case now on trial before Judge Epstein, but it is always a delight to interrupt it to read letters from you and to respond. I am more pleased than I can say by your reactions. I hope that not simply out of politeness, but out of interest, you will read the remaining articles and, if you are so minded, give me your views of them. I am thick-skinned enough to accept any sort of judgment.

Let me sum up the situation in the current trial. We have been offering evidence for five days—not the entire time, but substantial portions of each day. We have virtually completed our case and there is a two-day respite. On Friday the defendants will offer their evidence. I have learned through the grapevine that they are having difficulty in getting experts of any kind, but there is no point in assuming anything. It is my task to anticipate what they will offer and to arrange for evidence to overcome it.

We offered the testimony of Richard Ellmann, who is a well-known professor at Northwestern University and the author of a prize-winning book about James Joyce;[1] Barney Rosset of Grove press; Hoke Norris, the literary editor of the Chicago Sun-Times; and Frank Ball, the regional sales supervisor of McFadden Publications.[2] All of these witnesses were truly wonderful. The more they were cross-examined by the defense, the better they were. In addition, we were able to get into evidence the depositions of the various police chiefs against whose unlawful conduct we have complained. Then we were able to get into evidence a vast number of favorable book reviews, magazine articles, books and other material, showing your distinction as a writer and the high qualities of "Tropic of Cancer."

The one respect at which the Court balked at our testimony was in connection with the material that we have offered to show the community standards on sexual writing. We had a vast amount of so-called literature that is readily sold everywhere here, including the City Hall. We will have to content ourselves with a so-called offer of proof as to this material. That is really quite enough for our purposes.

I decided not to use the Lutheran minister at this time, but to save him for rebuttal, because it was clear that the Court felt that we had offered more than enough evidence and that it was now up to the defense to show what they have. If I could guess at this time, I would say that our rebuttal will consist of the Lutheran minister and a sociologist and, perhaps, some more documentary evidence. I think that the case is likely to be concluded next week. Then all of the attorneys will have to file briefs and the Court will probably take a couple of weeks thereafter to prepare an opinion. I think it may be a favorable one, but one never can tell.

There are so many other matters that I want to discuss with you and, perhaps, by the end of the day I will supplement this letter.

I want to thank you for all of the material that you have sent to me. Do, please, send on whatever you think will interest me. I have one trait at least in common with you. When I get absorbed in a subject I have an insatiable appetite for everything about it and at this time I am absorbed in you.

Sincerely yours, ELMER GERTZ

P.S. To my surprise, I was able to get the parties to agree to the Court's taking judicial notice of the facts with respect to Chicago's cultural position. The enclosed document is unlike anything that I have ever filed in court. I suspect that it may be unique.[3]

1.   Richard Ellman received the National Book Award in 1960 for *James Joyce* (New York: Oxford University Press, 1959).

2.   MacFadden Publications, Inc., distributed Grove's paperback edition of *Cancer*.

3.   This document is in UCLA's Miller-Gertz files.

ALS, 2PP.   Jan. 18th 1962

Dear Elmer Gertz—   I'm mailing you two issues of the Belgian revue Synthèses in which you will find what I think is a marvelous critique of my work by Prof. Antoine Denat, a Professor of French at the University of Queensland, Brisbane, Australia.[1] He came to Big Sur to see me a few years ago—in a taxi, all the way from San Francisco!—and I was out. Never have met him but have had quite some correspondence with him. Anyway, you'll see how refreshing it is to read the way a European looks at literature. We have nothing like it in America.

I wrote to Rosset to ask if he would bring it out in his "Evergreen Review." (I bet he doesn't—too much bother translating.)

It was so good of you to go into all this detail about the trial. Rosset too seemed to think it was going great.

As for "The Paper"—yes, I will leaf through, but it takes time. Every day books, mags, MSS, pour in on me. And my wife (in Big Sur) kills off most of the c/s[2] for me.

Maybe the Lutheran pastor ought to know that among European mystics I venerate these—Meister Eckhart, Jacob Boehme and the anonymous author of "The Little Book of the Perfect Life."

Must stop. Carry on!   Henry Miller

1.   "Henry Miller: Clown baroque, mystique et vainqueur," Part I, October 1961, pp. 32–44; Part II, November 1961, pp. 269–90.

2.   Miller frequently uses c/s for correspondence. Eve McClure, Miller's
      fourth wife whom he married in 1953 and from whom he was sep-
      arated, resided in Big Sur. Their divorce decree became final in June.

TL(CC), 1P., AIR MAIL   January 19, 1962

Dear Mr. Miller: Before going into the next session of the trial,
let me see if I am fully caught up with all of your letters and other
material.

I am distressed about Kenneth Patchen. He certainly merits
aid, but I would think that it is inadvisable for you to write to the
magazines. This ought to await the clearing up of the "Tropic of
Cancer" situation. If you feel very strongly about the matter, I
would suggest your sending me a draft of the kind of letter that you
propose sending out and I will tell you my frank opinion of it.

It is unfortunate that even a free spirit like you must be inhibited during the course of litigation, but that is the rule of the
game and the consequences of doing otherwise can be severe.

I read your very remarkable article, entitled "Love and How it
Gets that Way." It should certainly be published. It cannot appear
in the usual magazines because of its size, and yet it ought not to
be abridged. It seems to me that there are some literary quarterlies
that would be eager to publish it. Does not Karl Shapiro edit such
magazines, and are there not others?

When one reads your "Credo on Sex," it is difficult even for
the conventional person to quarrel with it. It is only when you
express yourself in one of your celebrated autobiographical novels
that the old maids and bigots go on a rampage.

Incidentally, I have gotten a lot of wonderful material on the
effect of erotica from Paul H. Gebhard, executive director of Institute for Sex Research, Inc. I suppose I was able to get this material because I am the attorney for the Indiana University Press.
Later I shall try to tell you more of it. Warmest regards.

                                        Always yours, ELMER GERTZ

ALS, 2PP.   Jan. 19th 1962

Dear Elmer Gertz—   Sitting here over breakfast pondering your request to say something about your writing, as revealed in "The Paper." Read a half-dozen or more in bed last night. (Liked very much the one on Tesla,[1] whom I always venerated and never learned enuf about. Great man, yes!)

That you can express yourself is obvious. The sole question is—do you want to give yourself to it wholly or only in part? The character of your writing would change once you devoted yourself to it completely. Now and then—you know who I mean—we have good writers who are also doctors, lawyers, surgeons (even) and so on. Usually Europeans. Usually their professional pursuits took second place.

As I see it, what you have done is to "write about." *To write* (*punkt!*) is another matter. You then become involved—and *responsible* in a different way. Responsible, perhaps, to God, let us say. You invite defeat, humiliation, rejection, misunderstanding. You speak solely as the "unique" being you are, not as a member of society. Do I make sense? Am I answering as you wish me to? "The Paper" itself, while interesting enough, is of no great consequence. It serves to feed the various egos involved. Once seriously engaged, the ego falls away. You are happy—and blessed—just to be an "instrument."

In my mind a writer or any sort of artist is, in the last analysis, no more important than a ditch-digger or garbage collector. We are all, no matter what our function or capacity, but instruments in the divine orchestra called humanity. Each one, however humble his task, is necessary. If we understood that we would take joy in fulfilling our respective roles. And the role of artist would then be seen to be the greatest privilege, simply because it permitted the "maker" (poet) the greatest freedom, the greatest joy.

Sincerely, Henry Miller

1.   Nikola Tesla, naturalized American electrical inventor born in Croatia, worked briefly with Thomas A. Edison. Among his many accomplish-

ments was the designing of the Niagara Falls, New York, power system. See John Joseph O'Neill, *Prodigal Genius* (New York: I. Washburn, Inc. [1944]); Arthur J. Beckhard, *Electrical Genius Nikola Tesla* (New York: Messner [1959]); Inez Hunt, *Lightning In His Hand* (Denver: Sage Books [1964]).

ALS, 1P.   Jan. 23rd 1962

Dear Elmer Gertz—   Am a little puzzled by what you say about Patchen and the magazines. That is, I'm not clear about what I ought *not* to do during litigation. I refuse radio and TV conferences always—for my own reasons—and avoid newspaper men. But where the Patchen business comes in I don't see. However, I'm still mulling it over in my head. I have a friend, Bill Webb, who sees him now and then, and I am waiting for word from him before doing any thing whatever. Meanwhile I've asked New Directions if they won't reconsider publishing his collected work.

I know Karl Shapiro well and of course he'd be happy to have the "Love" text.[1] But if I can, I prefer a magazine with a larger circulation.

Gebhard came to see me at Big Sur some years ago. They must have an extraordinary collection!

All the best meanwhile.   Henry Miller

1.   "Love and How It Gets that Way" (see H. M. 1/14/62). Karl Shapiro, Pulitzer Prize poet and critic who had been editor of *Poetry*, was at this time editor of *The Prairie Schooner* at the University of Nebraska, though on sabbatical leave for the 1961–62 academic year. His *In Defense of Ignorance* has a chapter on Miller entitled "The Greatest Living Author" (New York: Random House [1960], pp. 313–38), first published in *Two Cities* (Paris, France), Dec. 15, 1959. This essay, revised somewhat, served as an introduction to the 1961 Grove Press edition of *Tropic of Cancer*. In the *Cancer* version of Shapiro's essay, it is interesting to note, a section introduced as follows was omitted: "But I very much doubt whether any Judge Woolsey will ever admit Miller's banned books to legal publication. They are too intelligible. Even an innocuous little book like Allen Ginsberg's *Howl* had to fight its way through the San Francisco courts."—*In Defense of Ignorance*, p. 326.

ALS, 2PP.   Jan. 23rd 1962

Dear Elmer Gertz—   I liked very much your texts on your father and grandfather—*and* on Einstein. But if I had been a member of the Decalogue Society, I would have resigned after the castration of Einstein's most significant words.[1] I have only contempt and disgust for people who do this sort of thing. With Einstein it was like giving him the Judas kiss. Absolutely inexcusable. Sorry to have to say so.

I enclose a clipping about the American Nazi Party.[2] I wonder—what are the Jews of America doing about such things? The lines (obliterated) I underlined are absolutely shocking. (Note that the idiot lumps Zionists (sic) and Communists together.) And our government agencies regard such statements and doings as "ineffectual and unimportant." Evidently they learned nothing from the story of the house painter's rise to power. They do nothing about the John Birch Society either. But they get hot and bothered about landing a man on the moon!

When you're through with this clipping would you please send it to a friend of mine, a young editor whom I admire. Mr. Dieter E. Zimmer—c/o "Die Zeit"—Pressehaus—Hamburg, Germany. Say it comes from me. And if you have any copy of interest on the Cancer trial, send it to him also. My German publisher, Rowohlt, will soon launch a trade edition of the 2 Tropics. With the permission of the authorities, he brought out a limited, numbered edition in a de luxe format. He thinks the time is about ripe there now to risk a public edition. My Italian editor, Feltrinelli of Milan, published both Tropics in one volume, in Italian, but *in France*, not Italy.[3] Soon the Hebrew edition of these two books will be out—in a pocket edition, I believe.*

Enough. Don't let me keep you from your noble task.

Salut! Henry Miller

*I hope from Jerusalem and not Cos or Patmos![4]

1.   As recounted in Gertz's article, Einstein had taped remarks for a 1954 award dinner of The Decalogue Society of Lawyers at which he was to

be honored. The Society chose to omit that portion of Einstein's list of human rights having to do with "the right, or the duty, of the individual to abstain from cooperating in activities which he considers wrong or pernicious."

2. Louis Cassels, "U.S. Nazi Party Chief Reveals Aims," Los Angeles *Herald Examiner*, January 23, 1962.

3. *Tropico de cancro* [e] *Tropico del capricorno*, tr. Luciano Bianciardi (Milan: Feltrinelli, 1962).

4. On envelope in which letter was enclosed, Miller wrote: "Got clipping and letter to Rembar. HM."

ALS, 1P.   Jan. 25th 1962

Dear Elmer Gertz—   Here's a fast one, probably too late and probably "irrelevant" and all that—in the eyes of the judge. Have you ever thought to make reference, when defending the "obscene," to the famous Hindu manuals of love, like the "Kama Sutra" and the "Ananga-Ranga"? or to present photos (enlarged) to the court, showing the erotic (but religious) sculpture from the caves and temples of India?

I was just thumbing through a brochure (with illustrations) the other night—called "Erotic Aspects of Hindu Sculpture" by Lawrence E. Gichner—probably an acquaintance of yours. (You seem to know about everybody of any importance in this world.) It was privately published in 1949—no address given.

Anyway, it's a shot in the dark. Better far than any Lutheran's testimony. *The works*, what!   Henry Miller

TL(CC), 2PP., AIR MAIL   January 26, 1962

Dear Henry Miller: There is so much that you have written to me, about which I want to comment. I am deeply grateful to you for this very wonderful exchange of views. As soon as the case is out of the way, I shall catch up with all of the loose ends.

Now, I simply want to tell you that the trial before Judge Samuel B. Epstein has been completed and that all day Monday,

and perhaps Tuesday, the legal arguments will be heard. I open
and close, and the defendants speak in between. I have been preparing my notes for the argument very carefully, and I hope ⟨they⟩
it will give a good account of myself. Of course, the turn in argument depends a good deal upon the Judge. He may interrupt with
comments and questions. It is very fortunate that we have a judge
who, despite an innate prudery, is an honorable man through and
through, who will decide on what he thinks the law and facts are,
even if it hurts him. This is in marked contrast with some of the
judges elsewhere. In Philadelphia, for example, I understand that
the judge has been expressing his views about the "smut" in the
book, in the course of interrupting witnesses who express other
views; this, despite the fact that the Philadelphia Bar Association
has intervened in your behalf. One does not like to generalize, but
I am afraid that some judges, because of their particular religious
upbringing, are incapable of acting in a judicial manner when books
are involved.

So far as I can gather as of this moment, Judge Epstein believes that the obscenity laws, as interpreted by the Supreme Court,
are directed only against hard-core pornography. The Judge personally is opposed to censorship. At the same time, he thinks that
two or three passages in "Tropic of Cancer" are inexcusable. He
has read the law on the subject matter each night until about mid-
night and says that this case has been of more concern to him than
any during the fifteen years he has been on the bench. He is about
a year older than you, a man of financial means, not a professional
politician, a cultured gentleman, despite his strain of prudery. This
means that we have a better than even chance of winning, but I
would not be absolutely certain until the result is announced.

You will hear from me soon.

Faithfully yours, ELMER GERTZ

APS, 1S.   1/28/62

Dear Elmer Gertz—   I will be in Big Sur from Tuesday night
until following Tuesday most likely. Have read the copies of letters
to Rembar[1] with much interest. Here's wishing you the best of
luck!   Henry Miller

---

1.   Charles Rembar, New York attorney, coordinated efforts to defend
      Tropic of Cancer, in state after state, for Grove Press. See his book
      The End of Obscenity (New York: Random House, 1968) for an
      extended account of *Cancer* litigation.

TL(CC), 3PP., AIR MAIL   January 29, 1962

Dear Henry Miller: Over the week-end, I prepared my notes
and outline for the final arguments before Judge Epstein. Normally, I do not like to be burdened with any writing, as I depend a
good deal on improvisation, but I feel that this is much too important for that.

     In addition, I re-read your recent letters and thought of the
sort of reply I would write to them.

     Then I finished reading one of your books and glanced through
another one.

     Finally, to get my mind completely off of everything, I saw
Audrey Hepburn in "Breakfast at Tiffany's"—a real Hollywood
make-believe, utterly divorced from life, which I enjoyed tremendously.

     I put the two issues of the Belgian review "Syntheses" to good
use. This character, Dr. Zimmerman, who was one of the defense
witnesses, pretended that your work was never translated into
French, that French writers did not comment upon your work and
that your alleged reputation in France and elsewhere was fraudulent. I forced him, on cross-examination, to admit that your works
have been translated into French (including "Tropic of Cancer")
and that leading French writers have commented upon you. Then

I asked him if he knew how to read French, and by that time he was almost afraid to say yes. I then showed him the two issues of the magazine.

I, too, hope that the magazine is translated and published so that I can read it, as well as others.

I deeply appreciate the trouble to which you have put yourself in connection with "The Paper." What you say of it is true. I liked it because it gave me the opportunity to do more writing than I had been able to do for a considerable period of time. Articles of mine have appeared in many magazines and newspapers. At certain periods, I have written as much as the so-called professionals, but have always had to write under very great pressure. A few things of mine have given me pleasure. I will try to send one or two of them to you.

We concluded not to use the Lutheran pastor as a witness. We thought we had better leave well enough alone. Our witnesses have done so well and the defense witnesses so poorly that we wanted to be sure not to break the charm. It would have been intriguing to bring out the various ideas suggested by you, by him and what I had in mind, but it is better to win the case than to gamble on such a situation.

As you can judge from reading this letter, I am picking up yours page by page and that accounts for my jumping back and forth. I hope that you don't mind this.

I have often wondered if I have remained a lawyer, and not become a professional writer, because the path of the lawyer is easier than that of the writer. I don't mean that there is less work in it—nobody works harder than I do. A lawyer, more often than not, can see tangible results and has a degree of acceptance that even an immortal writer sometimes lacks. Even an imbecile can see the meaning of my victories in the Leopold case, the narcotics conspiracy case and, I hope, this case. But it takes a degree of subtlety which many people lack to appreciate the outpourings of a free soul who has nothing to give but his heart and soul and mind.

Of course, as you say, every occupation has its dignity and its glories, but the creative person, whether Michelangelo or Shakespeare, has something that the bricklayer never knows. Even a creator who lives in poverty and goes down in defeat and anguish has a glory that is unfelt by others.

What I meant to say with respect to your proposed Kenneth Patchen letter is that everything that you say nowadays can be used against you in one or other of the pending suits. I want to avoid this. But, of course, it can be carried to silly extremes. Perhaps, in writing to you, I was much too careful in my suggestion. If you want to let me look at what you write on the subject, I shall be glad to tell you how I react to it. It is always possible that, instead of harming you, such a letter could do some good. It might indicate that, even in the midst of your own troubles, you can think of others.

I can think of no magazine of large circulation that is a real possibility for your text on love. Even the university and college quarterlies don't publish articles of that length. Sometimes a freakish thing happens. The Saturday Evening Post or Life will take a work of literature (as, for example, Hemingway's "The Old Man and the Sea") when the subject matter is newsworthy. They may feel that about your article. Why don't you have your agent explore the matter?

I am sending a copy of Dr. Gebhard's letter, as you will find it interesting and useful. I would love to have your comments thereon.

What you say about The Decalogue Society and Einstein is unquestionably true. I squealed loud and long at the time, but did not resign. The fact is that the group has had a useful existence since then and reaches people who would be untouched by other organizations. If you are interested, I will spell this out.

I shall send the clipping to your young German editor, together with some material about the "Tropic of Cancer" trial. What you say about the American Nazi Party and other related matters strikes a response in me, but I am much too afraid of any abridgment of freedom of expression to feel comfortable about taking action against even the John Birch Society or people like them.[1]

When they become a clear and present danger to the peace of the community, we can act. It is always a matter of judgment as to when that time has arrived. I have the strong feeling it has not yet arrived, but people differ as to this. While fighting for your freedom of utterance, I can hardly fight against anyone else's freedom, even if you are creating literature and he is spewing forth venom.

There are so many things that I would like to discuss with you, but I shall have to leave them until after the oral arguments. I must rush to court. I shall be thinking of you while trying to persuade Judge Epstein to do what we think is the right thing.

Warmest regards.   Always yours, ELMER GERTZ

Enc.

---

1.   Gertz later sued the firm of Robert Welch, Inc., for publishing a libelous article about him in *American Opinion*, organ of the John Birch Society. The landmark case was decided in Gertz's favor by the United States Supreme Court in 1974 (*Elmer Gertz v. Robert Welch, Inc.*, 418 U.S. 323).

APS, 1S.   1/30/62

Leaving now for Big Sur. Back in week or ten days. If anything urgent (*or very pleasant*) write me there please.

Good luck! Henry Miller

TL(CC), 1P., AIR MAIL   February 1, 1962

Mr. Henry Miller
Big Sur, California
Dear Henry Miller: Late yesterday, we concluded the final arguments in the case pending before Judge Epstein, and he said that he would prepare a written opinion within two weeks. I think the

chances are good of our prevailing, but one can never tell. I was assured by everyone that my final arguments were excellent. The defense arguments were not particularly persuasive. If there should be an adverse ruling, it will not be because of them, but because the Judge cannot conquer any temperamental antipathy that he may have for sexual explicitness. As I see it, he is struggling now with certain forces within him. He is utterly opposed to censorship, book banning, and the like. At the same time, he has a dislike, I think, for your kind of candor. He seems to feel that there can be obscenity convictions only in the case of hard-core pornography and he does not seem to regard your book in that light. He has been subjected to a lot of pressure both ways, and has been honest enough to tell us about these pressures. My closing note was that one cannot be opposed to censorship in general; one must be opposed to it in specific instances. I stressed to the Judge that he ought to show the courage of Judges Woolsey, Hand and Bryan,[1] and give encouragement to all creative artists by declaring your book non-obscene and restraining police interference with it. I am hopeful that, in the end, he will recognize this. In his opinion, he may condemn portions of the book and regret that he cannot expunge them, but I think that, in the end, he will find with us. If not, there are higher courts.   Always yours, ELMER GERTZ

---

1.   In 1933, Judge John M. Woolsey of the Southern District of New York ruled that James Joyce's *Ulysses* was not obscene. His decision was upheld by Judges Augustus and Learned Hand (cousins) in the Circuit Court of Appeals. Judge Frederick van Pelt Bryan cleared *Lady Chatterley's Lover* in 1959. See Felice Flanery Lewis, *Literature, Obscenity, and Law* (Carbondale, Ill.: Southern Illinois University Press, 1976).

ALS, 1P.   2/1/62
                                                     Big Sur

Dear E. G.   Some odds & ends I found here—thought they might interest you.   H. M.

TL(CC), 1P., AIR MAIL   February 5, 1962

Dear Henry Miller: I received the two volumes of your "Hamlet" with a note that I am to return them to you at Big Sur when I have finished with them. Are you in any particular hurry?

I also received today, from Paris, the first volume of your "Nexus," passed by the United States Customs at Chicago.

I have not received the other books which you mentioned you are having sent to me.

Warmest regards.   Always yours, ELMER GERTZ

TL(CC), 2PP., AIR MAIL   February 5, 1962

Dear Henry Miller: In 1925 or so, when I was a student at the University of Chicago, I studied German by myself—I took no college courses in it—and I thought I knew a little about the language. I memorized the Lorelei (I still know it) and other poems by Heine, Goethe and the other lyric poets. At that time Jakob Wasserman[1] was at the height of his fame and was scheduled to lecture at the University, in German. With great anticipation, I attended. I was much impressed, deeply moved, by the rather short, rather swarthy, stockily built and handsome man, whose voice was so musical and rich. But I understood only about a tenth of what he said. Thereafter, I was discouraged from continuing my German studies, and I have never read any of Wasserman's books.

These things came to my mind as I read your little book, *Maurizius Forever*, these things and recollections of the Nathan Leopold case. It was as if this work of yours was written expressly for me. Maurizius was innocent of the crime for which he was unjustly convicted, but he had a sense of guilt; Leopold was guilty, although in a lesser degree than Loeb, and, strange to say, he had such strength of character during those thirty-four years in prison that it was amazing. During the period when I was trying to get him released, I used to visit him frequently, sometimes more than once a week, and although he wore a prisoner's uniform and we were surrounded by guards and the other indicia of institutional confinement, he talked softly, often in the manner of a philosopher, with aplomb, and never with the bedraggled defeatism of the too long frustrated. It is a story that I ought to tell some day; he wants me to do so.

The story of Leopold; the story of Maurizius; the story of crime and punishment in all ages; life itself in our so-called civilized age, with justice and injustice being interchangeable, and violence the law of life and death—these thoughts and others like them charged through me as I read that stirring outpouring of yours inspired by Wasserman's book. I must read the book that distant day when I have more leisure.

Last night, too, I read your little masterpiece, *The Laugh at the Foot of the Ladder*,[2] so wonderfully illustrated by your own paintings. I was thinking of it as I go through the tremendous mass of material that has piled up on my desk during the weeks of *The Tropic of Cancer* trial. How different from that outpouring is this little book. Do you think that you could sustain such an effort through 300 pages?

I, also, went through the Nicholson doctoral dissertation in which you, Lawrence and Whitman are compared.[3] There are both good and bad things in it. I find that the chief value of such theses is that they provide the fodder for those better able to digest the material.

Finally, I read through the transcript of my legal argument in the case, and, as usual, blushed. Court reporters simply cannot get such things with complete accuracy. I have to file the material with the Court. I called Judge Epstein's clerk for some guidance, and he put the judge himself on the line. Judge Epstein was kindness itself to me. He said that I had done very well and that I had earned a rest. He urged me to get away for a week. I wish that I could.

Remember me to Emil White in Big Sur.[4]

All our best to you.   Always yours, ELMER GERTZ

P.S. Thanks much for sending me those things that you found at Big Sur. Keep looking! Everything about you interests me.

1. Jakob Wassermann, an Austrian novelist, dramatist and essayist, fol-
    lowed *Der Fall Maurizius* (1928), Tr. *The Maurizius Case* (1929),
    with two related volumes (see H. M. 2/18/62, notes). Miller listed
    this *Maurizius* trilogy as among the hundred books that had most
    influenced him.
2. *The Smile at the Foot of the Ladder.*
3. Homer K. Nicholson, *O Altitudo: A Comparison of the Writings of
    Walt Whitman, D. H. Lawrence and Henry Miller* (Ph.D. diss.,
    Vanderbilt University, 1957. Reproduced by University Microfilms,
    Inc., 1962). Miller, who has frequently been compared to D. H.
    Lawrence and Walt Whitman, rejects the idea that his philosophy
    resembles Lawrence's: "Don't see much connection between the
    world of H. M. and that of D. H. L., however much I have admired
    his work. When it comes to 'idealism' I differ radically from Lawrence.
    I am closer to Zen in this respect."—Gordon, *Writer and Critic*, p. 17.
4. Emil White, a close friend of Miller and of Alfred Perlès, and a resi-
    dent in the Big Sur area, was editor of *Henry Miller: Between Heaven
    and Hell* (Big Sur, Calif.: Big Sur Publications, 1961).

ALS, 2 PP.   Pac Pal—2/8/62

Dear Elmer Gertz—   I got back last night and found several
pieces of mail from you—all very stimulating. I read with great
interest your "Bizarre Fellowship."[1] Once again, if you have more
copies, I wish you would send one to Herr Dieter E. Zimmer, c/o
"Die Zeit"—Pressehaus, Hamburg. There are certain German writers (like Lewissohn)[2] whom the younger generation hardly know at
all. And I doubt very much if they ever heard of Viereck.[3] I knew
the name but never read any of his works—only magazine pieces,
it seems. Leonard's[4] poetry I do, or did know, certainly.

I am more and more amazed by the number of interesting
people you knew. That's something which must show clearly in
your horoscope, as mine shows—*friends*.

Well, I wait to learn the great decision. I can understand how
difficult it must be for Judge Epstein—I sympathize with him. The
man of conscience has to undergo the tortures of hell.

More soon. Flooded with accumulated mail at the moment.

Henry Miller

P.S. The man I intend to nominate for the Formentor Prize this May is John Cowper Powys. His "Autobiography" alone entitles him to it, I believe. (To say nothing of his "A Glastonbury Romance.")[5]

1. Elmer Gertz, "A Bizarre Fellowship," *The Chicago Jewish Forum*, Vol. 3, No. 2, Winter 1944–1945, described the friendship of William Ellery Leonard, George Sylvester Viereck, and Ludwig Lewisohn.
2. Ludwig Lewisohn (1882–1955), American author and critic, born in Berlin.
3. George Sylvester Viereck, American poet whose allegiance to his German heritage in both World Wars eclipsed his early fame as a literary prodigy.
4. William Ellery Leonard, American poet (1876–1944).
5. See H. M. 1/6/62, notes. Postscript on second page (reverse of page one). Also on 2/8/62, Miller sent an unidentified item to Gertz, saying in a covering note: "Forgot to return this to you. Thank you."

TL(CC), 2PP., AIR MAIL   February 12, 1962

Mr. Henry Miller
661 Las Lomas
Pacific Palisades, California

Dear Henry Miller: It is always intriguing to explore the lines of communication between a writer and a reader. I am sure that my representing you in litigation and my being a correspondent of yours establish links between you, your work and myself that are different from those claimed by other readers. There is an extra quality, a mystic quality even, in our communication that may be lacking in the cases of others. But even before this possibly unique relationship was established, I thought of other ties between us. For four months in the summer of 1929 I lived in the Williamsburgh[1] section of Brooklyn, at 292 Bedford Avenue, in the office of Dr. A. I. Tobin, the dentist with whom I wrote the book on Frank Harris that appeared in 1931. Tobin and I, as excessive admirers of Frank Harris, had been in correspondence for some while; then we decided to collaborate on the writing of a book on Harris (the collaboration, but not the book, turned out to be a mistake). I was a law school student in Chicago and without financial means. He suggested that, somehow, I get to New York and when there I would live at his office during the week, having all of my meals with him; then week-ends I would live in his apartment in Brighton Beach, with his pleasant family, spending Sundays at the beach. I got an automobile ride to Detroit, took the overnight boat to Buffalo, where I got a milk train to Hoboken, and took the tubes to New York. My summer with Tobin was a fascinating one, despite the differences which developed when I learned that he could not write and did not know what genuine research was. I wandered up and down the streets of Williamsburgh[1] and all over Manhattan. I saw more of New York than I have seen in all the years since then. Having no money, I had to find values in libraries, museums, public places generally, streets, alleys, people, books, and, above all, my own thoughts. I wrote long letters to my beloved in Chicago, the girl I later married and who was my wife until her tragic death four years ago. Reading *Nexus I* (I have not yet read *Sexus* or *Plexus* because I do not have copies), I had the feeling often of living through your pages.

Then elsewhere, when you write of Emma Goldman[2] and Ben Reitman,[3] you strike other familiar chords. I corresponded with Emma Goldman and I knew Reitman intimately; indeed, I wrote a completely fanciful biographical novel about Ben.[4] That is another story worth telling you one day.

Now I must go to court on another, less interesting matter.

Always yours, ELMER GERTZ

---

1.   Williamsburg.
2.   Miller has said that the Russian-born anarchist lecturer and writer Emma Goldman influenced his life and thinking significantly: "But to get back to that year 1913, in San Diego, where I heard Emma Goldman lecture on the European drama . . . Through her, Emma, I came to read such playwrights as Wedekind, Hauptmann, Schnitzler, Brieux, d'Annunzio, Strindberg, Galsworthy, Pinero, Ibsen, Gorky, Werfel, von Hoffmansthal Sudermann, Yeats, Lady Gregory, Chekov,

Andreyev, Hermann Bahr, Walter Hasenclever, Ernst Toller, Tolstoy and a host of others. (It was her consort, Ben Reitman, who sold me the first book of Neitzsche's that I was to read—*The Anti-Christ*—as well as *The Ego and His Own* by Max Stirner.) Then and there my world was altered."—*The Books In My Life*, p. 306.

    Miller may have heard Emma Goldman lecture in San Pedro rather than in San Diego. In a 1939 letter to Huntington Cairns, Miller said he bought Stirner's book from Goldman "in San Pedro or San Diego." According to Richard Drinnon's *Rebel in Paradise* (Chicago: University of Chicago Press, 1961, p. 136), Goldman did not speak in San Diego in 1913, having been forced by the police to leave before she had an opportunity to lecture.

3.   Ben Reitman was Emma Goldman's companion and manager. Drinnon described him as an "eccentric Chicago physician of uncertain reputation as 'King of the Hobos.' "—Drinnon, p. 122

4.   The unpublished "Ben Reitman's Tale," by Elmer Gertz and Nathaniel Bruce Milton, was announced by the Windy City Press. The announcement, which contains Reitman's reaction to the manuscript, is in UCLA's Miller-Gertz files.

ALS, 2PP.   Feb 15th 1962

Dear Elmer Gertz—   Yours of the 12th with enclosures to hand. *All* very interesting indeed. *Williamsburg*, you say. That's the "14th Ward" I write about in *Black Spring*[1] and elsewhere. Hurrah!

    You say you don't own *Plexus*. Are there any others you lack? Let me know, and I will see that you get copies.

    Have you glanced at *Hamlet* yet? Please don't fail to return it when through reading. (Send to Vincent Birge *or* Eve Miller[2]— Big Sur.)

    It's possible now that I may get it republished thru a small publisher at Harvard.[3] We have to get Mrs. Fraenkel's permission.[4] She owns all the rights—and has held up republication out of spite—hates my guts.

    I've never been able to find out what my rights, as co-author, are. The book has been out of print ten years or more now. Usually an author can have his rights back again—after a certain lapse of time. But as we were *two* it gets more complicated. I can hardly ask to publish my own part as a separate book, what?

The "decision" must soon be ready. My guess is the Judge will rule against, but with some favorable comment.

Reading between the lines I gather that you and Rosset expect to win cases in superior court eventually. But this (favorable) ruling has nothing to do with the Dept. of Justice's approval of the book, has it? What I mean is, a Superior court *could* rule adversely too, no?

This in haste—forgive me.   Henry Miller

P.S. I've just discovered an *excellent* Bibliog. (1961) by Esta Lou Riley—Forsyth College—Fort Hays Kansas State College, Hays, Kansas.[5] Much better as guide and reference than the one put out by "H. M. Lit. Society."[6] (Paul K. Friesner, librarian there, is an ardent fan of mine.)[7]

---

1.   Paris: Obelisk Press, 1936.
2.   Vincent Birge often assisted Miller. For example, while the two were travelling together in Europe in 1961, Birge answered Miller's mail while the latter was preoccupied with his play *Just Wild about Harry: A Melo-Melo in Seven Scenes* ([Norfolk, Conn.]: New Directions, [1963]).
      Miller and his fourth wife, Eve McClure, separated in 1961. These letters reveal that thereafter he only visited Big Sur, where she continued to reside, for brief periods.
3.   Walker-deBerry Publishers, Cambridge, Mass.
4.   Daphne Fraenkel, widow of Michael Fraenkel, co-author of *Hamlet*.
5.   *Henry Miller: An Informal Bibliography, 1924–1960.*
6.   Thomas Hamilton Moore, *Bibliography of Henry Miller* (Minneapolis: Henry Miller Literary Society, [1961]).
7.   Postscript written vertically in left margin of first page.

ALS, 2PP.   Feb. 15th 1962

Dear Elmer Gertz—   I was indeed happy to get that incredible "intravenous deposition."[1] Never dreamed such books were openly on sale. Never dreamed they took such liberties with subject matter. Frankly, I've never read *any* of this literature, even the less offensive ones. Have you? I'd be curious now to read one or two on the list—the worst, preferably. Could you send me copies?

I suppose Rosset has a copy of this "deposition"? He ought to be able to make good use of it in the other cases being tried.

In my letter yesterday[2] I mentioned "superior" courts. I meant "Supreme" court.

There was a newspaper item yesterday in the L.A. Times (which I sent to Rosset) in which a psychiatrist (of L.A. County jails) testified that "Cancer" was a book for *animals and cannibals*, not human beings. I rather like the underlined—would make good sub-title for the book (later on.)

This on the wing again.   All the best! Henry Miller

P.S. Do you have any extra copies, by chance, of this deposition? Would like to send to a few friends. If I wanted to quote from it, whom would I have to get permission from? Would want to quote from the *jackets*, what you have quoted.

Regarding enclosed clipping from N.Y. Times—in those areas where the State has won the fight to keep the book out of circulation, is it not an offense to even "receive a copy through the mails" —in other words, "to be in possession of a copy"? This bookseller must obviously be catering to prospective buyers in the forbidden Zones.[3]

---

1.   Reference is to an intervenor's deposition.
2.   Either this letter or the previous one was evidently misdated, since here Miller corrects his letter of "yesterday," which was also dated February 15.
3.   Postscript commences in left margin of first page, vertically, and continues on second page (reverse of page one).

TL(CC), 3PP., AIR MAIL   February 15, 1962

Dear Henry Miller: I am glad that you have asked me which books of yours I lack. I am going to list now the books as contrasted with the special publications (brochures, etc.). I will greatly appreciate your sending these to me, provided you do not have to spend any of your own money for this purpose. If it is simply a matter of your instructing the publisher to send on the books without charge to you, that is one thing; if there is a charge, that's another thing. Of course, I will be glad to pay any charges.

The list of books, then, which I lack is as follows:

> *Black Spring*
> *Max and the White Phagocites*[1]
> *Tropic of Capricorn*[2]
> *Sexus*
> *Plexus*
> *Quiet Days in Clichy*[3]
> *The Time of the Assassins*[4]

The books will be doubly welcome if you inscribe them.

I have more than glanced at *Hamlet*. I have read many passages in the two volumes; and I hope to read the rest. I find it very stimulating. When the book is reprinted, I certainly want a copy for my library. Meanwhile, I shall return your copy within the next very few days.

In the books it is noted that all rights are reserved for the authors by Carrefour (342 East 19th Street, New York). Was there any formal copyright? Did you enter into a contract of any sort with Carrefour? If you do not know the answers to these questions and would like me to look into the matter, I shall be glad to do so, *without charge*. The work ought to be reprinted and I would regard it as a privilege to help you do so.

I was rather amused to learn that you have just discovered the bibliography by Esta Lou Riley. It is, indeed, an excellent one. I offered it in evidence in the case before Judge Epstein; and I have written to Miss Riley for another copy for my own personal use. The difficulty with much of my Henry Miller library is that I have had to part with copies when I introduced them as exhibits in the case. As soon as the decks are cleared, I shall go over the various bibliographies and take all the steps required for completing my collection. Unlike many other collections, this will be one of well-read books.

At first I felt completely certain in my own mind that the Judge would rule in our favor. I still feel that he will, but the delay gets me a bit edgy. I ran into one of the Judge's closest friends about an hour or so ago—he is the landlord of the building in which I office—and he told me that his gathered impression, after talking with the Judge, was that he is ruling in my favor. Of course, that is only an impression. Let us leave it at this. On the law and the facts, and on the sort of case we presented to the Court, and the poor defense put up by the opposition, we ought to win. Balanced against these facts is the foreboding one, that the leadership of this community is Roman Catholic and we cannot always tell what influences are brought to bear upon judges. I think Judge Epstein is less susceptible to these influences than anyone else, and that he is a superior person, but not necessarily a hero or martyr.

I don't wonder that you, a layman, are puzzled by the conflicting situation in the courts. So far as the Post Office, United States Customs and Federal officials generally, I would say that we are completely safe, but their rulings are not necessarily binding on the various states. This may mean a certain conflict in the rulings, until the matter goes up to the United States Supreme Court. A ruling by that Court that the book is constitutionally protected would mean that no community could suppress it. It is important to know that the United States Supreme Court, in our day, has never declared any work of literature to be obscene.[5] The clear tendency of the United States Supreme Court is to confine obscenity bans to so-called hard-core pornography; that is, out-and-out smut with no redeeming qualities.

Incidentally, have you read the editorial in the February 17 issue of the Saturday Evening Post?[6] I would say that, by and large, it is very helpful to us. I would say, too, that when the legal dust settles you ought to write a little essay on the question propounded by the Post: "After obscenity, what?"

Of course, I am grateful to you for sending me the early draft of your preface to *Stand Still the Hummingbird*.[7] Despite what you point out, the piece is an extremely interesting one and makes me very eager to read the contents of the volume. I am in such a state of mind that I have to be on guard against going overboard with respect to your writing. Perhaps, I ought to forget that and just read and react without worrying whether I am objectively right or wrong in any conclusion I reach. There is too much chewing over of opinions anyway by the literary critics and one ought to read sometimes without regard to the importance, unimportance, or any other fortuitous circumstance.

For two very busy people, we seem to have at least one quality in common—we love correspondence. Louis Adamic once described me as the best correspondent in America. Whether or not that judgment was then a sound one, it gave me great pleasure. Louis is another person about whom I ought to write an essay, as I was one of his very closest friends. He refers to me in his book *Dynamite*.[8] I notice that in your list of books read by you, you include a couple of his volumes.

Enough for today.   Always yours, ELMER GERTZ

---

1.   Paris: Obelisk Press, 1938.
2.   Paris: Obelisk Press, 1939.
3.   Paris: Olympia Press, 1956.
4.   New York: New Directions, 1956.
5.   Gertz used the term *literature* in a limited sense here, as meaning works of recognized value.
6.   "After Obscenity, What?," p. 80. The editorial made the point that "dirt and confusion are not enough," but conceded that "today's frankness has swept away a lot of undesirable hypocrisy and falsehood" and that "almost always censorship creates more problems than it solves."
7.   *Stand Still Like the Hummingbird*. ([New York]: New Directions, 1962).
8.   New York: Viking, 1931.

TL(CC), 1P., AIR MAIL   February 16, 1962

Dear Henry Miller: I forgot to answer one question you pro
pounded to me as to whether you might publish your letters alone.[1]
That question has both a literary and a legal aspect. From a literary
viewpoint, it is probably best that the correspondence be complete,
although there are certain of the letters that could well be published by themselves; for example, Letter No. 17 in Volume 2 is
one of the most moving things you have ever written. From the
legal viewpoint, the question will depend on certain facts which
I have not yet determined. I have written to the Copyright Office
to learn what their records indicate and if I hear further from you
I will be in a better position to advise you.

     I think you will be pleased with the attitude that even many
of the so-called respectables take on the matter of suppressing
"Tropic of Cancer." The enclosed letter from one of the top officials of Bell & Howell Company will delight you as much as it
pleased me.[2]   Always yours, ELMER GERTZ

Enc.

---

1.   A further reference to the Miller-Fraenkel correspondence in *Hamlet*.
2.   This letter was from Charles W. Gray, who said in part: "Incidentally,
      I am watching with great interest the progress you are making on the
      Tropic of Cancer case. I haven't read the book, but I'll be darned if
      I want a policeman telling me I can't."—Miller-Gertz files, UCLA

ALS, 1P.   2/16/62

Dear Elmer Gertz—   Please return the "corrected" copies later.[1]
I give them to my daughter (16) now.[2] She thinks she may write
some day.

     Well, you see that even a "master" (sic) has to sweat it out.
                                        Best! Henry Miller[3]

1.   Draft of preface to *Stand Still Like the Hummingbird.*
2.   Valentin (Val) Lepska Miller, born November 19, 1945.
3.   This note was written on paper with the printed heading:
     from the desk of . . .
     HENRY MILLER
     Big Sur, California
     But Miller often used whatever stationery was at hand, and in this
     instance he was apparently still at the Pacific Palisades address.

TLS, 2PP.   Pac Pal—Feb. 17, 1962

Dear Elmer Gertz,   To answer yours of the 15th . . . I have
to write the publishers for the books you would like—don't keep
any here. ⟨obliterated⟩ Max[1] is out—long out of print. Sexus may
also be difficult to get, either out of print or difficult to mail in.
(Would you mind if it were seized by the Customs? Frankly, that's
one book I never intend to have published here, and I wouldn't
want any stink over it through a rassle with Customs officials.)
Quiet Days in Clichy has been out of print but is supposed to be
reprinted—I will ask to have them send you it when ready. But
here again is a book which the Customs have not passed on, and
they ⟨obliterated⟩ may make a fuss about it. It's pretty strong. Do
you want that? Won't have a chance to inscribe them, until we
meet sometime somewhere. Incidentally, when I leave for Europe
—which may be around middle of March—I will go to Minneapolis to meet the H. M. Lit. Soc. members—never met any. Then to
N.Y. for a very few days. Maybe we can arrange to meet somewhere? Also to the Missouri Penitentiary in Jefferson City to see a
lifer whom I know thru long c/s.

    As for Hamlet. Just had card from the American publishers
saying they have hopes Mrs. F.[2] may come round. She is in process
of moving now. I imagine there was a formal copyright, but am
not positive. Imagine too I made a contract with F., but if so, don't
know where it might be—unless in U.C.L.A. archives.[3] Doubt this.
If you could find out I would be pleased. But if it means writing

to Mrs. F. I'd say don't bother—it might only put her back up. I know definitely that I do not own any publishing rights—I am entitled (presumably) to half of the royalties, that's all. The rumpus occurred when F. insisted on deducting from my royalties half of the loss incurred in publishing the first edition. Loss or expense, not sure which.[4] But it seems to me that, merely as co-author, I have the right to insist that the book be kept in print.

Very interesting to hear that the Supreme Court has never declared any work of "literature" to be obscene. You say, "in our day." Presume there haven't been many cases of this sort put before them.[5] Which reminds me—how do these buggers who are publishing that slimy stuff you wrote me about . . . how do they manage to get by? How is it no one is taking action against them? Baffles me.

As for my writings which I send you occasionally—mostly it was to help you in defending me, to show my other facets, etc. No need to give me critical opinions. I sent the last,[6] with all the corrections, because I thought it would give you a kick.

I never saw Sat. Eve Post thing. Hardly ever look at a magazine. What is there to read, eh?

Yes, we are inveterate letter writers, alas. It's something I would like to kill, but can't. Takes hours of my time each day. And the worst is that I must first answer all the business and fan letters (those worth answering). After that I can write a friend, but he gets the leavings, unfortunately. I began by writing letters, long ones, 20 to 30 pages—about everything under the sun . . . in lieu of writing books. Ours will naturally taper off, but if I give you the silence for a while don't think I have forgotten you. When I travel I don't write much. Nor even think much. How you can find time and energy to write all the letters you do beats me. You are a living dynamo. So, until I hear from you I'll only ask publishers to send you the Rimbaud, (N.D.),[7] Plexus, Black Spring and Capricorn, all free of custom inspection.

When Dutton's bring out the Durrell-Miller correspondence[8] —perhaps late this year—you must read this. It is exciting and extremely revelatory.

I am praying that the Judge will give you the green light. I wouldn't want to be in his shoes.

All the best now. Henry Miller

---

1. *Max and the White Phagocytes.*
2. Mrs. Fraenkel.
3. Lawrence Clark Powell, while chief librarian at the University of California at Los Angeles, established the Miller archives there. In 1931, while he was a graduate student at the University of Dijon, Powell was introduced to Miller, who for a short time taught at the Lycée Carnot. The two men struck up a close friendship in the early 1940s when Miller, then living a mile away from UCLA in Beverly Glen, appeared at the UCLA library asking for a work by Jacob Boehme. He had been referred to Powell by the publisher James Laughlin (New Directions), who reportedly said of Powell, "He's a librarian who reads books." Miller's *The Books in My Life* grew out of Powell's request that Miller write an article for him on the influential role played by books and libraries in Miller's development. See Powell's introduction to *The Intimate Henry Miller* ([New York]: New American Library [1959]), reprinted in Lawrence Clark Powell, *Books In My Baggage* (New York: World Publishing Company [1960]), as "The Miller of Big Sur," pp. 148–53; and Lawrence Clark Powell, "Letters From the Famous and the Faceless," *New York Times Book Review*, May 9, 1965, pp. 5, 34.
4. Fraenkel published the *Hamlet* correspondence under his "Carrefour" imprint.
5. Edmund Wilson's *Memoirs of Hecate County* was the book involved in the first literary obscenity case reviewed by the United States Supreme Court. In 1948 the Court, divided four to four, failed to rule in that case, thus allowing the New York conviction to stand. For Supreme Court decisions in literary cases thereafter, see Lewis, *Literature, Obscenity, and Law.*
6. Preface to *Stand Still Like the Hummingbird.*
7. *The Time of the Assassins: A Study of Rimbaud*, New Directions (1956).
8. Wickes, *Lawrence Durrell and Henry Miller: A Private Correspondence.*

TLS, 1P.   Pac. Pal. Feb. 18, 1962

Dear Elmer Gertz,   With your last letter and enclosures also
came a letter that had gone to Big Sur. Don't worry about Hamlet
—hold it as long as you wish. I see you received Nexus. I must
have asked my Paris publisher to send you books weeks ago; now
I have written again. You might give the duplicate copies to
friends, if you wish. Was very happy to receive "Civil Action NO.
6161784."[1] Never saw it before. And the extra copy of the other
deposition. Thank you.

I notice that there is mention of "Cancer" being copyrighted
(1961); I looked in the book and see it says so. On the other hand,
I was under the impression that none of my books which had been
published in Paris first, and without American copyright, could
possibly be given a copyright on being republished here. Am I
wrong about this? And if I am right, then how could the book be
given copyright by the Grove Press?

In your letter of Feb. 5th, you mention the Nicholson doctoral
dissertation; I don't know of this, but not important to see it.

No, I don't think I could sustain a 300 page story in the manner of the "Smile." Each work gets done once, and in its own way.
When I finish Nexus I may take an entirely new turn—or become
silent.

I was extremely interested in what you wrote me about Wassermann and the Maurizius trilogy. (I do think you should write
the Leopold story some day, and in very simple language. It should
be marvelous.) Do let me urge you to make time, forgive me, to
read the whole of the Maurizius trilogy, or at least, the first two
volumes.[2] Volume two deals with Dr. Kerkhoven and Etzel Ander-
gast. The former is a magnificent character, a saint of a psychiatrist, modeled upon three men whom Wassermann knew intimately, one being Jung and ⟨the other⟩ another a Dutch analyst,
now living in New York, with whom I have had a brief correspondence. You will reap a great harvest from this work, let me
repeat. I have never gotten over the reading of it, and never will.
It's like the last word on love and justice. Wassermann should be

revived; the younger generation would get much from him. His little book called "My Life as a German and a Jew"[3] is also worth glancing at.

I enclose a clipping about my "anti-Semitism."[4] I don't know where the Rabbi's statement appeared or if he had testified thus in court. But you must have heard about it. Well, there are Rabbis and Rabbis. Toward the end of Alexander King's book, "Mine Enemy Grows Older,"[5] he gives a portrait of a wonderful rabbi— the only kind. It's only 3 or 4 pages, near the very end. Have a look some time. Enough now!   Ever yours, Henry Miller

---

1.   Number evidently should have been "61 C 1784," designation of the *Cancer* case filed by Gertz in United States District Court for the Northern District of Illinois, Eastern Division, on behalf of Grove Press and Henry Miller against Robert Morris, et al.
2.   The three books of the trilogy are *The Maurizius Case* (tr. Caroline Newton; New York: Horace Liveright, 1929); *Doctor Kerkhoven* (tr. Cyrus Brooks; New York: Horace Liveright, Inc., [1932]); and *Kerkhoven's Third Existence* (tr. Eden and Cedar Paul; New York: Liveright Publishing Corp., [1934]).
3.   Tr. S. N. Brainin (New York: Coward-McCann, Inc., [1933]).
4.   " 'Tropic' Author Miller Defended Against Charge of Anti-Semitism," *Los Angeles Times*, Feb. 16, 1962, "Letters to the Times."
5.   New York: Simon and Schuster, 1958.

TL (CC), 4PP., AIR MAIL   February 19, 1962

Dear Henry Miller: I have returned both volumes of "*Hamlet*" to you at Big Sur. I have sent the volumes insured. Of course, I would not presume to write to Mrs. Fraenkel without your prior knowledge and approval. I have written simply to the Copyright Office in Washington to learn what their records indicate. Thereafter, I can advise you further. No matter how much trouble it occasions, this work of yours ought to be reprinted, as it contains some of your best writing. Challenged by Fraenkel, you did some of your best thinking without sacrificing your skill as a raconteur and as a limner of the human soul. I read the books more rapidly than I should because I was worried about keeping them on hand, in view of all of the circumstances. One day I hope to read them in a more leisurely spirit.

I have sent you a half-dozen paperbacks similar to the ones described in the Offer of Proof in the case before Judge Epstein.[1] I cannot send you the ones that we have marked as exhibits in that case because we will require them if it becomes necessary for an appeal to be taken. Our purpose in offering the books, as well as other material, was to indicate the degree of acceptability in the community of material appealing to prurient interest. To anyone, except certain kinds of police officers, the material in these paperbacks is infinitely "worse" than anything that might be read in "Tropic of Cancer" or any work of literary value. These paperbacks are intended to arouse sexual feeling; that is why they sell so well. I sometimes am persuaded that the reason the police officers interfere with the sale of genuine literature, such as "Tropic of Cancer," is that they want the public not to notice that there is no interference with the trash which embodies smut for smut's sake. Some of these things are sold even in the City Hall and the County Building. Of course, we are not advocating the suppression of this material, but, if there is to be any form of suppression, it ought to start with such trash, rather than with your kind of literature.

What you call a deposition is really an Offer of Proof. The Judge felt that it would be improper to receive the books in evidence, because he would have to devote endless hours in analyzing them and making comparisons with "Tropic of Cancer." Whether or not he was right as a matter of law, there can be no doubt that, as a practical matter, there is much to his viewpoint. Still, I felt that, to protect your interest, I had to make the offer. I thought that, even if the books were not actually in evidence, the Judge would be impressed by the language of the offer.

Thanks much for sending me the copy of the bibliography by Esta Lou Riley, the issue of the Claremont Quarterly containing the interview with you[2] and the drafts of the Preface for "Stand Still Like the Hummingbird." Regardless of whether the case is won or lost, I hope that you will continue to send such things to me within the limits of your time and energy, as I am deeply interested, and not simply as an attorney. I know that there are many others like me. Last Saturday night a Chicago doctor and his wife had dinner with us, simply because of their interest in your writings. It is a long, and probably interesting, story, the telling of which will have to wait.

I am much interested in your reference to your giving material to your daughter, now sixteen, who thinks that she may write some day. She was born in the very month that our younger son was born. He, sad to say, wants to become an accountant, and not a writer.

To revert again to the Offer of Proof, I sent an extra copy of it to you the other day and after the case is over I will see if I can send you any more. I don't dare part with copies while the case is pending and there is any likelihood of an appeal. I have sent copies to Rosset's attorney in New York, but I don't recall whether or not I have sent him one. In matters of a purely legal nature, I don't bother Barney. It is only when I think there may be some special interest on his part that I communicate with him.

I think that I used more devices in the local cases than in the cases in other parts of the country. Whether or not they will produce the result we want, we shall learn Wednesday.

The psychiatrist to whom you refer must have been the same sort of character as the one used here. I think I told you what I said in open court with respect to him and how Judge Epstein responded in agreement. Curiously enough, when I was with the internist to whom I referred earlier in this letter, the name of the psychiatrist came up and one of the other guests told of the very unfortunate situation that she had with him involving her own son. I always discount what patients say about their doctors, but she was pretty persuasive in her indications that this psychiatrist is incompetent.

You asked if you have to get permission to quote from the Offer of Proof and the answer is no, since the document is part of a court proceeding. If you quote from it, you should declare, for the sake of safety, that you are quoting from a court document.

You asked if mere possession of an allegedly obscene book is an offense and the answer is no. The old Illinois Statute which declared possession an offense was confessed to be invalid by the Attorney General of Illinois. There has to be a knowing public exhibition and sale. One of the opposing counsel in the case here showed me a mailing piece with respect to "Tropic of Cancer" which was the most obvious sort of appeal to pruriency. If it had been received in evidence, it would have been highly prejudicial, but the attorney did not even offer it, knowing that it would not be admitted, because it was not one of our mailing pieces.

The legal literature on "Tropic of Cancer" is a growing one and one day I would like to write an article on it.

Thanks much for going to all of the trouble of getting the books for me. I would love to have them because I am deeply interested in your writing. Your books have been a life experience for me, and not simply reading matter. I don't care if the books are seized by Customs, if you don't care. I prefer having them arrive safely and as soon as possible, but if you feel that you want to chance having them sent through Customs, that is all right with me.

As you should know, "Tropic of Cancer," "Tropic of Capricorn" and "Plexus" have been declared non-obscene by United States Customs. I do not know if there has been any finding of obscenity as to the others, but I assume from your letter that you have reason to believe that there has been such finding. If the finding was made prior to the "Lady Chatterley's Lover" case, the situation ought to be reviewed, but this is not the time. If I were to voice an opinion as to the time sequence, I would say that, first, we have to get a final adjudication on "Tropic of Cancer"; then on "Tropic of Capricorn"; and only then should we consider the other books. The public and the authorities seem to be growing up to your books, but it still would be dangerous to hurry them unduly.

I am deeply interested in your plans about going to Minneapolis, Jefferson City and New York in mid-March, and I am grateful to you for suggesting that we ought to meet somewhere. I quite agree with you. Of course, I would prefer Chicago, but, if it is not

Chicago, then Minneapolis or New York would be the places. If we win the case here, it ought to be in the nature of a victory celebration, but, win or lose, I want to see you. After the decision Wednesday, I will write to you again on this matter.

Since I am answering your letters as I pick them up, there is a certain degree of disorganization which is unavoidable.

What you say with respect to Fraenkel, I can understand. Despite your friendship, it is apparent from the "Hamlet" letters that intellectually and emotionally the two of you were often at swords' point. You were friends in spite of these differences. Part of the appeal of the "Hamlet" correspondence is the fencing that is more than swordplay.

I am sending you the editorial from the Saturday Evening Post because I think it important that a magazine of such vast circulation is opposed to censorship, even if critical of your kind of writing. The Post editorial is added evidence that you, Lawrence and Joyce are regarded as the leaders in modern literature, at least so far as the schools are concerned and the young writers as well. For that reason, I suggested that when all of the battles are over you might take up the question of the Post and answer it in your own way.

You and I have been commiserating about correspondence. While I am wondering how you find the time to do so much of it, you ⟨request⟩ ask similar questions with respect to me. I suppose that the answer is that correspondence supplies a certain need of ours, like the craving for salt and sugar. In letterwriting, we are facile, and we don't try to write literary masterpieces—unless you are writing to Fraenkel, Durrell or someone like that.

I am sure that I have omitted many things from this letter, but I have already taken up more than enough of your time.

Always yours, ELMER GERTZ

1.   Gertz made a note of five titles sent to Miller on February 19: *Call Me Sinner, Wall Street Wanton, Frigid Wife, Daisy, Community of Women.* The first two were Nightstand paperbacks, many of which have been involved in obscenity litigation (for example, see *Kansas v.*

A *Quantity of Copies of Books*, 191 Kan. 13, 379 P. 2nd 254; reversed 378 U.S. 205).

2.   George Wickes, "Henry Miller at Seventy," *Claremont Quarterly*,
      Winter 1962, pp. 5–20.

[*February 21, 1962*]

GLORY BE. WE HAVE WON.[1]   ELMER GERTZ

[*Wire to Miller at 661 Las Lomas, Pacific Palisades, California, 21
February 1962. From Chicago, Ill.*]

---

1.   For more about this and other *Tropic of Cancer* litigation in Illinois,
      see Gertz, *A Handful of Clients*, pp. 229–32, 244–303; Gertz, "The
      Illinois Battle Over 'Tropic of Cancer,' " *Chicago Bar Record*, Janu-
      ary 1965, pp. 161–72; Hoke Norris, " 'Cancer' in Chicago," *Evergreen
      Review*, July-August, 1962, pp. 41–66; Samuel B. Epstein, "A Book to
      Remember from a Chancellor's Trial Book," *Law Alumni Journal*,
      University of Chicago Law School, Fall 1976, pp. 17–20.
          Plaintiffs in the Chicago suit (prospective purchasers of *Cancer*,
      and the publisher and author, as Intervenors), sought to enjoin Chi-
      cago's Police Commissioner, as well as the Chiefs of Police in certain
      suburban municipalities, from interfering with the sale of the book.
      Judge Epstein might have avoided the obscenity issue by restricting his
      ruling to whether the officials cited had exercised "prior restraint" in
      banning the book, but felt that "the court would dodge its responsi-
      bilities if it [ruled] on such narrow basis and left open the principal
      issue . . . to be decided after arrests had been made." In summing up
      the reasons for his conclusion that the book was not obscene (based on
      the United States Supreme Court's guidelines in its 1957 *Roth* deci-
      sion: "whether to the average person applying contemporary commu-
      nity standards, the dominant theme of the material taken as a whole,
      appeals to the prurient interest"), Judge Epstein said:
          "Censorship is a very dangerous instrumentality, even in the hands
      of a court. Recent history has proven the evil of an attempt at con-
      trolling the utterances and thoughts of our population. Censorship has
      no fixed boundaries. It may become an oppressive weapon in a free
      society.
          "Taste in literature is a matter of education. Those who object to
      the book are free to condemn and even to urge others to reject it.

Organizations, such as church societies, and other sincere groups are free to condemn any book they deem objectionable. Such efforts would help to educate the literary tastes of the reading public. Reviews and comments in the press are calculated to such purpose. Such voluntary efforts are praiseworthy and consonant with democratic principles.

"In the words of Justice Douglas, in the *Roth* case: 'I have the same confidence in the ability of our people to reject noxious literature as I have in their capacity to sort out the true from the false in theology, economics, politics or any other field.'

"However, that is a far cry from censorship established by law whereby all readers are geared to the taste of the relatively few.

. . . .

"The constitutional right to freedom of speech and press should be jealously guarded by the courts. As a corollary to the freedom of speech and press, there is also the freedom to read. The right to free utterances becomes a useless privilege when the freedom to read is restricted or denied."

[*February 21, 1962*]

CONGRATULATIONS. JUST MARVELOUS. NO ONE
BUT YOU COULD HAVE DONE IT.   HENRY MILLER

[*Wire to Gertz at 120 South LaSalle Street, Chicago, Ill., 21 February 1962. From Pacific Palisades, California.*]

TL(CC), 2PP., AIR MAIL   February 22, 1962

Dear Henry Miller: The morning after our great triumph finds me fatigued, but extremely happy. I had not realized how worn out I am. I am going to see if, somehow, I can get a little relaxation. Whatever the wear and tear, it has certainly been worth it. The telegrams from you, Barney Rosset and others helped add to my joy. When you get a copy of the opinion, as you will in a few days, you will be happy all over again.

As I told you, the Judge summoned us to appear in his courtroom 12 o'clock noon and there was a surprisingly large attendance, including newspapermen, several members of my family, my secretary, some of my law associates and others. Promptly at 12 o'clock noon, the Judge opened the session, made a few appropriate remarks and then read the opinion, interpolating additional remarks now and then. After it was over, there was a receiving line in court of those congratulating me. I told the Judge that he had written an historic opinion. Laughingly, he said, "You would, of course, think so." But I told him that I believed it without regard to the fact that I had won; indeed, I do think that this is the most important decision in its way since Judge Woolsey's classic statement in the "Ulysses" case. In many respects, this goes beyond the "Ulysses" decision. I hope the Judge's words are widely reprinted, as he deserves the acclaim.

Now that the case is over, I will tell him about your compassionate viewpoint with respect to him while the case was pending.

There is one additional way in which you can reward me, and that is to send me a copy of the clothbound edition of "Tropic of Cancer" with an inscription by you.[1] You can date it as of February 21, when we won our great victory. Four years and a day prior thereto, I won my victory in the Leopold case. Of course, I have won other cases since then, but this one gives me the most satisfaction.

I am returning the various drafts of the Preface to "Stand Still Like the Hummingbird," except for the one that you have stated that I can keep. It is a fascinating thing, watching the progression from draft to draft. I don't wonder that your daughter wants the originals. For my gratification, I have made photostats of the first and second drafts so that I may have them as a memento.

There seems to be no end of material by and about you that I am eager to get. I have gotten many things through New Directions and Grove Press, most of which are exhibits in the case, and I have purchased other items from the Gotham Book Mart, Bern Porter[2] and others. I am sending herewith a list of some of the things that I yet lack. I would love to get them from you, if they are available and if you tell me how much I must pay. I do not want to put you to any undue expense.

With respect to the allegations in the Federal case about the book "Tropic of Cancer" being copyrighted, I was in error, and the allegations were corrected in the complaint in the case before Judge Epstein. We are going to have a running battle with pirates because of the lack of copyright on some of your books and it may be that we will have to work out devices to protect you. There are also other legal problems that may arise when the vigilante groups get after the book in the absence of police interference. These matters, too, I will discuss with you.

Monday night I was on a television program, on the subject "Should Broadcasters Be Free." One of the participants was Virgil Mitchell of CBS, who told me, privately, many interesting things about you. He has a tremendous admiration for you and for Emil White. I shall write Emil about it.

I shall certainly take your advice with respect to reading the "Maurizius Trilogy" and I shall write the Leopold story, as you suggest.[3] Right now, I would like to kick over the traces and just meander around without aim or destination. Of course, I won't do this, knowing my own exigent nature.

This will have to do for today. Always yours, ELMER GERTZ

---

1.   Miller inscribed a copy of Tropic of Cancer as follows:
      "For Elmer Gertz—
            A lover of freedom, truth and justice, a loyal friend, a lover of books and a peerless barrister. May Heaven protect him ever!
                  In gratitude and admiration—
                                    Henry Miller
                                    2/21/62
      On the eve of the great decision. 'Victory.' "
2.   Author of Henry Miller: A Chronology and Bibliography [Berkeley, Calif.: The Author, 1945]; publisher of The Happy Rock: A Book About Henry Miller [Berkeley, Calif.: Bern Porter, 1945]; and of works by Miller.
3.   Gertz told the "Leopold story" in A Handful of Clients, pp. 3–192.

TLS, 1P.   Pac Pal. 2/25/62

Dear Elmer Gertz,   To reply to yours of Feb. 22nd, with enclosures all around. Yes, do try to get a bit of rest! Most important. So far I haven't seen or heard a thing about the Chicago victory. The news seems to be suppressed. But it will leak out soon, no doubt. I think Judge Epstein did a heroic job of it. More than I expected of him. You've read about the defeat here, I suppose.[1] Did you notice that one of the jury stated (to newspapers) that "the literary merits of the book were never discussed." That's something, what!

I don't know Virgil Mitchell, or do I?

About the books you'd like to have. A pleasure, of course. Only, some of them are hard to find—for those will have to refer you to Gotham Book Mart. Such as: Patchen (a brochure) but which is (almost entirely) incorporated in the new book by New Directions, out in June: The Hummingbird. Of, By and About H. M., Plight of the Creative Artist. (Again, portions of these will appear in Hummingbird) Semblance of A Devoted Past. H. M. Miscellanea, Why Abstract—all long out of print.[2]

I asked Emil White to send you "Aller Retour N.Y."[3] I made revisions (considerable) and added a preface and a *post*face (Reunion in Barcelona) to this, but thus far it has appeared only in French (La Guilde du Livre, Lausanne.) All the others my friend Vincent Birge will send from Big Sur. Except "Angel is my Watermark" (handsome water color album) which will be sent you by Harry Abrams, N. Y. soon as it's ready—with English text.[4]

And now I must beg off. Have simply been flooded with correspondence these last few days—nothing to do with the trials either. I have my own trials.

Naturally I would like a copy of Judge Epstein's complete decision some day, if possible.   All the best ever, Henry Miller

P.S. Received *one* copy of T. of C. in HEBREW. Asked that you be sent one. Too bad you didn't have it for the trial.

Excuse typing! Off to-day!

P.P.S. *Do* congratulate Judge Epstein for me—for his honesty and sincerity.⁵

---

1.   On February 23, 1962, a Los Angeles jury convicted Bradley Smith, a Hollywood bookseller, of a misdemeanor for selling *Tropic of Cancer* (*Publishers Weekly*, March 5, 1962, p. 31).
2.   *The Plight of the Creative Artist in the United States of America* [Houlton, Me.: Bern Porter, 1944]; *Semblance of a Devoted Past* (Berkeley, Calif.: Bern Porter, [1944]); *Henry Miller Miscellanea* ([Berkeley, Calif.]: Bern Porter, 1945); Why Abstract? ([New York]: New Directions, [1945]).
3.   *Aller Retour New York* (Paris: Obelisk Press, 1935).
4.   *Henry Miller: Watercolors, Drawings, and His Essay, The Angel Is My Watermark!* (New York: Abrams [1962]). *The Angel Is My Watermark* (Fullerton, Calif.: Holve-Barrows, 1944).
5.   The two postscripts are written by hand, the second in the left margin, vertically.

ALS, 1P.   Feb. 26th 1962

Dear Elmer Gertz—   Today came the full decision of Judge Epstein. Wonderful! I see now that it truly marks an advance over Woolsey's. Will it affect the judges in other States? That's the big question.

The intelligent members of the L.A. community are incensed by the decision here. The defeat may turn into a victory. So it looks to me. Sometimes a defeat is more effective than a quick victory— you know that, no doubt.

I just wrote the enclosed today and send it off to you, since you express a desire to see everything. But please return both copies soon as possible. ⟨It⟩ The text will appear, as a lead, in an English Carmelite review.¹ Don't know how I happened to get into correspondence with Fr. Sewell, the editor. I am wondering if he will swallow it *all*. The whole next issue will be given over to Joseph Delteil. Most unexpected outlet!

More soon. My best!   Henry Miller

1.   "Joseph Delteil," *Aylesford Review*, Vol. IV, No. 7 (Summer, 1962),
      pp. [247]–250. Reprinted in *Joseph Delteil: Essays in Tribute* (Lon-
      don: John Roberts Press Limited, for signature by Joseph Delteil and
      Henry Miller, for publication by St. Albert's Press, 1962), pp. 3–6. In
      this article Miller said of his friend of many years, who received the
      Prix Fémina for his *Jeanne d'Arc*: "The most and the least I can say
      is that I love every word he writes. Just to glance at a line of his prose
      makes me dance." Perlès, in *My Friend Henry Miller*, reports that
      Miller visited Delteil at his home in Montpellier, France, in 1952; and
      that immediately thereafter, in Barcelona, Delteil and his American-
      born wife were with the group that celebrated the reunion of Miller
      and Perlès, who had not seen each other for fourteen years. See also
      Wickes, *Lawrence Durrell and Henry Miller*, pp. 372–73, for Miller's
      reaction to Delteil's *François d'Assise*.

Writing on March 1, Gertz pointed out that John Glenn, returning from the first American manned space flight, had landed in
the Tropic of Cancer on the day before Judge Epstein's favorable
decision in the Chicago case. In concluding his two pages of
largely personal remarks, Gertz said: "I am sadly in need of some
rest or, at any rate, recreation, and I look forward to seeing you
when you journey in this direction. When will that be?"

TLS, 1P.   Pac Pal—March 5, 1962

Dear Elmer Gertz,   For several days now I have been feeling
and acting like a sleep-walker. Too relaxed to think. Can't make
decisions, even to make love. I got all the enclosures—you're swamp-
ing me—and was especially interested in Jack Mabley's column in
the Chicago American. Curious to see what happens when those
ten thousand citizens get the 19 passages from "Cancer."[1] You ask
about favorable publicity here. I haven't seen any. (Except for a
brief paragraph by the Chancellor of U.C.L.A.) What I get is word
of mouth reactions. All the people I meet are incensed about the
L.A. trial. But I am traveling in the wrong circles, I guess.

About Glenn's orbital flight. Was told that the prosecuting
attorney here dragged that into his speech in summing up. Glenn

was in the air as he spoke; he opens Cancer to some page where I attack the scientists, and then points to Glenn's achievement. What humbuggery!

Entre nous, and I mean this as confidential . . . One of my astrologers wrote me recently that, so far as my name and fame are concerned, this year will see even greater acclaim and success. "Cancer" was launched at the most favorable moment; nothing can defeat it. We'll see. What I wonder is—when they launch Capricorn are these trials to begin all over again? No word as to when Grove intends to bring it out so far.

Shirley McLaine[2] was quoted in Variety as saying that if marooned on a desert island and had to bring ten books along she would bring ten copies of "Cancer." (I met her the other day.)[3]

Those pocket books you sent me—I've scanned three and find nothing very reprehensible or censorable in them. The language is pretty clean. The worst is by implication. These don't match the ones you described in your "Offer of Proof."

Norman Mailer is supposed to have inserted some highly censorable stuff from one of his works in progress in his "Ads for Myself."[4] He's deliberately trying to write something that will be censored, I am told.

Enough. . . . Must get my thinking cap on.

Sincerely, Henry Miller

1.   See Jack Mabley, " 'That Book' to Get Shock Treatment," Chicago's American, March 2, 1962, p. 3. Mabley said the Chicago chapter of Citizens for Decent Literature was mailing a six-page letter with 19 extracts from Tropic of Cancer to 10,000 people in its effort to foster public protest. A copy of this broadside is in UCLA's Miller-Gertz files. Mabley had excoriated the book in his column as early as October 31, 1961, immediately after Grove's paperback edition was published, and had testified against it during the trial.

2.   The actress's last name is MacLaine.

3.   Miller told, in The Henry Miller Literary Society Newsletter (September 1962) of making "the rounds of Hollywood studios" with his friend Joe Gray: "Met Shirley MacLaine, Robert Mitchum, Marlon Brando, Cary Grant and Dean Martin, all very much alive, especially Dean Martin. Was invited to a private showing of 'Cape Fear' in

which Mitchum does a phenomenal piece of acting. I also made a point to see 'The Hustler,' which I consider the best American film in many a year, and 'A Walk on the Wild Side,' which was a bitter disappointment after reading the book."

4.   *Advertisements for Myself* (New York: Putnam [1959]).

T1(CC), 2PP., AIR MAIL   March 6, 1962

Dear Henry Miller: I have not been myself lately, but have been so tied up in trial work and other professional activities that I have not been able to take the sort of rest that I need. I did stay in bed for parts of three or four days, but apparently what I need is some consecutive relaxation.

Your inscription in my copy of "Tropic of Cancer" moved me more than I can say. I try not to go overboard with sentimentality, but it is difficult not to become emotional when one receives such warm praise. It was worth while spending myself in this case in order to read your comments.

In the same mail delivery, there arrived a copy of "The Happy Rock," beautifully inscribed by Bern Porter.

And now, just a few moments ago, several other books arrived, for which I am extremely grateful. I want you to tell me, frankly, if you have been put to any expense whatsoever in connection with the various books that you have sent me. I want to pay any and all out-of-pocket expenditures. It is sufficient that you go to so much trouble in my behalf without your spending money which might better be devoted to other purposes.

Oh, yes, yesterday I received from your French publisher "Tropic of Capricorn" and "Black Spring." I am reading "Black Spring" and my wife "Tropic of Capricorn." We have established new comradeship in reading your works together.

I am trying to confine my work today to the barest essentials so that I can get away early.

Some of the enclosures will interest you, particularly the letter

that I received from the young man who assisted me in the preparation of the case.[1]

Warmest good wishes.   Always yours, ELMER GERTZ[2]

Encs.

---

1.   Letter from Sidney Karasik dated March 2, 1962; in the Miller-Gertz
      files at UCLA.
2.   On the original of Gertz's letter, Miller wrote: What about "DAM-
      AGES"?

TL(CC), 2PP., AIR MAIL   March 7, 1962

Dear Henry Miller: So much material comes in that it is, indeed, overwhelming. I try to send you only the more important
items, as I do not want to submerge you. The material sent today,
for example, appears to me to be of tremendous importance. I
have been in communication with Barney Rosset with respect to it
and we will be able to report some developments to you very soon.

I hope that you feel that you can be completely frank with me.
If you would be happier hearing less about this matter, even though
you are the one most involved, don't hesitate to say so. I know that
sometimes I get into the state of mind, in which I say: "To hell
with everything; let things take care of themselves." Should you
feel that way, I want you to tell me.

My hope is to act as a sort of clearing house for you when developments of any kind take place, so that I can put them in those
terms that will convey the most meaning to you. Too often, lawyers
are involved in technicalities and they fail to see that their clients
are concerned only with the results and the reasons behind these
results.

As soon as I learn whether or not there is going to be an appeal, I will be in the position to obtain for you the books included
in the offer of proof.

My head is spinning with figures. A small group of us met with

Roger Stevens, who is the Chairman of President Kennedy's Cultural Committee. They have plans for a great national center for the performing arts and have evolved a gimmick whereby the local communities will also benefit in a direct way. Since I am concerned with attempting to restore the old Auditorium Theatre here, the group thought they would like to talk with me. The net effect is the loss of a couple of hours of time and a headache. I shall be glad to get home in order to resume my Miller reading.

Always yours, ELMER GERTZ

Encs.

ALS, 2PP.   Pac Pal—3/8/62

Dear Elmer Gertz—   Yes, those enclosures *are* interesting. So Judge Epstein is upset by Mabley's column! Can't blame him. He sounds like a Fascist.

One thing I haven't heard about in connection with the victory is the question of "damages." "We" sued for several million dollars. Didn't we even get $10.00—the usual compromise in such cases?

I seem to read between the lines that you will handle other cases for Grove in other towns—is that right? Would be wonderful. And now you are "fully armed"!

No use telling work-horses like you and me to take it easy. I have been a bit successful at it lately—but it won't last. If you get easy in the mind it's quite enough.

No, you owe me nothing for books—I owe you infinitely more. But I'll let you make me a gift, to remind me always of you when I take up the pen. Send me a decent pen (not a fountain pen!) You see how mine dribbles. Not an expensive one—just a working one. I hate these new pens (refills) but we have to get used to them, like ⟨to⟩ with rockets and missiles and sonic booms. Okay?

I think more books are on the way to you.

Had warm letter (and gift books) from Alexander King recently. Suppose you know him too. I read only one book—and enjoyed it thoroly—"Mine Enemy Grows Older."

More anon. Ever yours, Henry Miller

P.S. You should try to get a book called "The Hundred Dollar Misunderstanding" by Robert Gover (American) pub. by Neville Spearman, Ltd.—112 Whitfield St. London, W. 1. How it gets by the British censors is beyond me. It's a riot!
P.P.S. I won't go to Minneapolis on way to N.Y.—much too cold for me. Will see you on way home, late May, early June—with Schwartz.

Forgive me![1]

---

1. The first postscript is written vertically in the left margin of the second page; the second postscript at the bottom of that page.

TL(CC), 2 PP. AIR MAIL   March 9, 1962

Dear Henry Miller: With the thoroughness that I like to think is sometimes characteristic of me, I did some research on the subject of mechanical pens and I am sending the result under separate cover. It meets all of your requirements. It is useful, it is not expensive, it won't dribble. One of the women in the office says that she uses it for all of her considerable amount of dictation taking and that it lasts for months. But just in case it does not last that long, I am also sending a couple of refills. I agree with you completely with respect to the mechanical madness of America. Even zippers are sometimes beyond me. They are the best argument for nudity that I know.

Let me explain how our millions of dollars vanished. It is true that we originally asked for damages in the suit before Judge Epstein; then I began to think of the problems facing us in order to prevail. It occurred to me that a judge might be reluctant to find against police officers if he had to assess damages in addition to restraining them. I concluded that it was best to withdraw our demand for damages and rest content if we succeeded in having the book declared not obscene and persuaded the Court to restrain interference with the sale. However, I have good news. We still have the theoretical right to obtain damages. We have another suit pending in the United States District Court here—remember, I have told you about it. In this suit, which is based upon the violation of your civil rights by the police chiefs, we ask for damages. We will proceed with that suit if the defendants in the case before Judge Epstein do not waive appeal. Thus, you and I may be on the road to becoming millionaires, which may not ruin my career as a lawyer, but will certainly wreck you as a writer.

As soon as the situation clarifies itself, I will let you know. You would be surprised what sort of complications there are, even when one wins. For example, there is a police prosecution against a bookseller in [*name omitted*], a village near Chicago. The Village Attorney has asked that the suit be dismissed, but the Judge, who is notorious as the keeper of a kangaroo court, has thus far refused to dismiss the case. It comes up Wednesday and I am going to ask for a change of venue if he does not dismiss the case then. I also have several other motions in mind. You may read that the Judge has sentenced me to jail for contempt of court, if I am provoked into telling him exactly what I think of him. I have often had that temptation during ⟨the⟩ my thirty-two years as a lawyer, but, thus far, I have resisted it. I say this, not in praise of myself, but as an indication of the cowardice even of so-called courageous lawyers. You will remember that, in the Scopes case, Darrow, who spoke out against the moron presiding at the trial, then apologized to him in order to exonerate himself from his sentence for contempt.[1]

Everyone around me is trying to persuade me to get away and I would like to, but when I look at my calendar and think of all of the matters that require attention, I despair a bit. I will probably take some long week-ends and occasional days in the middle of the week. I should take with me some of the literature mentioned by you in your letter. As I am getting to my late boyhood, I really ought to read some of the stuff suggested by you.

As long as you don't mind it, send on all the printed matter that you think will interest me. Where others eat rare meat, I devour rare books, with or without the aid of wines and brandies. More later.   Always yours, ELMER GERTZ

---

1.   The year before the famous Scopes evolution trial (1925), Clarence Darrow, who was adamantly opposed to capital punishment, served as defense counsel in the sensational Leopold-Loeb murder case. Of the more than one hundred clients charged with murder whom he defended, none was ever sentenced to death.

ALS, 1P.   March 9th '62

Dear Elmer Gertz— Yes, do keep ⟨me⟩ sending me material *you* think important. The last was exciting. That Hoke Norris[1] sure can handle himself—a good head. He must feel as if he were waging a hopeless battle. (Like fighting the Pope in Italy.) Do give him warm greetings from me. He has courage. The Mableys we will have with us always.

When I am abroad, better cut c/s down to absolute minimum. Letters "forwarded" often go astray or take months to reach me. I think I will give you Rosset (Grove Press) as address, since I'll be moving about, and don't want to be obliged to give fresh new addresses to all my correspondents. Easier to sieve thru him. Better hold off mailing me those books—until I give the go signal.

That Citizens' Committee should help sell a lot of copies of the book, eh what! Chicago is getting to be a hot spot. I feel truly sorry for Judge Epstein. Take care of yourself!

All the best. Henry Miller

---

1.   Reference is probably to Hoke Norris's article in the *Chicago Sun-Times* "Critic At-Large" column of March 7, 1962 (Section Two, p. 14), entitled " 'Flood of Filth,' " a reply to Jack Mabley's column in the March 2, 1962 *Chicago's American* (see H. M. 3/5/62, notes).

Norris, who died July 8, 1977, enjoyed a distinguished career as a novelist, short story writer, editor, journalist, and director of the

Office of Public Information at the University of Chicago. While serving as literary editor of the *Chicago Sun-Times* he not only testified on behalf of *Tropic of Cancer* during the Chicago trial but wrote many articles in support of freedom of expression, as is evident from references in this volume. Norris was invited, with Miller's approval, to join a small dinner party which the Gertzes hosted in Miller's honor in November, 1962 (see H. M. 10/26/62).

Gertz informed Miller on March 12 that Hamlet was apparently not copyrighted in the United States, and forwarded a letter from the Register of Copyrights in this regard. He also enclosed a letter from a former client, published in a suburban newspaper, that castigated Gertz for befriending Leopold and Miller.

ALS, 2PP.   March 12th '62

Dear Elmer Gertz—   I am writing this letter with the beautiful pen you sent me, for which all my thanks.

Yours of the 9th, with enclosures, again most interesting. I thought, when I first heard about it, that it was just too good to be true—suing the police for damages. Still, it's done now and then.

Your Dr. Litman[1] doesn't seem to be up on the literature (of psychiatrists and their ilk) regarding the beneficial effects of "obscenity" (not pornography.) I think Havelock Ellis was the first to sound that note.

Rebecca West![2] I met her once or twice at my place in Paris around 1935–36—through Anaïs Nin.[3] She impressed me. Are you trying to pull her leg?

Don't get cited for contempt of court. I want to preserve my image of the masterful lawyer who never, under any circumstances, loses his temper—*in court!* As for me, I'd go plain berserk, I know. Stupidity is one of the few things I find difficult to tolerate. (So did the Buddha, incidentally.)

I'll send you shortly—for future reading—the proof pages (*un*corrected) of my "Hummingbird" book. I had another set which I corrected.

I think you will get a real kick when you read the Durrell-Miller c/s which Dutton will bring out. And this is only a half or less of the whole c/s, I understand.

There is still a greater one to come—between my life-long friend Emil Schnellock[4] and myself—saw it at U.C.L.A. library the other day. I wept! And they have only recovered a half or a third of it. There's a mystery attached to the missing letters. I once, in Virginia, saw the entire works. But these apparently lost items have a way of turning up eventually.

Enough! Abi gesundt! Henry Miller

P.S. In one of the early Durrell letters he quotes this from an unknown English poet—

"When out of the gorse
Came a homosexual horse."

1.   Gertz had forwarded a letter from Robert E. Litman, M.D., Beverly Hills, California, dated February 27.
2.   English novelist and critic. A copy of Gertz's March 8 letter to her, forwarding Judge Epstein's decision and referring to her testimony in the Lady Chatterley's Lover case, is in the Miller-Gertz files at UCLA.
3.   Anaïs Nin, American novelist born in Paris, was one of Miller's closest associates while he lived in France. See Gunther Stuhlmann, ed., The Diary of Anaïs Nin, Vol. I, 1931–1934 (New York: Harcourt, Brace & World, Inc., 1966); Henry Miller Letters to Anaïs Nin (New York: G. P. Putnam's Sons [1965]).
4.   American artist who attended P.S. 85 in Brooklyn with Miller. Schnellock died in 1960. Semblance of a Devoted Past contains two dozen of Miller's letters to Schnellock, written during the years 1930–39.

APS, 1S., AIR MAIL   3/13/62

Just a card to-day. Coming down with a cold. Amazing that Fraenkel too never thought to get an American copyright. But who wants to pirate Hamlet, eh? So, we're in the same boat as Leopold and Loeb! What next? Ich gebibble. *Abi gesundt!*   Henry Miller[1]

1.   This picture postcard, postmarked Pacific Palisades, California, bears the printed legend:

"HENRY MILLER Val's Birthday Gift
Watercolor and Ink, 11½" x 17¼"
Collection of Valentin Miller"

"Val's Birthday Gift" is reproduced in Henry Miller, *To Paint Is To Love Again* (Alhambra, Calif.: Cambria Books, [1960]).

APS, 1S.   [3/13/62]

Same day. On the cover of Vol I. Tropic of Cancer (Israeli edition)[1] it says: "The book all Israel has been waiting for." (sic) In Hebrew, of course. You'll be getting a copy in a few weeks. Funny, making 2 Vols. of it. Clever lads!   Henry Miller[2]

1.   *Hugo shel sarton*, tr. Ednah Kornfeld (2v.; Tel-Aviv: Desheh, 1962).
2.   This card, postmarked March 13, 1962, Pacific Palisades, California, bears the printed legend:

"HENRY MILLER Deux Jeunes Filles
Watercolor and Ink, 11½" x 14"
Collection of Henry Miller"

"Deux Jeunes Filles" is reproduced in Miller's *To Paint Is To Love Again*.

TL(CC), 1P., AIR MAIL   March 14, 1962

Dear Henry Miller: Interestingly enough, I obtained a copy of *The World of Lawrence Durrell*, edited by Harry T. Moore,[1] at the very time that I got your letter, in which you refer to your correspondence with Durrell. I am almost excessively eager to read the correspondence, as I have a special feeling for the letters passing between human beings who have the capacity for cerebration and emotion. Your letters have a particular quality that makes me feel that I am clasping your hand each time I get even the briefest note.

    There is no chance of my being cited for contempt of court, because I will not be out to [*name emitted*] tomorrow; instead, my

young associate, Sidney Karasik, will be there, and I will be enroute
to New Orleans. I suddenly got so fatigued that it was easy for my
son, his wife and my wife to persuade me that we ought to go on a
holiday. I expect to be at the Thunderbird Motor Inn (1910 Tulane
Avenue, New Orleans, Louisiana—Phone 525-7272) until next
Tuesday. That is all too short a time to be away, but it will be a
lifesaver.

I am eager to see the proof pages of your Hummingbird book;
indeed, I am eager to see whatever you write or what is written
about you. I am handling you as I handle a case to which I become
attached. I get so absorbed in the details that every now and then I
have to remind myself of the necessity for calling a halt. At the
moment, I see no necessity for calling a halt. It is much too provocative.

Stay well. I hope that I will sound more interesting when I get
back.   Always yours, ELMER GERTZ

---

1.   Southern Illinois University Press, 1962.

ALS, 2PP.   March 16, 1962

Dear Elmer Gertz—   Again a batch of exciting mail from you—
particularly as regards the raid on the actors.[1] (They look so serious,
these readers!) At this rate the book will soon be on the best seller
list again. Dick Ellmann, professor, also sounds too serious. So
many, of the professor stripe, can't believe it's autobiography. Even
that man from Harvard (New Republic).[2] They've never had it
served as biography of the whole being, including the interstitial
glands, cells and glow-worms, that's the trouble. Even the exaggerated episodes are closer to truth than to fiction.

When you take a vacation cut your bridges behind you—never
leave addresses and phone numbers. Die to the world—utterly—
even if only for 36 hours. Otherwise, the "world" will kill you. I
haven't a single Jewish friend (always a professional, of course)

who knows how to take a real vacation. I think sometimes the Jews are farther from the orient than any Westerner. The Orient for us (I include myself, notice) is what sleep is to the body cells. To forget, to just not give a damn, to laze away the days—what a gift!

Take it still easier, please.   Henry Miller

P.S. one exception—my friend and beau-frère, Bezalel Schatz—but then he was raised different—in his father's wonderful school in Jerusalem, where creative activity, music and play were the paramount things. Man, he sure can relax!

P.S. Don't go to see the film—"A Walk on the Wild Side." It broke my heart. Utterly unlike the book[3]—a real slaughter. And not one line out of Dove's mouth that resembles Dove of the book. Dove's language, by the way, gets me more than any character's in all fiction. It's a Céline-like creation.

I'm sending you a brochure called "1001 Ways to Live without Working." (To Chicago) I know it won't cure you but you should get a few good laughs. Laughter is even better than resting.   H. M.[4]

---

1.   Four actors were arrested at a nightclub for reading excerpts from *Tropic of Cancer*. Gertz finally agreed to defend them (see Gertz 4/20/62).
2.   Reference is probably to David Littlejohn, whose article "The Tropics of Miller" appeared in *The New Republic* on March 5, 1962 (pp. 31–35).
3.   By Nelson Algren (New York: Farrar, Straus and Cudahy, [1956]).
4.   The first postscript is written vertically in the left margin of the first page. The second postscript is the only portion of the letter on the second page (reverse side of page one).

On March 21, writing on another "Val's Birthday Gift" postcard, Miller acknowledged receipt of an inscribed photograph of Gertz. Gertz responded on March 28 with a three-page letter in which he mentioned, among other personal items, his unpublished novel about Ben Reitman (see Gertz 2/12/62, notes) and the forthcoming marriage of his daughter "Midge" (Margery Ann). A large portion of the letter was devoted to the status of *Cancer* litigation in Chicago:

"The situation, in brief, is that Mayor Daley ordered the Corporation Counsel's office to appeal the case because of the tremendous pressure upon him from Catholic sources. As I explained in one letter, a copy of which was sent to you, the appeal is to the wrong court, but that may be deliberate.[1] It is also important to bear in mind that the other defendants, the suburban police chiefs, have all signed waivers of appeal and have agreed to be bound immediately by the decree. We, thus, have the anomalous situation in which anybody in Chicago may order the book by mail or may go to the suburbs and get copies. Not only psychologically, but legally, I think that this will impress the court on appeal as being rather foolish.

"I suspect that there will be some pressure on the Appellate Court, but I think it can resist it. Certainly, the Supreme Court would resist it.

"I understand that, in the period between the Judge's filing his opinion and the taking of the appeal, the book was selling fantastically well. Kroch's alone ordered 2500 additional copies and the Levy Distributing Company almost 30,000. This is important in ascertaining the damages if we ultimately prevail. Of course, at that point, we would be inclined to press for damages.

"The reporting on this case has not been as good as it might have been. Anyone reading some of the newspapers would assume that the Judge had enjoined the further distribution of the book. What he enjoined was interference with the distribution of the book and that is quite the reverse of what the newspapers said. But since an appeal is pending, the appeal acts as a supersedeas, which is lawyers' jargon for saying that the effect of the decree is stayed for the time being. In my judgment, there could be no valid prosecution at this time. Of course, the police may attempt such prosecutions, but they would ultimately fail, if not in the trial court, then on appeal; this regardless as to how the upper courts rule on the case before Judge Epstein.

"I suppose that by now you are prepared to agree with Charles Dickens that the law is an ass. Certainly, those who administer it are often asinine."

On the original of this Gertz letter, Miller wrote: "Bob— Please file with rest of his papers. Henry."

---

1.   Police Superintendent Orlando Wilson's appeal was filed with the Appellate Court of Illinois, First District, on March 16. Gertz felt

that it was in the interests of his clients that the case be heard by the Illinois Supreme Court without delay and that since constitutional questions were involved there were grounds for proceeding directly to that court. In subsequent letters Gertz tells Miller of his efforts in this regard.

ALS, 1P.   March 28, 1962

Dear Elmer Gertz— No letter from you recently—it's like a gale suddenly subsiding. Hope it's not due to change of heart! I did get all the clippings, etc. And had dinner the other night with Stanley Fleishman who is handling the appeal here.[1] I like him!

I leave Friday morning early and stop off two days at Jefferson City, Mo. to see a "lifer" at the Penitentiary there.[2] (One of my fans.) Hope I can do something for him with the Parole Board.

For future mail suggest you use Grove Press as address. Don't send me clippings etc. unless very important, eh? When I travel I don't (usually) write many letters. Must *relax*, as I urged you to do. We live only once—at least, in *this* guise. I need a bit of fun.

More from somewhere.   Ever my best to you! Henry Miller

P.S. And warm greetings to Judge Epstein, please. There was a wonderful 2½ hour debate on Hunter's T.V. program recently. Four women—excellent. Especially Mrs. Frances Sayres.[3]

1.   Reference to the Bradley Smith case (see H. M. 2/25/62, notes). For an account of the earlier Marin County jury trial, which resulted in a verdict of not guilty for Franklin B. Pershina, a book dealer in San Rafael, California, see Donovan Bess, "Miller's 'Tropic' on Trial," *Evergreen Revue*, Vol 6, No. 23 (March–April 1962), pp. 12–37. On May 2, 1962, Geraldine and Laurence McGilvery, operators of the Nexus Bookstore in La Jolla, were cleared by a San Diego Municipal Court.
2.   The long-time correspondent whom Miller saw for the first time on this visit to Missouri State Prison in Jefferson City was Roger Bloom. At fifty, he was serving a life sentence for being an habitual criminal. As will be seen, Gertz soon joined in Miller's effort to have him paroled.
3.   Postscript written vertically in left margin.

ALS, 2PP.   April 4th '62

Dear Elmer Gertz—   Got yours of March 28th here.[1] Curious
how you know all the people—like Ben Reitman—who also were
in my life, but only slightly.

　　Didn't see Rosset—he's in California at the moment.

　　But, I had lunch to-day with Alex. King and his adorable wife.
Great session, indeed. I'm up to my ears meeting people—a bit
pooped out. Leave for London Friday. Address there, until April
17th c/o Alfred Perlès—69, Parliament Hill, London, N.W. 3.

　　Forgive me for being so brief.   All the best! Henry Miller

P.S. Remind me some time to tell you about my friend Roger
Bloom whom I visited in the Missouri State Penitentiary. He knew
Leopold—in Joliet prison, I believe.[2]

1.　　Written on stationery with printed heading, "One Fifth Avenue, New
　　York 3, N.Y."
2.　　Postscript written separately, on second page (reverse side of page one).

TL(CC), 1P.   April 6, 1962

Mr. Henry Miller
One Fifth Avenue
New York 3, New York

Dear Henry Miller: I have your little letter about your immediate plans. You mention that you are leaving for Europe Friday.
If it is next Friday, rather than this one, I may be able to see you.
I will be at the Waldorf Astoria in New York with my wife from
either April 11 or 12, to and including April 15. I would love to
hear from you and to learn if there is any possibility of our meeting.

　　I got a very delightful letter from your friend Roger Bloom.
Now and then I shall write to him, in the hope that it will enable
him to pass the time more cheerfully.

Believe it or not, Jack Mabley telephoned me yesterday and invited me to have lunch with him. I accepted. Mabley said, among other things: "I hope that you realize, Elmer, that this means that I have the utmost respect for you, even when we differ."

I spent a good deal of time with Hoke Norris, going over the draft of his article about our trial here, which will be published in the next issue of the Evergreen Review. It is an excellent article and I think that you will enjoy it.[1]

I was delighted to get a call from the airport from Peter Viereck.[2] Although we have corresponded for many years, I have not seen him since he was a young man.

All my best to you.   Sincerely yours, ELMER GERTZ

cc: c/o Grove Press, Inc.

---

1. " 'Cancer' in Chicago," Evergreen Review, v. 6, No. 25 (July–August 1962), pp. 41–66. This issue of Evergreen Review also featured on its cover, the following endpaper, and first two pages, a "Statement in Support of Freedom to Read," signed by more than two hundred authors, journalists, and publishers, which commented favorably on Judge Epstein's decision.
2. Pulitzer Prize poet, son of George Sylvester Viereck.

ALS, 1P.   from London—4/14/62

Dear Elmer Gertz—   When I can get down to it I must begin again trying to do something to get Roger Bloom out on parole. Very kind of you to offer to write him occasionally. I had two momentous meetings with him in the Pen. Also good talks with the director of prisons (for the State)—Colonel ⟨obliterated⟩ Carter[1] and with the Protestant Chaplain. The Warden left me ice cold.

Amazed that Jack Mabley acts this way. How do they do it— left hand-right hand biz., I suppose.

Also had wonderful meeting in N.Y. with Alex. King and his wife.

Publisher here is mailing you a book called "Hundred Dollar Misunderstanding."[2] (I got a kick out of it—the girl's language.) No trouble with censors over it. Mails copies to US. No complaints. Don't understand. They have also published Tanizaki's "The Key" over here—without interference. Beats me.

I'm off for Paris Tuesday and on the 27th will arrive in Mallorca. Better write me to Paris unless I advise otherwise. Tom Moore says the appeal has gone to the "wrong court." (?)

Forgive brevity. You see, I don't think very well in traveling. And yet I don't make the mind "empty," as the Chinese recommend.   All good wishes! Henry Miller

---

1.   Colonel J. D. Carter, Director of Corrections. The Protestant Chaplain was the Reverend E. C. Grandstaff. (*Henry Miller Society Newsletter* No. 9, May 1962.)
2.   See H. M. 3/8/62.

TL(CC), 2PP., AIR MAIL   April 20, 1962

Mr. Henry Miller
c/o Agence Hoffman
FF Blvd. Saint-Michel
Paris (5e)
FRANCE

Dear Henry Miller: This has been a period of excessive work. The only reason that I find it livable is that the work is of great interest and importance and all sorts of stirring events have occurred.

When I was in New York last week-end, for example, I attended an interview of Justice Hugo Black of the United States Supreme Court. It was a truly moving and historical event. Justice Black, as you may know, believes completely in the First Amendment. He is against obscenity prosecutions and even against libel suits. In his mind, there can be no exceptions to the fullness of scope of the Amendment. Listening to him, I was almost completely persuaded.[1]

So that you will understand the situation thoroughly, let me bring you up to date on the "Tropic of Cancer" situation here in Chicago—I am not referring to the situation elsewhere. The Corporation Counsel, acting for Superintendent of Police Wilson, has deliberately appealed to the wrong court; this for the purpose of delay, so far as I can judge. Barney Rosset and his associates are disturbed over the consequent losses of sales. I have, therefore, promised to attempt some move or other to speed up the appeal, and I am now working on it. When the papers are drawn, I shall send copies to you, because I believe that they will interest you. I hardly suppose that I will succeed in this move, but one can never tell. At any rate, it is worth attempting.

At first, I was not going to represent the four actors who read portions of "Tropic of Cancer" some weeks ago, but, on reflection, I decided to appear in their behalf. The matter came up in court yesterday and I had some hope of throwing out the whole proceeding, but the prosecutor begged off on some pretext or other and the matter was continued until May 15.

I shall write to Roger Bloom as soon as I have a moment to spare. He intrigues me, of course. I am as bad as you, in involving myself with this person or that, and this cause or that, without regard to time, health, money or other considerations. I suppose that it is the nature of the beast. I suppose, too, that I would be much less happy if I were more niggardly in my expenditure of energy.

I have just purchased a copy of the magnificent book published by Harry Abrams, dealing with your water colors.[2] Of course, I shall go through it tonight. Bit by bit, I am completing my collection of Miller-ana.

Thanks much for mailing a copy of the book mentioned in your letter. I have not yet received it, but I am sure it will be very amusing.

Don't feel under any compulsion to write, although I always am very happy when I hear from you.

Have an exciting time and return in shape for the battles.

Always yours, ELMER GERTZ

1. The occasion to which Gertz referred was a banquet in Justice Black's
    honor on April 14, the climactic feature of the American Jewish Con-
    gress's 1962 convention, during which Justice Black was interviewed
    publicly by Professor Edmond Cahn of the New York University Law
    School (see the *New York Law Review*, June 1962, pp. 549–63). In
    introducing Justice Black, Professor Cahn said: "[*Justice Black*] draws
    his highest inspiration from the First Amendment in the Bill of Rights,
    which forbids the Government to abridge our freedom of speech, free-
    dom of press, freedom of religion, and freedom of association. Since
    his appointment to the [*United States Supreme Court*] bench in 1937,
    he has incessantly called on the State and Federal Governments to re-
    spect these freedoms literally, completely, and without exception." As
    the following exchange reveals, Justice Black held that the First
    Amendment prohibits any censorship of so-called obscenity:

    > CAHN: Is there any kind of obscene material, whether defined as
    > hard-core pornography or otherwise, the distribution and sale of
    > which can be constitutionally restricted in any manner whatever, in
    > your opinion?
    > JUSTICE BLACK: I will say it can in this country, because the courts
    > have held that it can.
    > CAHN: Yes, but you won't get off so easily. I want to know what
    > you think.
    > JUSTICE BLACK: My view is, without deviation, without exception,
    > without any ifs, buts, or whereases, that freedom of speech means
    > that you shall not do something to people either for the views they
    > have or the views they express or the words they speak or write. . . .
    > I do not believe there is any halfway ground for protecting freedom
    > of speech and press.

2. *Henry Miller: Watercolors, Drawings, and His Essay,* The Angel Is
    My Watermark!

APS, 1S., AIR MAIL   Paris—April 21st

Dear Elmer Gertz—   Though our correspondence has tailed off
I think of you often. It's good to see old friends like Rattner and
Brassai.[1] Tomorrow I lunch with *Ionesco.*

All the best! Henry Miller

---

1. Abraham Rattner, American artist, knew Miller during his Paris days,
    and accompanied him on the early part of the trip (1940) that Miller
    described in *The Air-Conditioned Nightmare* ([New York]: New Di-

rections [1945]). Rattner designed the cover for that book, as well as the frontispiece for *Scenario* (Paris: Obelisk Press, 1937). Miller wrote about him in an essay in *Remember to Remember* ([New York]: New Directions, [1947]), entitled "A Bodhisattva Artist." Halasz Brassai, internationally famed Hungarian photographer, was in the Miller-Perlès circle in Paris in the 1930s. "The Eye of Paris," in *Max and the White Phagocytes*, is an appreciation of Brassai.

Miller's lunch with the avant-garde, Rumanian-born French playwright Eugène Ionesco was at Le Vesinet, the country home of his publisher, Edmond Buchet. While in Paris Miller also met for the first time the American authors James Jones and William Styron.

From Paris, Miller flew to Mallorca to join the authors and publishers attending the Formentor Conference and to assist in choosing the recipient of the Formentor Prize, which was awarded to Ewe Johnson of Berlin. The Henry Miller Literary Society Newsletter of May 1962 (No. 9) reported: "In addition to Miller, the other U.S. judges are James Baldwin, Harvey Breit and Herb Gold. Prix Formentor is the first and only international award for unpublished works of fiction. Each May the winning manuscript is awarded $10,000 and is published simultaneously in France, Italy, Germany, England, Spain, Portugal, Denmark, Sweden, Holland, Finland, Norway, Canada and by Grove Press in the United States. Last year's winner—the first—was 'Summer Storm' by Juan Garcia Hortelanc."

APS, 1S.   May 9th—Formentor

Dear friend—   Caught the flu here (in Paradise) but better now. Will be in Berlin in a week but write c/o Agence Hoffman, as ever. Haven't seen mail for 2 weeks. It's all waiting for me in Paris. Expect to arrive in Minneapolis end of May. Hope I can see you there chez Schwartz—*not* Chicago! All the Best! Henry Miller

TL(CC), 2PP., AIR MAIL   May 15, 1962

Dear Henry Miller: I am sorry to learn of your illness and I
hope that you are now fully recovered and that the chasing hither
and thither will not wear you out. I look forward to seeing you at
the end of May. Please give me the full particulars so that nothing
will go wrong.

Let me bring you up to date on the *Tropic of Cancer* appeal.

As you know, the Chicago police superintendent, the only defendant not accepting the results, filed a notice of appeal to the
Appellate Court of Illinois, an intermediate reviewing court, which
does not normally hear constitutional questions. I was certain that
the purpose of appealing what is essentially a constitutional case to
the wrong tribunal was to delay the matter as long as possible, since
the notice of appeal filed within a short period of time acted as a
stay order; that is, the sale of the book might be held up by police
action during the pendency of the appeal. Accordingly, I thought
of a procedure that, so far as I know, has never been tried previously. As appellee, I filed what is called a Short Record in the
Appellate Court and then filed a motion either to dismiss the appeal
or transfer it to the Illinois Supreme Court. After the filing of briefs
by both sides on my motion to dismiss or transfer, the Appellate
Court, much to my pleasure and surprise, transferred the case to
the Supreme Court. I think that this will lop off about a year of
stalling. Now I am going to see if I can persuade the Supreme Court
to set aside the stay order. If I succeed in this result, and it is unlikely, then the book may be sold in Chicago, pending the result of
the appeal.

I hope that this makes sense to you, although I realize that it
is not always possible to express legal concepts in laymen's language.

After you left the country, I was in New York for a few days
and spent some time with Barney Rosset and his associate Mr. Perlman. I also talked with Charles Rembar and Stephen Tulin.[1] We
compared notes about the various *Tropic of Cancer* cases throughout the country and agreed upon certain aspects of procedure.

The Chicago case will be the subject of a long article in the Evergreen Review. I think it comes out around June 1.

After all, I was prevailed upon to represent the four actors who were arrested for reading portions of *Tropic of Cancer*. I filed a motion to suppress the evidence and to dismiss the case and also changes of venue from a number of the more bigoted judges. The matter has been continued to June 28. The three prosecutions against City booksellers have been continued generally.

I had one personal joy a few days ago. My older son, who is in military service, got leave from his outfit and came in to town to be sworn in specially as an attorney. I appeared with him before my old law school friend, Justice Schaefer of the Illinois Supreme Court. There were about a dozen young men and women who were sworn in at the same time and Justice Schaefer asked me to address the group. When I got back to the office there was a letter from President Truman, congratulating me on Ted's admission to the bar.

I am rather on edge because of illness in the family. My two older brothers both have been extremely ill; the one with a coronary. As soon as I get some emergency work out of the way I am going to the hospital to learn what I can.

I look forward to seeing you. Always yours, ELMER GERTZ

---

1.   Stephen Wise Tulin, of Polier, Midonick and Zinsser, New York, was one of the attorneys who assisted in coordinating *Cancer* cases for Grove Press. Milton Perlman was a Grove Press official.

APS, 1S., AIR MAIL   Berlin—May 18th

Dear friend—   Haven't had any news, about trials, etc. but presume it can wait till I get to Minneapolis (about end of May). All quiet here. Hope you received "The Hundred Dollar Misunderstanding" from London.

All the best ever!   Henry Miller

ALS, 1P.   Berlin—May 27th '62

Dear Elmer Gertz—   Only got yours of May 15th yesterday—
held up by French Postal strike. I've got to have my heart checked
when I arrive in N.Y. or else in Minneapolis. But don't feel bad—
just not tops.

I wrote Schwartz to keep in touch with you so that we can
meet when I get to Minneapolis—where I will stay two or three
days certainly. I arrive in N.Y. May 31st and have asked Grove
Press to book me a plane for Minneapolis June 3rd. Hope you can
come there without too much inconvenience.

I get all you say about the Chicago business. From the Supreme Court of Illinois I suppose we go eventually to the U.S. Supreme Court—or no? It would be tough just going from one *State*
Supreme Court to another, eh? I wonder how Stanley Fleishman
is making out in Los Angeles.

Sorry to hear about your two brothers. This heart trouble seems
to hit most every home. Must be the pace we live at.

Weather here is miserable—Paris the same. No spring yet
in Europe.

Well, à bientôt!   Henry Miller

I like the German bookshops—great variety of books.[1]

---

1.   Postscript written vertically in left margin. Miller reported in the Sep-
        tember 1962 issue of the *Henry Miller Literary Society Newsletter*
        that from Formentor he returned to Paris for a few days before going
        to Berlin; and that in Berlin he looked up the author and adventurer
        Jack Bilbo, and at the Springer Gallery saw for the first time, in fin-
        ished form, the bust of him that Marini had sculpted the previous
        summer, in Italy.

TL(CC), 1P., AIR MAIL, "HOLD FOR ARRIVAL"   May 28, 1962

Mr. Henry Miller
c/o Grove Press, Inc.
64 University Place
New York 3, New York
Dear Henry Miller: Eddie Schwartz has told me that you will
be in Minneapolis Sunday, and he has invited me to share his hos-
pitality. You are going to be his house guest and I am going to be
at a nearby motel, as I understand it. This delights me; but before
setting forth for Minneapolis I want to make certain as to your
plans.

I don't know whether or not the letters I sent to you to the
Paris address or any other have arrived, but, in any event, I can
bring you up to date when I see you Sunday.

I hope that you are well and that you enjoyed your European
trip thoroughly.   Sincerely yours, ELMER GERTZ

[*June 1, 1962*]

ARRIVING MINNEAPOLIS SUNDAY NIGHT HOPE TO
SEE YOU THERE MONDAY
BEST OF GREETINGS   HENRY MILLER

[*Wire to Gertz at office, 1 June 1962. New York City.*]

*Gertz met Miller for the first time the evening of June 3, 1962,
when he and Edward Schwartz picked Miller up at the Minneapolis International Airport. During the next three days Miller also
met Tom Moore, secretary of the Henry Miller Literary Society
and the author of Bibliography of Henry Miller, and Robert C.
McClure of the University of Minnesota Law School, authority
on obscenity litigation; renewed his friendship with Orvis Ross,
organist and piano teacher in Rochester, whom Miller had not
seen for forty years; and taped a radio interview with Audrey June
Booth, KUOM, University of Minnesota.*

Gertz, in giving his impressions of their meeting in the Henry

Miller Literary Society Newsletter No. 10, September 1962, wrote in part:

"I could feel that creative mind of his at work on me. I could visualize the process by which so many men and women have been immortalized in his autobiographical novels. Would I squirm if I found myself as real as life on one of his pages?

"Talking with Henry I had a sense of his complete integrity, even when he outrages the conventional code. Henry Miller is an innocent, even when he scandalizes.

. . . .

"When I returned to Chicago, my wife was much concerned about getting my impressions of a man and writer whom she, too, values. She was annoyed at me for depicting a thoughtful, courteous, by no means brash creature. 'All right,' I said, 'I found him swinging from the chandelier at the airport, screeching profanity at all the world.' That picture did not satisfy her, either.

"The fact is that a valid portrait of Henry Miller requires depth of understanding and subtlety of brush work. It is something to be attempted only when memory mellows one and all that is extraneous vanishes."[1]

---

1.   See also Gertz, *A Handful of Clients*, pp. 232–35.

TL(CC), 2PP., AIR MAIL   June 8, 1962

Dear Henry: Greetings upon your return! I hope that you arrived back home refreshed and content and with not much of an accumulation of work. Do, please, look into any matters pertaining to your health that require attention. We want you with us for a long while to come. I must say that you looked and acted extremely well and there is no suggestion of any ill health.

It was one of the great experiences of my life, this meeting in Minneapolis. I have often thought of the many striking things said by you. I am sure that they will form a permanent part of my memory.

I am delighted with our friends Eddie and Tom. There are

certainly few people like them. If I had speculated as to the kind of persons capable of forming the Henry Miller Society, I would never have come up with them as my vision. I cannot imagine any persons capable of arousing more enthusiasm for you.

I am sending you copies of the McClure articles on obscenity.[1] They are tough going in part, but, in view of the tremendous amount of *Tropic* litigation, it might be well for you to have some intimate knowledge of the legal aspects.

I am hard at work in examining the transcript of the record, which runs into many thousands of pages, so as to be certain that the City does not throw any curves. The work is not as tedious as it might ordinarily be, because of the excitement of the subject matter.

I am sending a copy of Hoke Norris' latest article, dealing with the situation in Maywood, a village near Chicago.[2]

When I catch my breath I will write more.

Warmest greetings to you.   Always yours, ELMER GERTZ

---

1.   There is no record of the articles Gertz enclosed, but see: William B. Lockhart and Robert C. McClure, "Literature, the Law of Obscenity, and the Constitution," *Minnesota Law Review*, 38 (March, 1954), 295–395; "Censorship of Obscenity: The Developing Constitutional Standards," *Minnesota Law Review*, 45 (November, 1960), 5–121; "Obscenity Censorship: The Core Constitutional Issue—What Is Obscene?," *Utah Law Review*, 7 (Spring, 1961), 289–303.
2.   "Critic At-Large: Censorship," *Chicago Sun-Times*, June 8, 1962, p. 36.

Before returning to California, Miller paid a second visit to Roger Bloom in the Jefferson City, Missouri, penitentiary. From Jefferson City on June 11 Miller sent Gertz a five-page, handwritten letter on legal size paper about Bloom, of whom he said that "in 24 years he has only been at liberty twice and then for less than six months." The letter gives Miller's and Bloom's thoughts about prison officials and the parole board, and names influential people whose assistance might be elicited, among them being ex-Governor Blair.

> *Apparently Miller enclosed a memorandum from Bloom about*
> *someone who owed him money, a matter which comes up in sub-*
> *sequent letters. Bloom not only wanted the money for legal fees*
> *in connection with his efforts to secure parole but because, accord-*
> *ing to Miller, he believed there was "a way of getting out—by*
> *paying."*
>   *Miller's next letter reveals that he marked the envelope of*
> *this communication "Confidential." As will be seen from later*
> *correspondence, he was concerned about whether it reached Gertz*
> *safely.*

ALS, 2PP.   from Kansas City Airport
                                           June 12th '62

Dear friend—   An amazing thing happened this morning after
my second visit to Roger Bloom. As I was about to leave a man
asked me if he could give me a lift. Said he saw my name on the
register—had never read my books but eager to meet me. In a few
words, as we drove along, I told him of Roger Bloom and my reason for visiting the prison. As we pulled up to my hotel he asked
if I was free to lunch with him and if so would take me to the airport. I agreed. He gave me his card—was a well-known lawyer,
fairly rich, I gathered, *and* only too happy to be of service to me—
free of charge, he added.

He said he would look up the file on Roger, and let me know
what his chances were. Sort of implied that if he had a chance,
Roger, he would take it on. (He didn't add for free, but Heavens
only knows what his thought was.) He was a typical Missouri
gentleman, took me to his home to introduce me to his wife and
daughter, then to his Country Club for lunch. Seemed proud to
show me off to his friends—and wants badly to read some of my
work (Cancer especially). I had a most favorable impression and
was happy I had acted on my intuition yesterday—as I wrote you.
Hope you got this letter, marked "Confidential." The impression I
got from him was that if it was at all possible to do something for
Roger *he* could do it. (I discovered in the course of conversation

that he was a friend of long standing with Ex-Gov. Blair, his brother and father.)

In the Penitentiary I also had a good talk with a Mr. Hughes, secretary of the Parole Board. He seemed like an "enlightened" individual, somewhat of a psychologist too. Was glad I had called on him and urged me to write him if there was any thing I thought he could do for me.

A wonderful morning, really. And in Kansas City, at the Frank Glenn Bookshop, I met a Jean Benedict who knew good friends of mine and was most charming.

I am getting my plane for L.A. in a few minutes. Must stop. Let's see what happens next! Cheers! Henry Miller

P.S. The lawyer's name is—
Edgar M. Eagan
Central Trust Bldg.
Jefferson City—Mo.

APS, 1S.   June 15th '62

Dear Elmer Gertz—   Got copies of your letters. What a *long* one you wrote Roger. Makes me feel even more cautious—about using your precious time and energy. Am writing this in a drug store—no stationery to hand. Very interesting too that the Radio interviewer wrote you as she did.[1] I do think it was about the best (radio) interview I ever had. Tom Moore is trying to get permission to use the T.V. talk I had with Perlès in London.[2] More soon. All the best! Henry Miller

---

1. Audrey June Booth of KUOM, University of Minnesota (see *Henry Miller Literary Society Newsletter* No. 10, Sept. 1962).
2. Two-hour tape made for release in Canada, cut to a half hour when shown.

ALS, 2PP.   June 18th 1962

Dear Elmer Gertz—   Though I thought I saw references to the two letters I mailed you, from Jeff City and Kansas City, in the copy you sent me of your long letter to Roger Bloom, I still feel uncertain that you got them. Especially concerned about delivery of one marked "Confidential." I'm not pressing you for an answer immediately—maybe none is required—but would love to have a line saying you *did* receive them.

I will be at a friend's house in Northridge, California until this Friday evening. If there's any thing urgent for me to know, would you please telephone me there—[*number omitted*]. (Dr. Robert Fink's home.)

The printed material you sent me just arrived. Will read it shortly. Just got my kids off this morning to spend a 2-week vacation in Big Sur—six kids in a big station wagon. Now I'm waiting for a phone call to know if they arrived safely.

The phone number at 661 is [*omitted*], if you ever need it. (care of ⟨obliterated⟩ VERZEANO.)[1]

No time for more now. Have been on the go since 6:00 A.M.

More soon.   The best! Henry[2]

---

1.   Reference to Janina Lepska Miller Verzeano, Miller's third wife who left him in 1951, mother of Valentin and Tony Miller.
2.   Written on stationery of Langdon's Uptown Motel, Rochester, Minnesota.

TL(CC), 2PP., AIR MAIL
June 19, 1962

Mr. Henry Miller
c/o Verzeano
661 Las Lomas
Pacific Palisades, California

Dear Henry: My letter to Roger Bloom was something in the nature of a reply to you as well, but I ought to add certain words of caution.

I know from the Nathan Leopold case, as well as other matters that I have handled, that men who have been incarcerated for a long period of time and have been unsuccessful in their efforts to get out tend to seek desperate remedies. Very often Parole Boards and other public officials are corrupt, so that there is a measure of truth in reports about buying one's way out of prison. I know when I first became Leopold's attorney, some "gentleman" from St. Louis called upon me and professed to be deeply interested in Leopold's future, and he advised me that Leopold would be released only if certain people were paid off and that he was the one to make contacts. I made certain that there were concealed witnesses to the conversation and tried not to offend the "gentleman" until after I had taken various steps in Leopold's behalf. But in the end I made it clear to him and others that in no circumstances would we seek to buy Leopold's freedom. Of course, Leopold himself was unenthusiastic about this attitude on our part, but his family was in complete agreement with me. Money had gotten him into trouble in the first instance, and they were determined that it would not get him into trouble again. Even without any moral or legal consideration in the matter, on sheer expediency one could not afford to do the wrong things in his case.

This is not quite as apparent in the Roger Bloom case, because Roger does not have the notoriety that Leopold had and has, but you do have such fame or notoriety, and if you were involved, however innocently, in any action that could be misconstrued, it would be more mischievous than even these various obscenity cases.

You must tell Roger that all you can do is to offer advice and discuss the matter with me, and that you cannot act as a go-between or anything else that might be misconstrued. You can tell him, as kindly as possible, that an inexperienced person like yourself can do more harm than good, and that your principal interest in life must be in your work. You can make him feel that you are going to encourage him in every way and be as helpful as possible, but there are certain things that you cannot and will not do. I don't think that I need to spell out what I mean.

Of course, I would love to be helpful to Roger, but, for the moment, I think I ought to confine my activity to trying to collect the obligation owing to him. I suspect that, if the other party communicates with me after I write to him, we will learn some very interesting facts. My wife, who is often very shrewd in such things, suggested that all is not as represented with respect to "Grayson."

There is so much that I would like to say, but I want to give you the opportunity to catch up on some of your work, and I don't want you to overdo.

Incidentally, my son is being transferred from Fort Chaffee in Arkansas to Ford Ord near Monterey. He is a very bright young man, and his wife has a good deal of artistic ability. I have told them to say hello to you some time or other this summer.

I have not yet received the water color from Berlin. I wonder if it could be at Customs or delayed some other way. Perhaps, you ought to make inquiry.

My very best to you.   Always yours, ELMER GERTZ

TL(CC), 1P.   June 19, 1962

Dear Henry: The other day I sent you a copy of a book that you might otherwise not read. It is entitled *Mater et Magistra—An Encyclical Letter of His Holiness Pope John XXIII*.[1] This is worth having, because it is a very special printing of one of the classical statements on social justice issued by the present Pope. The editor and publisher are Jewish, the one who defrayed the expenses is

Protestant, and, as I suggested to Eddie, I believe that the Pope is Catholic.

The current issue (June 23) of the Saturday Review has an extremely good article by John Ciardi at page 39 thereof.[2] It puts the problem with respect to censorship in the most understandable light. Ciardi is aware of the problem from the legal viewpoint as well as other more important considerations.

Incidentally, I have just finished talking with the Chief Justice of one of the courts—not Chief Justice Epstein—and I find that he regards you as one of the great authors of modern times. He told me that he had given that opinion to the Corporation Counsel of Chicago, but apparently it did not help there.

Sincerely yours, [*Elmer Gertz*][3]

---

1. New York: Paulist Press, 1961; [Boston]: St. Paul Editions, [1961]. The edition that Gertz sent Miller was: Chicago, The Discoverers Press, 1962.
2. "Manner of Speaking: The Book Banners."
3. No typewritten signature line; original signed as usual.

Gertz brought Miller up to date on matters pertaining to Roger Bloom in a three-page letter dated June 20. He reported that there were difficulties in attempting to collect the debt for Bloom, chief among which was that Bloom "apparently obtained money for Grayson through a robbery," and cautioned Miller as follows:

"You are eager to help Roger get out of prison, and you believe that he will lead a useful life if he is paroled. I am intrigued by him and am eager to be of assistance to you; but, very frankly, I must tell you in the strictest confidence that I am not yet completely satisfied in my own mind that he can succeed on parole. Unfortunately, some men are simply not built for freedom. I am making discreet inquiry and when I have learned something I will let you know. There are men who are brilliant, kind, filled with promise, and yet they are unable to manage their lives."

Gertz also said he was sending a copy of Nathan Leopold's book, Life Plus 99 Years (Garden City, New York: Doubleday, 1958), and thanked Miller for the inscription in a copy of Stand

Still Like the Hummingbird. That inscription reads: "For Elmer Gertz—one of the most amazing men I have ever met—and so gentle, modest, humble withal. In friendship Henry Miller Minneapolis 6/5/62 'Remember to remember'"

TLS, 1P.   661 Las Lomas, Pac. Pal.
                                      June 23, '62

Dear Elmer Gertz,   First day at the typewriter. Just catching up. Find quite a few letters, enclosures, books, etc. from you. Oof! Will get down to the reading of things soon as I can. I did see Ciardi's article in Sat. Rev.

As to the "wanted" list, will do my best. Slow work. Am writing Berlin again about the water color. Don't understand delay. But if lost in mails don't worry—will do another.

I will be here until mid-August, and then to Edinburgh, if all's well. Would your son come all the way down here—I don't expect to be in Big Sur at all this Summer.

Now about Roger Bloom. Everything you write me about him is perfectly clear. It's true he was in a desperate frame of mind when he gave me the dope on Grayson to forward you. I am sure he thinks differently now. Also, I am acting very cautiously and slowly —for all the reasons you mentioned. Believe me, I too have weighed his problem from every angle—I mean, what might happen upon his release. Both the secretary of the parole board, Mr. Hughes, with whom I had a good talk and who seemed fairminded, intelligent, etc., and the attorney, Mr. Eagan, whom I met by chance, spoke of the difficulty they have with men like Roger— i.e. confidence men, defaulters, safe crackers, etc. But, rare as it may be, men do change sometimes; and I would like to give Roger the benefit of the doubt, myself. Mr. Eagan wrote me briefly that he had visited Roger "and found him to be perfectly reconciled to his situation. He has no distorted views about the probability of ultimate release." Rather curious statement, revealing Roger's tact, I believe. I expect to hear further from this man, after he has gone over Roger's file. If it appears to him that Roger has a chance, I presume he will ask me if I want him to handle the case and then talk about costs. The preliminary work he offered to do gratis, of his own accord. He has the manners of a Southern gentleman, outwardly at least. Roger, on the other hand, had written me before seeing Mr. Eagan, that "the men" did not think he had much pull, that to them he was "a minor." Which pleases me rather than disappoints me. I think and feel he is above taking bribes, in any form. I still feel it was lucky (for all concerned) that I did not reach the man Roger wanted ⟨obliterated⟩ me to see.

Meanwhile Anaïs Nin, with whom Roger is also in correspondence, is urging him to ask for the intervention of a psychiatrist. She feels that the prison authorities proceed on traditional lines and are immune to the pleadings of people like us (meaning artists, etc.) I told Roger to hold off on this too for a while. Her idea may be a good one, but I don't feel like "rushing" the prison people. Work slowly and quietly and through regular channels, is what I think best at the moment.

I will stop now; wish I had a secretary. Every time I see my mail come in my heart sinks. I saw the heart specialist again yesterday, got a new cardiogram reading, and for the moment all seems quite good, nothing too serious. It was a mistake to have taken the digitalis which the Spanish doctor recommended, especially in big doses; it also made the first cardiogram a crazy reading. I'll know more about everything in a week or so.

By the end of next week my kids return; then the real chores begin. Give warm greetings to your wife, who sounds so wonderful, and take good care of yourself. After 3 days "vacation" in the Valley, chez Fink, I feel used up. Too much talk, no activity.

Henry Miller

TL(CC), 2PP., AIR MAIL   June 26, 1962

Dear Henry: This has been a real Henry Miller day. I received the Hebrew edition of *Tropic of Cancer*, I read two articles about you in the current issue of Saturday Review and one article in News-week.[1] Then our thoughtful friend, Eddie Schwartz, telephoned to say that my water color had arrived and it was so beautiful that he was tempted to steal it, but he is sending it to me in the fastest way. He, also, told me that the Milwaukee case involving your book had been decided adversely, in a rather apologetic decision by the judge.[2] I have not yet seen it.

The United States Supreme Court yesterday seems to have made it even more difficult to get convictions in obscenity matters. The New York Times summarized the case better than other news-papers, but I still do not know precisely what was decided. Of course, I will get the various opinions of the members of the Court. They seem to have split all over the lot, not as far as the result was concerned, but with respect to their reasoning.[3]

Of course, you got my copy of the letter to Roger Bloom. I hope I took the right line with him. I do not want to hurt him, but I feel that the least I could do for him is to be completely honest in the expression of views. I have a strong feeling that pursuing Grayson might be disastrous. The important course is the more direct one of trying to get Roger out of prison. There are so many things that I must do this summer, but I shall try to visit him, if only to let him know that there are people who are deeply con-cerned about him. It would be well, first, to know what the other gentleman of my profession is doing. I must not appear to be inter-fering with him, not simply as a matter of professional courtesy, but because he may feel inhibited if he has to account to anyone else. Don't hesitate to tell me anything that occurs. I shall com-ment upon it as frankly as I can. I shall certainly write to you with-out inhibition, even when I might temper my words in communi-cating with Roger.

Interesting as your letter is, it indicates that you are in need of some time ⟨obliterated⟩ wholly to yourself, without conversation or other interplay between people. In the circumstances, I had bet-ter cut short this letter so that you can do as you please without the necessity of communication.

Thanks so much for your words about my wife. She is, indeed, wonderful.   Always yours, ELMER GERTZ

---

1.   John Ciardi, "Manner of Speaking: Tropic of Cancer," *Saturday Review*, June 30, 1962, p. 13; Harry T. Moore, "Portrait Gallery and Pet Gripes," ibid., p. 18; "Off Stride," *Newsweek*, July 2, 1962, pp. 82–83. (Both "Portrait Gallery and Pet Gripes" and "Off Stride" were reviews of *Stand Still Like the Hummingbird*. For other reviews of that book, see "The Dry Pornographer," *Time*, June 29, 1962, p. 78; Annette K. Baxter, "Random Brushstrokes of a Radical Optimist," *New York Times Book Review*, July 8, 1962, pp. 6, 7.)
2.   For an account of the Milwaukee trial without jury (May 15–18, 1962), the adverse decision on June 22, 1962, and the Wisconsin Supreme Court's reversal (May 20, 1963), see E. R. Hutchison, *Tropic of Cancer on Trial* (New York: Grove Press, Inc., 1968), pp. 178–201.
3.   Manual Enterprises v. Day, Postmaster General (370 U.S. 478) involved the magazines MANual, Trim, and *Grecian Guild Pictorial*, which featured nude or almost nude photographs of young men. Six United States Supreme Court Justices declared the magazines not obscene, but as Gertz says they failed to agree on the reasons for their positions. Justice John M. Harlan, who wrote the opinion for reversal, with which Justice Potter Stewart concurred, said in effect that the magazines would have prurient appeal only for a limited (homosexual) audience. See Rembar, *The End of Obscenity*, pp. 190–93.

ALS, 1P.   June 26th '62

Dear Elmer Gertz—   Wonder if you have read of this already? About the most wonderful statement (from a judicial mind) I have ever seen.[1]

Think Grove Press ought to know about it. If they do already, no use mailing them the clipping. Mail it back to me, then.

Is this the man who traveled extensively in Asia and Africa? *And*, who else on the Supreme Court Bench sides with him, can you tell me?

This in haste.   Henry[2]

---

1.   Reference is to interview given by U.S. Supreme Court Justice Hugo Black on April 14, 1962. See Gertz 4/20/62.

2.   Written on stationery of Langdon's Uptown Motel, Rochester, Minnesota.

TL(CC), 2PP., AIR MAIL   June 27, 1962

Dear Henry: I don't wonder that you are much excited by Black's statement on the First Amendment. I had the rare privilege of being present in New York when Justice Black was interviewed by Professor Cahn[1] and made the remarks summarized in the Los Angeles Times, as well as countless other publications. I expect to get several copies of the full text of the interview and will send one to you. Meanwhile, I am returning your copy of the cutting.

As I told my wife, who was with me at the time, I felt that I was present at an historic occasion. Although I did not agree with what Justice Black said on the subject of libel, I found almost everything else that he said true and inspiring.

Undoubtedly, Grove Press knows about the interview. It has been played up in New York, as well as elsewhere.

No, Justice Black is not the man whom you mean. Justice William Douglas is the one who has traveled so extensively, not only in geographical terms but intellectually as well. The Warren Court is really the Black Court, and Douglas is the Chief Lieutenant of Black.

On the obscenity issue, the Court appears to be increasingly our way, with the exception of Justice Clark.[2] Just Monday the Court gave an opinion in an obscenity matter, of which we will make good use in connection with the *Tropic* appeal.

I have finally received the water color from Berlin and it is truly wonderful. It will find a pleasant place in our living room.

                                        Always yours, ELMER GERTZ

---

1.   Professor Edmond Cahn (deceased), New York University School of Law.
2.   Justice Tom Clark cast the one dissenting vote in *Manual Enterprises* v. *Day*.

TLS, 1P.
Pac Pal, Calif. June 28, '62

Dear Elmer Gertz,   I can't get over it, what wonderful letters you find time to write—not only to me, but to every one, including friends of friends. Your letter to Roger Bloom is a gem. It will certainly bolster him up. You are not only a lawyer, counselor, friend, but a philosopher and father confessor as well.

I haven't heard further from Mr. Eagan, the attorney there, but wrote him yesterday that I am waiting to hear from him after he has gone through the files. Meanwhile Roger writes again, of his good impression of Eagan, of whom "they" were previously rather dubious, remember? I also informed Eagan that you were not handling the case. Of course, if you should ever visit Roger and meet some of the people there—the Warden, Colonel Carter, director of State prisons, and so on, and a Dr. Handler, pathologist (Jewish, with whom I had several family sessions, delightful) you would learn more in 24 hours than I would in a month. Tom Moore is visiting him soon now.

Today I had a phone call from my friend Orvis Ross of Rochester. I'll see him here tomorrow—and go on "reunioning" some more. This year my life has been full of *rencontres* with old friends—all very wonderful indeed. I'm also getting more and more calls for help from all sides—advice, money, all sorts of demands. No matter, so long as you're healthy.

I see my doctor today and will know definitely about my heart condition. Think the report will be quite favorable. My children arrive tomorrow night; then the battle begins.

Am so glad the water color from Berlin finally arrived and only hope it is one you will like. You will get more with time.

And that Hebrew edition of Tropic—isn't that a strange looking little book—and only the first half? I wonder if you will show it to Judge Epstein? No censorship there, in Israel, so far as I know. Doubt there will be. Am amazed that nothing has been done against the Argentine edition, in Spanish.[1] Now a contract has been made for a Portuguese version, in Brazil. The last barriers seem to be giving way. Of course Great Britain is the last stronghold. But this Fall Plexus and Nexus will be brought out in London, unexpurgated. And the publishers, Weidenfeld & Nicolson intend to go to court, if need be.

Your reference to the Supreme Court . . . are you referring to Justice Black's statements on the First Amendment, or is it something other? What a fuss they are making about the "prayer" business.[2] As if all these hyaenas who are protesting know anything about prayer! What nonsense and hypocrisy—and wilfull misinterpretation again. Once the Supreme Court gives in to these reactionaries what little democracy we have in this country will be finished. Things are completely upside down to-day—the Conservatives are radical and vice versa.

I haven't yet had a chance to glance through the books sent. The Whitman book, though, has not come yet. I am still reading— a few pages at a time—Thomas Merton's "New Seeds of Contemplation."[3] Feel very close to him—minus the Holy Ghost and Virgin Mary biz., of course. He's truly courageous—not like the clergy. He also gives me a new slant on the proper conception of a "saint."

Will stop now. As Fritz von Unruh says (title of book) "The End is not yet."[4] More soon, naturally. The best.   Henry Miller.

P.S. Did you ever get "The Absolute Collective" by Erich Gutkind? If not, I could lend you my copy (much marked up!). But no hurry. Something to read on a vacation.[5]

---

1.   Buenos Aires: Editorial Rueda, 1962.
2.   The case referred to here is *Engel* v. *Vitale*, 18 Misc. 2d 659, aff'd. 11 App. Div. 2d 340, aff'd. 10 N.Y. 2d 174, 370 U.S. 421 (1962). At issue was the recitation, in some New York State public schools, of a prayer composed and recommended by the Board of Regents: "Almighty God, we acknowledge our dependence upon Thee, and beg Thy blessings upon us, our parents, our teachers and our country." The United States Supreme Court ruled that, despite the nonsectarian character of the prayer, the recitation was a religious activity, and therefore was prohibited under the First Amendment of the Constitution. See H. M. 8/7/63, notes, for information about a similar decision by the Supreme Court in 1963. For a comprehensive discussion of litigation over religious exercises in the public schools, see Leo Pfeffer, *God,*

Caesar, and the Constitution (Boston: Beacon Press, [1975]), pp. 168–227.
3.   [Norfolk, Conn.]: New Directions [1961].
4.   New York: Storm [1947].
5.   Postscript written vertically in left margin.

ALS, 1P.   June 28th '62

Dear Elmer Gertz—   With yours of June 27th came the Whitman book[1] and the Leopold one. Look exciting.

I've just come from the doctor's—good news. I'm ⟨obliterated⟩ to forget every thing, he says. Just live wisely. Heart is off, prostate somewhat enlarged, all other organs in good shape. No pills, no medicines to take. Walk on!

I was so grateful I stopped outside his office and rendered a silent prayer to the Creator.

Sometimes—many times—I feel that I have a guardian angel who watches over me.

May he or she or it do the same for you! We are never alone. No more now.   Henry Miller[2]

---

1.   Walt Whitman's Civil War, compiled and edited by Walter Lowenfels, with the assistance of Nan Braymer (New York: Knopf, 1960).
2.   Above the salutation Miller wrote "2nd letter," referring to its being the second written on June 28.

TL(CC), 2PP., AIR MAIL   June 29, 1962

Dear Henry: Our friend Hoke Norris is at it again—thank God!
I am sending you his latest piece, which you will find of particular interest.[1] In the next few days the Evergreen Review article on our Chicago trial will appear. I suggest that you send a note to him, as I am sure it will please him greatly. His address is Chicago Sun-Times, Sun-Times Plaza, Chicago, Illinois. You might say to

him that you know through me of his helpfulness, not only as a witness in the case but as a staunch defender of the right to read. Of course, I don't have to instruct you as to what to say, but I would like to know that Hoke receives a personal word from you.

I am also sending you with this letter a report on censorship, issued by the Commission on Law and Social Action of the American Jewish Congress. Despite the mouth-filling words, that is a very important organization. I have been connected with the CLSA since its founding and am president of the Greater Chicago Council of the American Jewish Congress.

You will recall that the Black interview took place before a meeting of the AJC. I am going to obtain a copy of the full text for you.

I am having a copy of the magazine Focus/Midwest sent to you, because it contains an article I wrote about our case here.[2] Unfortunately, the editor saw fit to make a couple of interpolations, with the result that in one place he understated the number of defendants in the suit and in the other he garbled the legal test for obscenity. But, notwithstanding this, you may find the article interesting.

I have just received a copy of the little book, the Italian edition of *Obscenity and the Law of Reflection*,[3] which was sent to me, undoubtedly, at your suggestion. I cannot read the Italian, but I prize the book nonetheless. The illustrations are extremely good.

Several times I have seen *Days of Love and Hunger*[4] listed among your books as having been published by American World Library of Literature (1955). I have never seen the volume, however. Did it actually come out, and are copies available?

Always yours, ELMER GERTZ

Encs.

1. "Critic At-Large: Henry Miller (contd.)," *Chicago Sun-Times*, June 29, 1962, p. 32, a review of *Stand Still Like the Hummingbird*.
2. "Test Case: Tropic of Cancer," *Focus Midwest*, Vol. 1 No. 2 (July 1962), pp. 12–14.

3.   Milan: Vanni Scheiwiller, 1962; Yonkers, N.Y.: [Oscar Baradinsky at the Alicat Book Shop], 1945.
4.   On 6/30/62 Miller explained correct title was *Nights of Love and Laughter*.

APS, 1S., AIR MAIL   6/30/62

Dear Elmer Gertz—   The Whitman book just came—a beauty!
—and your letter, *etc. etc.* "Days of Love & Hunger" is an error.
Title was changed to "Nights of Love and Laughter" (a Signet
pocketbook.)[1] I have just written Hoke Norris. A *wonderful* review, I thought. Haven't seen Time or News Week—never read
any mags.   Cheers! Henry[2]

---

1.   [New York]: New American Library [1955].
2.   Card postmarked Pacific Palisades, California, bearing printed legend:
          "KENNETH PATCHEN Painting Poem
          Mixed Medium, 9½" x 17½"
          Possession of the poet"

ALS, 1P.   July 3rd '62

Dear Elmer Gertz—   Just a brief word to say I have now read
about 80 pages of Leopold's book and find it quite wonderful. His
portrait of Darrow is very touching. Lucky you were to have known
him!

I just received (3) copies of the 2nd vol. of the Hebrew edition of *Cancer*. Did you get one of the first volume? Does it mean
any thing? If so, I'll send you Vol. 2.

By the way, some of these legalistic documents you send me,
while important, bore me a bit. When it comes to law and to "my
case" (Cancer) all I ask for is the "essence." There is such a lot of
jargon, waste, etc. in professional documents—law, psychiatry, etc.
You understand. We writers also give off a lot of "waste" too, I

know—and I am just as hard on them as does it, believe me. Talking with Orvis Ross, about "repetitious phrases" in music, was delighted to discover he found it insupportable too—even in the great, like *Beethoven* and Brahms.

Enough or I won't stop!   The best! Henry Miller

TL(CC), 2PP., AIR MAIL   July 6, 1962

Dear Henry: I have several unanswered letters of yours. I have read all of the letters with the utmost interest, but my energies have been depleted in various ways. For one thing, I have been emotionally involved in attempting to save the life of Paul Crump, a young Negro who is scheduled to die on August 3, unless the Governor extends executive clemency. I am not Crump's attorney, but I am working almost as hard on the matter as if I were. I think I sent you one article that I wrote for a Negro newspaper about the case and I have written another article for a magazine. I have stirred up editorial comments, columns, special news items. This is one of the most extraordinary cases imaginable. Crump, who was virtually illiterate when he was first arrested, is now a cultured and completely decent person. It would be shocking beyond words if he were actually put to death. There is more than a chance that he will be, because of certain defects of our Governor. Incidentally, I am going to be a witness at the ⟨parole⟩ ⟨pardon⟩[1] clemency hearing and I am generally helping Crump's attorney, a young man whose name you ought to remember. He is Donald Page Moore, who has already won two historic cases in the United States Supreme Court and will win many more before he reaches the end of his career. At sixteen, Moore was virtually a hillbilly in West Virginia. He quit high school and enlisted with the Paratroopers. He saw action in Korea. When he returned, he suddenly was filled with ambition. All sorts of rules had to be broken to get him into law school, but he ended as one of the top students at the University of Illinois Law School.

The combination of Crump and Moore intrigues me intellectually and moves me emotionally.

I understand that the next issue of Life and Time will contain big articles about the case.[2] Time interviewed me about three or four times.

I knew that you would find the Leopold book an extremely interesting one. He actually wrote it himself. My contribution consisted of using the legal blue pencil and here and there adding a few words.

I received two paperbacks in Hebrew, containing all or some part of the text of *Tropic of Cancer*. I assume that they came through you and I want to thank you.

I shall try to avoid sending you merely legalistic material; but now and then something of that nature is important and even interesting.

It seems as if almost every issue of the Saturday Review contains something about you and *Tropic of Cancer*. In the current issue there is a piece by Malcolm Cowley, in which he refers to you.[3] It is an interesting exposure of the mind of a man who was once radical and has grown conservative. He is still basically honest.

I have yet to answer the most recent letter from Roger Bloom. I shall do so in the next very few days.

One of my problems in the next couple of weeks will be that my secretary will be away on her vacation. When you have a good secretary, you grow dependent. A substitute is coming in. That is almost as much of a gamble as the result of a lawsuit. Anything can happen. I have had some horrible creatures during the three or more decades that I have had secretaries. Also, I have had some very wonderful secretaries. My first wife was my secretary. That is how I met her. That was the last time she took any dictation from me.

I should have begun this letter with words of thanks for the good news about your health. I hope that you will continue not to overdo. At this moment I feel very weak myself. I am sure that it is not physical.

The other day my brother left the hospital, after eight weeks. He is now at home. Recuperation is likely to take a very long while.

I am grateful to you for your reference about my getting more water colors with time. One of my projects will be to create a Henry Miller gallery. Sometimes I laugh when I tell my daughter, who is going to be married this year, that when she gets out of the house I am going to turn her room into a museum for my best manuscripts, books and pictures.

Somebody is waiting to see me. She is only a client, but even clients are entitled to rights occasionally.

Always yours, ELMER GERTZ

1. On Gertz's original, the cancelled reading "pardon" does not appear.
2. "The Last Mile?," *Time*, July 20, 1962, p. 22; Ronald Bailey, "Facing Death, A New Life Perhaps Too Late," *Life*, July 27, 1962, pp. 26–31. See also Louis Nizer, *The Jury Returns* (Garden City, N.Y.: Doubleday & Company, Inc., 1966), pp. 1–137.

    Crump, one of three men who participated in a Chicago robbery on March 20, 1953, in which a guard was killed, was scheduled to die in the electric chair on August 3, 1962. An impressive number of prominent people, including law enforcement officers, were convinced that he had been rehabilitated during his nine years in prison and were urging that his death sentence be commuted. Gertz, who remained Crump's sole attorney after the commutation of his death sentence, was one of those most active in his behalf.
3. Malcolm Cowley, "Artists, Conscience, and Censors," *Saturday Review*, July 7, 1962, pp. 8–10, 47. Cowley, who had defended *Lady Chatterley's Lover* in court, did not volunteer his services on behalf of *Tropic of Cancer* because he discovered in himself an "unexpected residue of moral conservatism." He wrote, "I was glad it would be bought by adults . . . but I didn't know that I was eager to have it displayed on newsstands for 95 cents, since it wasn't, so it seemed to me, the best sort of work for the immature."

ALS, 1P.   July 6th '62

Dear Elmer Gertz—   I am passing the enclosed letters on to you to read and return.[1] Don't know what I am to infer from this information—but will know more, as you see, in another few days.

Barney Rosset, of Grove Press, whose edition of Miller's *Tropic of Cancer* in 1961 precipitated the battle against the continuing censorship of Miller's autobiographical novels in the United States. *Courtesy Grove Press*

Charles Rembar, New York attorney and author of *The End of Obscenity* (1968), who directed Grove Press's defense of *Cancer. Photograph* © *1977 Jill Krementz*

Stanley Fleishman, the attorney involved in one of the California *Tropic of Cancer* cases, who was often consulted by Miller.

The late Hoke Norris, Chicago *Sun-Times* book editor, who wrote favorably about the works of Henry Miller and supported Elmer Gertz's struggles against censorship in Chicago. *Courtesy Field Enterprises, Inc.*

Judge Samuel B. Epstein, the chief justice of the Superior Court of Cook County, Illinois (now the Circuit Court). In recognition of his trenchant *Tropic of Cancer* opinion (February 1962), which held that the book was constitutionally protected, and which judges in other states cited in concurring decisions, Judge Epstein received the 1962 Intellectual Freedom Award of the Illinois Library Association. *Photograph by Fabian Bachrach*

Henry Miller in Minneapolis, June 1962, on the occasion of his first meeting with Elmer Gertz. *Courtesy Edward P. Schwartz*

Edward P. Schwartz, president of The Henry Miller Literary Society, Elmer Gertz, Henry Miller, and Thomas H. Moore at the Press Club in Minneapolis, June 1962. Moore was secretary and founder, with Schwartz, of The Henry Miller Literary Society. *Courtesy Edward P. Schwartz*

The first of Henry Miller's gifts of his watercolors to Elmer Gertz. It was sent to Gertz from Berlin in 1962, inscribed "For Elmer Gertz from Henry Miller." *Photograph by Henry R. Hechtman*

"The Nude and the Clown," one of a dozen or so watercolors painted by Henry Miller while a guest in the Gertzes' home in Chicago in 1962. The painting is signed by Henry Miller and dated "Chicago 10/4/62." *Photograph by Henry R. Hechtman*

Henry Miller in his home in Pacific Palisades, California, in 1963. On the reverse side of this photograph Miller wrote: "To Elmer Gertz/The (Wailing) Wall/chez moi/Henry Miller/12/15/63." *Courtesy Elmer Gertz*

Gladys Fuller, Elmer Gertz's secretary at the time of the correspondence. She is now administrative director of the Law School at the University of Chicago. *Courtesy Gladys Fuller*

Elmer Gertz in his study with a copy of his book, *A Handful of Clients* (1964). *Daily Courier-News, Elgin, Illinois, photo*

Elmer and Mamie Gertz with Charles Mathes (left) and Edward P. Schwartz, Press Club, Minneapolis, August 1965. *Photograph by Peter Marcus, Minneapolis*

Elmer Gertz receiving City of Hope Award, May 15, 1966. *Left to right:* Judge John V. McCormick, Judge George Leighton, U.S. Senator Wayne Morse (Oregon), Elmer Gertz, Solomon Jesmer, and Judge Samuel B. Epstein.

Elmer Gertz with a group of "beat" poets, Chicago, February 1959. *Left to right*: Paul Carroll, Allen Ginsberg, Elmer Gertz, Gregory Corso, and Peter Orlovsky. *Photograph by Rialto Service Co., Chicago*

Elmer Gertz, with a portrait by Edward Weiss of the famous criminal lawyer Clarence Darrow. *Photograph by Chicago Photographers*

Nathan Leopold on his release from prison, with Elmer Gertz, Chicago, 1958. Gertz's efforts on behalf of prisoners, notably Leopold, Bill Witherspoon, and Paul Crump, formed a bond in his friendship with Henry Miller, who took a personal interest in Roger Bloom, a prisoner in the Missouri State Penitentiary. *Photograph* © *1958 Chicago Sun-Times*

Henry Miller on a visit to Roger Bloom, the prisoner with whom he corresponded extensively, Missouri State Penitentiary, Jefferson City, Missouri, 1962. The photograph was sent to Henry Miller by Roger Bloom with an inscription, on the back, "Please excuse the manner in which this appears—my back, that is—this was taken at our recent visit—more later, I trust" and signed "Roger."

For Elmer Gertz —
one of the most amazing
men I have ever met
— and so gentle, modest,
humble withal.
    In friendship.
        Henry Miller
        Minneapolis
        6/5/62
" Remember to remember "

Inscription by Henry Miller in a copy of *Stand Still Like the Hummingbird*, presented to Elmer Gertz at the time of their first meeting in Minneapolis, June 1962. *Courtesy Special Collections, Morris Library, Southern Illinois University*

For Elmer Gertz —
a lover of freedom, truth
and justice, a loyal friend,
a lover of books and a
peerless barrister. May
Heaven protect him ever!
In gratitude and
admiration —

Henry Miller
2/21/62

On the eve of the
great decision.
"Victory"

Inscription by Henry Miller in a copy of *Tropic of Cancer*, sent to Elmer Gertz on February 21, 1962, when Judge Samuel B. Epstein ruled that *Cancer* was not obscene and, hence, was constitutionally protected. *Courtesy Special Collections, Morris Library, Southern Illinois University*

Jan. +9.ᵗ 1962

Dear Elmer Gertz —

Sitting here over breakfast pondering your request to say something about your writing, as revealed in "The Paper." Read a half-dozen or more in bed last-night. (Liked very much the one on Tesla, whom I always venerated and never learned enuf about. Great man, yes!)

That you can express yourself is obvious. The sole question is — do you want to give yourself to it wholly or only in part? The character of your writing would change once you devoted yourself to it completely. Now and then — you know who I mean — we have good writers who are also doctors, lawyers, surgeons (even) and so on. Usually Europeans. Usually their professional pursuits took second place.

As I see it, what you have done is to "write about". To write (punkt!) is another matter. You then become involved — and responsible in a different way. Responsible, perhaps, to God, let us say. You invite defeat, humiliation, rejection, misunderstanding. You speak solely as the "unique" being you are, not as a member of society
(over)

Do I make sense? Am I answering as you wish me to? "The Paper" itself, while interesting enough, is of no great consequence. It serves to feed the various egos involved. Once seriously engaged, the ego falls away. You are happy — and blessed — just to be an "instrument".

In my mind a writer or any sort of artist is, in the last analysis, no more important than a ditch-digger or garbage collector. We are all, no matter what our function or capacity, but instruments in the divine orchestra called humanity. Each one, however humble his task, is necessary. If we understood that we would take joy in fulfilling our respective roles. And the role of artist would then be seen to be the greatest privilege, simply because it permitted the "maker" (poet) the greatest freedom, the greatest joy.

Sincerely,

Henry Miller

Early two-page holograph letter from Henry Miller to Elmer Gertz, January 19, 1962. *Courtesy Special Collections, Morris Library, Southern Illinois University*

Aug. 5th 1964

Dear Elmer —

Here is my chronology up to date. Had
to give it to some Australian for some encyclo-
paedia or what. May be a little mixed up at
points in my travels — but not seriously.
Now then, could you have a Xerox (?) copy made
for yourself (if you want it) and another for
Mme Jacqueline Langmann — Préverenges —
(Vaud) — Switzerland. She is one of my
best astrologers and is going to do a book
about my life and work from the astrological
standpoint — i.e. show the concordance
between crucial moments in my life and
the planetary aspects which substantiate the
events. This is what I had wanted Sidney
Omarr to do in his book — but he was
too lazy, I guess. Imagine if we had
something like this for enigmatic figures
like Rimbaud, da Vinci, Bosch, Dostoievski
— or, above all — Gilles de Rais !!!

Just got four albums from the Jewish
Music Archives Society — think I asked
them to send you their catalogue. To me
it's a God send. For years and years I
have been searching for records of Cantors
Sirota and Rosenblatt. Now I have

them and my heart leaps to my throat as I listen. There's one of Sirota's — R'zei — which really sends me. Imagine, when I was 18 and earning about $52 a month in the Atlas Portland Cement Co., I used to save up to buy a Sirota — single-faced disc at $7.50 !!! God, what a difference to-day! How easy it all is now. But because of the sacrifices I made whatever I got went through and through me — and stayed with me.

"Blessed are the poor"!

Don't forget — tell mamie not to overlook getting (from library) "The Lost World of the Kalahari" by Laurens van der Post. Here is a man after my own heart. And what a man was that earliest of all mankind — the Bushman!

Enough! Cheers!

Henry

Two-page holograph letter from Henry Miller to Elmer Gertz, August 5, 1963 (accidentally dated 1964 by Miller). Typically, the letter reflects the wide range of Miller's interests. *Courtesy Special Collections, Morris Library, Southern Illinois University.*

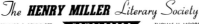

The HENRY MILLER Literary Society

EDWARD P. SCHWARTZ
President
121 North 7th Street
FEderal 8-5681

NEWSLETTER
DECEMBER, 1961 — NUMBER 8
MINNEAPOLIS 3, MINNESOTA

THOMAS H. MOORE
Secretary
3748 Park Avenue
TAylor 3-4784

BOOK BURNERS HARASS STORES SELLING 'TROPIC OF CANCER'

BIBLIO SELLING WELL

Sale of the Henry Miller Bibliography, edited by Thomas H. Moore, secretary of the Society, has exceeded original estimates according to Edward P. Schwartz, president.

Amazingly enough, many of the orders came from outstanding college and university libraries. Bulk sales were also heavy, the largest coming from Gotham Book Mart, New York, which stocked 100 copies.

As in the type, there errors, deleti the "Master Sometime d will collate on to biblio

The 32-pa graphs of 1 in a water table of cont

Books by to Periodica to Books (19 ry Miller, Books Con Miller, Doct Miller, Chart First Editio of Henry M Henry Miller icals (1924-1 Miller Biblic Numbered addressing M usual trade five or more

CORRECT

Correction published " (Henry Mill apolis, $1.50 "Nexus" lated into th published b Denmark, 19

Book-burning, an excuse for the strong to "save" the weak, which went out of fashion with hoop skirts and fear of witches but came back to haunt civilized people with the ascendancy of Hitler in the 30's, is again rearing its singed and cracked head over this and other free lands.

Grove Press published the American edition of Henry Miller's 1934 'Tropic of

BRONZE BUST AVAILABLE

● Galerie Springer Berlin has six original casts of the Henry Miller bust sculpted by Marino Marini in honor of the writer's 70th birthday. Anyone interested (especially libraries, institutes or individuals) should address their inquiries to Galerie Springer Berlin (W 30, Kurfurstendamm 16). Pix by Foto-Gnilka, Berlin.

MILLER AT HIS BEST

● Say what you will, Henry Miller is at his best after a satisfying meal and pleasant companionship as evidenced in the above Polaroid pix by Eddie Schwartz at Elmer Gertz' Chicago home early in November. Left to right are Lois Solomon Weisberg, Henry Miller and Hoke Norris, literary editor of Chicago's Sun-Times and author of "We Dissent." Lois is the former editor of "The Paper" which brilliantly battled for worthwhile causes like the recent Paul Crump case in Chicago.

↓↓↓↓↓↓↓

'El Foldo'?...

It's just an old Spanish expression (via "Variety") and it means the Henry Miller Literary Society Newsletter may discontinue because the financial burden is too great for the Society.

President Edward P. Schwartz feels that the original goal has been achieved: "GET MILLER READ IN HIS OWN COUNTRY!" This was the cause-celebre which instigated the Newsletter in the first place and was so stated in the original mimeographed news release issued late in 1957.

Even Miller, when he visited with Society members in June, 1962, expressed the same opinion. He said: "YOU HAVE ACCOMPLISHED YOUR ORIGINAL OBJECTIVE. THERE IS NO OTHER REASON TO CONTINUE WHEN IT MEANS A FINANCIAL LOSS TO THE PARTICIPANTS."

All around us we see wonderful publications going down the drain of accumulated deficits. Basic production costs are going up faster than the contributions can ever match, dollar for dollar.

As of this issue, No. 11 (of the printed variety), we owe nearly $1,000. We still feel that this is a voluntary operation and any contributions should come from voluntary sources or not at all.

Secretary Tom Moore advances this theory. Let's tell our present 688 free "subscribers" (many have already contributed liberally in the past and they are excluded), that we would like a "show of hands" within the next 30 days and IF the contributions equal the deficit, we can at least break even. IF the surge of money passes the present deficit, we then can proceed further, probably back to the mimeographed letter originally published.

ADDED INFORMATION: Postage rates increase Jan. 7, 1963. Labor costs are due for escalation Feb. 1, 1963. Everything else follows the leader. IT'S UP TO YOU!

↑↑↑↑↑↑↑

OPERA S

● Antonio Bib letter No. 7). opera based Foot of the L Borge Sornum

---

The HENRY MILLER Literary Society

EDWARD P. SCHWARTZ
President
121 North 7th Street
FEderal 8-5681

NEWSLETTER
DECEMBER, 1962 — No. 11
MINNEAPOLIS 3, MINN.

THOMAS H. MOORE
Secretary
3748 Park Avenue
TAylor 3-4784

TRINITY COLLEGE SCORES A 'FIRST' WITH MILLER DAY

(Editor's Note — Trinity College, Hartford, Conn., scored an American "first" with a combination showing of Henry Miller watercolors, playing of Miller recordings, exhibition of Miller books and a panel discussion—covered by The Trinity Tripod — below.)

●

Oct. 9 — The banning of books on moral grounds seems to be closely linked with the segregation p r o b l e m in the South, said Barney Rosset, publisher of Grove Press, at a panel discussion before a large group in the Library Conference Room.

"Freedom to Read" was the topic considered by the panel which included Anne Lyon Haight, author of "Banned Books," Stuart Sherman, Librarian of the Providence Public Library, Herbert F. West, Professor of Comparative Literature at Dartmouth, and Mr. Rosset.

More books are banned on moral grounds where serious segregation splits exist, according to Mr. Rosset, who suggested there might be a connection between the two problems.

The banning of books brings us near the erosion of one of our basic freedoms, that of the press, said Mr. Sherman, who last year won a court struggle allowing him to place Henry Miller's 'Tropic of Cancer' on his library's shelves.

The problem is not whether a book is moral; it is whether an adult should be restricted to reading only books which are considered fit for children, Sherman said. "The price of a free society is no censorship," added Mr. Rosset.

The "commercial angle" forces or encourages many authors to put scenes with sex into their books, Professor West pointed out. Books are often hurt by this, he said, but censorship is "foolish." He classified Miller as a "good writer with a fine sense of humor."

John F. Skelly, counsel for Trumbull Huntington in the Hartford case concerning Miller's "Tropic" last winter said concessions must be made in order to protect many books from being banned.

Publisher Rosset answered that as a pragmatist he realized such concessions would have to be made; the process toward a complete freedom to read would have to be gradual, he thought.

Many books are b e i n g published now which several years ago would have been condemned, said Rosset. Agreeing with this, Professor West noted that Catholic Church officials, at least in Hanover (where Dartmouth is located), have stated that college students could read any book assigned by a professor.

The views taken on this problem by the Supreme Court are far more liberal than those taken by many lower courts and city officials, Mr. Sherman said.

Miss Haight, discussing the history of banning books, pointed out that books, such as the works of Homer and the Bible, have been banned for political and religious as well as moral reasons.

●

The Henry Miller Literary Society was supplied with programs, news clips, photos and other information from the Watkinson Library curator, Mrs. Marian Clarke and her associate, Jessie M. Kenny.

FAR EAST REPORT

Ooi Chiew reporting the Singapore news to "Variety" had the following item (Nov. 14, 1962): In nearby Malaya, police raided bookshops all over the peninsula seizing copies of Henry Miller's 'Tropic of Cancer' which first appeared here several months ago.

RADIO SCRIPT PUBLISHED

The three-part University of Minnesota KUOM broadcast heard on consecutive Wednesday nights (Aug. 15, 22 and 29, 1962) featured the voices of Professor Alan T-achtenberg, Penn State English Department; E l m e r Gertz, famed Chicago attorney who represented Grove Press and Henry Miller in a successful court action; and, in one of his rare personal appearances before any microphone, author Henry Miller. The program was handled in its entirety by Audrey June Booth, Supervisor in charge of Community Services at KUOM.

Plans are now in the making to run a transcript of the tapes and publish the broadcast in its entirety. Excellent comment from the general public leads the Society to believe that such an edition would be a valuable instrument in the constant fight of the public vs. the censors.

This office will notify members of publication date and cost in the near future.

MILLER ON CENSORSHIP

From a radio transcription heard over BBC during the Edinburgh Conference which featured the voices of Henry Miller, Lawrence Durrell and BBC's interviewer light, D. Geoffrey Bridson on Oct. 8, 1962.

Bridson: What do you feel about the question of censorship, which in fact you will probably be talking about this afternoon at the Conference?

Miller: It has been a dual thing really. It has been good and bad, I must say. I can't say (as for me personally) that it has been a totally bad thing. Without the censorship, without the banning of the books, why perhaps I wouldn't be read as much as I am. Despite the censorship, you see, the books got read and this is one thing I feel that censorship always defeats itself: that men have always been able to say what they want despite the conditions. If they can't say it in their own country it is smuggled out and published in another country. If they can't put it in writing they put it in words, and words travel, do you see? You can't suppress free speech, or free thought — it's impossible, it's utterly absurd, and today we see it more clearly. We're about at the end, I think.

(In the broadcast Lawrence Durrell tells about writing to Miller for the first time: "I was lent a copy of 'Tropic of Cancer' and simply as a fan letter to Henry' He was kind enough to reply, much to my surprise, and a sort of correspondence developed. I was then living on the island of Corfu. Eventually we met and the friendship has continued over the years").

'NAKED LUNCH' REVIEWED

Current reviews of "Naked Lunch" by William S. Burroughs (Grove Press — $6) in most of the leading magazines and newspapers, stress an affinity of Henry Miller's writing to adding machine heir Burroughs. However, John Wain in the Dec. 1 New Republic says they are writers of entirely opposite tendency. "Miller is an affirmative writer, Burroughs is not." And he spent over two pages telling New Republic readers why!

Issues of the *Newsletter* published by The Henry Miller Literary Society.
Courtesy Elmer Gertz

Assured him [*Eagan*] you merely wished to be of aid if necessary—in whatever way possible.

Seems the Harvard publishers may do *Hamlet*—since they have corroborated lack of copyright. You may hear from them, if they have last minute doubts about their right to publish. They would, of course, divide royalties equally between Mrs. Fraenkel and myself—which seems fair to me.

It would be wonderful to see this book—so little known—come out now, eh? Naturally, it won't have a big sale. But there is much in it of value—and different from my other writings.

No time for more now.   All the best, Henry

---

1.   Two letters about Roger Bloom, dated June 28 and July 3, from attorney Edgar M. Eagan of Jefferson City, Missouri. In the June 28 communication Mr. Eagan said in part: "I have known the Records Clerk for a number of years and the members of the Parole Board are very good friends of mine. . . . I shall evaluate the Bloom case very carefully and give you a report as soon as I've discussed the matter with the Parole Board." On July 3 he wrote:

"After addressing to you my letter of June 28th, I went over to the Parole Board and discussed Roger's case. It was an informal meeting in which I explained your interest in trying to get something done for Roger.

"An examination of the records indicates that Roger has done time in the states of California, Ohio, Illinois and Missouri. He also entered pleas of guilty upon two charges in Minn. upon which he received two 18 years sentences. They are running concurrently with his present one.

"Since the Parole Board has set the case back for one year for an additional review, it will be necessary for Research Laboratories to renew its job opportunity offer at the proper time. The Board approves the job and I think it was mighty fine of Mr. Fink to offer to assist.

"There are primary difficulties. He is serving under a life sentence, and is known to have committed six offenses."

TL(CC), 2PP., AIR MAIL   July 10, 1962

Dear Henry: Yesterday I wrote to Roger Bloom and sent you a copy of my letter. I also returned the two letters from Mr. Eagan. I made copies thereof for my file so that I have the essential information. I gave a good deal of thought to Roger's matter and concluded that this was the only thing that I could do at this time.

Mr. Eagan's letters to you throw a much more serious light on the situation than I had imagined. The Board will think not once or twice but many times before releasing a man who has committed a number of offenses and has against him sentences in other states which are now pending. Roger is a remarkable person and I would like to see him live in freedom but it is by no means a certainty that he can do so with complete safety to society and himself. This is an unsentimental thing to say but it is the sober truth.

I am delighted that the Harvard Publishers are going to issue your "Hamlet." It is one of my favorites among all of your books. This would be a very good time for it to appear.

I had another very interesting chat with Judge Epstein yesterday. We discussed the latest United States Supreme Court decision on obscenity and we agreed that it strengthens our position very much. The Illinois Appellate Court has just handed down another such decision which will be most useful in the case in which I am defending the four actors.

This is the day that the Evergreen Review article is supposed to appear. I am extremely eager to see it.[1]

Always yours,   Sincerely, [*Elmer*][2] ELMER GERTZ

---

1. Evidently a reference to the Hoke Norris article " 'Cancer' in Chicago," *Evergreen Review*, v. 6 No. 25 (July–August, 1962), pp. 41–66.
2. See Gertz 1/4/62, notes.

ALS, 1P.   July 12th '62

Dear friend—   A hasty note just to enclose Mr. Eagan's latest.[1]
I *know* how bad Roger's case must look—but I also have that firm
belief in man's ability to change. What *need* would he have to do
these foolish things again, when he now will have such good friends
and supporters?

So much to do here—forgive this scratch!   Henry

---

1.   Mr. Eagan implied in a letter of July 9 that Miller and Gertz should
      leave contacts with the Parole Board to him until "some time after
      the first of the year," when the matter of Bloom's parole would come
      before the Board.

TL(CC), 1P., AIR MAIL   July 13, 1962

Dear Henry: I am in receipt of a very fine letter from Roger
Bloom dated July 11th. I assume he has told you of its contents.
When I reply you will get a copy and you will then be able to tell
what he wrote to me.

I suppose you have noticed that Governor Blair died in mysterious circumstances the other day. There goes one of Roger's
reliances.

I am sending herewith a cutting of another article about the
Tropic suit here which I wrote. I suppose you have received the
Focus Midwest article. I am surprised that the Evergreen Review
one has not arrived yet.

A Judge Matthews in New Jersey wrote a remarkable opinion
in an obscenity case. If it should be published I will send you a
copy because you will enjoy reading it even if it is a legal document.

Eddie Schwartz expects to be in Chicago at the end of the
month. It will be a wonderful opportunity to recall those great
hours in Minneapolis.

Warmest regards.   Always yours, ELMER GERTZ

TL(CC), 1P., AIR MAIL July 16, 1962

Dear Henry: I have your note of July 12th. I returned Eagan's latest and made a copy of it for future reference.

Of course, I agree with you that as long as there is a chance that Roger will fulfill his obligations on parole we should do all we can to help him.

It appears clear from Mr. Eagan's letter that he does not want me to appear in the matter until it reaches its decisive point, if then. I can hardly blame him. Obviously no lawyer wants his style to be cramped by another attorney.

I received the copy of "Sexus" from Mexico. Thanks much. "Plexus" is the one volume of the trilogy that I now lack in addition to the other books mentioned by me some while ago.

Did I tell you that I finally did the tape for the University of Minnesota for a whole hour? I hope it is what they want.

Warmest regards.   Sincerely yours, ELMER GERTZ

ALS, 1P. July 17th '62

Dear friend—   Thank you for Focus and your text in Chicago Courier[1]—very good, *yours!* Just had phone call from Rosset re Mass. Supreme Court's decision.[2] Guess Justice Black's speech had something to do with this unexpected victory, eh?

Yes, I read of Blair's death. Strange coincidences lately. Haven't received copy of ⟨your⟩ Roger's letter to you yet. Think something's brewing there.

Re the Mark Twain enclosure—can you suggest anything?[3] Haven't read him in years. Would like to oblige the son or grandson—with aid of your fabulous memory!   In haste, Henry Miller

1. Not located.
2. The Boston trial (September 1961), the first in which *Cancer* was tested, resulted in an adverse decision, but the Supreme Judicial Court of Massachusetts, which in the not too distant past had ruled that

Dreiser's *An American Tragedy* and Caldwell's *God's Little Acre* were obscene, was the first high court to clear *Cancer*. See Rembar, *The End of Obscenity*, pp. 186–95.

3. Cyril Clemens, editor of the *Mark Twain Journal*, had written to ask Miller for a favorite Mark Twain story or quotation.

TL(CC), 1P., AIR MAIL   July 18, 1962

Dear Henry: I suppose you know of the wonderful victory won by Charles Rembar in the Supreme Court of Massachusetts. This victory, the one in Maryland and the one I obtained are cumulatively likely to achieve a finally favorable result throughout the country.[1] I shall have more to say about this later.

I suppose you know that the University of Minnesota was quite pleased with the tape I prepared for them on the legal aspects of ⟨this⟩ "Tropic of Cancer." They are enthusiastic generally about the Henry Miller program. This, too, should have national repercussions.

Of course, I am grateful to you for suggesting that I do a chapter in the book the Southern Illinois University Press is going to publish.[2]

I ran across an extremely interesting book the other day which would be a particular delight to you. It is entitled "Seven Friends" and is by Louis Marlow, which is a pseudonym for Louis Wilkinson, and was published in 1953 by the Richards Press in London.

There are long chapters on John, Theodore and Llewellyn Powys, Frank Harris, Aleister Crowley.[3] Marlow has a very deep appreciation of the Powys brothers.

More anon.   Always yours, ELMER GERTZ[4]

---

1. There were more than sixty *Tropic of Cancer* cases, roughly half of which resulted in unfavorable decisions. While it was natural for the book's defenders to hope that each win would be influential, *Cancer's* fate remained very much in doubt until the United States Supreme Court cleared it.

2. George Wickes, ed., *Henry Miller and the Critics* (Carbondale, Ill.: Southern Illinois University Press, 1964).

3.   Also on Oscar Wilde and William Somerset Maugham.
4.   Opposite the inside address, Gertz wrote by hand, "Dictated before yesterday's letter!"

TL(CC), 1P.   July 18, 1962

Dear Henry: I am sending herewith a copy of the letter that I just sent to Roger Bloom. I hope it helps keep him in a better frame of mind.

I am returning the letter from Cyril Clemens, who is a cousin of Mark Twain's.

Here is the quotation that I suggest:

"A lie can travel around the world while the truth is putting on its boots." (This, I give from memory, but it is substantially correct, I am sure.)

I am sure that Justice Black had a lot to do with the thinking of the court in the Massachusetts case and all of the justices have given thought to this matter. I think the mature opinion has been formed that it is wrong to censor anything with literary value. We simply must run the risk, if risk it is. Assuming as I do that the fight against legal censorship is being won, we will be faced with an even more serious fight against the private vigilante groups that take the law into their own hands. I have been asked to do a book on the subject, and I am tempted to do so, but must allow time for the more general volume about my cases that I have been asked to write. I shall tell you more of this project later.

Always yours, ELMER GERTZ

TL(CC), 2PP., AIR MAIL   August 2, 1962

Dear Henry: Now that the Paul Crump matter is disposed of —the Governor has spared his life—I can get down to other matters. This has been an agonizing struggle. Later I may send you some material about it, because I believe that the author of "Maurizius Forever" will be deeply concerned.

I wrote the chapter for the Wickes book. At first I was going to send it to you in advance; then I decided that you would prefer a completely objective and unedited view. I hope that you will like it.

Eddie Schwartz read the piece when he was here for a couple of days this week. He arrived in the midst of all of the Crump excitement, but my wife and I did manage to have dinner with Eddie and Mae, and the next day Eddie and I lunched together. In all, we put in several very happy hours. He proves that the greatness of heart is more important than some of the alleged virtues.

Barney Rosset wrote to me, telling the good news that "Tropic of Capricorn" will be published now, but without any indemnification of the booksellers. This is wise. I have urged Barney to publish "Black Spring" as soon as possible.

I have another letter from Roger Bloom. Because I think that you ought to know of his latest thoughts, I am sending a copy herewith.

I suppose that you are up to your ears, clearing the decks before you leave for Edinburgh. I hope that on your way back you will stop in either Minneapolis or Chicago, and preferably Chicago. Do let us know.

In connection with the Crump case, I had the very interesting experience of working with Louis Nizer, the author of "My Days in Court."[1] Nizer has achieved several noteworthy victories. His winning of the *Faulk* case[2] recently should put an effective end to McCarthyism.

I hope that you are well and happy.

Always yours, ELMER GERTZ

---

1.   *My Life in Court* (Garden City, N.Y.: Doubleday, 1961).
2.   John Henry Faulk, radio and television entertainer and a Vice President of the New York Local of American Federation of Television and Radio Artists (AFTRA), was out of work more than six years after being accused of being a Communist sympathizer. See Nizer, *The Jury Returns*, pp. 225–438.

ALS, 1P.   August 2nd '62

Dear Elmer Gertz—   With the copy of your letter to Roger came the news of Paul Crump's—what? Not victory, exactly, but alive to fight some more. I thought it a tough kind of mercy the Governor extended—life plus without possibility of parole. Wonder how you feel about it. God, but all this is so atavistic! So heartless.

It's so very, very good of you to write these long, kind, sincere letters to Roger Bloom. You do much better than I, I must say. I struggle each day to merely *answer* all the letters that come in.

Last night I took Tony[1] (whose foot is now in a cast—fractured a bone while surfing) to see "Judgment at Nuremberg." We were much impressed. What a problem is posed here! And what a comment at the end—none of the 99 convicted are now in prison!

More soon. I am involved in a number of interesting projects at the moment. Leave for Edinburgh[2] (via N.Y. & London) Aug. 15th. No chance to stop over on way over now. Maybe on the way back—in Nov. or December. Haven't seen latest Evergreen yet. You know, I suppose, that Grove is releasing Capricorn in September. My best to you and your dear wife!   Henry Miller[3]

1.   Miller's son, born August 28, 1948.
2.   Miller was preparing to attend an International Writer's Conference, a feature of the Edinburgh Festival (see Anthony Blond, "Unshockable Edinburgh," *Books and Bookmen*, October 1962, pp. 26–27). Among other participants were Norman Mailer, William Burroughs, Mary McCarthy, Lawrence Durrell, Angus Wilson, Malcolm Muggeridge, David Daiches, and Maurice Girodias. After the conference, Miller and Durrell went to Paris.
3.   Last three sentences and signature written vertically in left margin.

TL(CC), 2PP., AIR MAIL   August 3, 1962

Dear Henry: Our letters crossed. The Governor's commutation in Paul Crump's case, although phrased in absolute terms, is not as bad as you interpreted it. Translated into everyday language, it means that, if Paul Crump shows the same degree of rehabilitation during the ensuing years while he is in the penitentiary, his sentence will be cut further and he may even be released on parole.[1] It is quite possible that even now, because of a constitutional point, he may be eligible for parole at the end of eleven years from this date. The important point is that his life was spared and a blow struck at the institution of capital punishment. In addition, this was a specific recognition of rehabilitation as an element to be considered on clemency applications in capital cases.

Roger Bloom, too, had been much exercised over the Crump case; indeed, everyone who knows me has been stirred. In addition, there has been a strong feeling about this matter throughout the state and, perhaps, the country, because of the six-page Life article.

I will be cutting this letter short in order to visit with Paul Crump at the County Jail. When I see him hereafter it will be at a penitentiary in which the rules are much more severe than in any County Jail. The decisive period for Crump lies ahead. If he is equal to the problems that he will face during the next few months, then I feel cheerful about his future.

He has written a novel, entitled "Burn, Killer, Burn." It will be published very soon and I will see to it that you get a copy of it. I am proud of the fact that "The Paper," which Lois Solomon and I put out, was the very first Chicago publication to urge clemency for Crump.

I hope that your boy Tony mends rapidly. He is at the age when anything can happen, and generally does.

My reaction to "Judgment at Nuremberg" was the same as yours. It is one of the most impressive films produced by any American company.

My wife is delighted that you refer to her in such kind terms. She wants to be remembered.   Always yours, ELMER GERTZ

P.S. I have just returned from more than three hours that I spent, first with the Warden of the Jail, and then Paul Crump. I wish that I had your evocative genius, as I would like to set down all that was said, first by the Warden, and then by Paul Crump. It has been my singular good fortune to have had many remarkable experiences in my life, but it would be hard to think of one with more meaning and drama than this conversation in depth with a man snatched from the jaws of death. Tonight I am going to set down for myself an account of the conversation. Now I want merely to say that I have never felt more justified in any activity than in this effort to save Paul Crump's life. I know that his character is going to develop further in prison and that many memorable things will be said about him in the future. The explanation of such a miracle of character development, I do not know. I would love to discuss it with you one day.   E. G.

1.   In December 1976, the efforts of Gertz and others on Paul Crump's behalf bore further fruit—Governor Dan Walker of Illinois removed the words "without parole" from Crump's death commutation, making him eligible for parole consideration.

Both men wrote cover letters for enclosures on August 6. Gertz's enclosure was an account of his moving conversation with Paul Crump, as set forth in a letter to Gertz's son Ted. Miller forwarded "for safekeeping" a seven-page, typewritten recital of his early history, addressed to Huntington Cairns from Paris on April 30, 1939, saying, "I trust you to keep it confidential." (Most of the information in this document—part of the Gertz collection now on loan to the Morris Library, Southern Illinois University—has been published in various biographical sketches.) In his August 6 note Miller also told Gertz: "I saw Anaïs Nin yesterday after a lapse of 15 or 16 years. Wonderful meeting."

On August 7, Gertz assured Miller that he would guard the Cairns letter.

ALS, 1P.   Aug. 13th '62

Dear Elmer Gertz—   If I know how to read between the lines, I would say, on reading letter from Mr. Eagan, that it's in the bag.[1] I'll stop off at Jeff City on my way home and fix what's needed. Don't believe he is going to soak me.

Am off Wed. morning. Will be in Paris around Sept. 1st. Mail hereafter should go to me c/o Agence Hoffman—77 Blvd. St. Michel—Paris (5e).

Met Stanley Fleishman other night. Feels optimistic about the L.A. case.

Will be writing you from abroad now and then. Take good care of yourself. That letter to your son was simply wonderful.

My best now! Henry Miller

---

1.   The August 9 Eagan letter, which mentioned again that all three members of the Parole Board were his friends, contained no fresh information other than he had that day visited Bloom.

TL(CC), 2PP., AIR MAIL   August 29, 1962

Mr. Henry Miller
c/o Agence Hoffman
77 Blvd. St. Michel
Paris (5e), France

Dear Henry: Greetings! I hope that your trip has thus far been a glowing success, that you are enjoying every moment of it, and that you are well.

Barney Rosset has just sent me an advance copy of *Tropic of Capricorn*. It will be interesting to see what, if any, excitement will be caused by its appearance. Part of the time I think there will be very little effort made to suppress it, and the rest of the time I am not so sure of this.

From a legal viewpoint, I believe that *Capricorn* is less vul-

nerable than *Cancer*, because the legally questionable material is
concentrated in a few places, while it is throughout *Cancer*. In some
spots *Capricorn* is more outspoken than *Cancer*, but there are
dozens, if not hundreds, of pages with nothing objectionable from
a legal viewpoint in *Capricorn*. I hope it does not run into any difficulty, but if it does I would love to defend it, if only because one
particular friend of mine told me it will be harder to defend than
Cancer.

Frank Harris' autobiography is scheduled to be published in
unexpurgated form soon.[1] For sentimental reasons, I would love to
be the attorney there too, if there is trouble.

The Corporation Counsel of Chicago has just filed the printed
Abstract of Record in the *Tropic of Cancer* appeal here and has
gotten an extension of time, until September 26, to file the brief.
This means that I am hard at work on the appeal. The Abstract is,
in many respects, a bad one; in other respects it is pretty good.

I don't want you to spend time reading letters, as you are in
the part of the world where you can derive other pleasures. I want
you to know I am up and around and thinking of you.

All my best.   Always yours, ELMER GERTZ

---

1.   *My Life and Loves*, edited and with an introduction by John F. Gal-
     lagher (New York: Grove Press [1963]). Gertz not only urged Grove
     to publish the book, but sponsored the first meeting of the parties to
     the publishing agreement (see Gertz 10/23/62).

TL(CC), 2PP., AIR MAIL   August 30, 1962

Dear Henry: In my letter of yesterday's date I forgot to thank
you for the overly generous words about me that you wrote for
the Newsletter.[1] I got some vicarious satisfaction yesterday which
brought to mind that I had not thanked you. My childhood friend,
Arthur J. Goldberg, has just been named by President Kennedy to
succeed Justice Frankfurter in the Supreme Court of the United

States.[2] Arthur is a very great man. I think I told you that, following our victory before Judge Epstein, he congratulated me privately and, in a public address, commended Judge Epstein as deserving the support of the entire Bar for his courageous decision. From a purely selfish viewpoint, I would say that we now have, in place of the dubious vote of Justice Frankfurter on freedom of press issues, the certain support of Justice Goldberg, not because he is a friend of mine, but because instinctively he knows what freedom means. So that you may rejoice further during your absence from the country, I would say that we have three absolutely certain votes—Justices Black, Douglas and Goldberg; and we have two virtually certain votes—Chief Justice Warren and Justice Harlan. Justice Stewart is likely to be our way and it is not unlikely that the only Catholic, Justice Brennan, will go along with the majority. This leaves only Justices Clark and White in doubt.[3] Without being overly optimistic, I would say that there now appears to be a certainty that we will win the very first *Tropic of Cancer* appeal in the United States Supreme Court. It would be a shocking reversal on the part of the court if such were not the case.

Meanwhile, I have to win in Illinois, and others have to win elsewhere.

Needless to say, I am keeping in touch with Roger Bloom, Eddie Schwartz and Tom Moore. Have you been told that Eddie's wife Mae was in the hospital briefly?

Your *Hamlet* publishers have written me about their problem with Mrs. Fraenkel, and I have given them some advice on the matter. I suppose that they will follow through on it. I told them that she has no right to insist upon any special terms. I suggested that, perhaps, they should have me write to her to that effect.

Always yours, ELMER GERTZ

1. Miller said of Gertz, in reporting their Minneapolis meeting in the September 1962 *Henry Miller Society Newsletter* (No. 10): "And what an honor it was to have the pleasure of Elmer Gertz' company for three whole days! I hope we shall soon see him sitting on the Supreme Court bench, where he belongs."

2. Gertz and Goldberg were grade school classmates. They graduated from the Theodore Herzl Public School, in Chicago, in January 1921.

3. When the United States Supreme Court finally ruled on *Cancer* (having accepted for consideration an appeal from a Florida conviction), only five Justices supported the per curiam reversal that cleared the book—Justices Goldberg, Brennan, Stewart, Black, and Douglas. The four other Justices, without giving their reasons for doing so, opposed the granting of certiorari (*Grove Press v. Gerstein*, 378 U.S. 577 [1964], rev'g 156 So. 2d 537 [Fla. App. 1963]).

APS, 1S., AIR MAIL   Paris—8/30/62

Dear friend—   Expect to leave for Copenhagen very soon. Find Paris warm & cosy—after grim Edinburgh. (It's almost Winter there.) Now going to visit Hildegarde Neff. Am making some recordings, in English, for "La Voix de l'Auteur."[1]   My best! Henry

---

1. Miller and Lawrence Durrell made recordings from their books.

ALS, 2PP.   Sep't. 10th 1962 [Copenhagen]

Dear Elmer Gertz—   Got your two letters somewhere. I met Arthur Goldberg and his wife in Big Sur. First Justice of Supreme Court I have the honor to know. Now I'm leaving for Bavaria to stay at Hildegard Neff's[1] home near Starnberg-am-See while she ⟨obliterated⟩ plays Catherine the Great (for an Italian film company) in Zagreb and Rome. Will stay there till end of September, then to Berlin, I think.

My Danish publisher[2] brought out Lolita—but it's a flop here. Danes can't get excited about it.

Made (3) recordings while in Paris for "La Voix de l'Auteur" (in English.) World distribution.

Hope to do a little writing and painting when I get to Bavaria. It's quiet here. Weather off. Food quite good.

Been visiting my composer friend at the hospital.[3] He's doing well. Has a piano in his room. Think more than ever that the opera ("The Smile") will be a sensation.[4]

Expect to get things rolling in Berlin as regards my play. Will stop off to visit you in Chicago, if nothing prevents. Probably in November. Then I will see Mr. Eagan in Jeff City and talk money. Keep writing me c/o Hoffman, Paris.

All the best now to you and your lovely wife.   Henry Miller[5]

---

1. The actress's last name is usually spelled "Kneff."
2. Hans Reitzel.
3. Triestino composer Antonio Gino Bibalo, who was being treated for tuberculosis.
4. The opera based on Miller's *The Smile at the Foot of the Ladder* was produced in April, 1965, at the Hamburg Staatsoper.
5. Written on stationery of the Palace Hotel, Copenhagen. In the December 1962 *Henry Miller Literary Society Newsletter*, Miller said: "Went one day with my publisher to visit Palle Nielsen, the famous graphic artist whose marvelous book of linoleum cuts on Orpheus and Eurydice I am proud to own. . . . While there I tried my hand at a copper plate engraving—and caught the bug."

APS, 2SS.   Copenhagen—9/11/62

Dear Elmer Gertz—   If you didn't receive copy of *Sexus* I ordered from the Mexican bookshop, write to my publisher here (see back of envelope) to send you one. It's on sale all over here—in English. Can't find a copy of *Quiet Days* anywhere! Nor will publisher say when he brings out a new edition. *Sexus* now going into a paper back (cheap) edition in Danish. Is read & discussed in the schools too. Ho ho!   Henry Miller

Give my best to Eddie Schwartz, please.[1]

---

1. Written on back of unaddressed postcard, which as text indicates was enclosed in an envelope.

APS, 1S. Percha—9/28/62

Dear Elmer Gertz— Don't have your last letter in front of me.[1] Just a word to say I leave for Berlin in a few days, where I hope to get my play under way at the Schiller Theater.[2] Good news about *Hamlet*. AUSTRIA is the place to visit! Also, you must see some of mad Ludwig's castles. Wish I knew a "good" book about him! He intrigues me. All's well. My best! Henry Miller

---

1. The UCLA files contain a letter from Gertz dated September 17, though no carbon of this is in the Miller-Gertz collection at SIU, Carbondale. Reference is made to a trip Gertz had made to New York at which time he talked with Frank Harris's executor, Arthur Leonard Ross, about publication of an unexpurgated edition of *My Life and Loves* (see Gertz 10/23/62).
2. *Just Wild About Harry* was not produced at the Schiller Theater, reputedly because Miller would not agree to certain proposed changes (Wood, *Collector's Quest*, p. 153 n.1).

TL(CC), 1P., AIR MAIL October 12, 1962

Dear Henry: Just a hurried word to tell you a few things of interest.

The Corporation Counsel of Chicago has filed his brief in behalf of Police Superintendent Wilson. It is, in some respects, a diabolically clever document, filled with distortions. I am working day and night to respond to it, as I do not want to ask for even a day's delay. When you return I will tell you more of it.

For another thing, I had the pleasure of a visit from Orvis Ross. He was en route to New York for a performance of Die Meistersinger. Orvis is a wonderful fellow and I look forward to seeing him again on his return from New York.

Of course, I look forward to seeing you. Please let me know your plans as soon as they are fixed in your mind. Of course, we would love to have you as our house guest.

What a lovely lady Hildegarde is, to judge by her picture.[1]
And what a time you must be having in Europe.
All of our best.   Aways yours, ELMER GERTZ

---

1.   On the reverse side of the postcard Miller sent Gertz on September 28
      was a glossy photograph of Hildegarde Kneff.

TLS, 1P.   Berlin—Oct. 16, 1962

Dear Elmer Gertz,   Just a word to acknowledge your recent letters. I note that you are working like mad on this Chicago business.
And wondering, therefore, if it will be inconvenient for you should
I arrive in Chicago before Nov. 3rd. I am hoping to get away from
here by the end of October, and would spend only 36 hours in
N. Y. I'll write again when I have definite date. Am held up here
because of the theatre people.

        Meanwhile maybe you received a letter from Mr. Eagan? He
had written me to ask if I thought you could come to Jefferson
City to appear before the parole board in Roger Bloom's behalf.
I told him, of course, that I couldn't say—you would have to do
that. It seemed a little strange to me that he should have requested
this. But it also seems to me now that he has been talking to the
Board members and that something can be done.

        Don't bother to write me at length—I feel sorry that you are
put to so much trouble and work. As for Orvis Ross, yes, he is a
wonderful person. What a pity it is that the voluminous correspondence we had no longer exists. It is also rather remarkable, I
think, that after a lapse of about 35 years two friends should come
together again and reestablish a relationship—and quite as if no
time at all had intervened.

        While here I met Nicolas Nabokov, the composer, and cousin
of the author of Lolita. Quite a person. And, I imagine quite a
different character from his more famous cousin. He promised me
a tape of his Rasputin opera.

The great thing here is the George Grosz exhibition. Just fabulous. Now don't tell me that you knew him too! I suspect you might have. I never did meet him, alas.

I am typing here at Renate's home,[1] being unable to find a hotel in all Berlin. We have a regulation ping pong table in this big room and between paragraphs I get up and play with her two boys. I've made a number of water colors too—some of them pretty good, I think. Maybe I can add something to your collection.

But do tell me frankly if it were better I didn't come to see you before Nov. 3rd. Or, if it would be easier for you I could put up at a hotel there.

Meanwhile my very best to you and to your dear wife whom I hope to meet soon.   Sincerely, Henry Miller

P.S. Never heard what happened in the L.A. Appeals case—did we win or fail, I wonder? Stanley Fleishman was handling it. He's a man I like very much and esteem.
P.P.S. And so far no new eruptions over Capricorn. Strange indeed.[2]

---

1.   Renate Gerhardt translated a section from Miller's *Remember to Remember* under the title *Ein Weihnachtsabend in der Villa Seurat* (Hamburg: Rowohlt, 1960). The Gerhardt Verlag was preparing to publish *Just Wild About Harry* in German. In the *Henry Miller Society Newsletter* of December 1962 (No. 11), Miller wrote: "From Munich I flew to Berlin to visit the young Gerhardt Verlag which has started with a bang. Six unusual titles for Fall and Winter production, among them Artaud, Max Ernst, Breton and the Marquis de Sade. The Verlag is housed in an eight room apartment, the like of which one used to see on Riverside Drive, N.Y. Several rooms are large enough for ping pong tournaments or roller skating; the floors are all of polished inlaid wood."
2.   *Tropic of Capricorn*, together with *Tropic of Cancer*, had been ruled obscene in a 1950 Customs case in California (see Lewis, *Literature, Obscenity, and Law*, p. 208), but the Grove Press edition of *Capricorn* (1962) appears not to have been involved in litigation. Miller's second postscript was handwritten.

ALS, 1P.   Berlin—10/21/62

Dear Elmer Gertz—   Today at the Art Academy here I met
again the ⟨District⟩ Attorney General from Hamburg—Buchholz
—who is a good friend of Ledig-Rowohlt and a defender of freedom of speech. (Just won case here for Genet.) He asked if I
would get him whatever data might be valuable regarding the
Tropics' decisions in U.S. Rowohlt will soon bring out the Tropics
in a public edition and there may be a fight.

I told him of you and all you had accomplished. If you could
send him material (only essential data) please do. Send it to H. M.
Ledig-Rowohlt—Rowohlt Verlag—Reinbek-bei-Hamburg, West
Germany and ask him to forward it to ⟨Distr⟩ Attorney-General
Buchholz, that the latter requested it. Thank you! (*no great hurry!*)
                                    More later. In haste, Henry

APS, 1S   10/23/62

Dear E. G.—   Arriving next Monday night (the 29th) in N.Y.
Will stay till Wednesday probably, then take plane for Chicago.
Will be at the Grosvenor (35—5th Ave.) or, *for mail,* c/o Grove
Press.
                                    My best! Henry Miller[1]

---

1.   Postcard, postmarked Berlin, of The Wall separating East and West
      Berlin. In the *Henry Miller Society Newsletter* of December, 1962
      (No. 11), Miller wrote of his Berlin visit: "The first thing I did on
      arriving was to take a taxi and drive slowly around the Wall. Horrible
      sight. Made more so by the no-man's land established between the
      two cities. This dead area in which no one lives, moves or breathes,
      reminded me of an old Ufa film, vintage 1920. The Wall will go, that
      is certain. After the great Wall of China and the Maginot Line, how
      can this one endure?"

TL(CC), 2PP., AIR MAIL   October 23, 1962

Dear Henry: Forget anything about my work or anything else, and plan on being with us at any time that it suits your convenience. Mamie and I will be delighted to have you in our home; indeed, we look forward to it with tremendous excitement. We hope that it will be comfortable enough for you.

Most of the pressure with respect to the brief has lessened. I have corrected the galleys and expect to submit them to the printer today. I should get the page proofs tomorrow and finish my corrections of them at that time. This means that before the end of the week, or, at latest, Monday, the brief will be on file, several days ahead of schedule. We have already completed the so-called Additional Abstract and it should be filed today. I will present you with a set of these when I see you. At least portions of our brief are more interesting than most legal documents.

I am sorry that we dismantled our ping-pong table. The kids played, but, unlike you, I have very firm religious beliefs and practices with respect to exercise. My religion calls for strict abstinence from all forms of exercise. I am a fundamentalist in that respect. Mamie is the athlete of our family. She is a star tennis player and can still jump rope better than any kid.

No, I have not heard from Mr. Eagan, but I did get a very fine letter from Roger. When you are in town we can discuss my appearance before the Parole Board in his behalf. The other day I was so wound up that I dropped everything and went with Mamie to see "The Birdman of Alcatraz," a truly remarkable film.

No, I never met George Grosz, although I admired him tremendously. I first heard of him through Frank Harris. Incidentally, I brought Harris' executor[1] and Barney Rosset togther. Harris' autobiography will be published unexpurgated in the spring—I hope with a preface by me.

All of the briefs have been filed in the Los Angeles case. I received a copy of one of Stanley Fleishman's briefs, and a very excellent brief, too. Unfortunately, in California appeals go through an intermediate court first, before reaching the Supreme Court.

By the time you are in Chicago we will know when the oral argument in our case will be set. It will take place in Springfield.

Of course, I noticed with great joy what you said about adding to my collection of your water colors. Our walls cry for them.

Now I must ask you frankly about your wishes with respect to seeing people while you are with us. Of course, Eddie, Tom and, perhaps, Orvis, will come in from Minnesota.[2] There is also the possibility, I understand, that Bob Fink may be in town. Whom else would you care to have around at any time? We want to be guided by your do's and don't's in this matter. My own thought is that I would like to have my associate, Sidney Karasik, meet you. He is a very unusual lawyer in several respects, including his love of literature. He was a boyhood friend of my brother-in-law and used to sit virtually at my feet when a kid. Now he has somewhat more independence, but we still enjoy working with each other. I would also like to have Hoke Norris, the literary editor of the Sun-Times, and Dr. Richard Ellmann, our star witness. But in all cases I want to be governed by your wishes.

We look forward with much excitement to seeing you.

Always yours, ELMER GERTZ

cc: (bei Gerhardt)
    1000—Berlin—31
    Jenaerstrasse F., Germany

---

1. Arthur Leonard Ross.
2. Edward Schwartz, Thomas Moore, Orvis Ross.

APS, 1 S., AIR MAIL   Berlin—Thursday (25th)

Dear E. G.   It's probable now that I'll stay in N.Y. till Thursday instead of Wednesday. So much to do there. Hoping to find letter if O.K. to come at Grove Press Tuesday morning. If you wish to telephone (or give me your home number and address) try to get me at the Grosvenor Hotel—35—5th Ave. N.Y.

This in haste.   Henry Miller

TLS, 1P.   from Berlin—Oct. 26, 1962

Dear friends, (Elmer and Mamie)   Ich komme bald. Just got yours of the 23rd—fast work! Good, I will come Thursday, Nov. 1st, by plane. Will get ticket when in N. Y. An afternoon or early evening plane, if possible. Hope you will meet me. I don't have your home address, you know. If I am not at the Grosvenor at 35 Fifth Ave. N. Y. ask Grove Press, N. Y. (Barney Rosset, or Judith Schmidt, his secretary) where I am. Arrive there late Monday night.

About people to meet while in Chicago . . . I'll leave it to your excellent judgment. You know, ⟨I⟩ I'm not keen on meeting a lot of people. But your friends, that's another matter. And certainly Hoke Norris. But do please try to keep the newspaper men away from me, eh? I hope I can get by without any press interviews—just a chat with Norris.

Sounds wonderful that Harris' autobiography will be published and that you may do the preface to it. I have a hunch the L.A. appeals will go well too, this time.

I hope to be able to stay two or three days, at least, with you. Hope it isn't freezing there already. I have a fairly warm overcoat, thank God. And you probably have central heating, eh?

I am not a believer in exercise either—not deliberate work, I mean. But ping pong is something special with me. I want to be like a Zen monk at it eventually. Unfortunately my hip doesn't permit me to go at it as strenuously as I used to. Certainly I don't expect you to provide me with that sort of entertainment.

Yes, we'll talk about Eagan when we meet. Maybe I'll telephone him from Chicago.

The war scare was strong here for 36 hours; quiet now. The Europeans are used to this kind of thing. And Berlin seems intact.

Enough now. My best to you two. Eddie Schwartz will probably come, and if Ross could too that would be quite perfect. And
Dear Tom Moore. Fine.

I am going to the Schiller Theater now—last minute arrangements. The new press here (Gerhardt Verlag) is also starting off
beautifully. My play is the best seller so far—though it only comes
out late in ⟨this m⟩ in November.[1]   **Henry**

---

1.   Ganz Wild auf Harry (Berlin: Gerhardt Verlag, 1963).

On October 29 Gertz wrote Miller at the Grosvenor Hotel about
final arrangements for his Chicago visit, adding: "Our brief in
your case is filed, about ten days ahead of schedule. This is contrary to the Union rules, but I want to give the City no opportunity for asking for an extension of time. I suggest that you get
a copy of the brief from Barney Rosset, who has a number on
hand. Some of the brief is legalistic in language, but much of it
can be read with enjoyment, even by you!"

[October 30, 1962]

ARRIVING OHARE AMERICAN AIRLINES THURSDAY
615PM CHICAGO TIME

HENRY MILLER

[Wire to Gertz at his office, 30 October 1962. New York, N. Y.]

Miller said of the visit, in the Henry Miller Society Newsletter
of December, 1962 (No. 11):
     "Spent several days in Chicago chez Elmer Gertz, the at-
torney in the Chicago case. What a wonderful man, what a wonderful family! One can sit down and talk with Elmer Gertz from
now till Doomsday; he's inexhaustible. It was not surprising to me,
when I stepped into his office, to see on his desk the sculpted
figures of Bernard Shaw, Clarence Darrow, and Carl Sandburg.
He should also have had one of Frank Harris, about whom we
talked at great length. His good wife Mamie drove us about town

from one end to the other. I had a look at Maxwell Street, the marvelous Lake Front, the stockyards which, in their present state of dilapidation, are wonderful material for a photographer, especially one like Brassai, and finally we wound up at the Loop Synagogue where Abraham Rattner's stained glass windows are there for all to see. A wonderful synagogue, orthodox, whose atmosphere is far more inspiring to the devout than St. Patrick's Cathedral or Trinity Church, N.Y. Were I to live in Chicago I would go there every day to sit and meditate. And each day I would offer up a silent prayer for the health and well-being of Abe Rattner, one of the great, great artists of our time."

Gertz included a vivid description of Miller's visit in A Handful of Clients, pp. 235–40, concluding:

"I know of popular poets and artists who prate of democracy and are terrors as guests. They rearrange households, choose the menus, and invite the guests. They tyrannize over their hosts, who rejoice when they leave. Only the vanity of having a lion in the den can compensate their hosts for the loss of dignity and the lack of real communication. By contrast, Henry Miller is the most wonderful of guests—thoughtful, co-operative, undemanding, eager to add to the happiness of a household. It was to be expected that he and I would have long conversational bouts; but he was equally close to all members of the family. He talked to the children about matters that were of importance to them, and was genuinely interested in their concerns. Occasionally, he went on little shopping trips for my wife, Mamie, and they chatted together about household matters and about Russia, the birthplace of Mamie's parents. . . . Henry Miller is that rare person—a genius of letters with a genius for friendship."

From Jefferson City, Missouri, Miller sent a card (dated October 7, but obviously written November 7) saying he thought Roger Bloom's parole was "in the bag," and that he was going to Hannibal, Missouri, the next day.

Gertz, writing in care of Mr. Eagan in Jefferson City on November 7, mentioned "the Brooklyn situation," his reference being to a Tropic of Cancer case that plagued Miller for some months and is frequently mentioned in subsequent letters—the only Cancer case in which Miller was a defendant.

On November 8 Gertz informed Miller that he was forwarding Paul Crump's Burn, Killer, Burn (Chicago: Johnson Publishing Co. [1962]), and a copy of a Frank Harris letter that was in his files.

APS, 1S   From Hannibal, Mo. (11/8/62)

Dear Elmer & Mamie—   Just to let you know I got here. Town
is colorful & decrepit. He was born (Mark) in Florida, Mo.[1] I leave
for L.A. tomorrow. Eagan turns out to be quite wonderful. All the
best!   Henry

---

1.   Eagan took Miller to see Mark Twain's boyhood home in Hannibal;
      the message is written on a postcard bearing a photograph of the parlor
      of that home.

ALS, 2PP   Pac. Pal—California

                                                    11/10/62
Dear Elmer—   Got in last night—staying temporarily at the
Santa Ynez Inn (motel) on Sunset Blvd—near the ocean. Get mail
& messages at usual address (see back of envelope.)
     Barney telephoned to say nothing new on Brooklyn, doesn't
know yet the charges against us (!), but wondered if I might appear voluntarily in Bklyn in the next few weeks. Eagan (of Jeff
City) advised not to go, but let them come and take a deposition,
if necessary. I am doing nothing meanwhile, trusting it will blow
over without fuss.
     There's an immense slew of mail awaiting me—haven't looked
at a morsel yet.
     Eagan was quite wonderful, in every way. More on this an-
other time. Appeared before Parole Board and think I impressed
them. They are non-committal, but Eagan assures me it will go
through. Roger was full of joy and hope.
     I met judges, senators, all sorts there—and most of them had
read me—and seemed to like it.
     Fred Perlès' pocket edition ("My Friend HM") is now on
the stands (Belmont Books, N.Y.) Found *one* in Jeff City at the
hotel news stand.

My love to all the members of the family. More anon. It was a wonderful event for me to be with you.

(Roger said *Steve Allen* writes him wonderful letters.)

Now to wade thru all the paperasserie.

My best to you and Mamie.   Henry[1]

---

1.   Written on stationery of the Hotel Governor, Jefferson City, Missouri.

TL(CC), 3PP., AIR MAIL   November 15, 1962

Mr. Henry Miller
c/o Verzeano
661 Las Lomas
Pacific Palisades, California

Dear Henry: I have received letters from you, Eddie Schwartz and Roger Bloom, and they all form sort of a pattern. I have not heard from Barney Rosset or Cy Rembar about the Brooklyn situation, and I really must get some further information on the matter before I can advise you in good faith. In the pending litigation here I represent both you and Grove Press, and I feel that I must be fair to both of you. In your case, particularly, there is a personal tie which would make it impossible for me to be anything except completely honest in the advice I offer, even if there were conceivable situations in which I might be less than candid.

I have a twofold interest in the Brooklyn situation. First of all, I want to make certain that nothing happens which might hurt you. While I would defer to a certain extent to those having the responsibility for the defense of the Brooklyn proceeding, I would, in the last analysis, form my own judgment in order to advise you in the same manner I would want to be advised myself if I were a defendant in such a proceeding. It happens also that the Brooklyn proceeding has been dragged into the Tropic of Cancer appeal

here. The Corporation Counsel of the City of Chicago, who represents the appellant in our case, filed a reply brief the other day,
really a very poor document, except for one below-the-belt passage
which can be highly prejudicial. The following passage is inserted
on page 18:

"(It may be interesting to note that the authorities are still
concerned with Mr. Miller. His arrest has been ordered by a
Brooklyn, New York, court for having failed to answer criminal
charges of writing obscenity, represented by *Tropic of Cancer*. Chicago Tribune, Nov. 2, 1962, p. 2, col. 2.)"[1]

For this reason, I have been hounding Barney to enlighten
me and have been rather distressed that the information I seek has
not been forthcoming. From what he tells you, he does not know
either, which is strange indeed. For all I know, by the time you get
this letter I will have more information. I would suggest your telling Barney, if the question comes up again, that you do not want
to act in haste, that you want to think the thing through before
committing yourself to any course of conduct. My offhand impression is that Mr. Eagan is right, that you ought not to go to Brooklyn voluntarily. My reason for this is a simple one. The Brooklyn
proceeding is obviously one filed in bad faith. You did not write
the book in Brooklyn and you have nothing to do with its distribution there. This means that any action in Brooklyn charging
you with the writing of the book twenty-seven years after you
wrote it in Paris is motivated dubiously, to put it mildly. It is either
a publicity stunt on the part of the judge or District Attorney, or
someone who wants to prejudice our case here by doing something
elsewhere. Every legal proceeding has its own subtleties, and until
one is familiar with all of them, one hesitates to give advice, particularly to one as dear to me as you are.

Your visit is a permanent part of the lives of Mamie, the children and myself. We constantly talk about you. Following your
departure, Hank did one of the very best water-colors, Sue began
working on a new hanging, Ted began reading *Colossus of Maroussi*[2] like mad, and I have written countless pages of my book.

Mamie presides over everything with her usual grace and humor.

Roger's letter was a very happy one. He tells me that he is restrained from saying too much for reasons that you know. I am eager to get the full story from you. I am eager, indeed, to hear from you as to all that has happened since your departure. We look forward to your next visit with mounting anticipation.

I suppose Eddie Schwartz has written to you about the hope of the University of Minnesota to publish the interview with you, my legal talk and the critical review, in a pamphlet. I think that that would be a very good idea, provided we have the opportunity to do the most essential brushing up of the material. Anything beyond that would tend to take away the spontaneity of our words. I think the pamphlet would be strategically wise at this moment, in order to take the curse, as it were, off the Brooklyn situation. It will sit well with many people if the University in the great Scandinavian State of Minnesota thought enough of you and your writings to sponsor such publication; besides, I want to add to my Miller collection.

I have made inquiry of the United States Customs about the phonograph records that you sent to me. I do hope that I get them soon in order to recall that wonderful voice of yours. I wish that we could have taped some of the conversations we had during the days you were with us.

All of us send our very best to you.

Always yours, ELMER GERTZ

P.S. As you will be informed by the enclosed copy of a letter to Cy Rembar, Barney finally sent me a copy of the so-called information against you and others. Have you seen it? If not, I can send you a copy. The information would be characterized by me as knowingly false. It alleges, among other things, that you wrote the book between January 1, 1961, and June 30, 1962, in the County of Kings, which is where Brooklyn is located.[3] Of course, the District Attorney knows that the book was written and published in Paris in 1934. There are other falsehoods of such nature as to make one wonder about the integrity of the public officials involved in the matter.

1.   "Order Author Seized, Charge Book Obscene." According to this article, Grove Press claimed not to know Miller's whereabouts.
2.   San Francisco: Colt Press, 1941; [Norfolk, Conn.]: New Directions [1941].
3.   The second count of the charge alleged that Miller conspired with Grove Press and certain wholesalers in the writing and publishing of the book. For more about this *Cancer* case, see Rembar, *End of Obscenity*, pp. 209–15.

TL(CC), 1P., AIR MAIL   November 16, 1962

Dear Henry: While I was away from the office today Cy Rembar tried to reach me, and he was away when I called back. I suppose Monday I will know more about the Brooklyn matter.

I received that magnificent copy of *Into the Night Life,* surely one of the most beautiful books ever printed. The collaboration between you and Schatz is a memorable one. I shall treasure the work.

In response to my inquiry, I heard from the United States Customs. As of November 15 the office here has no record of receipt of any package. They suggest that I contact the shipper relative to a tracer.

Warmest regards from all of us.

Always yours, ELMER GERTZ

TLS, 1P.   Nov. 18, 1962

Dear Elmer,   Just got your various letters and enclosures, all very interesting. Rosset sent me copy of the charges in Brooklyn case, but no letter with it. I too am curious to know what Cy Rembar is doing about it; seems to me it should prove a boomerang for the Brooklyn prosecutors. You use the term "quash." Take it this means roughly—throw it out, non-valid, or some such. One little point I am interested in is whether, assuming the charge is proved false, non-valid, ridiculous, etc., does my failure to appear there still stand against me—I mean, would I still be answerable to them if ever I set foot in Brooklyn? A good reporter ought to be able to run down the real motive for this action and expose it, don't you think?

I don't know how much I told you of my meeting with the Parole Board in Jeff City; they were non-commital, as always, but I am certain they are going to do something now. Only some unexpected happening could reverse this possibility. Even the Warden seems to take it for granted. I told Roger not to act or talk as if it were a certainty. One day I'll relate the whole thing to you vive voce—much easier.

It would be excellent, yes, if the University of Minnesota published the texts you speak of. Haven't heard anything definite yet.

I was happy to see that Frank Harris letter. It reminded me that, in addition to the text I believe I wrote for Pearson's, I suddenly recall having written about Solomon's Temple for the Menorah Journal (now extinct, I suppose) way back in 1925 or '26.[1] I remember showing the text to my father who, as you know, never read anything else of mine except "Money and how it gets that way,"[2] which he took seriously. I remember his being impressed with my "erudition"—of course I had borrowed all the information from books. It would be wonderful if Tom Moore could trace this piece down, and that little thing I spoke of for "Black Cat."

Now, as to the recordings . . . It seems I only *thought* I had asked them to send you these. I order so many things for so many people, and you are always on my mind for each list, that I just took it for granted. Now I have written to the American distributor—Spoken Arts, in New Rochelle, to send you them; it will be quicker this way. Note their catalogue of recordings, the American one, I mean, as well as those put out by the Swiss firm (La Voix de l'Auteur).

Guess that's it for the moment; still answering the pile of

letters I found on arriving. Glad to hear all the members are so creatively active, radiant, and so on. Give my best to your jewel of a Mamie.

I'm house hunting here. The kids want us to be a "family" once more. I'd much rather go to Mexico and look for a new home, believe me.   All the best. Henry

---

1. For *Pearson's* article, see Miller 1/6/62, notes. No article identifiable as Miller's located in *Menorah Journal*.
2. Paris: Booster Publications [1938].

TL(CC), 3PP., AIR MAIL   November 21, 1962

Dear Henry: While I was picking up a copy of the Perles book, My Friend Henry Miller, I ran into the enclosed paperback edition of *The Erotic in Literature*, by David Loth.[1] You will notice that your writings, Durrell's *Justine* and Frank Harris' *My Life and Loves* are spread all over the cover of the book. It is an interesting one anyway.

I spent many hours earlier this week with Edward de Grazia, who is one of Barney Rosset's corps of lawyers. He is a man of some literary interest and is a good lawyer. He is the one representing Grove Press in connection with the Customs seizure of a manuscript by an author named John Schultz. I understand he succeeded in getting the manuscript back. Strangely enough, he, too, is puzzled by the Brooklyn prosecution and is not fully acquainted with all of the facts. He has promised to learn them for me, if possible, in advance of November 27, the time of the hearing in Springfield. I was rather surprised to learn that Cy Rembar has not actually filed any motion of any kind in Brooklyn—at least as of the date that Ed de Grazia talked with me. Apparently, de Grazia is the one who gave Barney the notion that you ought to appear voluntarily in Brooklyn. When he expressed the same thought to me, I disagreed strongly and tried to make him see why it would be a foolish move. It is clear that the prosecution is fraudulent and malicious. What reason is there to suppose that they would not subject you to some other such embarrassing result. If the case should be dismissed in Brooklyn, then you would not run any risk if you appeared in Brooklyn, at least so far as *Cancer* is concerned; *Capricorn* may be another matter.

There seems to be a sort of revival of censorship generally in some of the communities. I noticed that, in recent weeks a number of Chicago booksellers have been arrested, some as recently as yesterday. These are people who have had immunity for a long while. They have been the sellers of ordinary commercial pornography, for the most part.

I suppose that you have been brought up to date on the California situation, which is not as good as you had hoped. I assume Stanley Fleishman has explained the situation to you. Briefly, this is it.

There have been three prosecutions in California, one in San Marin County, one in La Jolla and one in Los Angeles. Juries acquitted booksellers in San Marin County and in La Jolla, but convicted the bookseller in Los Angeles.[2] This in itself is preposterous. Either the book is, or is not, obscene. It is not that much a matter of geography. It was believed that the original trial in Los Angeles had been bungled and Stanley Fleishman was brought in for the appeal as an extraordinarily capable man in this field. In California there are, as you know, several intermediate appeals before a case reaches the Supreme Court. On the first level, the jury verdict was sustained, but the court, on its own motion, as if recognizing that it had acted improperly, certified the case as an important one to the next appellate level. This would normally mean that, as a matter of course, the higher reviewing court would take the case; instead, with one judge dissenting, they turned down the appeal. Stanley Fleishman is now preparing to take the case to the United States Supreme Court. If the Supreme Court allows an appeal (and it is wholly discretionary in the court), this will be the first highest court test of the matter. It could be the most important case in the history of obscenity decisions superseding Roth[3] and earlier cases.

If, meanwhile, our case were decided in Illinois either way, it, too, might be taken to the Supreme Court, so that the Court would have cases from two jurisdictions to consider, with the background of the Massachusetts and Maryland results. All of this sounds very complicated, I know. Translated into simple language, it means that, because of the persistence of the censors, we will not be absolutely certain as to the standing of *Cancer*, or any similar work, until the United States Supreme Court hears a case relating to it. Since the California case is not as good as the Illinois one, it would be well if both cases were heard together by the court. If we lose in the Supreme Court of Illinois, we would surely try to get a reversal in Washington.

All sorts of anomalous results are possible. For example, we could win in Illinois and the City of Chicago could attempt to appeal, and the Supreme Court could refuse to accept such appeal. At the same time, it could refuse to accept an appeal from California. This, in effect, would be sanctioning two completely opposing results. It would be tantamount to the Court's saying that, for the present, any local result would be final, even if one local result contradicted the other.

I have asked Tom Moore to check into the matter of those old articles of yours. I am sure that he will come up with something or other. I understand that the Menorah Journal is still being published.

Thanks a million for ordering those records for me. I look forward to them with much excitement.

Sue is going to spend Thanksgiving Day framing your water colors for us. You will see our private exhibition of them when next you are here—part at the office and part at home and part in Sue's apartment.

All our very best to you.   Always yours, ELMER GERTZ

Enc.

---

1.   David Loth, *The Erotic in Literature* (London: Secker & Warburg, 1962).

2. See H. M. 3/28/62, notes.

3. In its 1957 *Roth* decision, the United States Supreme Court for the first time ruled directly on the broad question of the constitutionality of obscenity statutes, holding (with three Justices dissenting) that obscenity was "not within the area of constitutionally protected speech or press." *Roth* is also important because, in delivering the opinion of the Court, Justice Brennan enunciated a guideline for determining the type of material that could be legally proscribed which for some years was cited by lower courts as the test of obscenity—"whether to the average person, applying contemporary community standards, the dominant theme of the material taken as a whole appeals to prurient interest." (See Judge Epstein's ruling in the Chicago *Cancer* case, Gertz 2/21/62, notes.) Another section of Justice Brennan's opinion that would have significant bearing on future decisions was a statement that led to what would be called the "social value" test: "All ideas having even the slightest redeeming social importance—unorthodox ideas, controversial ideas, even ideas hateful to the prevailing climate of opinion—have the full protection of the guaranties [of the Bill of Rights], unless excludable because they encroach upon the limited area of more important interests." For a discussion of *Roth*, and of Supreme Court decisions on obscenity following *Roth*, see Lewis, *Literature, Obscenity, and Law*, pp. 183–247.

TL(CC), 2PP., AIR MAIL   November 23, 1962

Dear Henry: Wednesday evening Cy Rembar called me and I got a little more of the background of the Brooklyn situation, but not really enough. It is amazing how little anyone knows about it. According to Cy, each month while the Grand Jury was in session, Judge Leibovitz hounded it to indict you, Barney, et al., and each month the Jury failed, or refused, to do so. Then, finally, the local attorney, equivalent to our State's Attorney, was persuaded to proceed on an Information.[1] From what I can gather, he is not eager to push the matter. He would just as soon let it hang fire indefinitely. Cy Rembar feels, like Ed de Grazia and Barney, that you ought to appear voluntarily. Perhaps there is something wrong with my thinking, but I just don't see it that way. While I owe loyalty to Barney, I also owe it to you, and I feel it more strongly in your case. I can conceive of circumstances in which it might be expedient for you to confound the local authorities by appearing and demanding that the matter be completed. Public-relations-wise, that might be the best thing to do. But I am thinking, also, of your comfort and well being. Sooner or later, and probably sooner, you will have to reach a decision yourself.

I have just received from the English publishers the copy of the Nigerian novel about which you spoke with such enthusiasm. Thanks much for sending it to me. Mamie and I will read it with much interest, thinking as we do of your report of your conversation with the author.

I am sending herewith a copy of the report of the committee of the Illinois Library Association which gave its 1962 award to Judge Epstein.

Tom Moore sent me excerpts from the October issue of *Books and Bookmen* of London, which gives a rather interesting account of the Edinburgh festival.[2] To judge by this account, you were the center of attention and the one whose works were most praised. I wish I could have known of the view of Mary McCarthy before our trial here.[3]

Enough for the moment.   Sincerely yours, ELMER GERTZ

Enc.

---

1.   Instead of indicting the defendants, the Brooklyn Grand Jury suggested that they be prosecuted through the issuance of an "information"—a formal charge filed by a district attorney—which was permissible under Section 1141 of the New York Penal Code (see Rembar, *End of Obscenity*, pp. 209–10). The warrant for Miller's arrest was not dismissed until October 1964, some months after the United States Supreme Court decision ("'Tropic of Cancer' Accepted—at Last—in Brooklyn," *Publishers Weekly*, October 19, 1964, p. 35).

2.   Anthony Blond, in "Unshockable Edinburgh," *Books and Bookmen*, October 1962, pp. 26–27, said: "If Henry Miller was the hero of the week, William Burroughs was the heroin."

3.   Blond, p. 27, said further that Mary McCarthy "was the first to cite Henry Miller and William Burroughs as the most exciting and seminal writers of the 20th century."

ALS, 1P.   11/25/62

Dear Elmer—   I wonder if you could suggest the names of a few non-profit organizations which might be disposed to accept water colors of me as "gifts." If I could find one or two that would take 'em and put a valuation of $250.00 each on them, I could reduce my income tax considerably.[1] (I haven't any on hand now but would begin to make them if there was a chance to do this.) Wonder too if tax deduction would hold for gifts to European organizations? Think I could find bidders there too.

    Nothing new to speak of at the moment. No further news from Brooklyn either.

    Give my best to all the happy family.   Henry

P.S. You should be getting the recordings soon now.
P.P.S. It just occurred to me that perhaps the "Night Life" book would also be a good tax gift item too. It is priced at $250.00. Better for me to give to charity than sell to individuals.

---

1.   The tax laws in effect at this time permitted Miller to receive credit for gifts of his paintings, manuscripts, letters, etc., to nonprofit organizations. In 1969 the provision that allowed deductions for such gifts was rescinded, as was brought to the public's attention in the matter of President Nixon's papers.

ALS, 1P.   Nov. 27th 1962.

Dear Elmer—   Got your letters of 21st & 23rd with Enclosure (good!)—also the book, which I hope to scan soon.

    Thanks for bringing me up to date on the Brooklyn and other cases.

    I fell confident all will go thru satisfactorily. (It's in my horoscope!) But it does beat me why Barney's lawyers haven't done any thing of consequence as yet. I am quite sure I will not appear in Brooklyn.

I haven't spoken to Stanley Fleishman since I'm back. Am on the go constantly. Almost have found a house.

More soon again.

I'm reading with keenest interest a book (biography) of Chesterton, one of my favorites.[1] He was much better, bigger, than I had thought—even tho' an ardent Catholic. Best to Mamie.   Henry

---

1.   Maisie Ward, *Gilbert Keith Chesterton* (New York: Sheed & Ward, 1943).

TL(CC), 2PP., AIR MAIL   November 28, 1962

Dear Henry: You can tell from the enclosed copy of a letter to Barney what happened in Springfield yesterday. It was very exciting. I am trying not to go overboard, but the consensus seems to be that the court is with us. I should say, however, that it is always wrong to reach any conclusion based upon the effect the oral argument seems to give. Today, for example, I argued another case in the Appellate Court. Ted was present at the time. Ted, and everyone else, thinks that the court is going to rule in my favor, although this time it will take a reversal for me to win. The reason for this is that one of the judges bluntly stated that he tended in my direction and the other judge seemed to say the same thing. I would say that there is every indication of my prevailing in that particular case, but I would not be surprised at the contrary result.

In the same way, I felt that my opponent did not do particularly well in the argument in the *Tropic* case, and I seemed to be carrying the court with me, but too many surprising things have happened to me during the last thirty-two years for me to be cocksure. We won't celebrate until the case is actually won.

On the way to Springfield I stopped at Pontiac, where I saw Paul Crump. He has been moved from the Joliet Penitentiary to the one at Pontiac, which is a much better institution. Paul is very happy and bubbling over with hope. Only one thing disturbed him.

He is a Catholic, you know, and the Catholic chaplain at the prison was enraged at him by reason of his writing *Burn, Killer, Burn!* Paul, who is a self-respecting man, said, "Father, are you sure you are not unfair to me?" And the chaplain replied, "I am never unfair to anyone."

Interestingly enough, Sammy Davis, Jr. is much excited about the book. He has read it and wants to play the role of Crow in a movie based upon it. He is going to visit Paul soon.

Incidentally, Paul knows some of your writing and admires it greatly. He was shocked when I told him that you are near your seventy-first birthday. He assumed that you were in your early forties by the tone of your writing. When Paul was only twelve years old he read *Lady Chatterley's Lover* and was shocked not by the book, but by the controversy thereafter. The more I talk with him, the more intrigued I am by him. He is still in the process of finding himself and what he will ultimately do depends not only upon himself but upon others.

In the current issue of the New Republic there is an article on Burroughs[1] which is largely a paean of praise with respect to yourself.

Mamie and the children send their love.

More later.   Sincerely yours, ELMER GERTZ

1.   John Wain, "The Great Burroughs Affair," *New Republic*, December 1, 1962, pp. 21–23 (review of *Naked Lunch*).

TL(CC), 2PP., AIR MAIL   November 30, 1962

Dear Henry: I have that extremely interesting letter from you with respect to the tax situation. That is the sort of letter that I had never expected Henry Miller to write. You are taking a very sensible attitude on the matter and I believe that I can be of help to you.

There is no reason why you should not make tax deductible

gifts in the way of water colors and books. Others do it and you have the same right to do so. Not only will you accomplish the tax savings, but your works will be better displayed as a result.

I believe that I can "persuade" a number of schools, museums and institutions to accept gifts from you. Are you thinking in terms of the next few weeks in 1962, or are you thinking from a long range viewpoint? I hope the latter. Are you having anyone else give any consideration to this matter? For example, I heard that someone named Lou Feldman* has been concerned with this situation. Does the name ring a bell so far as you are concerned.

In order for you to make a tax deductible gift, at least two conditions must be met: (1) the donee must be on the approved list of the Treasury Department; and (2) there must be an acceptable valuation. It is easy enough to get the approved list from the Treasury Department and I will check every proposed donee on that list, so that no errors will be made. So far as the valuations are concerned, it would be best if someone other than yourself or the donee made the appraisal—preferably someone with standing as an art or book appraiser. Do you have anyone in mind?

I have discussed this general subject with my good friend, Ralph G. Newman, of the Abraham Lincoln Book Shop. He is one of the leading appraisers of literary material, books and manuscripts, but not art works, unless they are historical ones. He inquired about your manuscripts and I told him you were committed to U.C.L.A. He knows Lawrence Clark Powell.[1]

You asked about gifts to European organizations. No, they would not be included in the official list.

I gave Judge Epstein a full account of the oral argument before the Supreme Court and he was delighted.

The very best from all of us. Always yours, ELMER GERTZ

P.S. *House of Eldieff

---

1.   See H. M. 2/17/62, notes.

In a brief letter dated December 3, Gertz thanked Miller for the promised phonograph records, received that day.

ALS, 1P   12/3/62

Dear Elmer—   Don't understand your surprise. After all, I'm a realist. Don't know this Lou Feldman. I'm thinking in short *and* long terms. Found out a lot in last session with my lawyers and tax consultant. (Didn't know the "donee" had to be on the approved list. But will only deal with such like—to begin with—U.C.L.A.) Understand biz. of outside appraisers—yes. Very simple. My aim, God willing, is to get clever enough to not pay *any* taxes.

If I own other people's paintings and can get approved valuation on them, I assume these properties are also "donatable," yes?

Forming corporation now—to handle "Cancer" film—all proceeding nicely thus far.

Will have to make w.c.'s to "donate"—problem with them is to get big enough valuation—*and* where to place them. Could you show yours to some one just to give me approximate idea of their worth? (I figure about 200–250 dollars each. May be way off.)

Must write Crump one day after I have read a bit in his book. No time thus far. Just hate to finish the Chesterton biography. Everything else I pick up seems like so much trash.

More soon. "Love all around." Henry

Read all the "legal" enclosures with interest. Feel more and more confident of final outcome. The tide is with us—*just intuition.* (Plus a bit of astrology)[1]

1.   Postscript written vertically in left margin.

TL(CC), 2PP., AIR MAIL   December 10, 1962

Dear Henry: Sometimes an illness is a blessing. I have spent
three days in bed because of a very bad throat, fatigue and the like.
I used the time listening, with Mamie, to the three albums that
you sent me. The play and *To Paint Is to Love Again* we heard
twice. Your voice is truly impressive, Henry. There is nothing over-
dramatic or false in your delivery. It was as if you were in our dining room again, talking with us as during those wonderful days
and nights not too long ago. The play is better than you had led us
to believe. It should be a great success in Berlin. Are you making
any plans for Broadway or off-Broadway! Without being derivative,
it reminds me of the best moments of Saroyan's best.

I shall soon come up with a list of suggestions for gifts of
your water colors. My first request is that you send one to the Adult
Education Council of Greater Chicago (332 South Michigan Avenue, Chicago 4, Illinois). Mark it to the attention of Mrs. Fain, the
executive director. The Adult Education Council is on the list of
the Treasury Department, and gifts to it are tax-deductible. I am
chairman of the Arts and Letters Assembly of the A.E.C. and I
have a paternal interest in it. This was the group that staged both
the Shaw and the Darrow centennials. On January 9, I am chairing
a tribute to Hemingway, a product of our territory, and in the
spring an evening in honor of Faulkner. It will be appropriate to
have one of your water colors hover over our offices at that time.

Interestingly, Mamie and I have been invited to attend a black
tie affair in New York to mark the 85th birthday of Carl Sandburg.

When do you expect to be going East, and returning? Of
course, we want you to be our guest.

Mamie and the children send their love.

                              Always yours, ELMER GERTZ

P.S. I am glad that you have a tax consultant. He will tell you that
you can certainly donate other peoples' paintings and get an approved valuation on them. See if you can get some recognized art
appraiser to place valuation upon the pictures. I will also attempt

to get it from this end. I don't think your figure is too far off, but I shall check further.

It would be wonderful if you wrote to Paul Crump, as you suggest. It will serve to encourage him more than anything else that might happen. He does not have Roger Bloom's privileges of correspondence, but he can receive any letters.

> Between December 13 and 17 Gertz wrote three times, mainly about gifts of Miller's paintings to Roosevelt University, the University of Chicago, Northwestern University, and the Adult Education Council of Greater Chicago.

ALS, 2PP.   Dec. 18th 1962

Dear Elmer—   Forgive me for being so remiss. I am almost going nuts with all the problems which confront me. And you are so prompt, so industrious, so painstaking.

I am grateful indeed for all the information you've given me, all the "soliciting" you've done. But at the moment I don't have a single painting to dispose of. I've given every thing away. Perhaps next year

I must now prepare a sort of answer to charges for the U. S. Supreme Court. Stanley Fleishman hopes to present the "Cancer" case there soon. It's his idea that I write something on my own behalf—thinks it will carry weight.

Mostly I'm fatigued with all the harassing problems on hand. I get no real work done at all. I go from one situation to another.

Today I spent six hours with a tax consultant and it has left me discouraged. I may have to borrow money—and where?—to meet my coming payments. The more I make the worse off I am, seemingly. I gave too much away—as gifts, apparently. The old story.

But to hell with all this. I just wanted to let you know that I haven't been remiss deliberately. And also to say what a great boon it has been for me to know you and have you as a friend. And this goes for Mamie too. (How lucky you are!)

For me, despite family, friends and all that, I feel lonelier (almost) than ever before in my life. I would almost say—I have gotten nowhere. I end up as I began—a failure.

Let's hope it's all a bad dream. Tomorrow is another day.

My daughter Val hopes to become my secretary next June when she graduates from High School. This may be very wonderful —for both of us. She may become a writer too one day, alas!

Do give warm greetings to all the family. You are a blessed man in many ways. And you earned it!

Give Paul Crump greetings from me too, when you see him again, please. I am slowly reading his book. He can write. And what are our sufferings or privations compared to his? Alors—"Merry X'mas"!!!!   Ever yours, Henry Miller

TL(CC), 1P., AIR MAIL   December 19, 1962

Dear Henry: In Chicago's American I read today an Associated Press dispatch, as follows:

"Producer Joseph E. Levine says his company will make Henry Miller's controversial novel 'Tropic of Cancer' into a 2-million-dollar movie.

"Levine, president of Embassy films, said Elliott Kastner and Stan Shpetner will produce the movie. First shooting is scheduled in Paris, setting for the book, next summer."

Is there any truth to this report? I wish that you would tell me the situation because there is some information that I would like to give to you that might be pertinent.

The very best from Mamie, the kids and myself.
                                     Sincerely yours, ELMER GERTZ

Again on December 20 and 21 Gertz wrote of institutions that would like to receive donations from Miller—paintings, or *Into the Night Life*, or both: the University of Chicago, Cornell University, Indiana University, and the Newberry Library.

ALS, 1P.   Dec. 22, 1962

Dear Elmer—   Just got yours of 19th (with interesting enclosure.) Yes, the movie deal is a fact, though Joseph Levine is
only the financier—and I haven't heard yet if it's really a $2,000,000
deal. *My* corporation (Rellim Productions) (*Miller* spelled backwards) will join with Kastner & Shpetner's (2) corporations to
produce through a third *joint* Corp. (Venture). I haven't even
heard definitely that the money has been put up yet—tho' the fact
that it was released as news probably means that. I'll be at Big Sur
from the 23rd to the 30th. If any thing important arises phone me
there—[*number omitted*]. Phone is under H. D. Ross' name—my
nearest neighbor.   In great haste, Henry

P.S. I think most likely all has gone as reported.[1]

---

1.   Postscript written vertically in left margin.

Gertz's three-page letter of December 28, which spoke primarily
of his daughter Midge's wedding and other personal matters, included a question about when Miller was planning to return to
Europe, and a warning about Joseph Levine. "He spent a good
deal of time with me in discussing a moving picture about Clarence Darrow and said that he would pay me for my time. I billed
him a very moderate amount for a good deal of services and sent
him statements from month to month, without being paid a nickel
nor even receiving an explanation. I finally gave up billing him.
Somehow, I was not surpurised. This means that you should make
absolutely certain that you are completely protected in your dealings with him so that you do not have a repetition of this experience of mine."

ALS, 2PP.   12/31/62

Dear Elmer—   Out with the old year![1] I feel lousy, disspirited, low—tho' O.K. physically. Too many problems. No time ever to do my own work. I hope *you* will know enough not to kill yourself with work.

Won't be going abroad till June perhaps. About Levine—he's only the financier and deals with the two producers, not me. I'm as well protected as can be in such matters by the contract my lawyers drew up. Strange though to hear about him thus.

Last night I met my friend (ex-lawyer) Jo Edelman who used to be of Chicago and remembers you. He sends greetings.

Am waiting for Fleishman to read my first draft to the Supreme Court. When I retype I'll send you a copy, sure.

No chance yet a while to do any water colors.

Just reading (in Big Sur) "The Spinoza of Market Street"—I. B. Singer.[2] The rabbi! He gives a wonderful picture of one in one of these stories. I love Singer. He's not of *this* world. (Nor any other.)

Also by chance met Dick Rowan (in Big Sur) who wrote that article for Sun-Times. He's a photographer. Not very interesting as a person. Curious to see his name signed to text.

I feel more than ever guilty taking so much of your time about the water colors. However, no reason I can't proceed for next year. What I will have to shell out this year, despite deductions, makes me sick at heart. *Now* I really have money problems. Before it was only a matter of staying alive—much simpler.

After Jan. 15th I hope to be in a better mood. At least a fighting mood.

Take care of yourself—and Mamie too. And God bless you both!   Henry

1. Sentence written above the salutation.
2. Isaac Bashevis Singer, *The Spinoza of Market Street* (New York: Farrar, Straus & Cudahy, 1961).

1963:
January 6–December 28

January   Miller writes letter for United States Supreme Court in the Bradley Smith appeal from a *Cancer* decision. *Lawrence Durrell and Henry Miller: A Private Correspondence* published.

February   Miller moves to new Pacific Palisades home. *Black Spring* published by Grove Press. Gertz reviews Durrell-Miller *Private Correspondence* for *Chicago Daily News.*

March   *Cancer* published in England by John Calder. Miller's letter for U.S. Supreme Court published in *Chicago Sun-Times.* From March to August, Miller paints more than 100 water colors.

May   Miller writes preface for *The Best of H. E. Bates,* and text for Anne Poor's drawings in *Greece.* Exhibition of Miller's water colors at Ankrum Gallery, Los Angeles. *Cancer* held not obscene by Wisconsin Supreme Court.

July   World premiere of *Just Wild About Harry* in Spoleto, Italy. Gertz writing *Handful of Clients.* California Supreme Court rules *Cancer* not obscene, but New York Court of Appeals holds otherwise.

August   *Just Wild About Harry* closed as obscene at Edinburgh Festival.

September   *Plexus* published in England, and Durrell-Miller *Private Correspondence* in France.

October   *Henry Miller and the Critics* published, with essays by Miller and Gertz. *Cancer* published in Brazil, in Portuguese.

December   Gertz assists Miller with donations of his water colors.

TLS, 1P.   Jan. 6, 1963

Dear Elmer,   Here is a copy of the letter for the Supreme Court,
the second and I hope final draft.[1] If you see anything in it you
think ought to be changed please tell me and Stanley.

I am almost out of my wits with the problems now confront-
ing me, chiefly financial. If I get through this month I may take
new courage. It's really a test, an ordeal.

Meanwhile—God is love. And, I should add, I do believe there
is such a thing as "divine justice."   Henry

---

1.   Letter addressed to Stanley Fleishman, dated December 26, 1962—
      Miller's 71st birthday. For references to publication of the letter, see
      Gertz 3/12/63 and 3/19/63.

TL(CC), 3PP., AIR MAIL   January 7, 1963

Dear Henry: I seem finally to have gotten rid of my cold, or
virus, or whatever it was, but I don't feel wholly myself. Mamie
says that it is because I am on edge waiting for this thing and that
to happen, including the decision of the Illinois Supreme Court in
the *Cancer* case. Actually I feel confident about that decision, but
I am never really surprised at any result in a legal matter. The law
is a guessing contest and too often one guesses the wrong answer.
If the court should decide against us, there will be many persons
besides ourselves who will be deeply surprised.

Midge and Hank returned some days ago from their honey-
moon, spent in San Francisco and Carmel. They also drove by your
place in Big Sur, in your absence, and brought back to us a very
interesting account of the surroundings. They tell me that you have
to have both courage and strength to reside at Big Sur.

I am sorry about the postponement of your trip to Europe. I
suppose it is tied up with financial matters. Everyone seems to have
those problems, no matter what his alleged income bracket. At the

end of last year and the beginning of this year I had to dun more debtors than in years. As I phrased it in a letter to Barney Rosset, it has been all work and no pay.

I am intrigued by your reference to Joe Edelman. Yes, indeed, I remember him. While not intimates, we were friends, and I cherish a lively recollection of him. He had the proper contempt for most members of our profession and a due regard for the arts. As I recall, he was much interested in painters and painting. Please tell him that I send my very best wishes to him. Should he return this way, he should be sure to get in touch with me. You might mention, also, that a mutual friend of ours, one with whom he was fairly close—Lillian Gordon—passed away some months ago.

As I told you, I am intrigued by the piece that you are writing for the United States Supreme Court. I look forward to obtaining a copy of it. Please tell Stanley Fleishman to be sure to send me a copy of the petition for certiorari and anything else that he files.

Sue, who had been ill, finally got around to framing some of your water colors, with our aid, and they now add gaiety to our living room and dining room. Next some will be placed in my office.

Since your visit, Sue has sold several hookings. Everyone who sees them is very enthusiastic about them. We are trying to instill in her enough self-confidence so that she will spend more time in producing them as well as other works of art.

Ed de Grazia called my attention to a book that will probably interest you as a mixture of scholarship and pretentiousness. It is called *The Anatomy of Dirty Words*, and is by Edward Sagarin.[1] It is published by Lyle Stuart, who specializes in controversial writings.

Don't be concerned about taking up any of my time in the matter of the gifts of the water colors. We have laid some ground work and later you can follow through with the gifts. I think they are worth making, not alone for tax purposes, but to give your work a wider audience.

Needless to say, Mamie and I, and the whole family, are grateful to you for the very fine things that you say of us in your letter that appears in the current issue of the Henry Miller Newsletter.[2]

I hope that the Newsletter can be preserved, although I don't wonder that Eddie is concerned about the deficit. I think more than the deficit he is concerned about his health. That tremendous energy of his seems to be ebbing. Being in that state myself, I can understand his concern.

Mamie and I find the atmosphere of the household rather unreal, now that Midge and Ted have their own homes. Of course, they visit with us a lot, but a visit is not the same thing as a residence. The atmosphere will be even quieter when Jack leaves for college this summer. Mamie and I tell each other that we will both rejoice in the lessening of demands upon us. That really remains to be seen.

Mamie always lights up with joy when she reads your kind words about her. She is the best thing that has happened to me in many a year.   Always yours, ELMER GERTZ

1.   Introduction by Allen Walker Reed. [New York]: Lyle Stuart, 1962.
2.   Issue No. 11, December 12, 1962.

TL(CC), 2PP., AIR MAIL   January 9, 1963

Dear Henry: I salute you for a magnificent defense of *Tropic of Cancer* and your life generally. It is better even than the two letters you wrote for the Norwegian Supreme Court.[1] The letter will necessarily have an influence on the decision of the court as to whether or not it will take the case. I am sure than Stanley Fleishman has explained to you that the Supreme Court has the widest possible discretion in determining which cases it will consider. As the court is greatly concerned about the protection of First Amendment rights, relating to the freedom of expression, I feel that there is a likelihood of certiorari being granted. The difficulty is that some of the Supreme Court Justices do not read the petitions themselves, but pass them on to their law clerks, who make recommendations to the court. I think in this instance the Justices themselves will read the petition, particularly if it contains your letter.

Any fairminded person reading your letter would be overpow-
ered by the revelation of a great creative personality. I suppose it is
possible to make suggestions for textual changes here and there, but
it would serve no purpose. The letter as it stands is in classical form.

What I like particularly is your handling of the material with
respect to the "normal community standard." You make that phrase
a very silly one and it is likely to carry weight.

The Chicago papers still have a great to-do about *Tropic* and
you. I am sending herewith the latest Mabley column and one by
Sydney Harris,[2] one of our better columnists.

I feel rather elated. I have just won a sweeping victory in a
baby adoption case in the Illinois Appellate Court. The case is
likely to be a landmark one in its field. Now I am on edge awaiting
the Supreme Court's decision in the *Tropic* case and the lower
court's ruling in the *Compulsion* case.

I hope that this letter finds you more cheerful.

Always yours, ELMER GERTZ

Encs.

---

1.   Both letters may be found in Moore (ed.), *Henry Miller on Writing*,
     pp. 203–9.
2.   "Mabley's Report: War on Smut Finally Begins to Bear Fruit," *Chi-
     cago's American*, January 9, 1963, p. 3. Harris, on January 9, 1963,
     entitled his "Strictly Personal" *Chicago Daily News* column (p. 14),
     "Here's a Little Guessing Game." After inviting his readers to guess
     who had written several philosophic excerpts from Miller's works, he
     concluded: "Since moralizers are always picking out selected passages
     [*from Miller's books*] as an example of 'obscenity,' I thought it just as
     easy to find passages demonstrating Miller to be a serious, thoughtful
     and perceptive artist."

ALS, 1P.   1/12/63

Dear Elmer—   Glad to hear you think the "letter" good. That Sydney Harris column was very interesting. I wrote and thanked him.

Give my best to Sue. Delighted to learn she sold some hookings. Let her hook some more!

I never knew Eddie S. was in the red with the News Letter. Seems to me he could drop it now. The job's done, don't you think?

I may go up to Big Sur around Feb. 1st for a week or so, while "they" get the new place in shape. Hope to start in working on Nexus—Vol. 2—soon again, I wrote 100 pages in about 3 weeks. If I could only get 3 months uninterrupted time I could finish it.

Paris may be any time between April and June. I'm in no hurry to go.

Another victory, you say. Heavens, but you seem to have nothing but victories. Congratulations!

I have read a ways into Crump's book. Very vivid, very well done. But I don't really want to continue. These stories depress me. I feel I've lived a lot of it myself. But do give him greetings from me and say I *know* he is a writer—and no doubt a very wonderful human being too. I pray he gets out on parole before he's too old.

Henry

I always include Mamie in my thoughts even if I don't mention her. She's there always—just like X'mas—and shining like a gem. The new Income Tax regulations drive me mad. How long can a country go on in this crazy fashion? It's like ancient Egypt. I am a thousand times poorer now than when I had no money. (I sent you the play—advance copy.)   Cheers! Henry[1]
My best to Ted too![2]

---

1.   Postscript written vertically in left margin. Miller inscribed *Just Wild About Harry*: "For Elmer and Mamie—probably reads better than it sounded. Hope so. My best! Henry. 1/9/63"
2.   Postscript written vertically in right margin.

TL(CC), 2PP., AIR MAIL   January 16, 1963

Dear Henry: I have just finished reading the volume containing your private correspondence with Lawrence Durrell. The last
few pages I read at the office because I was too impatient to wait
until I got home. What a marvelous volume. Your letters have the
naturalness and sincerity of your conversation and best writings.
How fortunate Durrell was to get to know you and to win your
guidance, inspiration and approval. Unlike others, he recognizes the
very great debt he owes to you. His letters, too, had a tremendous
appeal to me, and I find that I am going to take a second look at
his writings. I don't find his work as easy to read as most people do.
This is probably a limitation in my own vision, rather than a fault
of Durrell's.

I am indebted to you for sending me an advance copy of the
play. It has not yet arrived. As you know, I have the taste of it, and
more, through hearing the recording that you sent to me.

I have conveyed to Mamie, Sue, Ted and Crump your greetings expressed in your usual inimitable fashion.

I told the editor of Crump's publisher what you said, and she
immediately asked if something or other could be quoted in Jet, a
leading Negro publication. I said I would have to get permission
from you. Are you willing to permit this?

You say I have nothing but victories. That ain't necessarily so.
But the adoption case victory was a sweet one. I am sending with
this letter a rather *shmalsy* account of the case that appeared in one
of the newspapers.

I have just become the attorney for Lenny Bruce in a proceeding against him in this highly moral city. He, too, is charged with
obscenity. Have you ever heard him?[1]

I am glad that you are trying to finish *Nexus*, Volume II. You
seem to have a sort of inhibition about completing that work,
almost as if you believed that it marked the end of a part of your
life that you wanted to hold on to. You have so much more to do
that you must rid yourself of any feeling of completion. Neither the
tax collector nor anyone else must dishearten you.

As soon as I hear the result of our *Tropic* case in the Illinois Supreme Court, I will let you know. I hope that you will remind Stanley Fleishman to be sure to send me a copy of the petition when he files it in the United States Supreme Court.

Affectionate greetings from all of us.

Always yours, ELMER GERTZ

Enc.

---

1. While performing in a Chicago nightclub in late 1962, the comedian Lenny Bruce was charged with obscenity. He called Gertz, who agreed to defend him, but Gertz did not hear from him again. Bruce was convicted, fined one thousand dollars, and sentenced to a year's imprisonment. This judgment was upheld by Illinois' highest court on Thursday, June 18, 1964, the same day that the court reversed the favorable lower court decision on *Tropic of Cancer*. On July 7, two weeks after the United States Supreme Court ruled that *Tropic of Cancer* was not obscene, the Illinois justices vacated their earlier ruling in the Bruce case and in November finally cleared him (People v. Bruce, 31 Ill. 2d 459, 202 N.E. 2d 497 [1964]). For a detailed account of Bruce's trial and conviction in New York in 1964, by the attorney who prosecuted that case, see Richard H. Kuh, *Foolish Figleaves?* (New York: Macmillan, 1967), pp. 175–211.

ALS, 2 PP.   Jan. 22nd 1963

Dear Elmer Gertz—   I've been at my friend Bob Fink's home the last four days and going back to Pac. Pal. today. I've got about 15 water colors done now. Have been rereading your letters referring me to various friends of yours in museums and elsewhere, but am too sick of details to get down to writing them and sending each one a water color. So I'm leaving every thing here with Fink pro tem. Maybe when I move into the new house I'll find time and energy.

I may go up to Big Sur this week end or next—if I do, my mail will be forwarded there. I want to get back to writing—would love to finish Nexus (II.) before I go to Paris. Can't see myself doing any serious writing while in Paris. The film will involve me in all sorts of activities. I need so much to find a good, competent secretary—or a new wife.

I haven't seen any mail since I've been here so don't know if you've written.

There's one little question perplexes me about the W.C. donations. Do I have to make the donation and then wait for the person to have it appraised? or, can I offer it, do you think, with the proviso that if the value set upon it is not high enough, I get the W.C. back? I have no idea what their value is. I am offering them only to reduce my income tax. Naturally, I want therefore to get as much as possible for them. My thought is—something like $200.00 or $250.00 each. I wonder if this will seem like a reasonable figure?

As for the Night Life book, that is definitely $250.00 per copy. And here I wonder if your friends realize that this is the true figure? (It originally sold for $100.00—but that's over ten years ago and in the meantime I lost a few hundred thru rats and other vermin.)

Oof! You see why I hate to begin writing these people. I'm sick of detail, trivia, money problems, and all that.

Best to you and to Mamie.   Henry
Note: *After* Feb. 1st new address will be—444 Ocampo Drive, Pacific Palisades[1]

---

1.   Postscript written horizontally at top of first page.

TL(CC), 3PP., AIR MAIL   February 7, 1963

Mr. Henry Miller
444 Ocampo Drive
Pacific Palisades, California
Dear Henry: This is a relatively long period of silence for me.
I have been up to my neck in work in connection with *Tropic of
Cancer* and other matters.

Briefly, the situation with respect to the litigation is that the
Illinois Supreme Court passed the buck on the case to the Appellate
Court, as per the enclosed opinion.[1] I think the opinion outrageous
and am going to apply for a rehearing, but the chances are that the
case will remain in the Appellate Court and be decided there, unless
the United States Supreme Court acts before then. You know, of
course, that Stanley Fleishman's petition in connection with the
California case will be filed in the United States Supreme Court on
February 11. Within a reasonable time thereafter, the United States
Supreme Court will decide whether or not to grant a hearing. If
it does, as we hope, the cases elsewhere in the United States, including ours, are likely to be held in abeyance, pending the final
decision of the Supreme Court. If the Supreme Court should deny
a writ, it is likely to prejudice our case and others. As you know,
either granting or denying of a hearing by the United States Supreme Court is not binding on other courts. But a final decision
on the merits is binding. I hope that the court is prepared now to
pass upon such basic issues as: Is literary value in itself tantamount
to social importance and does it take a publication out of the orbit
of obscenity; What is meant by the community—a city, a state, the
nation; Is obscenity limited to hard-core commercial pornography?[2]
Despite the many obscenity cases the courts have decided, the
United States Supreme Court has not expressly and explicitly
spoken on these points. Until now, the court has apparently not
thought the situation ripe for such rulings on its part. But the
intensification of activities on the part of the book-burners may
compel it to act.

Justice Douglas, in a recent pamphlet of his, called *Freedom of the Mind*,[3] expressed the matter perfectly, when he wrote: "The critical procedural area is that dealing with prior non-judicial restraints, where the issue of obscenity is tried by a local official acting in an administrative capacity. There the power to delay a decision, magnified by slow-moving processes of judicial review, becomes the power to destroy, and, unless closely supervised, results not only in economic death for the publisher or distributor, but in the demise of free expression as well." The vice of the decision by the Illinois Supreme Court, transferring our case to the Appellate Court, is that the court had not the remotest appreciation of these realities.

I assume that you [*are*] now in your new home. I hope that you are comfortable in it and that it gives you the incentive to finish *Nexus* and to do other work.

With respect to the matter of the gifts of your water colors, you can send them on to me, if you choose, for distribution to the various donees mentioned by me in my various letters. I can draft letters of gift and have them conform to the legal requirements, so that the valuations are acceptable to you and to the Treasury Department. We want to handle this in such way as to minimize the amount of work on your part. While the valuations must be in line, you have a certain measure of control over them in the selection of the appraisers. I can advise you more on this point later, when you are in the mood for such discussion.

I have not heard from you as to whether or not Jet may use your comment on Paul Crump. It would do him some good. Of course, he is thrilled that you have paid any attention to him.

A long review that I have written of your correspondence with Durrell will appear in the magazine section of the Chicago Daily News in about a week or so. I hope that you will like it. In any event, it represents my honest opinion of the work, and a very high opinion indeed. The correspondence has all of the qualities of a novel.

Durrell's opinion of *Sexus* led me back to that book. It contains, of course, some of your best writing. Other portions require a strong stomach. *Sexus* must be judged, of course, as part of the total work, *The Rosy Crucifixion.* Since I don't have *Plexus,* I am not in the position to judge.

I think you ought to suggest to Barney that he republish your book, *The World of Sex,* particularly if we should prevail in the Supreme Court.

I will have to cut this letter short, because I have the distressing business of a funeral. One of my dearest friends passed away. I have never known anyone to have more dignity and courage in the face of death.

I will try to write soon and in more detail with respect to the matters raised in your letter.

Mamie and the children send their most affectionate greetings to you.   Always yours, ELMER GERTZ

---

1.   To hasten a decision which he hoped would end *Cancer* litigation in Illinois, Gertz wanted Police Superintendent Wilson's appeal to be decided by the Illinois Supreme Court, on constitutional grounds. The argument presented on Wilson's behalf was that the matter in dispute was one of "fact"—whether or not *Cancer* was obscene—and therefore should be heard by the lower, Appellate Court.

     When Wilson's notice of appeal was filed to the Appellate Court of Illinois, First District, on March 16, 1962, Gertz succeeded in having the case transferred to the Illinois Supreme Court. As Gertz's letter of 2/7/63 indicates, the decision handed down following oral argument before the Supreme Court was to retransfer the case to the Appellate Court, on the grounds that there was no "debatable constitutional question" to give the Supreme Court jurisdiction to entertain the appeal. In that opinion, Justice Daily said for the court: "There are but two issues presented by this appeal, first, whether the book *Tropic of Cancer* is in fact obscene, and, second, whether the trial court applied erroneous legal tests of obscenity. Neither issue requires a construction of the constitutional question." (See Elmer Gertz, "The Illinois Battle Over 'Tropic of Cancer,'" *Chicago Bar Record,* January 1965, pp. 161–72.)

2.   Justices of the United States Supreme Court have seldom spoken with one voice in obscenity rulings, but for over a decade the Court has declared that literary value places a work outside the realm of obscenity, and has not held material to be obscene unless it was considered to be "hard-core pornography." The community standards issue, addressed in recent years by the Court, is still very much alive.

3.   [Chicago?]: American Library Association [distributed by] Public Af-
      fairs Pamphlets [New York, 1962].

ALS, 2PP.   from Big Sur
                                                      2/11/63

Deal Elmer—   I notice you have been sparing me—just copies
of important letters. I am still here and have not yet written a line.
Too many interruptions again—and then one storm after another—
with road blocks, broken mains, septic tanks out, etc. Usual stuff.
However, I have been painting—now made 35 since I started a
couple of weeks ago. When I get back to L.A. I'll take care of all
those people you were so good as to put me in touch with. (More
and more now I feel my asking price of $250.00 per W.C. is O.K.)
Not vanity that prompts me to say this. Last night I woke up at
2:00 A.M. with marvelous dreams of the pictures I'd like to paint—
and saw in my dreams just the right technique for them. Wonder
if it will stick when I pick up the brush again. I really think I made
a break through—found my style. We'll see!
     Did Rosset send you a copy of "Black Spring" which is com-
ing out very soon? And have you seen "A Private Correspondence"
(Miller-Durrell letters) which Dutton is just launching? I think it
is an exciting work. Let Mamie be the judge!
     No further news about the Brooklyn affair so far. Nor the Su-
preme Court biz. In March Calder of London brings out the British
ed. of "Cancer." What will happen then, I wonder?
     The new home in Pac Pal is being readied for my return. I
need a bit of an anchorage. Get tired of moving about, dragging
things along—like Caesar and his impedimenta.
     By the way, as with that biography of Chesterton I wrote you
about, I am now once again fired by a critical work on Kazantzakis'
"Odyssey." Do read it. On pages 74 & 75 you will find what seems
to me the most penetrating insight into my character and tempera-
ment, tho' it's about K———, not me.[1] I was transfixed, terrified,
when I read it. No wonder I despise Homer's Ulysses so much. It's

my own self I'm staring at. Let me know if you see what I mean.
Must stop.   Cheers! Henry
The title of the book is Nikos Kazantzakis and his Odyssey: A
Study of the Poet and the Poem—by Pandelis Prevelakis (Simon
& Shuster, N.Y. 1961)[2]
returning to Pac. Pal. this week-end.[3]

---

1.   Pandelis Prevelakis, *Nikos Kazantzakis and His Odyssey*, tr. from the
      Greek by Philip Sherrard, Preface by Kimon Friar (New York: Simon
      and Schuster, 1961), pp. 74–75:
          "Both Kazantzakis and Odysseus are molded more by the move-
      ment of their own thought than by outside events. They do not like
      to be conscripted, and they very rarely are; they sacrifice human hap-
      piness to their higher destiny; they are continuously conscious of the
      presence of "God" and they identify him with the primordial force
      which drives man to surpass himself; they burn with the desire for
      action and suffer from the irony of things; both have a mania for far
      places and wish to taste all earth's fruits; they are inspired by the
      heroes of the past and are jealous of their exploits; they live at times
      like hermits, persistently searching for a satisfactory view of the world
      and man; they look on poetic creation as one of the principal means of
      deliverance; they undertake things beyond their powers; they know that
      the mystery of the universe is not to be resolved by logic and yet they
      worship Mind, the Master Mason; they seek total fulfillment—to reach
      their limits, and to leave only the lees to death; they absorb the ideas
      of their time and master them with a personal intellectual discipline;
      they are detached from human concerns and resolutely, even cruelly,
      sacrifice beings and objects to the struggle; they apply rigid standards
      even to their friends; they affirm opposites and despise the coward and
      the conformist; they spurn social conventions, which weaken creative-
      ness and originality, and they stimulate their sensibility in the cosmic
      vortex; they transcend the erotic instinct and dissolve sensible reality
      itself with their thought; they attribute mystic significance to the
      dreams of sleep and to waking premonitions; they train themselves in
      solitude—this is the 'fundamental passion of their being.' They keep
      their eyes open before the dazzling sights of the world, but consider
      nature to be indifferent, if not hostile, to man. They are heartened
      rather than discouraged by the pessimistic understanding of the uni-
      verse, and they oppose an insatiable appetite for life to the absurdity
      of death. They grasp sensible and abstract things as a unity, like primi-
      tive men; they are impelled forward by their own nature and by their
      devotion to the One to ever greater isolation. They act disinterestedly,
      for the sake of the struggle and not for finite ends; they profess a fire-

worshiping theory, which reconciles extreme pessimism with indomi-
table heroism; they measure themselves against the great spiritual
leaders, with the aim of realizing, if not a new religion, at least the
sense of absolute freedom. They live an intense and resolute life, are
restless, and have the mentality of the beseiged. They struggle without
God, and gaze haughtily at the ultimate Nothing, but often they behave like desperadoes."

   Miller forwarded a two-page typewritten excerpt from this section
of the Prevelakis book, on the second page of which the following undated note was handwritten:
"Dear Elmer—

   "This is the passage that gets me—and the elaboration of same
which follows.

Henry

"Returning to Pac Pal this Sunday.

Henry"

2.   Postscript written vertically in left margin of second page.
3.   Postscript written horizontally at top of first page.

TL(CC), 2PP., AIR MAIL   February 19, 1963

Dear Henry: I am sending under separate cover a copy of the
review I wrote of your correspondence with Durrell. Mr. Van Allen
Bradley, the literary editor of the Chicago Daily News, telephoned
to say that he and other editors of the Daily News were very enthusiastic about my review.[1] I hope that you like it. I have read
reviews of the book in Newsweek and the Saturday Review, and it
appears quite likely that the book is going to be a great success,
not only critically, but perhaps in sales as well.

   I was much troubled when I talked with you the other night,
and then when I heard from Charles Rembar in response to my
letter to him, a copy of which was sent to you. Rembar has probably
talked with you by now or at least made the effort to do so. His
viewpoint remains that it would be best for you to appear voluntarily, make bond, and then let the case hang fire until the United
States Supreme Court passes upon Stanley Fleishman's petition.
He thinks it would be a mistake for you to wait until an extradition proceeding gets under way, although it is quite possible that

such proceeding could be defeated. I want to be fair to Cy, Barney and the others, and, above all, to you. I think that you ought to give more thought to the situation, make inquiry wherever you please, and then reach a conclusion. I cannot help feeling such great distrust for the characters in Brooklyn that I would not welcome your appearance there. Cy is less inclined than I to regard their action as being in bad faith.

I am sorry that your various problems have prevented your finishing *Nexus*. I hope that you get it out of the way and are then in the position to think ahead as to what more you want to do. I have the strong feeling that if a real effort were made, your play could be produced on, or off, Broadway with great success. Have you really made any effort to secure its production? I know Roger Stevens (not intimately) and I know others who could advise us in such matters.

I would love to see your new water colors and the technique that you have developed for them. As soon as you are ready to proceed with the various gifts and you want me to do anything else, please don't hesitate to let me know.

Barney sent me a copy of *Black Spring*. Does this exhaust the list of your books that he is publishing? I think he ought to publish *The World of Sex*. There is no reason why it should remain unpublished in this country. Is there any new word with respect to the *Hamlet* correspondence? Does the Durrell volume interfere in any way with this?

I suppose you know that the United States Supreme Court, by an eight to one vote, threw out some obscenity set-up in Rhode Island and wrote a very strong opinion in so doing. Justice Brennan, the one Catholic on the court, wrote the opinion.[2] After I read it I may write more to you about it.

The analogical portrait of you in the K. book is startling.

More and more I hear conversation about you, some of it showing real insight. Unlike you, I belong to several groups, including the Chicago Literary Club. In spite of its stuffy title, it is a splendid group and affords me real relaxation on Monday nights. Last night one of the doctor members, inspired perhaps by my review, talked at some length to me about your writings and what they meant to him. Despite the efforts of the Pygmies to ban your books, they are reaching a considerable audience.

Do tell me your plans and when particularly we may expect to see you.

Mamie and the children send their love.

Always yours, ELMER GERTZ

1.   "Miller and Durrell . . . Private Correspondence," *Chicago Daily News*, February 16, 1963, "Panorama" section, pp. 10–11.

2.   *Bantam Books, Inc.* v. *Joseph A. Sullivan*, 372 U.S. 58 (1963). The Commission to "Encourage Morality in Youth," created by the Rhode Island legislature and appointed by the Governor, had made a habit of warning a principal distributor of paperbacks that (1) the Commission regarded certain books, such as *Peyton Place*, as unsuitable for sale to minors, and (2) that local police departments were being so notified as well. The wholesaler, Max Silverstein, had reacted by collecting and returning unsold copies of the books listed as objectionable, fearing the consequences should he ignore the Commission's notices. His fears were reinforced by visits from policemen, checking to see whether he had ceased distributing the books. Justice Brennan, writing the almost unanimous (8 to 1) United States Supreme Court decision of February 18, 1963, said in part: "It is true that the books have not been seized or banned by the State, and that no one has been prosecuted for their possession or sale. But though the Commission is limited to informal sanctions—the threat of invoking legal sanctions and other means of coercion, persuasion, and intimidation— the record amply demonstrates that the Commission deliberately set about to achieve suppression of publications deemed 'objectionable' and succeeded in its aim. . . . In thus obviating the need to employ criminal sanctions, the State has at the same time eliminated the safeguards of the criminal process." See Morris L. Ernst and Alan U. Schwartz, *Censorship* (New York: Macmillan, [1964]), pp. 237–40.

ALS, 2PP.   Feb. 20th 63

Dear Elmer—   Back from Big Sur with a fine cold. Spoke to Rembar over phone last night. He told me all he could. Seems to think I should appear in Brooklyn voluntarily rather than be extradited or resist extraditing. Says my movements won't be restricted after I appear. Mere formality but they insist on it. Didn't offer much hope on quashing the case, but says it may never come to a trial.

I am supposed to think it over in next few days and then apprise him of my decision. He thought they might agree to letting me appear when I pass thru N.Y. on my way to Paris—April or May.

Do you have any further thoughts or suggestions, I wonder?

Every thing in disorder here—painters, carpenters, etc. But place itself seems very good—and the kids are happy I am with them again.

I *would* appreciate getting help in writing the various institutions and mailing them paintings. I just can't ask *you* to do it—it's a great imposition. Could Sue or some one else handle it, do you think? Next week I'll collect all I did—except for a dozen I already disposed of among friends—and then let you know—or you me. How's that?

Those who wanted copies of the Night Life book can have them—thru Eve in Big Sur. But I do want to make sure that they understand what the price is—$250.00 per copy.

I sold *one* ⟨obliterated⟩ water color at $250.00 the other day to a stranger—a fan. Don't think there will be much trouble getting these appraised at that figure—or even a bit more.

Meanwhile I may send you all those letters you sent me— re the W.C's and books.

No more now. Hope you are well now. And Mamie too.

My best! Henry

P.S. The BBC London are trying to get me over for TV show on Cancer end of March but I am holding off. I want to stay put here for a little while at least.

P.P.S. Oh yes—if Sue or whoever would do the work suggested I will be happy to pay for services.

TLS, 1P.   Feb. 21, 1963

Dear Elmer,   Just beginning to feel normal again and like the
new home very much, and think I get down to work very very soon
now. This morning I had to see my lawyers here (who handle the
Film, trust funds, etc.) and mentioned the Brooklyn matter with a
result that they will now contact Rembar and see what they can do
to help. I have just a few more days left before advising Rembar
what to tell them—am I appearing voluntarily or not. I still don't
understand myself why the case can't be quashed; as best I understand Rembar, seems that tho the facts (date and place) mentioned
are crazy the rest stands. Nor can I understand why they in Bklyn
want to risk being held up to ridicule, what purpose is served by
making me appear there. Do you suppose they want the satisfaction of giving me a prison sentence, even if I don't actually serve
one? I guess I have to trust in my guardian angel, as always when
I am in a crisis. I certainly don't want to hide away now—it means
so much to the children that I am with them now—and, I have so
much work to do and relish the peace and quiet here, which I don't
have any more in Big Sur.

To finish Nexus may take months—but if I get two or three
solid months work on it I will be content—and a good way thru.
As for my play, that's in the hands of MacGregor at New Directions; he's tried a lot of people already with no success. Colleges
appear to be biting, but I am leery of them—not good enough, not
enough funds for technical matters, etc. I don't want it to start off
as a flop. It will be produced when the time comes—always works
that way with me.[1] No use knocking your head against iron doors.

Yes, Black Spring is all Barney contracted for so far. I'm not
so certain, as you, that World of Sex is a good next one. After a
court victory maybe, yes. Plexus and Nexus would be better first, I
think.

Latest on Hamlet is that the young publishers are again thinking to risk it. Nothing definite yet.

By the K book you mean the one on Kazantzakis? Happy to

hear you are reading it. I just can't get over it. The only other great critical work I have read in last six or eight years is "Arthurian Torso" by Lewis Spence, on a fairly unknown novelist and poet.[2]

Met one of the producers today; looks as if I won't have to leave for Paris till May or so. They are waiting for script to be written first. Suits me fine. So I stay here, unless I am hailed to Brooklyn.

I'll write about the water colors, send them and list soon—that is, if some one other than you can do this dirty work for me. My morale has jumped 100%. All the best now. Oh yes, I read Fleishman's petition and it struck me as a classic—I told him so. Soon all will clear up—maybe miraculously—you'll see. I feel the tide has turned.   Henry

1.   The world premiere of *Just Wild About Harry* was at the Theatro Caio Melisso in Spoleto on July 7, 1963. The play was also scheduled to be performed by the Cambridge Players at the Edinburgh Festival in the Summer of 1963, but "on order of the Lord Chamberlain the curtain was rung down on the second night of the production in Edinburgh on grounds of obscenity."—Woods, *Collector's Quest*, p. 157, n.2

2.   Charles Williams, *Arthurian Torso*, with commentary by C. S. Lewis (New York: Oxford University Press, 1948). No critical work by Lewis Spence was located.

ALS, 1P.   2/28/63

Dear Elmer—   Here are your letters re the W.C's and Night Life book. I checked requests for N.L. in red pencil—just to remind you to be sure they agree on price—$250.00 per copy.

My friend Fink is sending, or has already, 15 W.C's.

I am taking it for granted now that some one will do the dirty work, not *you!*

This in haste.

Got (3) pages written (Nexus) yesterday. A struggle to make time, not to write. But am full of hope now. Now or never. Henry

P.S. I put Stanley Fleishman in touch with Rembar re Brooklyn case. He proposed some delaying tactics. Waiting to hear from both soon. Decided *not* to go![1]

1.   Postscript written vertically in left margin.

TL(CC), 3PP., AIR MAIL   March 7, 1963

Dear Henry: I don't remember when I have been more pre-occupied, perturbed and out of sorts. Generally I not only can take hard work and the criss-crossing of activities, indeed, I relish it, but in recent weeks it has caused some strain and a feeling of disquie-tude. Mamie tries to relax me in various ways and sometimes suc-ceeds. I wish it were possible to get away for a while, but this is hardly likely for the time being.

It has not been all work and no play. I have read a lot and have even done some writing. I have even managed to have lunch and breakfast on a couple of occasions with Mayor Daley. On one of the occasions I chatted with Police Superintendent Wilson, our opponent in the *Tropic* case, as well as in other legal matters in which I am involved. The City is opposing us, as you know, most strenuously. At the same time, the Mayor and other public officials have shown signs of friendliness towards me, and I was even named to an official committee of the City which chooses the recipients of human relations awards given annually by the community.

I continue to be amazed and delighted at the number of re-views of your private correspondence with Durrell. Most of the reviews are very laudatory. I notice, too, that the bookshops have very big displays of that book and *Black Spring*. Some of them have more copies of your other books than I have seen in a long while. I think that the atmosphere is changing decidedly.

I suppose that you know that Mae Schwartz has not been well since her return from California. I talked with Eddie as soon as I heard the news, and I have written to him since then. Both of them certainly lead too strenuous existences. I am the last one in the world who should make such an observation!

I received from Bob Fink a package of your water colors which are to be used for the tax deductible gifts. These are extremely good water colors, some of the best of your work that I have seen. Before distributing any of them, I will want to make certain that we have all of the necessary problems resolved. Yesterday, when I lunched with an accountant friend of mine, I discussed with him some of the relevant issues, and he told me of a case just decided by the Tax Court where a painter made gifts of some of her own paintings and the Government disallowed a large part of the deductions claimed by her. This was sustained in the Tax Court. It emphasizes anew the necessity of our having the right sort of appraisals and record of prior sales. What you told me about the recent sale is extremely important. You should jot down for yourself, and for me as well, a record as to the purchaser, the date, the amount and a description of the water color in question.

I am going to get a copy of the Tax Court case to which I have referred and will probably send it to you, together with my translation, as it were, of the contents of the opinion.

I will prepare all of the letters of gift and will send them to you for signature. I will determine whether or not it is wise for me to sign them or whether they ought to have your personal signature. I will also arrange for the sending of the water colors to the institution donees. Don't worry about the work entailed on my part. Most of it will be done by my secretary. Once we get the matter really under way, it will move swiftly and efficiently. Initially, there are bugs that have to be removed from the machinery.

I am much interested in the conclusion that you and Stanley Fleishman reached about the matter of the Brooklyn proceeding. I know that you concluded not to go to Brooklyn for the time being. I would be much interested in having a summary of just what Stanley Fleishman concluded and his reasons for so doing.

How are you finding your new house? I hope it is comfortable and that the adjustment to it and the children is easy.

You will remember that you were very much taken by the paintings of young John Doyle, a fellow student of Sue's at the Art Institute. You asked her to have Doyle send you some of his work at the time you get into your new house so that you might make a selection. Sue has talked with him on the matter and he is thrilled beyond words at your interest. He, or Sue, will send some of his things to you.

Are your plans any more definite with respect to going to Europe? When do you think you will go? Will you be able to stay with us en route? We would love to have you. We often think of the stimulating experiences of your last visit.

I cannot express an opinion with respect to *Plexus*, because I have never read it. It is one of the few of your books I have not been able to get; that, and *Quiet Days at Clichy*. Of course, I would love to have them.

Sexus continues to linger in my mind. It is certainly one of the most moving of all of your books. There were moments when I felt almost as Durrell felt. One has to assume that a creative artist knows what he is doing and is right when his critics are wrong. Mamie appears to be even more attuned to your work at times than I am. Even those portions of *Sexus* which distress me a bit delighted her. She is probably a more complete person than I am.

I don't think I told you that Ted is now practicing law with another firm. He loves it, and they are quite pleased with his work. I manage to get together with the kids once or twice a week. Mamie calls Tuesday night "family night" because Ted and Sue, as well as Midge and Henry, have dinner with us. We talk about everything under the sun, including my eccentricities. My kids have a humorous detachment towards me, as well as a very deep affection, and it is a lot of fun having them around.

Later I will look at your letters to see if I have missed anything.

Warmest greetings from all of us to you.

                                        Always yours, ELMER GERTZ

ALS, 2PP.   3/8/63

Dear Elmer—   Answering right away—or never! First, I enclose
Stanley's letter to Rembar—all I know thus far. No word from
Rembar in ten days or more. (Rosset is in Europe at moment.)

About the W.C. donations. Seems to me we must first of all
be clear as to Government's stand on such gifts. It baffles me.
Maybe the *case* in question was a special one. Surely the institutions
you are dealing with ought to know if there might be kick-backs or
not.

As for the one I sold at $250.00—yes, I have his name, date,
etc. No description of W.C. Can't even recall which. (I sent him
three, from which to choose one. Never heard any more—this 2 or
3 weeks ago.) Maybe he'll return *all*. But he paid in advance.

Meanwhile my friend Patricia Hardesty who will produce film
of my "Smile," says I ought to ask $350 or even $500 a piece. Says
she has seen old ones of mine priced at $250 and more.

I'm trying to sell a few at $250.00 to establish values. How-
ever, the value is there or not, depending on government's attitude.
But if we have recognized appraisers, how can they haggle (greatly)
over price? It's not sky high.

What does John Doyle want for his work? I hope I can afford
one, at least.

I will be going to Paris late May or June, it now seems. We're
waiting for finished script. I see Joe Levine, the money man tomorrow.

I am writing to Paris once again now for a copy of Plexus for
you. That Girodias[1] is a slow bastard. *Quiet Days* seems just impossible to find. I searched all over Paris. Can't understand why he
doesn't bring out a *new* edition. Some one (other than me) ought
to suggest it to him.

The English publisher who paid a good advance on "Plexus"
now refuses to do it. We will get another. Don't know his reason
either. (Weidenfeld & Nicholson)—London.

Don't know whether I stay or stop over on way to Europe—
will know better later. The new house is excellent.

I haven't written another line in Nexus. Fresh interruptions every day. Eventually I won't give a damn. Be happy just to be alive and breathing. I can't work under pressure—it must be a joy or not at all.

Glad to hear of your good family life. My best to them all—and especially Mamie. I think of you all often. Got your review of the c/s. *Excellent*. Saw only one other—S.R. No matter. *Book very expensive!*

Hope you make out in your fight with Courts. Just reading Al Capone's book—his life. What a background, what a city Chicago was then!   More soon. My best. Henry[2]

P.S. Enclose clipping in German by good man—Marcuse[3]—whom I met in Hamburg. Do you know any one who could translate it for me?[4]

---

1. Maurice Girodias succeeded his father, Jack Kahane, as publisher of Obelisk Press. For references to Kahane's publication of *Tropic of Cancer* see Perlès, *My Friend Henry Miller*, pp. 101–4; *Diary of Anaïs Nin*, Vol. I, pp. 135, 141, 321. Girodias assisted Barney Rosset in making arrangements for the American edition.—Hutchison, *Tropic of Cancer on Trial*, pp. 42–44
2. Last paragraph through signature written vertically in left margin on second page.
3. Herbert Marcuse, political philosopher, a founder of the Frankfurt Institute of Social Research, who emigrated from Germany to the United States in 1934. His *One Dimensional Man* (Boston: Beacon Press [1964]) was especially influential.
4. Postscript written vertically in left margin of first page.

TL(CC), 3PP., AIR MAIL   March 12, 1963

Dear Henry: I am returning the Stanley Fleishman letters. I have made copies thereof for my files. I think Fleishman's viewpoint is a reasonable one. But, to make doubly certain, I have written to Mr. Charles E. Roberts, the attorney of Syracuse, New York, handling the defense of the *Tropic* appeal there.[1] I have asked him his best estimate as to the time likely to elapse between the argument of the case on March 25 and its determination by the court. It is quite possible, too, although Fleishman does not say so, that the United States Supreme Court will decide within the next few weeks whether or not it will entertain the California appeal. In any event, I agree with Fleishman's conclusion. Of course, it may not be acceptable to the characters in Brooklyn, who may seek to extradite you despite the pendency of the higher court cases. In that event, through Fleishman, you can seek to defeat such move.

Incidentally, if you have an extra copy of the Los Angeles Times reprint of your letter to Fleishman,[2] I will appreciate it if you will be good enough to send it to me.

I am sending herewith a copy of the Tax Court case to which I referred in my earlier letter, because it, too, involves the gift of paintings. Of course, the artist in question claimed tremendous deductions for each painting, where you are far more modest in your claims. In addition, the sale upon which she relied to establish fair market value must have impressed the court as being phony. At any rate, I suggest that you read this opinion and phrase any questions that occur to you. Meanwhile, I am checking further for guidance and will then give you my considered advice, after which we can proceed with the actual gifts.

The information you give in your letter about prices sounds reasonable to me, and I have no doubt that we can work out the mechanics perfectly.

What you tell me about your friend Patricia Hardesty interests me. At your suggestion, she has written to me about her Saturday Evening Post article on you, and I have given her a good deal of material and have told her that she should feel free to ask me for more if necessary. I think that a Saturday Evening Post article will be of tremendous help to you at this time, with cases pending here, there and everywhere.

When will Patricia Hardesty produce the film of *Smile*? Has she considered dubbing in your voice? The recording of *Smile* that you did is magnificent, as I told you.

I will try to get someone to make a good translation of the German article.

Don't worry about the John Doyle work. I am confused as to whether he is presenting one to you or will expect payment, but, in any event, it will be very modest in amount. John is achieving a very great success at a surprisingly early age. Everyone who sees his work gets excited over it and buys. He looks as if he is on the verge of starvation, but actually he is doing all right and has a wife and several kids.

I will be intrigued to hear about your meeting with Joe Levine, the money man. I think I have told you something of my own contacts with him which were not very happy.

Thanks much for your efforts to get *Plexus* and *Quiet Days* for me.

Have you talked with Barney about publishing *Plexus* and *Nexus*? Would you want me to suggest it to him?

Tomorrow marks the fifth anniversary of Nathan Leopold's release on parole, and, unless something goes wrong, he will be discharged. It is assumed by everyone, including myself, that the formal order will be entered tomorrow. Meanwhile, the newspapers and other publicity media are hounding me. I, too, think it a very remarkable human story. Certainly nobody in the history of the parole system has ever acquitted himself as well as Leopold. I am sending herewith a copy of a statement he has prepared, which is to be released only when he is discharged from parole. You may want to clip it into your copy of *Life Plus 99 Years*.

I am intrigued by what you say of Al Capone. Strangely enough, when I was a kid in college, I was commissioned to ghost write his autobiography. He set forth only one condition—that the book be a preachment against prohibition. Then something miscarried, and the project fell through. I never met Capone. I was present in the office of a newspaper publisher when another exciting crime story broke—the escape of Dillinger from the Indiana Penitentiary. I was talking to Victor Watson, the editor of the Chicago Herald Examiner, about everything under the sun, except crime, when suddenly bells began to ring like mad and Watson ran out of the office, where he was sitting with me, and everything seemed to be in a state of excitement, similar to the outbreak of a

World War. I sat back and took in the whole scene, and it has lingered in my memory as further proof of what Frank Harris once wrote—that a newspaper does not succeed until it covers the interest of a twelve-year-old kid.

Affectionate greetings from all of us.

Always yours, ELMER GERTZ

Encs.

---

1.   On August 13, 1962, Marguerite Fritch, John Armstrong, and Allan Hammerie of the Economy Book Store in Syracuse, New York, were convicted in a *Cancer* case by a six-member police court jury. A year and a day later, following a reversal of this judgment by an intermediate court, the New York Court of Appeals held, by a four to three decision, that *Cancer* was obscene. In the Chief Judge's opinion the novel offered "no glory, no beauty, no stars—just mud." However, the case was sent back for retrial on the *scienter* issue—whether those selling the book were aware of its character (*People v. Fritch*, 13 N.Y. 2d 119, 192 N.E. 2d 713 [1963]). See Rembar, *End of Obscenity*, pp. 199–203; "Torrid Zone," *Newsweek*, July 22, 1963, pp. 50–51.

2.   "Here Are My Reasons for 'Tropic of Cancer'—Miller," February 24, 1963, "Calendar" section, pp. 1, 16.

TLS, 1P.   March 14, 1963

Dear Elmer: About two or three days ago I had a letter from Cy Rembar in N. Y. saying that the District Attorney in Brooklyn was reluctant to wait until the Supreme court of N. Y. handed down a decision in the appeal from Syracuse. Rembar said he could appeal to the Gov. of N. Y. to stay proceedings. I called him on the phone and told him to do that, appeal to the Governor. Rembar didn't sound too sure of the results, but thought it wouldn't hurt to try.

(Meanwhile, yesterday, my daughter Val, tells me that her teacher—in Government and Law—told her one can't be extradited unless for a very grave crime, like treason and such. I told her the lawyers didn't seem to be so sure.)

Now comes this letter from Rosset, which I answered just now by wire, saying I preferred appealing to the Governor rather than to go N. Y.[1] More and more I feel I shouldn't go unless I am forced to. There's not only the N.Y. Supreme court decision to be rendered soon, but possibly the U.S. Supreme Court. I should think the Governor would see the logic of waiting on these verdicts rather than having me appear on an absurd and incorrect charge. And don't I have some rights, as an ordinary citizen?

Rembar said over the phone that Stanley Fleishman had offered him only one case, from Pennsylvania, on resisting extradition charges. Seemed to imply that that might be weak. Now I wonder, what is the law on this business of extradition? Does it vary with each state, is it unclear, vague, etc.?

If you know anything that might support Rembar in his appeal please let him know promptly, will you? I know that there will be more publicity once the appeal is made, but somehow I prefer that to going to N. Y. and being humiliated or made a fool of. What do you think?

I'll be here, so far as I know, all day today and this evening and tomorrow too. Friday afternoon I may go to a friend's house in the Valley to stay overnight—to listen to that tape from the Minnesota University—the interview with Audrey Booth, remember?

I may also have to go to lunch tomorrow with Joe Levine (the movie financier) and the producers, but if I do I'll try to leave word with the telephone operator here where to reach me; in any case, I should be back by five or so in the afternoon, in case you wanted to telephone me.

I hope I'm not putting you to too much trouble. You and Stanley make sense when you talk—Rembar leaves me vague usually. Right now Stanley Fleishman is away for a few days. I sent Rembar's letter to him, to be forwarded. But I think I've covered the essentials herein. This in great haste.   My best. Henry

1.   Barney Rosset of Grove Press had, by letter of March 12, expressed concern about Miller's decision that he would not appear voluntarily in the Brooklyn proceeding: "In the eyes of the world it would make us look ridiculous, and would lead to more trouble, if you refused to

come than if you did come. Please consider this carefully, and think about coming, before we might be forced into the action of appealing to Governor Rockefeller, and having further actions in an effort to prevent the court from forcing you to come."

ALS, 1P.   3/15/63

Dear Elmer—   Just got your fat letter. No time to answer in full now. Just enclosing the clipping.

I met Joe Levine Sunday and go to see him again, with the producers and script writer. Must confess I liked him. More shortly.

Henry[1]

---

1.   Scratched out at the top of this letter is a typewritten heading, "Mona's talk——3," which appears to indicate that it was written on a discarded manuscript page, possibly from the second volume of *Nexus* on which Miller had been working intermittently.

ALS, 1P.   3/17/63

Dear Elmer—   To answer more of the queries in yours of 3/12/63. I read the clipping about Hilda Rebay's abstract paintings and tax revision.[1] I know who she is. I agree with the Revenue people—too much for such shit! Don't think we need worry about figures I suggested. Seem more and more modest to me. (I now have another prospective buyer at $250.00. Wants to choose one out of three or return if he doesn't like. A lawyer in Great Neck, N.Y.)[2] I'm also asking my friend, Bob Fink to offer one at auction to Sotheby's, London—just to see what *they* think.

Mrs. Hardesty hopes to do the film of *Smile* some time this year. No, my voice won't be dubbed in. (She's going to try now to get Marcel Marceau as Auguste (sic).).

Am waiting for things to clear before deciding on who publishes Plexus & Nexus here. Barney should have them, of course. New Directions is interested, if Barney doesn't want them. Frankly,

I think my books are coming out a bit too fast. Prefer spacing them.

Yes, I read about Leopold. How very wonderful! And what a crucifixion they put him through, eh?

That Capone book is really a moral diatribe. His happy end—free of crime—was another great surprise. He had character—*plus* a wonderful wife!   All for now! Henry

---

1.   Miller spelled the artist's name incorrectly. Baroness Hilla von Rebay, an ardent devotee of the nonobjective school of painting who died in 1967, was the first director of the Guggenheim Museum (1937–1952). She was born in Strassburg, Alsace; studied painting in Düsseldorf, Munich and Paris; and before coming to the United States in the 1920s exhibited with avant-garde groups in Germany, becoming acquainted with many of the budding artists of the day—among them Klee, Kandinsky, Chagall, Delauney, Léger—whose paintings she would later acquire for the Guggenheim collection. In an introduction to *Solomon R. Guggenheim Museum: Acquisitions of the 1930's and 1940's* (New York: 1968), published as a tribute to Hilla Rebay, Thomas M. Messer implies that she overvalued the works of certain artists, including her own (which continued to be exhibited up to 1962), but he honors the taste that was responsible for the acquisition of an impressive number of the museum's most valuable paintings.
2.   Miller sent Gertz an article from the *Medical Tribune*, March 8, 1963, about the art collector Dr. George P. F. Katz, an internist of Great Neck, Long Island, on which he wrote: "Elmer—this man just bought one of my W.C's—at $250.00.   HM"

ALS, 1P.   3/17/63

Dear Elmer—   Just received letter from Rembar enclosing copy of his letter to Gov Rockefeller's Counsel in Albany, which I have just sent to Stanley Fleishman. (I talked to Stanley to-day over phone.)

Rembar asked if I agreed with him that it might be wiser *not* to send the letter to the Governor yet. After I talked wtih Stanley I sent Rembar a wire saying I do agree with him.

Rembar's point is that the Ass't. District Attorney in Brooklyn has given him his word that they will not begin extradition proceedings without letting Rembar know before hand. He adds that there is still some possibility that "they" will not bring extradition proceedings. Says Rembar in conclusion—"it is my feeling that we should hold off on the letter, the risk of stirring things up outweighing the risk of perfidy." (His letter seemed very good to me—I mean, the one to the Governor's Counsel.) That's it.

In haste again, Henry

TL(CC), 3PP., AIR MAIL   March 19, 1963

Dear Henry: Do you know that the Chicago Sun-Times has reprinted your letter to Stanley Fleishman,[1] giving it great prominence, without mentioning that it is a letter to Fleishman or that it is part of the Petition for a Writ of Certiorari filed in the United States Supreme Court in connection with the California case? In this instance, I think the publication of the letter is all to the good. Our friend, Hoke Norris, you know, is literary editor of the Sun-Times. I suspect that he wanted to create the right atmosphere at this time, while our petition for rehearing in the Illinois Supreme Court is pending. Besides, he probably wanted to strike back at Paul Malloy, one of the columnists on the Sun-Times who does not like your work and follows the line of the so-called Citizens for Decent Literature. Finally, I think he was embarrassed because he had Bill Veeck, the famous baseball impresario, review your correspondence with Durrell, and Veeck wrote a rather silly review. For friendship's sake, I have not reproached Hoke.

This article by you was announced in an institutional advertisement that the Sun-Times placed in the Chicago Daily News[2] the day before it appeared, and also on the second page of the Sun-Times. (The Sun-Times and the Daily News are both published by Marshall Field.) I hope that the article was read by the right people.

I am sending you a copy of the page containing your article and also a copy of the advertisement that appeared in the Daily News.

I am returning the letter that Barney sent to you with respect to the Brooklyn case. It was good talking to you over the telephone the other day with respect to that case and to receive your two additional letters with respect to it. I do hope that you will keep me fully informed and that you will urge Stanley Fleishman to do likewise. If I hear anything further I will let you and Fleishman know. What is necessary in connection with the various *Tropic of Cancer* cases is communication between the parties.

I don't understand what is meant by the statement that the Assistant District Attorney in Brooklyn will not begin extradition proceedings until he lets Rembar know. Had he not begun such proceedings? I thought inquiry in connection with the matter had been made in Pacific Palisades some weeks ago.

Generally speaking, one state is supposed to honor the request for extradition of another state; but there are circumstances when the request may be denied—when, e.g., there is doubt if a crime has been committed, or where certain elements of due process may be violated. Years ago the United States refuseed to extradite Jake Factor to England, despite the gravity of the charges against him, because he was wanted as a witness in the Tuohy kidnapping case.

I shall check further into the law with respect to extradition and offer suggestions to Rembar.

What is the latest word on the University of Minnesota tape? Are you going to sanction its publication?

I'll be much interested in your further report of Joe Levine. Interestingly enough, he was, also, negotiating for the Paul Crump book.

The additional information on values is quite helpful. I hope soon to complete my study of the matter, so that we may proceed without further delay.

Marcel Marceau would, indeed, make a marvelous Auguste.

You are quite right that your books are now appearing too rapidly. They should be better spaced, so that they don't compete with each other.

Despite my preoccupation with so many matters, I finally got to read *The Maurizius Case*. I am more than half through with it. It is an experience.

I talked with Leopold last night. He phoned me from San Juan and got the call through to Midge's apartment, where Mamie and I were having the first dinner cooked for us by our daughter! It was a gourmet feast.

This Saturday I will have the very interesting experience of lunching with President Kennedy.[3] Mayor Daley invited a group of us. It is strange to have a couple in the White House who know something about artistic creativeness.

The best from all of us.   Always yours, ELMER GERTZ

---

1.   Reference is to Miller's U.S. Supreme Court letter (see Miller 12/18/ 62, 1/6/63; Gertz 1/9/63, 3/12/63). Published as "Miller: Who Shall Interpret Freedom?" *Chicago Sun-Times*, March 17, 1963, "Showcase" section, pp. 1, 2.
2.   March 16, 1963, p. 20.
3.   This was President Kennedy's last visit to Chicago.

TL(CC), 1 P., AIR MAIL   March 21, 1963

Dear Henry: As you know, one of the pleasing aspects of the present situation with respect to you is that the young people, particularly those in colleges, have a very great appreciation of your work. The latest expression of this is a long article about *Tropic of Capricorn* that appears in the current issue of the Roosevelt Torch, published by the students of Roosevelt University.[1] I am getting an extra copy of this for you and will forward it as quickly as I can. The author of the article, Ronald M. DeWoskin, holds a B.A. in English at Roosevelt University, where he is in his candidacy for his M.A. His thesis topic is *Henry Miller*. I offered to be of assistance to him.

In the barber shop this morning, I glanced through the movie section of the April issue of Esquire, written by Dwight McDonald. In it he has some very provocative things to say about Joe Levine, and particularly with respect to *Tropic of Cancer*. I think you ought to read this piece.

I finished Wasserman's novel, *The Maurizius Case*. At this

time, with the Leopold matter so much in mind, it was a particularly moving experience. Outside of the fact that Maurizius was innocent and Leopold guilty, there are many other points of difference between the two careers; also, many similarities. Here is another item relating to Leopold's release that you may care to tip into your copy of *Life Plus 99 Years*.

Sincerely yours, ELMER GERTZ

Enc.

---

1.   Ronald M. DeWoskin, "New Medium of Conversation: Tropic of Capricorn," *Oracle*, Vol. I, No. 2, March 18, 1963, pp. 1, 4. In the left margin of the original of this letter, adjacent to Gertz's reference to *Capricorn*, Miller wrote, "Send Rosset."

TL(CC), 1P., AIR MAIL   March 25, 1963

Dear Henry: I am sending herewith some material with respect to the situation on the giving of gifts. There is a lot more, but this will serve to educate you along general lines in the matter.

For the year of each gift, you should make an attempt to find the lowest market value, by obtaining a fair appraisal from more than one reputable art appraiser. You yourself may not determine the value. In any event, all such gifts are certain to be scrutinized. The Internal Revenue Service has warned taxpayers that charitable contributions of non-cash items, especially art objects, will be closely examined. Taxpayers are required to establish the fair market value of such contribution, but the Internal Revenue Service is not required to accept appraisals by experts, and consideration will be given to all available evidence. We must start, however, with such appraisals.

One thing that you have to remember is that works of art by the same artist vary in value. Not every one of your paintings has the same value as the others. But, for convenience, we are trying to standardize the values.

Thus far, I have been handling this matter on a catch-as-catch-can basis, in between many other things. I would like to make a really thorough examination of all of the cases and regulations, unless you prefer to have the one who prepares your tax returns or represents you in income tax matters do so. Let me hear your frank opinion on the matter.

    Warmest regards.   Always yours, ELMER GERTZ

Enc.

ALS, 1P.   3/25/63

Dear Elmer—   Here's the latest! I've just written Rembar that even if I wanted to oblige, the situation hardly permits. I am not only trying to finish Nexus (and make paintings to reduce my taxes) but more important, I am helping the script writer on the Cancer project. And this must be finished a month from now. We have no time to lose.

    I rush, rush every day, to do what must be done. Last night I gave out utterly—thought I had a heart attack. Too much work, too much pushing. And too many problems—of all sorts.

    As I told Cy, if I were to go to NY. now, it would set me back a month. Too much of a nervous ordeal at this time. I asked him— why can't they wait till I pass thru N.Y. on my way to Paris—end of May?

    Evidently, they are trying not to put the extradition thru. Hoping, I suppose, that I will give in and go voluntarily.

                            Enough! Henry

P.S. A letter from a German-Berlin Art Gallery, where my work has been shown, says he estimates my paintings to be worth 3 to 5 hundred dollars per. Have a good friend at Guggenheim who says they pulled a boner on the Rebay deal. I knew it.   HM[1]

1.   Postscript written vertically in left margin.

ALS, 3PP. 3/26/63

Dear Elmer—   Jesus, don't put yourself to more trouble over these paintings of mine! It's amazing and ridiculous how complicated governments make every thing. The way I look at it—very simply—is that at this stage of the game, considering my age, experience and reputation, a valuation (minimal) of $250.00 per W.C. is modest and legitimate. No matter what the size or age of W.C. Who can decide such trivia as whether one is worth $57.50 and another $165.00 and so on? If this simple view of ⟨obliterated⟩ the matter isn't tenable then I'll drop the whole business.

Meanwhile I will do what I can to sell a few at $250.00 or more—just to establish a fair value. If you think any of those institutions you recommended would pay such a figure, in cash, why sell them a *few*. And if they will then also take "donations" (at this figure) let me know how many they would be willing to take. I certainly think that appraisals by their appraisers should meet with Revenue men's approval. We are not dealing in "precious objects."

It occurs to me that a man who could be helpful in this matter is my old friend Huntington Cairns (our "unofficial censor"),[1] now Treasurer at the National Gallery of Art, Wash. D. C. Twenty years or so ago he arranged a show for me in Washington, if I am not mistaken. He may own a few of mine still. Ask him what he values *those* at now. You might add, of course, that my work has improved somewhat in the interim and that there is a lively interest in these things.

I often wondered why Rembar or Rosset didn't consult him about the Brooklyn business. Especially this question of extradition.

Incidentally, Justice Arthur Goldberg's wife gave me an exhibition in Wash. a few years ago. She has a gallery. Prices were lower then—but her word or valuation might have some weight. And what about Abrams,[2] who distributes my big album of W.C's?

Enough! I just sent that reprint which Schwartz put out—⟨obliterated⟩ Ciardi's text in S.R.[3] and my thing on "Cancer" (for

Supreme Court) to 26 of my foreign publishers. (and there are still more.) I think that will start the fire works abroad. Before I get finished with this Brooklyn affair I will make them forever ridiculous in the eyes of the world. I only hope some of the journalists in the Iron Curtain countries play it up. What material for them!

Steve Allen just sent me a text he wrote, defending himself against slanderers and maligners. He writes pretty damn well. But why must people always stress that they are "anti-Communist"? Seems weak to me.

I remain—just a plain, simple anarchist, with a small a. I'm agin every thing we respect.

"Every thing we are taught is false." Rimbaud.

Et comment! D'accord!   Henry

---

1. As a young Baltimore attorney, Cairns opposed in court the Customs Bureau's seizure of Longus's *Daphnis and Chloë* and two other books. He won the case, and in 1933 the Treasury Department began consulting him in reaching obscenity decisions.

    The Cairns-Miller friendship dated from the late 1930s. In the *Henry Miller Letters to Anaïs Nin* we learn that for some time after Miller's return to the United States in 1940 he received his mail through Cairns, who was then assistant general counsel to the Treasury Department. Although Cairns left that post in 1943 to become manager of the National Gallery of Art, he was still advising government agencies on obscenity rulings in 1960, when Miller was being urged by Barney Rosset to let Grove Press publish an American edition of *Cancer*. Before consenting, Miller asked Rosset to query Cairns about whether in his opinion the book could be defended successfully against obscenity charges should that become necessary. On February 24, 1960, Cairns wrote Rosset that he would like to oblige Miller, but felt that he should not offer an opinion in view of his "official connection with the Government." Cairns later told E. R. Hutchison that after the Supreme Court's *Roth* decision (1957) he had informed the Customs Bureau of his judgment that *Cancer* was no longer subject to prohibition. Customs lifted its ban when the 1961 Grove edition was published, apparently on advice of the Department of Justice. See Morris L. Ernst and Alexander Lindey, *The Censor Marches On* (New York: Doubleday, Doran & Company, Inc., 1940), p. 15; Ernst and Schwartz,

Censorship, p. 123; Hutchison, *Tropic of Cancer on Trial*, pp. 48–49; Rembar, *End of Obscenity*, pp. 168–69.

2. Harry N. Abrams, publisher of *Henry Miller: Watercolors, Drawings, and His Essay, The Angel Is My Watermark!*

3. John Ciardi, "Manner of Speaking: Tropic of Cancer," *Saturday Review*, June 30, 1962, p. 13.

TLS, 1 P.   March 28th '63

Dear Elmer: Rushing the enclosed to you as I want to answer Rembar quickly as possible.[1] As you know, in my last letter to Rembar I said—"Why can't they wait until I pass through in May . . . ?" Fortunately he hasn't passed that remark on to the Brooklyn people. I shouldn't have said that much, I fear. All I meant to convey was that I was not accepting the fare to go there in the immediate future.

The more I think about this thing, the more I feel I should not commit myself to agreeing to appear. The only thing that disturbs me, in such a decision, is Rosset's pleas to think seriously on it, to bear in mind that I may cause more trouble for all concerned by refusing to appear than by doing so voluntarily. I can't figure out why Rosset is so jittery about it. Would I, in refusing to appear, make myself out to be such a fool and a coward as he seems to imply? It was he, Barney, who undoubtedly urged Rembar ⟨t⟩ not to send the drafted letter to the Governor yet.

My inner feeling is not to go, to stand pat, to resist extradition proceedings, should it come to that point.

I'm not asking you to decide for me, but I would appreciate what you have to tell me now, at this point—i.e., how you feel about the matter. (I will mail you a letter later, just received, from a convict named Bill Witherspoon, Death Cell, Chicago, who speaks most highly of you.) We all revere your judgment and insight.

If you will, answer me special delivery, eh?

I'm knocking out a water color or two every day now. Some

good, some not so good. A gallery here wants to show (and sell, if possible) at an exhibition May 5th. Good idea. To get more evaluations.   This in haste. Henry

1.   Charles Rembar had advised, by letter dated March 22, of an unusual offer "from Brooklyn" to pay Miller's fare if he would appear voluntarily, and five days later asked Miller to say whether he would definitely appear in May if the District Attorney in Brooklyn agreed to wait that long. In the March 22nd letter Rembar also informed Miller that the *Cancer* case then pending in the New York Court of Appeals would be postponed for about a month.

TL(CC), 3PP., AIR MAIL, SPECIAL DELIVERY   March 29, 1963

Dear Henry: Again I have fallen badly behind, but much of the time I have been working on matters of concern to you. Let me see if I can bring you up to date, commencing with your air mail special delivery of March 28.

First of all, I am returning herewith the two letters that you received from Rembar, the one dated March 22, and the other dated March 27.

As I have said earlier, I simply don't understand why Barney, Cy and the others are in such a God-awful hurry for you to appear in connection with the Brooklyn case. I should think that they would be able to make this clear to you so that a decision would be easy. I tried to get Cy to explain himself; perhaps he did, but I did not grasp his meaning then. We have a situation in which a reviewing court in New York, the highest court in California, the Illinois Supreme Court[1] and the Supreme Court of the United States, are all considering whether or not *Tropic of Cancer* is obscene or constitutionally protected. The Brooklyn case will depend upon what these various courts decide. Yet the Brooklyn authorities are insistent upon your appearance. It seems to me that they should be glad to postpone the burdens of a trial, pending the disposition of the matter elsewhere. If they are not inclined to do so, what is their true motivation? Do they think that they could influence the result in the other courts? Do they have other motivation that we cannot surmise? Cy does not find their proceeding to be in bad faith, but you, I, John Ciardi and others feel that it is obviously a phony. This would suggest that they would try to embarrass you in some way were you to appear. If you were a young man, I would say you might get some fun even out of their mischievousness. You might have the opportunity to tell them to go to the devil, or to obtain material for use in one of your books, something that would pin them down for all time as knaves and fools. Despite your vigor, you are not young, and you ought not to tax yourself unduly. The question becomes, is it better to fight extradition, which would be embarrassing and nerve-wracking, or to appear voluntarily? You and I, joined by Stanley Fleishman, seem to have one answer, and Barney and Cy another. I have learned long since not to be so cocksure about my views as not to admit the possibility of being wrong. I hope that this restatement of the problem helps clarify your thinking and enables you to reach a decision. Frankly, having to choose between loyalty to you and loyalty to Barney, it is easy for me to stand by you. But I am Barney's attorney and professionally it is my obligation not to appear to thwart him. In other words, I am riding several horses and I am probably going off in several directions, but I hope that you can understand.

Gene Lovitz sent me a copy of Bill Witherspoon's letter to you. I hope that his life is spared, but I hope also that I will not be called upon to represent him, except, perhaps, in an advisory capacity through some other attorney. I don't like to have a man's life depend upon my competence, or incompetence, good luck, or bad luck.

I am delighted that a gallery wants to show your water colors. This will enable us to get more evaluations. I can proceed to make all or some of the gifts in your behalf at this time, or postpone them a bit. The benefits will all come during the current year and one week or one month more does not matter.

I share your views as to the unnecessary complications involved even in the making of gifts, but I don't want you to have even more complications because we overlook something or other. Let's leave it this way. I will not bother you anymore with correspondence on the matter, but will carry through as best I can. Then, in the end, I can advise you as to any reports you must file, any claims you must make, etc. If you have a regular accountant or tax counsel, I could even pass on the information to him, rather than to you.

I received a very fine letter from George Wickes, who liked my review of your correspondence with Durrell. He sent me the table of contents for the book, *Henry Miller and The Critics*. Of course, I am flattered to be sandwiched between you and Aldous Huxley. The book looks like an exciting one. I wish it were possible for it to come out in the next few days or weeks, so that I could make the Illinois Supreme Court realize how absurd it is not to declare a book constitutionally protected when a state university thinks enough of it and its author to publish a book about both. The reason I have not said anything to the court as yet on that theme is that I am fearful of forcing the hands of would-be censors who might prevent the publication of the book. After it is out, then we don't have to worry about those characters.

There are so many things that you touch upon in your letters that I am tempted to refer to, except that I do not want to weary you by too long a letter of my own.

The Chicago Daily News has asked me to review *Black Spring*. I will send you the review when it appears. I tried to compress the essence of the book into a very small amount of space. I hope that I have succeeded.

Mamie and I celebrated a very important event yesterday—the fourth year since we first met. I have been reviewing my life with her and many other recent events in the course of doing some additional work on the book of mine that is to be published this summer or fall. I can hardly spare the time, and yet there is such a drive to do it.

Affectionate greetings from all of us.

Always yours, ELMER GERTZ

Enc.

1.   The appeal from Judge Epstein's *Cancer* ruling was once more before
     the Illinois Supreme Court. After that court had determined that the
     case should be sent back to the Appellate Court (see Gertz 2/7/63),
     Gertz applied for a rehearing, which was granted on March 27; how-
     ever, as Gertz's subsequent letters indicate, the Illinois Supreme Court
     held the case over from term to term for more than a year before
     handing down a judgment.

ALS, 1P.   3/31/63

Dear Elmer—   Thank you so much for your fulsome reply—
the 29th. I wrote Rembar that I will simply *not answer*, as he suggested I could do, if I wished.

About the W.C. donations—yes, do go ahead and make gifts
and advise me as you proceed. Believe some kind of letter from me
is necessary to explain why I make each institution this gift. Maybe
you can ⟨frame⟩ formulate one for me.

What about the gifts of the Night Life books? That should be
easy, no? That book Wickes is editing won't be out till next year,
I guess.

About the taped interview—have given Tom the name of Van-
guard Recording Co—thru kindness of Joan Baez. Fink still has
the tape.

And now you're on your 5th lap with Mamie. Keep on! Peace
be with you!   Henry

Had a rather touching letter from the editor of the Carolina Israelite
—forget his name.[1]

---

1.   Postscript written vertically in left margin.

TL(CC), 1P., AIR MAIL   April 2, 1963

Dear Henry: You would have been delighted had you been
present in my office when two representatives of the Adult Educa-

tion Council were present. You will remember that we agreed to give one of your water colors to them. These two people know a good deal about art. In fact, both of them paint. I asked their opinion as to the value of your painting, and they named an amount far in excess of what we had been considering. I asked them if they would get for us a written appraisal, and they agreed to do so. They will write a letter acknowledging the gift; and our letter of gift will be dated prior to that time. I will send it on to you for signature as soon as I can.

The situation with respect to the *Night Life* book is certainly as you suggest. There can be no doubt about the substantiation of the values.

You refer to a rather touching letter that you received from the editor of the Carolina Israelite. His name is Harry Golden. In view of his closeness to Carl Sandburg, I would love to know what he said. Sandburg acted rather foolishly, you may remember, in connection with *Tropic of Cancer.*

Do take care of yourself.

Warmest regards.   Always yours, ELMER GERTZ

TL(CC), 2PP., AIR MAIL   April 3, 1963

Dear Henry: While I have a supply of water colors for distribution to the various donees, I don't have the copies of *Into the Night Life.* Are those going to be sent by Bob Fink? Just what will the arrangement be?

April 5, 1963

As usual, I got tied up on work.

Through Ralph Newman[1] and my own resources, we will be able to get other universities and public institutions to acquire your work. This will be good for a variety of reasons.

As you know, Mr. Eagan wrote to me about Roger Bloom. I am sending a copy of my reply. I have, also, written to Roger. I hope he makes it. He promises to visit with me briefly. I hope that you do, also.

I received another letter from Stanley Fleishman. It is interesting that the two of us are in such agreement, as to the extradition. We must be right!

This may amuse—or annoy—you. The literary editor of the Chicago Daily News has become fearful that he will be looked upon as partial to your attorney. Accordingly, my review will appear under a pseudonym. As I wrote Roger, I now know what it is to use an alias. Eddie is circulating copies of both of my reviews. Anyone reading them will know that both were written by the same person.

I enjoyed the letter from George Wickes. I think that he will become one of the most illustrious of the learned critics—like Geismar, Kazin, Moore and Company.

The head of the parole board in Puerto Rico sent Leopold a magnificent letter on the occasion of his becoming "a completely free man" (as if any of us ever is!). It reads, in part, as follows:

"Your final discharge has not been a mere formality after a stated lapse of time of good conduct. It has been honorably won by you and based on the patience, courage, faith and love for other people shown by you. Cases like yours compensate in abundance for the occasional disillusions that are incidental in the administration of our parole work."

This proves that public officials are sometimes human beings!

Affectionate greetings from Mamie and the rest of us.

Always yours, ELMER GERTZ

---

1.   See Gertz 11/30/62.

TLS, 1P.   April 5, 1963

Dear Elmer,   Heartening to ⟨get⟩ hear that the Adult Educ. group thought so highly of my work; do hope they will get a still higher appraisal. You know, I have to find ways and means now, at my present rate of earnings, to reduce my gross income (by donations) to the extent of twelve to fifteen thousand dollars a year.

Have to get rid of a lot of water colors to do that, what! Last year it was all mss. and documents.

Since I don't know if George Wickes also wrote you I am enclosing his letter to me and a copy of my reply.

That letter of Harry Golden was addressed to Charles Siegferth a mutual friend in San Francisco. Herewith a second letter he sent Siegferth. The first contained a sentence to the effect that he (Golden) "loved that bastard (HM) almost like a brother." Siegferth has the first letter. By the way, Siegferth is a bore of a letter writer, so don't get yourself involved.

I'm also enclosing two letters regarding my paintings. I just wrote Friesner,[1] Kansas (a very nice fellow) that you would be writing him and sending him several—if they can accept more than one. Also mentioned that you had had an evaluation higher than I estimated, and that if his people saw fit to put a higher figure on the work, fine. The one from Wenning[2] indicates further institutions likely to be interested, if we have enough to send round.

In the last two weeks I have made a number of paintings, and am sure they are good, most of them. I seem to have a painting streak on—probably because I can't find time for continuous writing, and probably because my mind is now concentrated on painting. In this next month I hope to produce quite a few. I am now on my 60th painting, since Jan. 15th. I think the L.A. show on May 5th (one day only) will start things humming. I feel the price will go up too. (Et pourquoi pas? as Picasso always says.)

Just had another letter from Bill Witherspoon. An excellent letter, full of insight, feeling, understanding. I will answer again.

Am rather glad Southern Illinois Univ. isn't rushing the George Wickes job. Next year will be just as good. And, meanwhile, if you wanted to quote from it, you could.

Had letter from Stanley F. . . . Glad to see he is of the same mind as us, as regards the Brooklyn affair.

Give my best to Mamie. Ask her if she would like to read a long, heavy novel called "The Brothers Ashkenazi" by one of the Singer brothers, the other one.[3] I have two copies. It's supposed to be a gem.   My best. Henry

And hello to your secretary! I hope she isn't smothered under all the work she's doing for me.

1. Paul K. Friesner, librarian, Fort Hays Kansas State College. See H. M. 2/15/62.
2. Reference is no doubt to Henry W. Wenning, rare book collector of New Haven, Connecticut, mentioned as a Miller aficianado in Henry Miller Literary Society Newsletters.
3. I[srael] J[oshua] Singer, *The Brothers Ashkenazi*, tr. from the Yiddish by Maurice Samuel. New York: Alfred A. Knopf, 1936.

ALS, 1P.   4/6/63

Dear Elmer—   Maybe some day some where you can ring in the enclosed.[1]

Edith [Hamilton] says his [*Aristophanes'*] words are imprintable. Does that mean that we have read only watered down versions? Could you ask some friend of yours—a Greek scholar, perhaps—if there exist unexpurgated translations?

Mailing Mamie the Ashkenazi—thru book store—to-day. Just in time for Passover.   Cheerio! Henry[2]

1. Typewritten excerpt from "Aristophanes and the Old Comedy," a chapter in Edith Hamilton's *The Greek Way* (New York: W. W. Norton & Company, Inc. [1942]), pp. 157–58.
2. On the flap of the envelope Miller wrote: "Just got yours of the 3rd— 5th. Eve will mail N.L. books out—give me the names and addresses. HM"

TL(CC), 1P., AIR MAIL   April 10, 1963

Dear Henry: I am sending herewith a copy of my review of *Black Spring*, which has just appeared. As I told you, it had to be published under a pseudonym.[1]

There are a number of things that I want to write to you in

response to recent letters. I hope to be able to write tomorrow, but I wanted this review to be in your hands.

Affectionate greetings from Mamie and me.

Always yours, ELMER GERTZ

Enc.

---

1.   Arthur Wainwright [pseud. Elmer Gertz], "Delirium and Joy in the 'Best' of the Early Miller Novels," *Chicago Daily News*, April 10, 1963, p. 34. The following excerpt from Gertz's review, ascribed to "Arthur Wainwright," was quoted on the flyleaf of Grove's paperback edition: "There is a growing opinion that *Black Spring* is the best of the early Miller novels, although, admittedly, *Tropic of Cancer* must still be regarded as one of the most daring works of its generation. . . . This book is seemingly as unplanned as life, and as bittersweet. There is delirium and joy on every page."

ALS, 2PP.   4/11/63

Dear Elmer—   This should please you! I opened your last, put the clipping aside, forgot who sent it to me (so much mail to read!), read it with the keenest delight and said to myself—"Who could this fellow Wainwright be—he's damned good." And then suddenly I remembered—it's you! Bravo! I hope Schwartz reprints it. That book somehow got lost (by the critics) and I've always loved it myself, utterly formless though it is.

By the way, a John Wain of London has written a very good critique of Cancer (new British edition.)[1] Eddie is reprinting it. 40,000 copies sold already—edition exhausted. And no prosecution yet. A bit of luck—so far!

Tell Mamie I'm now steadily reading "The Brothers Ashkenazi." It's really an epic work. What a picture of Lodz. Really formidable.

Hope she received her copy—along with bunnies (Kosher) and Easter eggs.

Enough! Good cheer!   Henry

Unidentified. See, however, John Wain's review of *Naked Lunch*, "The Great Burroughs Affair," *New Republic*, December 1, 1962, pp. 21–23, which is as much about Miller's writing as about Burroughs'.

TL(CC), 1P., AIR MAIL   April 12, 1963

Dear Henry: I have just been given a photocopy of a master's thesis by Ronald M. DeWoskin, entitled *Wisdom of the Heart.** The very fine young man who wrote it said he would be glad to send you a copy if you are interested.

He is about to become affiliated with the University of Wisconsin and hopes ultimately to do his doctor's dissertation on you. You won't recognize yourself by the time all of these young scholars get through with you.

Incidentally, our boy Jack will be enrolling at the University of Wisconsin soon. He is the youngster who is Val's age, you will recall; and he is much in need of training in writing. It will be good to have someone at the university to goad him.

I still hope to write to you on the other pending matters before the end of the day.

Warmest regards.   Always yours, ELMER GERTZ
*An Introduction to the Works of Henry Miller

APS, 1S., AIR MAIL   4/15/63

Dear Elmer—   Great news! Just informed that there will be no prosecution of "Cancer" by British authorities. Perlès heard it over the air in London. Maybe this will help in our battle here.   Henry[1]

---

1.   Postcard bears legend:
     HENRY MILLER Deux Jeunes Filles
     Watercolor and Ink, 11½" x 14"
     Collection of Henry Miller

> Gertz sent Miller two letters dated April 16. In one he informed
> Miller that the Guildhall Galleries in Chicago wanted to arrange
> an exhibition of his water colors. In the three pages of the other
> he primarily commented on numerous references in Miller's re-
> cent letters, but included the following about Harry Golden: "He
> is a strange character, a useful person who has long since written
> himself out. He does wonderful work in the South, where he helps
> to contain the bigots."

APS, 1S.   4/17/63

Dear Elmer—   I suppose I *ought* to read the young man's thesis.
Let him send it along. God, but I'm swamped with things to do and
read and write. Now on my 70th painting. After the show May 5th
I will have more to send you—if you can handle more (?) This in
haste.   Henry

TL(CC), 2PP., AIR MAIL   April 30, 1963

Dear Henry: I am returning herewith the simply delightful piece
that you have written about painting.[1] I have made a copy of it for
my file. As soon as the piece appears in print I would like to get
a copy. In your amusing way, you say some very serious and provocative things about painting. I am having Sue and Hank read
the article for their own enlightenment.

The enclosed copy of a letter from me to Stanley Fleishman
will bring you up to date on the legal aspects of the *Tropic* situation.
Soon all of the pieces will be in place and I think the result will
be pleasing to us.

When I talked with Cy Rembar yesterday, he told me that
the Brooklyn District Attorney has promised that no steps will be
taken towards your extradition without prior notice to him. I suspect now that no steps will be taken at any time, although one
cannot tell. Incidentally, Cy was extremely friendly to me. Apparently he does not resent my intervention in the matter. I am
not sure that this is equally true of the others.

I am going to see Justice Douglas tonight and then lead a discussion on his views tomorrow night at North Park College, a Lutheran institution. Then, next Tuesday night, I am going to have dinner with Justice Goldberg, several members of the Illinois Supreme Court and others. I am sure that all of these people will be thinking of the *Tropic of Cancer* case when they see me, but none of us will be able to say a word on the subject!

I am sending the sample pages from the Southern Illinois University Press book, *Henry Miller and the Critics*. Typographically it is very attractive. George Wickes was good enough to send me the manuscript of the book, the publication date of which is apparently advanced again. The book has real flavor. It is too bad that it will have to compete with so many other things for attention.

I looked at the current announcement number of Publishers' Weekly and I find that two books about you are scheduled for publication in the near future; this in addition to the Wickes volume. One is by Widmer and the other by Bower, I believe (I am referring to these from memory).[2]

If the Supreme Court of either Illinois, California or New York should release a resounding opinion in favor of *Tropic of Cancer*, it is likely to create renewed interest, and certainly later in the year the United States Supreme Court opinion will do that. There is really nothing that can be done about this new groundswell of interest. Like the lady who is being raped, you simply have to lean back and enjoy it.

Warmest regards from all of us.

Always yours, ELMER GERTZ

1. The article referred to appears to have been "Are We Getting Anywhere," *Artforum*, Vol. 2, No. 1, July 1963, pp. 27–30.
2. Kingsley Widmer, *Henry Miller* (New York: Twayne Publishers, Inc., 1963). The second title was not located in *Publishers' Weekly*, but may have been a book announced in the *Henry Miller Literary Society Newsletter*: H. Bowden, *Henry Miller* (Waldwick, N.J.: Bern Porter).

APS, 2SS.   4/30/63

Dear Elmer—   Thanks for copy of Crump letter. Now I get the
reason for their *seeming* liberality.

My play has now been taken for the Spoleto Festival in July—
I told you of the Edinburgh Festival (August).[1] *Cheers!*

I also see that *U.S.* Supreme Court will take the case in the
Fall. Hurrah!

Now I've got to find another opera Co. to do "The Smile."
Hamburg opera put it off indefinitely.

Will you want any more water colors—for donations? Will
any of these institutions take more than *one?*

I'm now on my 82nd one!

All the best!

Got Mamie's good letter. Long live the Ashkenazis!!   Henry

---

1.   See H. M. 2/21/63, notes.

TL(CC), 2PP., AIR MAIL   May 2, 1963

Dear Henry: You asked me about the unexpurgated translation
of *Aristophanes.* By sheer coincidence, a New York book shop is
offering the very work. With the thought that you may be interested, I am sending you the relevant page showing Item 11. I am
also sending another page with a reference (No. 105) to Hemingway. This may interest you.

The amount of activity in connection with you in the courts,
publishing circles, everywhere, is fantastic. You must find it difficult to keep up with yourself. Still, you must finish *Nexus.* Then
you can say, "To hell with everything and everyone except myself."

I am sure that the various schools and other institutions will
be glad to accept more than one of your water colors. If you send
more to me, I promise to dispose of them. The matter is going

very slowly, but I will find the time before too long and everything will then be in order.

You certainly must have the world's record for production of water colors. The amazing thing is that they are so good. Does Lawrence Durrell produce good paintings?

I have finally read the *Alexandria Quartet*, all at once. The novels are overpowering, even when I protest against the preciousness of some of the writing. Even more of it has the power and beauty of the best poetry. I would love to talk to Durrell one day.

Mamie, who is generally not a rapid reader, is almost through with The Brothers Ashkenazi. She talked so much about it that I am afraid that I will have to read the book as well.

Amusingly, her mother, who has always impressed me as a prim and proper person, picked up a copy of *Tropic of Cancer*. We held our breaths when we heard this. Last night, in talking to Mamie, she surprised us by her praise of the book. We surely have misunderstood Mother.

Warmest greetings from all of us.

Always yours, ELMER GERTZ

In an undated letter on stationary "from the desk of . . . EDWARD BLAU," Miller evidently referred to the forthcoming May 5 exhibition of his water colors in saying he thought Gertz might like to see something he had written "to go with the show." He added: "I'm afraid I may sell more pics than I intended to. Seems L.A. is all agog already."

APS, 1S.   5/8/63

Dear Elmer—   I spent 3 solid hours today FILING c/s of one month! Another 2 hours answering letters overlooked. Another hour reading current day's mail. which may explain why I don't answer always in full and in kind.

Had a marvelous show Sunday of w.c.'s. Waiting to hear results—quite a few sold, I believe, and at *my* figures! Couldn't go, as my twisted muscle still cripples me. Easing up SLIGHTLY now—after 2 weeks.   Henry

Am on 85th water color now![1]

---

1.   Postscript written vertically in right margin.

TLS, 1P.
                                                May 12, 1963

Dear Elmer,   First off—congratulations on receiving the Civil Liberties Award![1] Quite an honor. And who deserves it more than you?

Were talking about you last night; had Joe Edelman here and Stanley Fleishman, for dinner. Stanley and Joe both, for different reasons, seemed optimistic about Supreme court outcome in October. (More and more I remember the words of my astrologer-friend in Lausanne, over a year ago, about Cancer and its destiny. Nothing but triumph and victory.) We'll see. So far, so good—even the headaches.

I'm still in pain but it's begun to ease up a bit since yesterday. Continue to paint—am on the 88th one now. The show was a howling success. Sold 11 in 4 hours—crowd too big to handle. They would have sold everything, had time permitted, and had I given the O.K. But I wanted some of my work back—for donations, and a few for [my] own walls. Which reminds me again—do you wish me to send you more soon? Must also say there was never a question about the price of my work. I could have asked more, apparently. And I would like to, where donations are concerned, as it would save me that much work. You never did tell me what that Adult Education group in Chicago estimated their value to be. Didn't they think more than was asked? I acquired, through exchange, a sculpture of Don Quixote by Berenice Kussoy, Jewish young woman from N.Y.—all her sculpture made of bits of iron, ⟨h⟩ junk, odds and ends. Really quite wonderful.[2]

Am to see Joe Levine in a few days—here. We are having trouble (*entre nous*) with our producers—they have fallen out—quite a mess. Usual Hollywood stuff, I imagine.

I wrote a preface last week for "The Best of Bates" (collection of his short stories—British writer).[3] Wrote it in great pain and thought it no good—got letter saying it was "magnificent"???? Also wrote 16 pages preface or text for illustrations to book on Greece, by Henry Varnum Poor's daughter, Anne—will be an art book.[4]

But the main thing is painting—getting more enthusiastic every day. Also getting possessive—want to hold more now. Will have quite a gallery here soon. Walls already glow with old and new work.

About donees. Been thinking—wouldn't it be better if a few institutions took a number, rather than scatter one or two to a bigger number of places?

Must get out and try to walk a bit now. Couldn't walk at all till yesterday.

Carry on, good cheer, love all around.   Henry

---

1. Gertz was honored by the Illinois Division of the American Civil Liberties Union on May 25 at the Hotel LaSalle, Chicago. The award was "for exemplary service in the cause of literary freedom and equal justice under law."
2. See "Henry Miller introduces Bernice Kussoy: Sculptress," *Genesis West*, Vol. 1 No. 4 (Summer 1963), pp. [362]–[363].
3. Herbert Ernest Bates, *The Best of H. E. Bates* (Boston: Little, Brown, [1963]); published in England as *Seven By Five* (London: Michael Joseph [1963]).
4. *Greece*. Drawings by Anne Poor, Text by Henry Miller (New York: Viking Press, 1964).

TL(CC), 2PP., AIR MAIL   May 16, 1963

Dear Henry: What a hectic week this has been. We are likely to learn the thinking of the Illinois Supreme Court before the end of this month. Meanwhile, I have learned of yet another review of a lower court opinion in a case involving *Tropic of Cancer*. I don't know whether or not I told you, but some judge in Milwaukee had come to an adverse decision. Ages went by; I thought that the time for appeal had long since passed. Then, suddenly, I learned that the case was being appealed and is now in the Wisconsin Supreme Court.[1] I received a copy of one of the briefs in that case, but not of the others. In this brief, the opinion of Judge Epstein is stressed. Several pages of the brief quote extensively and effectively from Judge Epstein. It is fantastic that the matter is now in four state supreme courts and the United States Supreme Court. I cannot recall another book in history that has had a similar struggle.

I see no reason why the museums and other institutions won't be willing to accept several paintings, rather than just one. I am trying to goad Ralph Newman, so that I can get some of the material that he has on this matter. I should also get from you all available material with respect to the exhibition and sale of your water colors at the recent show. If there is a catalog or announcement, please send it to me, together with the information as to which water colors were sold, to whom and for how much. This will enable me to substantiate the values.

I wish that I could have been present when Joe Edelman and Stanley Fleishman had dinner with you and one of the topics of conversation was myself. I, too, agree with them, that the decision is likely to be favorable in the United States Supreme Court and probably in all or most of the state supreme courts. So far as the highest court of the land is concerned, it generally does not grant certiorari—that is, take a case—unless there is good reason for believing that the party seeking the review is right.

Reverting again to the exhibition and sale of your paintings last held, was there any newspaper publicity? It would be well if I had copies of the newspaper articles.

What are your plans about going abroad? When will you go? How long will you stay? Will you give us the very great pleasure of having you as our guest?

What you say about the hours you spend in filing your correspondence and in answering letters, I can sympathize with you.

Even with a very competent and devoted secretary, I am simply overwhelmed with the amount of time that I must devote to such things. I went to New York for a family wedding for a week-end and lost a total of a day and a half at the office. Now I am being punished. I have been working day and night, and have fallen more behind, rather than less. The broken promises to clients pile up. I no longer give a damn whether I keep my word or not.

I hope that you are now feeling better and that you don't extend yourself. When you have reached 100 water colors, we ought to have some sort of celebration which ends with our burning all the academic drawings embalmed in the worst museums.

Affectionate greetings from all of us.

Always yours, ELMER GERTZ

---

1.   Circuit Judge Ronold A. Drechsler declared *Cancer* obscene in June, 1962. His decision was reversed by the Supreme Court of Wisconsin in May, 1963. For more about the Milwaukee case see Hutchison, *Tropic of Cancer on Trial*, pp. 170–201; Gertz 5/22/63.

ALS, 2PP.   5/18/63

Dear Elmer—   I answered the enclosed by asking if they knew what the book was like—didn't want to cause them embarrassment, especially since Her Majesty, the Queen, is the *Patron*.[1] But, if it should turn out that they wrote with eyes open, wouldn't it be wonderful? Something to call to the attention of all the Supreme Courts, I'd say. Let's wait and see. Return the letter later, yes?

What ever happened to the paintings you were going to send me by that young genius whose work I saw at your Son's home? I'm still interested—and may buy something.

Now that Paris is put off for a couple of months I hope to do a little writing (Nexus II) as well as painting.

How wonderful it is not to be in pain. I was almost going nuts. It's not gone yet, of course, but temporarily smothered, so to speak. I read an interesting article on this subject—Pain—in Time

Mag. May 17th—under title "Therapy."[2] Have written the medicos for literature if there is any. To my mind, the conquest of pain is of far greater importance than all our space exploration. It would be an incredible boon to mankind. And, like with the Negro problem, I don't think it matters a damn how it's accomplished—drugs, hypnotism, magic, witchcraft, whatsoever. The thing is to lick it, eradicate it. Most of the world lives perpetually in pain of one kind or another. I never knew what it was until three weeks ago. I've had it! as they say.

I am enclosing the article from Time—don't need it now.

Best to Mamie and yourself—and all the happy members of your family.   Henry

---

1.   Miller received a request for permission to transcribe *Cancer* in Braille from the National Library for the Blind in London.—*Henry Miller Literary Society Newsletter*, No. 12, October 1963.
2.   "Therapy," *Time*, May 17, 1963, p. 93. At some point Miller forwarded this page to Gertz with handwritten notation in top margin, "Forgot to enclose."

ALS, 2PP.   5/18/63

Dear Elmer—   I enclose the only clipping about the show—printed a day before it opened.[1] Were no reviews of work shown because affair lasted only 4 hours. I've asked gallery for list of sales, prices, names & addresses—and an announcement, issued by some organization.

By the looks of things now, I may not be going to Paris till *August*. Saw Joe Levine again—like him more and more. A rough diamond and a straight shooter, I feel.

Will send you more w.c's soon—just as soon as I can part with them. Such a pleasure to see them here on my walls.

I'm now taking injections and ultra-sonic massages, which have helped greatly to reduce the pain. Am a bit weary, of course, after 3 weeks of no let up of pain. Relaxing now.

I have a feeling I'll see you on my way to Europe, yes.

I did my 91st w.c. the other day. Did I tell you that Jo Edelman visited Max Ashkenazi (Usher Cohen, in reality) in his chateau in Lodz some years ago? What a story!

More anon. Ouf!   Henry

P.S. one of my w.c's auctioned off (silently, by ballot) for the Museum, fetched $260.00.

---

1.   Claire Wolfe, "Sunday Big Day on Gallery Row," Los Angeles *Citizen-News*, May 4, 1963, which announced the Miller exhibit at the Ankrum Gallery, Los Angeles, and featured a photograph of one of his paintings. On the clipping Miller wrote: "This was the 1st W.C. I did here in new house. Have kept it."

ALS, 2PP.   5/21/63

Dear Elmer—   I'm enclosing two letters which may be useful in connection with my W.C. "donations." Please return later. The portrait of me by my life-long friend Emil Schnellock, mentioned in Springer's[1] letter, I have not received yet—nor the w.c's, nor the copper plate prints. I mention it (portrait) because, should U.C.L.A. not accept it as a donation (his figure—valuation seems high for a mediocre piece of work) maybe one of the institutions you are dealing with would be interested in acquiring it. (?) U.C.L.A. agrees to take 4 or 5 of my w.c's—donations. I got a number of the ones I cherish framed—to keep for myself. Will be able to send you eight or ten shortly, though—is that too much or too little?

Am enclosing clippings—no need to return. Did you get what you wanted from England?

Oh yes, I think I may be able to give you a (battered) copy of "Semblance of a Devoted Past". Or have you one already?

Did you get a copy of "Plexus"? Girodias (Olympia Press) seems in bad straits financially again. Because of loss he takes running swanky Night Club & Restaurant. He's worried about censorship in France. Says France has now become Puritanical (sic) Could be true. Maybe soon the French will have to get my (banned) books from England and America. What a farce it all is!

I know you're being honored this Saturday. I may forget to send cable congratulations. So I give them now—once again! Vive la liberté! Up Gertz! *Hourrah!*   Yours ever, Henry Getting injections and ultra-sonic massages for my stretched sacro-sciatic muscle. Keeps pain numbed. Will take weeks to heal. But I can paint and write even if I can't dance or fuck or raise my right arm to salute a bastard like Governor Wallace of Alabama.

P.S. Re Wallace-Kennedy—To what lengths can a governor go in flouting the law! Funny, how soft the rulers sometimes are. Tough on "bad words" (obscenity) and weak where human lives are at stake.

The whole business is disgraceful, ridiculous and disgusting.
HM[2]

---

1.   Rudolf Springer, of Galerie Springer in Berlin, who arranged for Mario Marini to sculpt Miller head in honor of Miller's seventieth birthday.
2.   Postscript written vertically in left margin of second page.

TL(CC), 2PP., AIR MAIL   May 22, 1963

Dear Henry: I have several of your letters to answer. The biggest item of news relates to the Milwaukee case. The Wisconsin Supreme Court has reversed the trial court 4 to 3 (close but sufficient!) and declared the book constitutionally protected. I have sent you a couple of newspaper cuttings about the matter, and when I get the opinion itself I will forward a copy of it to you. The A.C.L.U. *amicus* brief filed in the case quotes pages of Judge Epstein's opinion very effectively. I wish that our court would get around to it. And what does Stanley say about the likelihood of an early decision in the California Supreme Court. Such decision will have an effect, good or bad, on the U. S. Supreme Court case. Incidentally, the current issue of *Esquire* has a very good article on the U. S. Supreme Court and literature written by the reporter who recently won a Pulitzer Prize.[1]

Next week's issue of the *Saturday Evening Post* will contain an article on Nathan Leopold,[2] who, incidentally, is about to go with his wife to Europe for three months—the trip that was postponed for 39 years!

When will the Post article on you appear? ⟨Five or six words obliterated⟩

The Brooks introduction to the volume of *Paris Review* interviews refers constantly to you. Brooks was apparently intrigued by you.[3]

As soon as you get the material on your show that I have requested, please send it to me. *Important!*

Sue has sent you a couple of paintings by John Doyle, that brilliant young artist friend of hers. I hope that you like them. Sue, like an artist, puts off all things for tomorrow!

I get more and more intrigued by what you say of Joe Levine. I will have to see for myself!

I've begun reading Gerald Durrell's little book about his family, Larry included.[4] Are you familiar with it?

Long ere this I should have expressed my joy that you are now feeling much better, and, particularly, that the pain is gone. I hope that it does not return. About four years ago, for the first and only time, I had an attack of bursitis. I thought I had cancer, or worse. Mamie was my one solace then. She took over the driving of the car, taking me everywhere. My life has been eased by her ever since then.

It is good to know that we will see you when you are en route to Europe. This will make our summer a very happy one. Please let us know when to expect you, how long you will stay, etc.

Mamie was ever so excited to learn of Joe Edelman's visit with Max Ashkenazi. The Singer book was a great and moving experience for her. One day I, too, will read it.

Of course, I was intrigued by the letter from the National Library for the Blind. It would be almost cruel to subject some of the blind to the torments of sex! I am returning the letter. Do tell me what you learn.

Eddie Schwartz may be in town for the A.C.L.U. affair. How good of him.

Affectionate greetings from all.

Always yours, ELMER GERTZ

Enc.

1.   Anthony Lewis, "Sex—and the Supreme Court," *Esquire*, June 1963, pp. 82–83, 141–43.
2.   Leonard Lyons, "The Rehabilitation of Nathan Leopold," *Saturday Evening Post*, June 1, 1963, pp. [66]–68. Leopold was paroled March 13, 1958, after serving 33 years, six months, and two days.
3.   *Writers at Work: The Paris Review Interviews*, Second Series, with introduction by Van Wyck Brooks (New York: Viking [1963]). See also George Wickes, "Henry Miller," ibid., pp. [165]–191.
4.   Gerald M. Durrell, *My Family and Other Animals* (New York: Viking Press, 1957).

APS, 1S.   5/26/63

Do see Playboy—June issue—for text by Hugh Hefner—beginning p. 69, *very trenchant!*[1] And who would suspect to find the like in such a mag?

There was an interview with Bertrand Russell in a previous issue—real dynamite![2]   Henry

1.   Hugh M. Hefner, "The Playboy Philosophy," *Playboy*, June 1963, pp. 69, 71–78, 176–77.
2.   Bertrand Russell, "Playboy Interview: A Candid Conversation with Britain's Impassioned Pacifist," *Playboy*, March 1963, pp. 41–42, 46–50, 52–53.

TLS, 1P.   May 28, 1963

Dear Elmer,   Herewith statement of sales made by Ankrum Gallery that Sunday. Could you get a Xero(?) copy made for yourself and return this to me, so I can give to my tax accountant, please? You'll notice that some paintings went for $150.00; they were the smaller ones. I bought a piece of sculpture by Berenice Kussoy (Don Quixote on horseback)—I love it. Ask Sue if she ever saw this woman's work—sculpture made of bits of old iron, junk, etc.

They forgot to send me the announcement of the show—but you will get one direct from them. You may also get from them an official letter inviting me to send a "donation" to a school (bona fide for revenue purposes) in Aspen, Colo. I think I sent you some time ago a letter from the Fort Hays Kansas College, also requesting a donation. Soon now I'll be sending you more paintings. I'm beginning to get greedy—so many I'd like to keep for myself. Have a number beautifully framed now, and it's the first time in my life I have had this privilege of seeing more than two or three of my paintings framed—in my own home.

Had a letter from Eddie Schwartz saying the luncheon went off beautifully—he was impressed.

If ever some one with a camera should come along and offer to photograph the water colors of mine chez vous and Sue (in black and white or color) I would love to have a print of each—for the record.

Would you please tell Sue that I am returning soon the two paintings of Doyle. I feel a little embarrassed about doing this, but they are not quite what I expected somehow. Maybe at Sue's I saw his best things. I don't think these two are bad, mind you, simply not what I'd like to keep and hang here.

I made my 96th w.c. the other day, and hope today to make one or two more. And then—to part with them! I made a number of small ones, but I think I should send only the larger ones— in order to get the top valuation. Am still curious to know what valuation the Adult Education Counsel placed on the ones you mentioned.

A further, disquieting thought . . . I trust the ruling by the Revenue people doesn't mean that the valuation of donations is to be based on the "least" amount paid for one's work during the year???? Have a dim remembrance of some clause to that effect. Logically, it seems to me, whatever price or value was put on them by the institution's appraiser should be acceptable—why shouldn't the price vary with the institution and the painting?

Enough. . . . By the way, Playboy offers a full set of reprints of their 7 "serious" articles to date for one dollar. There is a very fine issue of the Texas Quarterly (Winter 1962) which you and Sue too might enjoy seeing—Univ. of Texas, Austin. Maybe I already asked them to send you a copy. Read the Celine correspondence with Milton Hindus.[1]   Up the Ashkenazis! Henry

---

1.   "Louis-Ferdinand Céline, Excerpts from His Letters to Milton Hindus," with an introduction by Milton Hindus, pp. 22–38. Also in the Winter 1962 *Texas Quarterly* was a reproduction of a Lawrence Durrell painting; an article by Stanley G. Eskin on "Durrell's Themes in the Alexandria Quartet"; reproductions of serigraphs by Sister Mary Corita, an art teacher in Los Angeles (the Community of the Immaculate Heart Sisters) with whom Miller studied silk screening for a time; and an article about Sister Mary Corita that quoted from Miller's *The Smile at the Foot of the Ladder*.

ALS, 1P.   6/1/63

Dear Elmer—   I'm enclosing announcement of exhibit at the Ankrum Gallery and something on Thoreau I find marvelous and would like to have back.[1] (Don't recall who wrote this or who sent it to me—found it at Big Sur weeks ago.)

The article in "Cavalier" will be on the stands any day now —by Lionel Olay—an interview.[2] I'm furious about the first paragraph. Had expressly requested him *not* to mention private matters. Aside from this, the thing isn't too bad, I guess.

I go to some violinist's home tonight to hear chamber music. Josuha Heifetz will be there and *Piatagorsky* (?) the cellist.[3] Should be interesting.

On w.c. #98 now!   Cheers! Henry

---

1.   The "something" on Thoreau has not been identified.
2.   Lionel Olay, "Meeting with Henry," *Cavalier*, July 1963, pp. 6–9, 84–87.
3.   Gregor Piatigorsky.

APS, 2SS.   6/1/63

Dear Elmer—   I just received a package from the Springer Galerie in Berlin, containing my w.c's, copperplate prints[1] and the portrait by Schnellock. Now I need that translation by Emil White, attached to Springer's letter, which I sent you recently. It tells me what to do about the copper engravings.

Sent you other items today by regular mail.

Hear that Cancer case comes up in Calif. State Court this coming week.   Henry

Have you read the "Black Muslims" in "Life"?[2]

---

1.   Writing about his Summer, 1962, European trip, Miller said: "From Paris I went to Copenhagen to visit my Danish publisher, Hans Reitzel. . . . Went one day with my publisher to visit Palle Nielsen, the famous graphic artist whose marvelous book of linoleum cuts on Orpheus and Eurydice I am proud to own. . . . While there I tried my hand at copper plate engraving—and caught the bug." Later in the same article Miller said that in Berlin he "made some more copper plates which the Galerie Springer will have printed shortly." See *Henry Miller Literary Society Newsletter* No. 11 (December 1962).
2.   Gordon Parks, "What Their Cry Means to Me," *Life*, May 31, 1963, pp. [22]–[33], [78]. Postscript written vertically in left margin on second side of postcard.

APS, 1S., AIR MAIL   6/11/63

Dear Elmer—   I did my 100th water color to-day, after a lay-off
of 10 days. The 99th—a big one—is quite something. Love to you
all.   Henry

APS, 2SS.   6/11/63

Mrs. Elmer Gertz
6249 N. Albany
Chicago (45.)
⟨California⟩ Illinois
Dear Mamie—   Elmer all right? It's so unusual not to hear
from him regularly that I feel a bit disturbed. I trust he's not ill.
Nothing urgent for him to tell me—just that he's O.K.
      I just read "The Slave" by I. B. Singer, brother of the Ash-
kenazi author.[1] Again, a moving book—of Poland in the 17th
century.   Cheers now! Henry

---

1.   Isaac Bashevis Singer, *The Slave*, tr. from Yiddish by the author and
      Cecil Hemley (New York: Farrar, Straus and Cudahy, [1962]).

TL(CC), 2PP., AIR MAIL, SPECIAL DELIVERY   June 14, 1963

Dear Henry: Mamie and I were deeply touched by your letter
to her inquiring about me. My unexpected silence has been due
entirely to the very great pressure of work. I got involved in some
litigation and other legal matters that have taken up so much of
my time that days have gone by without my realizing it. There is
so much I want to say to you, in addition to answering several
letters from you. I intend to write Monday morning without fail.
      Incidentally, I received a very beautiful letter from Abe Ratt-
ner, as beautiful almost as some of his paintings.[1]

I felt very badly when I learned the news from Roger Bloom. He sent me a very manly letter in which he tries to conceal his disappointment as best he can. Have you heard from his attorney as to why matters miscarried?

In addition to the professional matters that have kept me pre-occupied, I have had family and extra-curricular activities of a time consuming nature. Midge was graduated from college and Jack from high school, and Mamie has been completing arrangements for a Sabbatical. She needs a respite after twenty-five years of teaching.

Still no word from our Supreme Court as to your case. More to test the sentiment of the Court than for any other reason, I appeared before the best of our judges, Justice Walter V. Schaefer, and obtained leave to file some additional citations of law; namely, the ruling from the Wisconsin Supreme Court, the decision of the British Government,[2] and the granting of certiorari by the United States Supreme Court.

Justice Schaefer said that the Court was familiar with these recent decisions, but he gave no hint as to when the Court would pass down the too-long-delayed decision. They may be waiting for New York or California to decide the cases pending there. I am in touch with the situation everywhere in the country.

Last Saturday, the University of Chicago gave awards to Justice Schaefer and Judge Epstein, and in Epstein's case, the award was similar to the one I received from the University several years ago. The citation expressly refers to: "Judge Epstein's decisions opposing literary censorship (which) won him the 1962 Intellectual Freedom Award of the Illinois Library Association and other recognition." I am sure that Justice Schaefer took note of this.

I chatted with both judges without, of course, referring to the case that was on the minds of all of us.

Mamie and the children send their love to you.

Always yours, ELMER GERTZ

---

1.   In November 1962, immediately after seeing his friend's stained glass windows in a Chicago synagogue, Miller wrote Rattner from Gertz's

office and, at Miller's suggestion, Gertz and Edward Schwartz appended a few lines of appreciation. Rattner's letter to Gertz was a response to that communication.

2. As Gertz explained in *A Handful of Clients* (pp. 295–96), when *Cancer* was published in England the Government stated it did not plan to prosecute. Gertz wrote the British Public Prosecutor for confirmation of this decision, and on April 22, 1964, received the following reply from the office of the Director of Public Prosecutions:

"re *Tropic of Cancer*
"Dear Sir:
  "There has been no official statement with regard to the above book except that the Attorney General has stated that he was not going to institute proceedings under the Obscene Publications Act 1959 against Messrs. Calder, the publishers, in respect of the impending publication of the above book.
  "The following considerations are material:—
  "Under the Obscene Publications Act the definition of obscenity is tied to the circumstances of a sale. Thus the sale of a book to a child might offend against the Act while the sale of the same book to an adult might not.
  "Accordingly a decision not to prosecute in order to prevent a book being published does not and cannot preclude a subsequent prosecution if the particular circumstances of a sale are such as to justify a prosecution.
  "In this country criminal proceedings may be instituted by anyone.
  "Accordingly a decision by the Attorney General or the Director not to prosecute does not and cannot prevent the institution of criminal proceedings by any private person who feels aggrieved by the publication or sale of the book.
  "The following are defences to charges against the Obscene Publications Act, (1) that the book was not obscene, (2) that its publication was justified as being in the public interest on the grounds of the book's literary merit.
  "The former is solely a question for the Court and no evidence may be called. 'The book must speak for itself.' But expert evidence may be called as to the book's literary merit.
  "Accordingly whether a prosecution is likely to succeed depends to a considerable extent on the quality of the evidence available as to the book having or not having substantial merit.
  "If when a book is about to be offered for sale criminal proceedings are instituted and an acquittal follows, the sale of the book is likely to be greatly increased.

"Having regard to all these considerations the Director decided not to institute criminal proceedings at this state.

"I trust that these observations will be of assistance to you.

Yours sincerely,
Maurice Crump"

The four pages that Gertz addressed to Miller on June 17 were principally an item by item response to several of Miller's recent communications, but included mention of the fact that Bern Porter had "issued some more publications by or about" Miller. Gertz also commented that "while Sue was in Monterey, she picked up some sculpture made of bits of metallic junk," and asked how Miller liked the Schnellock portrait "on second view."

Miller's letter of June 19 was similar, though briefer—a one-page, closely typed answer that ranged over topics touched on by Gertz two days earlier. Among other things, he explained that he had crossed Bern Porter "off my list," asked if the sculpture Sue picked up was by Berenice Kussoy, and said of the Schnellock portrait that "there is something in it that smacks of the commercial artist." A personal note of interest was: "Eve (my exwife) and her husband Harry Dick Ross arrive today for the kids' graduation and will stay till week end. Lepska[1] left for Europe, on a guided tour, the other day and will return middle of August; I take care of the household." In a postscript he added: "Forgot to say I spent a very wonderful day at the College of The Immaculate Heart in Hollywood, the Art Dep't., where I was royally received, entertained and instructed by the Sisters, who are now famous throughout the world for their work. They will come to visit me soon and show me how to make serigraphs. Really joyous, liberated souls—Sisters Magdalen Mary and Mary Corita. Hurrah!"[2]

---

1.   Janina M. Lepska, Miller's third wife. The marriage, consummated in 1944, ended when Lepska left Miller in 1951. Their daughter Valentin was born in 1945, and son Tony in 1948.
2.   See H. M. 5/28/63, notes.

APS, 2SS. 6/26/63

Dear Elmer— Don't forget, if you will, that I want to donate as many "Night Life" books to various institutions as possible—at the regular price of $250.00 per copy. I gave Schatz (Israel) $5000.00 to build a home in Ein Hod and in return I am to pay myself back thru sale of N.L. books. I think I sold just one, so far this year. If people only knew it existed I think I could unload quite a few. I have a lot of announcements (A Dream of a Book) if needed.

In haste, Henry

TL(CC), 3PP., AIR MAIL June 28, 1963

Dear Henry: What an interesting and beautiful book! I refer to *Semblance of a Devoted Past*, which you were generous enough to send to me. I shall read every word of it. The first letters, of the period of *Tropic of Cancer*, which I have already glanced through, are intriguing, indeed.

What you say of Bern Porter puzzles me. In view of it, how can he presume to publish additional works by and about you? Before I had heard from you, I sent a little note of inquiry to him, asking for the details of the publications, but I have not received a response as yet.

The current issue of *The Reporter* has an article about **Giono**[1] which I am sending with this letter.

We are much disappointed that you will not be with us this summer. Perhaps, something or other will change your plans. It will be interesting to observe the contrast between the care of the children today and the problems of the earlier period, covered in the Big Sur book.

Midge is living with us while Hank is in camp. He and Ted have to spend a couple of weeks each summer in military camp for the next six years. Ted goes there soon, and Sue will then live with us. This is pleasant for Mamie and me, having the girls with us again, but very lonely for them. Damn this bellicose world!

Mamie's boy, Jack, is spending the summer in Mexico, where he will enhance his knowledge of conversational Spanish and Mexican folkways.

In response to an S.O.S. call, I visited with Paul Crump last Saturday. He is sorely distressed because of the primitive minds and base characters of those in charge of the prison. They seized the manuscript of a new novel that he is writing on the ground that it is obscene! They are, also, making it difficult, if not impossible, for him to get reading matter. I am trying to see what I can do, without worsening the situation.

Roger Bloom is more fortunate, at least in certain respects—despite his recent disappointment. He at least can read, write and think, and does not have to contend with the malice of his jailers. What have you heard to explain Eagan's failure?

The ways of prisons are strange. Some months ago I filed a suit for a federal prisoner who was almost blinded because of the negligence of the custodial help. The case was held in abeyance while the United States Supreme Court was considering a somewhat similar situation. On the last day of the session—the same day it passed on the prayer and Bible reading matters—it sustained such prisoner actions. Now I can go to town in behalf of this prisoner.

Yesterday I spoke at a farewell party for a brilliant and wonderful Jesuit priest, Father Kenealy, an authority on constitutional law and a warm personality. The party took place at Loyola University, a Catholic institution, and most of those present were well-known clergymen and lay leaders of the Church. I was rather surprised when I was asked to make the speech of the occasion, and particularly when a well-known priest introduced me in glowing terms. At the time I thought that he did not know of my connection with the *Tropic* case, but later in the evening he discussed that very case with me. He did not commit himself on the merits, but he admired my way of handling the case! One of those present was a very fine white lawyer from New Orleans, a Catholic, who has sacrificed himself financially through his defense of Negroes. He won a very important civil rights case in the United States Supreme

Court'a few weeks ago. Another such victory and he will be on the ash heap!

Finally, I was able to have a young associate of mine check the law very carefully, and now I will be able to proceed on the gifts. You will get a separate letter on this soon and, perhaps, the young man's notes, so that you may be informed.

Good or bad, I would like to get a photograph of the Schnellock portrait.

Sue says the sculptor in metal and junk whose work she purchased was male. She is not familiar with the woman mentioned by you.

You mention the graduation of your children. Both? Is there something special that Mamie and I could send them, something they would like?[2]

Gladys, my secretary, is back. Now matters move more easily. I hope that I can steal some time this summer for complete relaxation. Mamie is trying to go to gym daily and to play some golf, in addition to caring for the house. She is taking a Sabbatical to study Russian and art.

I have been hearing from the Leopolds while they are in Europe—the trip Nathan had to postpone for 39 years! Yesterday he was supposed to have luncheon in the House of Lords in London with two peers! I have finished the section of my book devoted to him; likewise the section devoted to the *Tropic* case.

Affectionate greetings from all of us.

Ever yours, ELMER GERTZ

---

1. Jean Giono, French novelist (1895–1970), whose home Miller visited in 1939, with Henri Fluchère. Article not located.
2. In the left margin of Gertz's original, adjacent to this paragraph, Miller wrote, "No!"

ALS, 3PP.   July 1st '63

Dear Elmer—   Before I answer some of the points raised in your last I want to tell you that in talking to my tax accountant today— a good man and knows his stuff—I gather that there is a *possibility* that no "self-created" donations may be made. Meaning, I could sell (*donate*) a Matisse but not my own work. However, this is not final. There is a mix-up in Wash. re. the new tax proposals. I'm waiting to hear from you and the young man you mention. Before making additional donations we had better wait till near the year's end when we will know more. I'm beginning to wonder if this proposed law would also exclude donations of MSS. and other documents of mine.

The Reporter text on Giono was written by a French woman I know, who gave me excellent write ups. Sad to think a man like Giono should have lost faith in his fellow man. Like Picasso, he's a compulsive artist. Gives me the shudders—his daily work program. (BUT read his "Blue Boy"[1]—a beauty.)

Haven't heard a word from Eagan. He must be away. Seems the fault was with the Federal end—but might be remedied yet.

Val graduated from High School and Tony from Junior High. Don't send any gifts! They get plenty—too much.

I may yet see you before the year is out. Who knows?

Now we have to get another script for the film—*and* get rid of the 2 producers. The more I see of Joe Levine the more I like him. Beneath the crass shell there's something touching about him.

Do you have "Max & the White Phagocytes"? If not, I may be able to get you a copy.

Yes, *Semblance* was a beautiful production. This bugger of a Porter has a knack of doing good book jobs. But impossible as a person.

I made my first silk screens Saturday—with the aid of two nuns and seven helpers. Will save one for you.

I repeat—tell Mamie to get "The Slave" by I. B. Singer (Straus, Farrar & Rinehart publishers.) It goes right to the marrow.

Just finished "The Lost World of the Kalahari" by Van der *Post* (?)² —simply marvelous. He dropped a sentence or two about the primitive Bushman woman never conceiving in time of famine or drought. Somehow, for a long time I have felt that this population explosion is a psychic (or cosmic) disturbance—portending preparation for a vast *de*population of the globe (atom bomb or whatever). It is not normal to procreate so prolifically. Birth control is no answer. *And,* I don't believe there will be a food shortage either. On the contrary! *But*—if you have never read about this wonderful (earliest) man, the Bushman, it's a must. He makes *us* look sick—and we *are* sick! What we have lost is incalculable.

I want to find out how reliable Van der Post is—he was born in Africa, nursed by a Bushman woman—and writes nostalgically about them. I'm more interested in them than in the (North) American Indian.

Give my best to Sue and Midge. Is Sue painting? Now I will do some etchings—and eventually creep back to writing. The kids keep me busy in strange ways. I give them lots of rope.

All for now. Give my best to Paul Crump too, please. What nonsense this, about obscenity from a lifer! Wonder if the President couldn't do something?   Henry

---

1.   Jean Giono, *Blue Boy,* tr. from the French by Katherine A. Clarke (New York: Viking Press, 1946).
2.   Laurens Van der Post, *The Lost World of the Kalahari* (London: Hogarth Press, 1961).

TL(CC), 1P., AIR MAIL   July 2, 1963

Dear Henry: In glancing through the current issue of Publishers' Weekly, I learned of the death of one of your favorites, John Cowper Powys. Did you know of this? I don't suppose anybody has written more warmly and appreciatively of Powys than you.

When I was in school, I occasionally heard him lecture and

was deeply impressed by his dramatic manner of presenting literature, but I don't really know his best works.

The very best from all of us.   Always yours, ELMER GERTZ

TL(CC), 2PP.   July 5, 1963

Henry Miller: By the time we get through with you, we are
going to make a tax lawyer out of you! Then you will cease to
paint, write, read or think; you will simply make money and vege-
tate. Is that not a beautiful prospect?*

I am sending herewith copies of three memoranda prepared
by my young associate. I believe they give you all the information
that you require, and, perhaps, more than you want. The last
memorandum relates specifically to the comments in the letter of
yours dated July 1, which I am now answering.

No, I do not have a copy of *Max and the White Phagocytes*,
although I have read the title story. Do please get a copy for me
if you can. *Max* is one of my favorite pieces by you.

One day I will read some books by Giono. At the rate I am
going with my own work, this is in the distant future. I spent the
4th of July doing about 20 or 30 pages of the chapter on the
Compulsion suit. Meanwhile, Mamie read almost 400 pages of
Plexus, in between gardening. This makes it imperative that we
get *Quiet Days at Clichy*.

I suppose you know that the California Supreme Court has
unanimously reversed the lower courts and holds *Tropic of Cancer*
to be constitutionally protected because not obscene.[1] I am annoyed with our situation here. Judge Epstein wrote by far the best
opinion of any judge anywhere, and our court is doing nothing
about it. I am sending you a copy of the letter that I have sent to
Barney Rosset today. It incorporates an idea that I have.

I do hope that we see you before the year is out. As much as
I enjoy corresponding with you, there is nothing more pleasurable
than meetings, particularly when the company is select.

Of course, I am absorbed by what you say with respect to Joe Levine and the *Tropic* film. I shall have to make a second effort at knowing him, to see if my first impression can be wiped out.

I look forward to seeing the silk screen that you are preparing. With the kind of assistance you had, the theme ought to be a holy one.

Mamie will get *The Slave* by I. B. Singer. She does not always follow my suggestions, but yours she does.

I have appointments in connection with Paul Crump today, tomorrow and Sunday. I hope as a result we can ease the situation. There has been a very great splurge of new publicity about the case. It is tending in the direction of an undercurrent in favor of the abolition of the death penalty. Crump's problems won't be solved until, somehow, we can get him out of prison.

This holocaust of which you speak so cheerfully, I hope that it does not occur until I get a chance to read *Nexus*, Volume II, and my own book.

I hope that all is placid in the Miller household. If Val and Tony get to be too much for you, ship them to us. Mamie is an expert in the management of the unmanageable.

Affectionate greetings from all of us.

Always yours, ELMER GERTZ

Encs.

*P.S. I would like to write to the art director of the Art Institute of Chicago to ask him if he would like a gift of some of your water colors. We could then get some sort of appraisal from this source and it might set a pattern. In view of what you have said, I do not want to write this letter without your prior approval.   E. G.

---

1.   This judgment pertained to a civil action, brought by a bookseller and a prospective customer against the Los Angeles city attorney (*Zeitlin v. Arnebergh*, 31 Cal. Rptr. 800), whereas the California case referred to frequently in preceding letters, which was being handled for Grove Press by the attorney Stanley Fleishman, was a criminal suit brought against Bradley Smith (see H. M. 2/25/62, notes). It was the latter case which the United States Supreme Court had previously agreed to

review, following an affirmance of Smith's conviction by an intermediate appellate court. Five months after the California Supreme Court ruled in the *Zeitlin* case that *Cancer* was not obscene, the United States Supreme Court refused to review that decision, and vacated the conviction in the Smith case, returning it to California (see Gertz, 12/19/63). Thus the book was cleared in California, but Grove Press lost an opportunity to have further litigation averted by virtue of a United States Supreme Court ruling. (See Rembar, *End of Obscenity*, p. 203.)

ALS, 2PP. 7/10/63

Dear Elmer— Just got yours of July 5th—what a slew of data! Still studying the dope. Though I see that the only new aspect is more paper work, which can be done. Will inform my tax a/c of what your friend says. Maybe he meant 1964, if any drastic change.

Yes, by all means ⟨get⟩ write the art director of the Art Institute of Chicago.

I will send you copy of "Max"—to keep. I take it, all you lack now is *Quiet Days*—right? I've got scouts out every where looking for copies. Soon as we get favorable decision from U.S. Supreme Court, I will give the green light to Rosset to publish World of Sex *and* perhaps *Quiet Days*. (Plexus & Nexus too.) But not *Sexus*.

The kids are taking care of me. Val is very good—cooks, cleans, irons, etc. beautifully. The boy is lazy—a play boy. (What happened to Playboy "HEFNER"?)[1]

Note what you say to Barney. Don't understand N.Y. & Illinois procrastination. Maybe they are waiting on the U.S. Supreme Court decision.

I just finished "Satan in Goray" by I. B. Singer—TREMENDOUS! Wish there were more of his to read. I dote on him. He's great.

Well, that's all for now. See next week's "Time" for write-up of my play at Spoleto Festival. They'll really slaughter it, I know.

Best to you all! Henry[2]

P.S. If you know any one who would like to BUY my water colors (at $250.00 per) do let me know. I can use some hard cash now.

Just heard that there may be a British paper back of "Cancer" arranged for soon—with "Panther".

Tell Mamie to see French film—"Sundays and Cybele" (Wonderful)[3]

---

1. Gertz, in his letter dated June 17, 1963, had said that "the Chicago Police arrested Hugh Hefner, the publisher of *Playboy*, because of some nude pictures of Jayne Mansfield."
2. Material from the beginning of the last paragraph through the signature was written vertically in the left margin of the first page.
3. Postscript is on a second page (reverse of first page).

APS, 1S.   7/10/63

Dear Elmer—   Just got wire from Rosset saying N.Y. State Supreme Court judged Cancer "obscene" by 4 to 3 decision. Wow! He has also just released Capricorn in paper back. Suppose that will be next on the calendar there. Am wondering how this decision will affect the Brooklyn case! Perhaps they will try again now to make me appear there. Though I intend to stand firm and remain here.   Cheerio! Henry

TL(CC), 1P., AIR MAIL   July 11, 1963

Dear Henry: I got your card telling the fantastic and unbelievable news that the New York Court has ruled four to three that *Tropic of Cancer* is obscene. This means that the attorneys will apply for certiorari to the United States Supreme Court, and this is all to the good, because of the precarious state of the appeal from California. I mean that, in view of the California Supreme Court decision, the United States Supreme Court might tend to hold the present case moot; but, with this new application from New York, the matter will be decided. It is reasonable to assume that certiorari will be granted. I just hope that the attorneys proceed with more than deliberate speed—with real speed! This means, too, that the Brooklyn case may proceed and they may try to extradite you. I quite agree with you that you ought to stand firm and not go to New York. This situation is so preposterous that it can only be resolved by a clear-cut decision by the United States Supreme Court.

After the California decision, I assumed that we had heard the last of this obscenity business with respect to *Tropic of Cancer*. It only goes to show that nothing in this world is certain. Rembar had misgivings about the case when I talked with him, although his associate Roberts was more confident.

Now, I am wondering again how all of this will affect our Illinois decision.

Affectionate greetings from all of us.

Always yours, ELMER GERTZ

bc: Karasik

P.S. What I say in this letter is based on the assumption that the New York case is in shape for an application for certiorari. I talked with Rembar and he is not sure.

TL(CC), 2PP., AIR MAIL   July 12, 1963

Dear Henry: The excitement about the New York opinion caused me to forget to answer your earlier—pre-New York—letter.

You will write to me, of course, after you have digested the various memoranda my associate prepared. Meanwhile, I am writing to the Art Institute of Chicago—copy enclosed. I hope the New York decision does not cast a shadow over this as well as other matters. I talked with both Rembar and Roberts in connection with the case. It seems that the judge who wrote the opinion for the court (if any one can be said to be the court's opinion in view of the abundance of opinions filed in the case—six, I understand) received an award from Citizens for Decent Literature (the Catholic censorship group) just a couple of weeks earlier!

Thanks much for telling me that you will send me a copy of *Max*; I look forward to getting it. The only major work I lack now is *Quiet Days in Clichy*. There are some offprints and works subsequently published in other volumes; but, except for these, my H. M. collection is complete, I think—thanks to you, Gotham Book Shop, Bern Porter and a few others.

When the United States Supreme Court decides, as we hope it will, you may safely re-publish the other works (save for *Sexus*). You now have at least two forms of immortality—as a creative spirit and as the most litigated author in history. Barney will miss a real bet if he does not publish a book about the *Tropic* cases. Barney needs real counselling now, and I hope he gets it. (Incidentally, I returned his letter yesterday, keeping a photostat of it. The letter illustrates what I mean. Before embarking upon such ventures, he should have consulted attorneys in various parts of the country, and not alone the East.)

The Hefner case is still pending in the courts on motions to dismiss. A change of venue was recently granted. Hefner's assistant is a friend of mine, who helped me in the Leopold case. She was rather irked that Hefner did not ask me to represent him.

I saw both the *Time* and *Newsweek* reviews of your play, and liked neither.[1] Can it be that I have lost my objectivity? My image of the play derives from your reading of it, and that was great. What are your second thoughts?

We are troubled by the illness of Midge's husband, Hank. He was ill when he went to Marine summer camp, worse all through those two weeks, and so bad when he returned that he landed in the hospital. We will know the full extent of his illness later today.

The very best from all.   Always yours, ELMER GERTZ

---

1.   "Theatre Abroad, Tropic of Corn," *Time*, July 12, 1963, p. 57: "The play is standard, consistent Miller all the way; that is to say, it is a show of dirty drivel"; "Tripe Topic," *Newsweek*, July 15, 1963, p. 53,

quoted with approval John Francis Lane of *The London Observer:* "It's a bright student play by a very old man."

On July 12 Miller wrote Gertz: "Here's something just came in I thought you might like to read. Return it some time, please." This may have been a letter from Barney Rosset dated July 9 on which Miller wrote: "Elmer—Thought you should see this. Henry." Rosset spoke of Tropic of Cancer *matters, and of having rushed to bring out a "paperbound edition of CAPRICORN," copies of which were being forwarded to Miller.*

Gertz informed Miller on July 16 that he had written the Art Institute of Chicago, and the next day thanked Miller for sending a copy of "Max."

APS, 2SS.   7/18/63

Dear Elmer—   A hasty word to ask you *not* to make any sale or donation of my w.c.'s just yet. Will give you reasons later. Just had long talk over phone with tax accountant.   In haste, Henry

TL(CC), 1P., AIR MAIL   July 25, 1963

Dear Henry: Immediately after obtaining your consent, I wrote to the Art Institute of Chicago with respect to the gift of some of your water colors. Then I got your card about holding up gifts. Immediately after writing I heard from the director of Fine Arts at the Art Institute that he will be delighted to look at your water colors. Now I am at a loss to know what to do. I think, for a lot of reasons, I ought to go ahead, but I won't do so until I hear from you. Please write immediately.

Have you heard anything from Barney or anyone else with respect to the New York situation?

Always yours, ELMER GERTZ

TLS, 1P   July 26, 1963

Dear Elmer,   Sorry about delay in writing you. I've grown a bit
lazy recently—good for me. Also had many interruptions again of
one kind and another.

The reason why my tax accountant asked me to hold off on
sales or donations of my paintings is because he has been trying to
get payments (back payments) for me from the Social Security
people. On my birthday this Dec. 26, I will be 72 and entitled to
regular monthly payments, no matter what my activities. But until
then I am not supposed to be actively engaged in painting, at least
to extent of making them for sale or donation. The accountant
thinks that toward end of this year, say October or November, it
may be O.K. for me to resume. Sounds a little strange, maybe, but
I skip all the technicalities, never getting this stuff clear anyway.

However, I see no reason why you couldn't show the paintings
to institutions meanwhile—if it can be quietly done!—and hold off
closing deals until later this year. It would probably help to determine what the paintings may really be worth, don't you think?

You see, the accountant has represented my painting activity
to being largely an avocation, and not a money making venture—
which has been true up until recently.

As for Barney and the N. Y. situation, I have heard nothing
new so far. I haven't had time to read the articles on Levine yet.
He is presently having difficulties with the two producers (of the
film), but it's no ⟨obliterated⟩ fault of his. So far I am in complete
agreement with him, and continue to like him. I also find—and he
admitted it himself—that he is not such a great "business man".
More of all this viva voce, when we meet again.

I am getting into good shape physically now. Am taking massages, which are just wonderful—besides swimming and bicycle
riding. Reason I get lazy is because with physical condition improved the brain doesn't work overtime, I guess.

I've found another wonderful writer—Laurens Van der Post,
the African (white) author, whose books I am going through now

one by one. Let me signal for you or Mamie this one—"The Lost World of the Kalahari"—by Morrow, N.Y.

Enough for now. Cheerio! Henry

P.S. My London agent is negotiating with a paperback firm there now for a coming paperback of "Cancer" in England—about a year or so from now—big deal. Presume you've seen Capricorn in paper back (Grove Press) just out. The Brooklyn people have made no move yet. I'm hoping they may not.

ALS, 2PP. Aug. 3rd '63

Dear Elmer—   The two paintings came and I am delighted to have them. I take it they are by the young man—friend of Sue & ⟨Jack⟩ Ted, yes?[1] Great thanks!

Enclose clipping. Have asked for copy of this form letter. Reminds me that I never saw the one the Chicago die-hards published.[2] Have you an extra copy of that leaflet?

Am getting into fine shape physically and will soon be working again.

More soon! Henry

P.S. Had letter from Roger Bloom the other day. He says Eagan is writing me. A long mysterious silence!

Roger says he's waiting eagerly for a word from *you*.

I believe Orvis Ross will be visiting me soon. Spent a wonderful evening last night with the concert pianist Jakob Gimpel.

Stay well!

And do read soon—"The Lost World of the Kalahari" by Laurens Van der Post (Morrow & Co. NY.)[3]

---

1.   Gertz had written on June 17 that he was sending as a gift the John Doyle paintings Miller had admired while in Chicago.
2.   See H. M. 3/5/62, notes.
3.   Postscript written on page two (reverse side of first page).

TL(CC), 2PP., AIR MAIL   August 5, 1963

Dear Henry: At last I sent you the two John Doyle paintings you liked so much when you saw them in my den and in Sue's parlor. They are gifts from Ted, Sue, Mamie and me. We hope that you enjoy them as much as when first you saw them.

Sue and Ted have done so much to their apartment. If you should see it, you will be pleased with the changes. One of your paintings has an honored place in it.

Did you notice that in a letter to the editor, printed in last week's issue of *Saturday Review,* the Books Editor of *Newsweek* calls *Tropic of ⟨Cancer⟩ Capricorn* one of the ten best books published in the last ten years?[1] And I suppose that you saw the review by Harry Gregory of *Black Spring* in *Gent.*

I have heard from Southern Illinois University Press that Wickes' volume of H. M. criticism will be out in October, with advance copies going to us in September. The press has offered to send me advance page proofs. I am trying to make up my mind as to whether to get copies of the book to members of our Supreme Court. Stanley Fleishman may want to get it to the United States Supreme Court.

What characters these Citizens for Decent Literature are! They are humorless as well as stupid. I have sent Hoke Norris a copy of the article from the L.A. *Times* as he is a student of such inanity. When justices of the highest court of a state (New York, e.g.) swallow that viewpoint, then I am afraid.

Barney has sent me a letter, telling me something more of the New York situation. It is not good there! It won't be straightened out, short of a United States Supreme Court decision; and it affects the distribution of *Cancer* throughout the country, since New York is the home base.

I shall try to get you a copy of the weird pamphlet the Chicago Citizens for Decent Literature put out; if not, I'll send you a photostat.

I have just become the attorney for Kroch's and Brentano's (largest book retailers in America) in an obscenity action. They're

accused of selling *Memoirs of a Woman of Pleasure (Fanny Hill).*[2]
At least, for a change, a big fellow is bothered, and not some poor
hole in the wall shop. Have you read the book, and what do you
think of it?

I shall try to write to Roger Bloom in a day or two. I must go
to Cleveland to take a deposition. When I get back I'll write.

Give Orvis Ross my best when you see him.

I am happy that you are well. Everyone says that I look well
myself, but I'm worn out. I desperately need some relaxation, and
don't know when I'll get it.

I'll let the Art Institute man select some water colors, if he
wants them, but won't formalize the gift until later, for the reasons
stated by you.

So much to say. Perhaps, more later.

The very best from Mamie and the kids.

Always yours, ELMER GERTZ

1. Richard W. Boeth, Books Editor, *Newsweek,* included *Tropic of
    Capricorn* in a list of the "ten best novels published in English" dur-
    ing the last ten years (*Saturday Review,* Aug. 3, 1963, p. 15). Also
    named were: Calder Willingham, *Eternal Fire;* Vladimir Nabokov,
    Lolita and *Pale Fire;* J. P. Donleavy, *The Ginger Man;* John O'Hara,
    From the Terrace; Kingsley Amis, *Lucky Jim;* John Updike, *Rabbit
    Run;* Norman Fruchter, *Coat Upon a Stick;* and Robert Penn Warren,
    The Cave.
2. In 1963, after two centuries of being shunned by reputable publishers
    and dealers, and universally regarded as just about the ultimate in por-
    nography, John Cleland's *Memoirs of a Woman of Pleasure* (*Fanny
    Hill*) was published by G. P. Putnam's Sons. Three years later, on
    March 21, 1966, the United States Supreme Court held that the novel
    was not obscene (*A Book Named "John Cleland's Memoirs of a
    Woman of Pleasure"* v. *Attorney General of Mass.,* 383 U.S. 413).
    For a discussion of this decision and of preceding litigation, see Rem-
    bar, *End of Obscenity,* pp. 222–490.

ALS, 2PP.   Aug. 5th 1964 [1963]¹

Dear Elmer—   Here is my chronology up to date. Had to give it to some Australian for some encyclopedia or what. May be a little mixed up at points in my travels—but not seriously. Now then, could you have a Xerox (?) copy made for yourself (if you want it) and another for Mme. Jacqueline Langmann—Prévér-enges—(V*aud*)—Switzerland. She is one of my best astrologers and is going to do a book about my life and work from the astrological standpoint—i.e. show the concordance between crucial moments in my life and the planetary aspects which substantiate the events. This is what I had wanted Sidney Omarr to do in his book²—but he was too lazy, I guess. Imagine if we had something like this for enigmatic figures like Rimbaud, da Vinci, Bosch, Dostoievski—*or*, above all—Gilles de Rais!!!

Just got four albums from the Jewish Music Archives Society— think I asked them to send you their catalogue. To me it's a God-send. For years and years I have been searching for records of Cantors Sirota and Rosenblatt.³ Now I have them and my heart leaps to my throat as I listen. There's one of Sirota's—*R'zei*—which really sends me. Imagine, when I was 18 and earning about $50.00 a month in the Atlas Portland Cement Co., I used to save up to buy a Sirota—single-faced disc at $7.50!!! God, what a difference to-day! How easy it all is now. But *because* of the sacrifices I made whatever I got went through and through me—and stayed with me.

"Blessed are the poor"! Don't forget—tell Mamie not to over-look getting (from library) "The Lost World of the Kalahari" by Laurens van der Post. Here is a man after my own heart. And what a man was that earliest of all mankind—*the Bushman*!

Enough! Cheers! Henry

---

1.   As is evident from Gertz's August 16 reply, this letter was written in 1963 rather than 1964.
2.   *Henry Miller: His World of Urania*, with Foreword by Henry Miller and Preface by James Boyer May [London: Published by Villiers Pub-lications for 9th House Publishing Co., Hollywood, Calif., 1960].
3.   Gerson Sirota and Joseph Rosenblatt. See Irving Howe, *World of Our*

Fathers (New York: Harcourt Brace Jovanovich, [1976], p. 193); Samuel Rosenblatt, *Yoselle Rosenblatt* (New York: Farrar, Straus and Young [1954]).

ALS, 1 P.   8/7/63

Dear Elmer—   I bought Fanny Hill in 1928 in Paris but couldn't read it through. Tried again later—no go. It bores me stiff. Recently an English publisher asked me to write a Preface for a new edition—I refused. (Wonder if it gets by in England and not here? Interesting reversal of usual pattern.)

Notice with great interest how some Southern communities flout the Supreme Court's ruling on the Bible.[1] What does our government do in such a case? Arrest a whole community—city, state, states? And if they can get away with this in the South, then why can't N.Y. citizens as regards "Cancer" or any other book?

Do you really think the U.S. Sup. Court will be influenced by Tom's and Wickes' books (mine)?[2] Aren't they "extraneous"?

I'm returning piece on Crump. Don't know what to make of it. More than ever now you should read *this* one of Van der Post's (so pertinent!)—"The Heart of the Hunter"—discusses all the things close to your heart—seriously—not a novel!

Must stop. Henry

1.   The United States Supreme Court had held, in *Abington School District v. Schempp*, 374 U.S. 203 (1963), that reading of the Bible and recitation of the Lord's Prayer in public schools, as part of school exercises, was "in violation of the command of the First Amendment that the Government maintain strict neutrality, neither aiding nor opposing religion." See Pfeffer, *God, Caesar, and the Constitution*, pp. 206–8.
2.   Thomas H. Moore, ed., *Henry Miller on Writing*, [New York]: New Directions, [1964]; George Wickes, ed., *Henry Miller and the Critics*, Carbondale, Ill.: Southern Illinois University Press, 1964.

TL(CC), 3PP., AIR MAIL   August 16, 1963

Dear Henry: Again I owe you a letter, and again I must plead the extraordinary demands upon my time. I feel as you did some months ago, just thoroughly disgusted on several counts. I hope that, like you, I will find myself in a cheerful mood. I am sure that some relaxation would help, but it is difficult to get away at this time. I have several appellate matters with deadlines and several trials that are set, and other pressing commitments.

Certain commitments I have met. I have delivered to the publisher the last chapter of my book, A *Handful of Cases*,[1] which is scheduled to come out early next year, and I delivered chapters in four other books, which are composite works. I owe a few book reviews and that is all. I wish I could say the same in other respects.

The American Bar Association had its national convention in Chicago and I would not have attended ordinarily, because it is not the kind of organization that appeals to me, but my friend Justice Arthur Goldberg was scheduled to speak and I would not miss him. When we chatted, he said, interestingly enough: "Elmer, I understand that you are in some censorship cases." I hastened to reply: "But we had better not talk about them." And he responded: "Yes, we had better not talk about them." I would not take the chance of his disqualifying himself in the *Tropic* or other cases in which I am involved.

While I think of it, I want to thank you for the very beautiful art magazine which you sent me. I enjoyed reading your article, a copy of which you sent to me in manuscript.[2] I liked the reproductions of your paintings. I am not forgetting about photographing the ones that I have, but it has been difficult to arrange at this time.

Mamie is in the midst of reading *The Slave*, and I will get the other book that you recommend. I will try to read both myself.

I am returning the original and a copy of the chronology that you prepared. I read it with very great delight. Of course, it gives me pleasure to know that you regard the period that we have spent together as worthy of record. I hope that you will, somehow, manage to visit with us again before too long. Is there any increased likelihood of this?

I have heard from the director of Fine Arts of the Art Institute of Chicago that the curator who will look at your water colors is away, and that as soon as he returns an appointment will be made.

I received another letter from Roger Bloom and will surely answer him, because I know what letters must mean to him. They have that effect upon me also.

Your comments on *Fanny Hill* intrigue me. I had never read it until I became the attorney. Of course, all forms of censorship, even of junk, fill me with anger, and I said as much in an interview with the Chicago Daily News. I might be embarrassed when that interview appears, but I thought I would chance it. I will send you a copy.

The reason I think the courts will be influenced by the books of Tom's and Wickes' is that a test of obscenity, or non-obscenity, is the degree of acceptability of a particular work. If it is a subject of serious writings, published by State university presses, then a court may be inclined to regard the book as acceptable. Another test is the motivation of the author. The material gathered by Tom from your writings would indicate the seriousness of your motivation in *Tropic* and other books. In brief, this is why I would like to have the books called to the attention of the courts. The manner of doing it will depend on the attorneys involved.

The article from the Los Angeles Times about the sealed envelope containing some of the more explicit passages from *Tropic* is fantastic. I showed the article to Hoke Norris. People who believe in censorship have aberrations of all sorts.

I share your interest in recordings of some of the cantors. Rosenblatt, in particular, gave me great joy. I like liturgical music in general. The less religious I become, the more I like of the practices and symbols of faith.

Enough for today.   Always yours, ELMER GERTZ

---

1.   Published as *A Handful of Clients* (Chicago: Follett Publishing Company, 1965).
2.   Probably Miller's "Are We Getting Anywhere" (see Gertz 4/30/63).

TLS, 1P.   Aug. 21, 1963

Dear Elmer,   Please don't feel you owe me letters. I know how
frightfully busy you are.

    I read about some of the Bar Association discussions, and got
the impression that the "lawyers" were ultra-conservative. Yesterday
I had a letter from Witherspoon's friend Lovett,[1] about the problems he has with the authorities in getting stays, etc. If he is talking
truth, then it is all frightful, abominable. I don't see much progress.
Also, talking to Stanley Fleishman on phone yesterday, I got the
dope on the U.S. Supreme Court and N. Y. State court issue. What
a mix up that is! Apparently, according to N. Y. law, Rosset can
not send Cancer out of State. Nor is it certain the Supreme Court
will accept the case—as yet. To a layman all these obstacles could
be eliminated in jig time, if there were the right will. It's all archaic.
And absurd. Letter from Barney this morning says he *is* ⟨sending⟩
selling books to other States, but drawing on reserves held outside
N. Y. He adds, "Whether or not this is legal no one seems to
know." Voila! Add to this that Stanley tried to persuade Barney's
new N. Y. lawyers to take Federal Court action to stop all this
nonsense, but doesn't know if they will pay heed or not. All this
is confidential, of course.

    I have just written my tax accountant to find out the earliest
date at which we can begin making gift donations of water colors
to the various institutions you had in mind. I hope by Nov. 1st, as
it will take a few weeks to settle all details, I imagine. I haven't
made a W.C. in weeks now—still taking it easy.

    By separate mail I'm sending you a photo which shows the
Schnellock portrait of me. I may get better, single shots of this,
shortly. I am with the nuns doing silk screens at my home in this
photo.

    I still haven't had a word from Eagan in Missouri. Seems ex-
tremely queer to me.

    As for Fanny Hill, of course I don't think it should be censored.
All I meant was that it was a dull book for me.

    But about Tom's book on my "writings"—that will be published by New Directions, not a University Press. Wickes' will be done by a Univ. Press. You shouldn't have any trouble getting advance copies or page proof copies.

Now we are getting offers from other countries about producing my play—latest Denmark and Holland. Production in London seems almost certain—and Rome (in Italian) a little later. Also in Paris, possibly in both English and French. The Spoleto affair was a mess, due to the producer, who just slaughtered it, I am told by the actor who played Harry in it.

Wonder if Justice Douglas will resign before case goes to Supreme court? *And*, who will replace him—that's the big question. It was wonderful to read about his third marriage—to a young chick. And his wife's marriage a few days later. Years ago this would be enough to finish a Supreme Court judge's career, what? Everybody loves Douglas.

After "The Slave" you must read "Satan in Goray" by Singer.[2] That tops them all—and is in its way absolutely unique. (At least for us poor Gentiles. I think even the Jews must shudder when they read it.) Enough. Best to you all. Who knows—I may be seeing you before I think. I leave it open.   Henry

P.S. Give my best to Hoke Norris, please.[3]

---

1.   Gene Lovitz (see Gertz 3/29/63).
2.   Isaac Bashevis Singer, *Satan in Goray* (New York: Noonday Press, 1955).
3.   Postscript handwritten vertically in left margin.

TL(CC), 2PP., AIR MAIL   August 26, 1963

Dear Henry: I am in receipt of the very interesting picture of your pals, the nuns, in the presence of Emil Schnellock's portrait of you. That is certainly one for the books.

I do hope that when you send me a copy of the Schnellock

portrait you inscribe it to me. I would love to have a good picture of you on my walls. If you would prefer to inscribe some other picture, rather than the Schnellock one, please do so.

Mamie has finished *The Slave*, by Singer, and she was so deeply moved by it that I can scarcely await the time for my reading it. We are both indebted to you for your suggestions with respect to books and writers, so long at it does not interfere with our reading your books.

I suppose you know that Rembar won the *Fanny Hill* case in New York.[1] I assume that the case will be appealed and one cannot be sure about the result, in view of the insane opinion with respect to *Tropic of Cancer* so recently handed down by the majority of the New York Court of appeals.[2]

I received a very fine letter from Justice Goldberg the other day. He is eager to see my book, A *Handful of Cases*. It should be out early next year.

Do let me know what your tax accountant finds out as to the date when we can begin making donations of your water colors.

I finally wrote to Roger Bloom. Perhaps, he has heard something more from Eagan. This whole situation has a rather fishy odor.

Did I tell you that Hoke Norris is going to be one of my witnesses in the *Fanny Hill* case here? My difficulty in that case is that my client is too eager to avoid controversy. I cannot say that I blame it, but this sort of puts us in wraps.[3]

Out of sheer stubbornness, I suspect that Justice Douglas will remain on the bench for a while. If he quit now, it would be like admitting that he does not have the right to lead his own kind of private life. I have heard him say on several occasions that he was one of the judges responsible for eliminating the tax exemption with respect to judicial salaries and that he feels that places him in the same position as any other citizen, subject only to the limitations of propriety in pending cases. He is right, of course.

Almost any time after Labor Day it is possible that our Supreme Court will hand down a decision in the *Tropic* case. We should be prepared for anything, but I will be shocked out of words if the decision is an adverse one.

Mamie and I send our most affectionate greetings.

Always yours, ELMER GERTZ

1. In New York, after being cleared by the trial court, *Fanny Hill* was held to be obscene in an intermediate appellate judgment, then declared not obscene by the Court of Appeals (*Larkin* v. *G. P. Putnam's Sons,* 14 N.Y.S. 2d 399, 200 N.E. 2d 760 [1964]).
2. See Gertz 3/12/63, notes.
3. This case did not go to trial; however in another *Fanny Hill* case Gertz testified during the trial as an expert witness for the defense and, when a conviction was forthcoming, filed an *amicus* brief. On appeal, the conviction was reversed.

TL(CC), 2PP., AIR MAIL   August 27, 1963

Dear Henry: I have just received a copy of the Brief of American Library Association as Amicus Curiae filed in connection with the *Tropic of Cancer* case now pending in the United States Supreme Court. You ought to obtain a copy of it from Stanley Fleishman. Although legalistic in form, it is really an exciting intellectual statement against obscenity statutes and their enforcement, without regard to the merits of *Tropic of Cancer* or any other book that may be involved. The heart of the brief is set forth in the following language:

"Though the literary merit of Henry Miller's *Tropic of Cancer* has been attested to by many scholars and critics, it is not the purpose of this *amicus* to take sides in evaluating the book in terms of literature. However, we unequivocally believe in the right of the individual to read or reject any book. In the exercise of self-determination in this respect, the individual rejects many books because they are dull, because they fail to speak to him in terms of his own experience, background, or interest, or because they offend his sensibilities. Let him who is offended put down the book he finds offensive and let him warn others of what he has found. In a great sense, this function is not solely that of the professional critic, or librarian, or any one who pretends experience and knowledge in evaluating literature, but, rather, it is the function of any one who can read, and on the basis of that reading, voice opinions."

I had a long conversation with Cy Rembar with respect to his victory in the *Fanny Hill* case in New York. The pseudo-morality of Fanny Hill seems to prevail over the unashamed robustiousness of *Tropic of Cancer*.

My associate has just returned from a trip to Greece and he brought back the enclosed circular in which reference is made to your views.   Always yours, ELMER GERTZ

Enc.

TL(CC), 1P., AIR MAIL   [*undated*][1]

Dear Henry: Your friendly relationship with the nuns calls to mind one of the most interesting stories of the twentieth century— the life of Dame Laurentia McLachlan, Abbess of Stanbrook in England. I first learned of the story when the *Atlantic Monthly* (or was it *Harper's?*) published excerpts from the correspondence between Bernard Shaw and this wise and witty Benedictine nun. Then a book about her, *In a Great Tradition*, was published by Murray in Britain and by *Harper's* here. This I read with great excitement, despite the theological content of much of the book. Finally, I acquired, just about a week ago, a book entitled, *The Best of Friends*,[2] dealing with the correspondence of Sir Sydney Carlyle Cockerell, for over a half century the director of the Fitzwilliam Museum and the intimate of Ruskin, Morris, Shaw, Hardy and many others. The biggest section of the book deals with Sir Sydney's correspondence with Dame Laurentia. I strongly recommend these things to you. As Shaw said, the lady was "an enclosed nun without an enclosed mind." She was "lively, learned, witty and loved by everybody; a happy woman, a fighting, holy human being . . ." She was one of the great authorities on liturgical music and illuminated manuscripts and other religious and secular matters. A devout Catholic, she loved all men of good faith. She was in the class of Father Kegan in Shaw's *John Bull's Other Island* and the canon in Carroll's *Shadow and Substance*. I would love to have your impression of her.

All our best.   Ever yours, ELMER GERTZ

P.S. Have you read Morris West's *Shoes of the Fisheerman?*[3] Is it just a clever work or really good?

1. From Miller's September 14 response to this undated letter, Gertz appears to have written it during the early part of the month.
2. *In a Great Tradition* (London: J. Murry, [1956]); *The Best of Friends*, ed. Viola Meynell (London: Rupert Hart-Davis, 1956).
3. Morris W. West, *The Shoes of the Fisherman* (New York: Morrow, 1963).

ALS, 1P.   9/7/63

Dear Elmer—   Here's a snap shot of the Schnellock portrait of me. May have better ones later. Just got seemingly very important book by Dr. Ludwig Marcuse (prof. of lit & philos.) called "Obszon." Quite a few pages devoted to me. Am handing it to Stanley Fleishman to look over in case he can use references to it in U. S. Sup Court case. Was published by Paul List Verlag—Munich— 1962.[1] Maybe a Chicago library has a copy.

More later.   In haste. Henry[2]

1. English version: Ludwig Marcuse, *Obscene* (London: Macgibbon & Kee, 1965). See pages 255–99 for chapter on Miller entitled "Los Angeles 1962: The Most Obscene Writer in World Literature."
2. On the flap of the envelope Miller wrote, "Believe car will be delivered in next 10 days!"

TLS, 1P.   Sept. 10, 1963

Dear Elmer: More, for the moment, about this book of Dr. Marcuse—"Obszön." I have almost finished with it now—the part about myself, latter part of book. Very hard sledding for me, since I'm too lazy to consult the dictionary. I called Stanley Fleishman about it, thinking maybe he could read it in German and make use of some of it in his brief. Says he can't read German. Also, it may be too late to insert more references in his brief, though he said he might if I got it to him soon.

Today I wrote Rowohlt in Hamburg, my publisher, to see if he could get a professional translation made—of just the part about me—and what it would cost. I met Dr. Marcuse in his office in Reinbek a couple of years ago. Don't know why he, Rowohlt, did not publish the book instead of Paul List—but maybe Marcuse was tied up with List Verlag.

I also wrote List to find out if any British or American publisher is translating it for publication in near future—haven't had reply as yet.

My friend Emil White, of course, could read it, but it would take loads of time and he would not give me a professional translation. Just the gist of it.

Have you any thoughts on the subject? The book looks very important to me. A scholarly work, and strong in language. Of course, maybe it's a bombastic piece of work—that I can't tell. I asked Rowohlt to tell me what the critics thought of the book.

Marcuse used to teach in this vicinity—one of our big universities, but last I heard he was in a sanatarium somewhere in Germany or Switzerland.   Enough—must stop here. Henry[1]

---

1.   Signature both typed and signed by hand.

TLS, 1P.   Sept. 14th, 1963

Dear Elmer,   Yesterday I had a long session with my tax accountant, a wonderful man, by the way, and of the faith, and he
said we could now go ahead and make the donations of water colors. Should try to get it all settled by Dec. 10th, the latest. It seems
that if I am not to be utterly ruined by the income taxes, I must
try to make donations up to $20,000 this year. Staggering sum. And
in any case, I must also make a further cash payment before end of
year of around $10,000. I gave away so much money again that now
I am at my wits' end to make ends meet. However, I expect to
make it . . .

As best I remember, I gave you something like 15 to 18 paintings, did I not? Do you think you can place all these with bona fide
institutions—and with what result, financially? And if there were a
real show of interest, do you suppose you could place more? I estimate roughly that at best the ones I gave you to dispose of won't
yield much more, maybe less, than $3500.00. Bryn Mawr will prob-
ably take almost $2,000.00 worth, and U.C.L.A. another $1200.00
worth. All this comes to less than $7,000.00, assuming all goes well.*
I can, of course, dispose of more of my MSS. and other documents,
but hate to do this if I can avoid it. I ought to have an ace in the
hole in case of an emergency, I feel.

You returned a copy of a letter from a lawyer named Philip H.
Meltzer regarding a possible donation to Contemporary Art Associates at Aspen, Colorado. Are you bearing this in mind too?

Anyway, now I shall get back to painting again, in case there
is need for much more of my work—for donations.

I am just rereading a recent letter of yours about books dealing
with nuns. I doubt that I will have time now to look into these,
however fascinating. No, I never read "Shoes of the Fisherman."
(I am now slowly reading a marvelous documentation on Celine,
put out by a French revue called L'Herne.) And I have mss. to
read and report on—by others, naturally. Like yourself, it's a per-
petual battle with me to find time to do my own work. This is the
negative side of "Success."

About "success." The accountant was horrified to learn that after earning about $140,000 these last two years I had less than $5,000 to my name, of which I gave the government yesterday $3500. I've got to change my ways, drastically, if I'm not to become a bankrupt individual. (I don't need to tell you, I guess, that I spent hardly anything of all this on myself.)

Well enough of all this. To work! At least I'm still healthy.

My best to Mamie, the youngsters—and a Happy New Year to you all!   Henry

*I may persuade U.C.L.A. to take two portraits of me, as donations, which may come to $1500 or so. (One of them will be Schnellock's. The nuns are now making color photos of this for you and me.)

P.S. Enclose something Emil White sent me. Suppose Rosset gets this mag. If not, maybe he ought to read it . . . Rowohlt, Hamburg, writes that he has already sold 50,000 hardbound copies of new trade edition of "Cancer" (in German, and it's still going strong).

P.P.S. And how about further donations of "Into the Night Life" at $250.00 per?[1]

---

1.   Final postscript written by hand, vertically, in left margin.

TLS, 1P.   Sept. 24, 1963

Dear Elmer,   Further about the damned water color donations. (made six new ones, two or three Jewish themes) in last two days. Must keep working if I'm to make it. Waiting to know if I can send you more, or if it's too much of an imposition. I assume your good secretary is doing the major part of the work on this, and you may be sure I will take care of her later and am deeply grateful. Talking with Lepska last night, she suggested that I try more institutions, among them these—the Seattle Museum of Modern Art, the Phillips Memorial Gallery, Wash. D.C., Sarah Lawrence College, Bennington College, Dartmouth College, Boulder Colorado University, San Francisco Museum of Art, and so on and on. . . .

At Dartmouth I have an old friend, the English Professor, Herbert West, if he's still alive and teaching. At Boulder I have Wallace Fowlie, Head of the French Dept. Years ago I met the head of the Phillips Gallery, but maybe he's dead now. I think I'm known at Bennington—Fowlie used to teach there.

Now then, should I write them direct to find out if they are interested, or would you? Don't hesitate to say if I am giving you too much work. I'm quite aware of all that is involved. But I'm sort of standing on my head now—must get an awful lot accepted and by the 10th of Dec. at the latest.

I also wrote Tom Moore to see if he could suggest any places in the mid-West, and Carmelita Keller, a dear friend in Houston, Texas, who has connections with galleries and museums in Texas.

If I can do 20 or 25 new ones in the next three weeks or so—and place them!—my problem would be solved.

Did I tell you I started a one act play, a burlesque? Takes place in a court room, the author on trial for writing obscene book; my idea is to make a thorough travesty of legal procedure and terminology, the judge a half-wit (as featured in old time burlesque), the language crazy, the witnesses all caricatures, etc. etc. Am piecing it together—do bits here and there at a time. If I can do what I have in mind it should prove a riot. My mind is jumping again—always does when I am pushed to the wall.

Tomorrow I will have a visit from Ziva Rodann, an Israeli actress from Haifa and Tel Aviv—a young beauty, they tell me.[1] She is crazy about my books. We will go together to see " 'Tis Pity She's a Whore" at U.C.L.A. theatre. One of my favorite plays—this and "Le Cocu Magnifique" by Crommelynck.

Enough now. Ta ta. Carry on.   Cheers! Henry

1.   Miss Israel of 1960. For a picture of her, and of Miller's portrait of her, see the *Los Angeles Times*, Sept. 17, 1964, Part 7, p. 1.

Once more Gertz sent a three-page response, on September 30, in which he carefully addressed most of the topics in Miller's recent letters. He said the Singer book *Satan and Goray* was out of print; that his secretary, Gladys Fuller, was proceeding to handle gifts of the water colors and Miller could send more paintings if he wanted to; and that he would make donations of *Into the Night Life* but had no copies. He also reported that Eddie Schwartz "had read in a column that the District Attorney in Brooklyn had withdrawn the charges against *Tropic of Cancer* and you." Of the Chicago case, Gertz said: "I had been keyed up to expect a decision in our Illinois *Tropic* case; instead, the court, once again, passed the case. Theoretically, it may be decided at the end of October, but one can never tell. The Court may be so divided that it will want to await the United States Supreme Court decision, in which case months may go by; and once the United States Supreme Court decides, there is no point in our decision—unless the United States Supreme Court simply remands the case. You know there is that technical possibility because of the latest California decision involving the book."

TLS, 2PP.   October 2nd, 1963

Dear Elmer,   Sorry you had to write me such a long letter, considering all the burdens you have. Note what you say about Chicago lack of trial and the rumor about Brooklyn matter, of which I know nothing. Plexus has just come out in England, published by Weidenfeld and Nicholson, who will also bring out Nexus. In France the Durrell-Miller c/s has just come out, by Correa, with great fanfare—and serialized in Figaro-Litteraire. The French TV wanted to come here to interview me about it, but I reneged. I saw Ben Grauer[1] about ten days or so ago and he is trying to get together material, for some time next year, to make stage presentation of readings from my works—with about five or six actors—something like the "Spoon River Anthology" done here at UCLA recently. I had a long letter from Leonard Ross (lawyer) who edited (?) the Frank Harris book. He says it's in its 2nd edition already.[2]

I'll give you more dope, or rough copy, later on, of the burlesque play. I am writing it helterskelter, in bits out of order, as ideas hit me. It violates all court procedure, of course, the judge doing a lot more talking and questioning than usual. Does one call the attorney for defense just that, or is there another way of refer- ring to him. When do witnesses usually come on? Of course I can disregard that too. Am undecided whether to have a jury or not— at first thought to have them with huge masks, representing jackal, hyena, fox, etc. And what about audience? Is there always an audi- ence? This may mean too many people in the play. I have all sorts of crazy notions but wonder if I can squeeze it all into one act of about, say, one hour and quarter or one hour and a half. I take it the box where the accused stands (and perhaps the witness too) is at left or right of the judge. (I may use three judges—for more funny business) But wait and see. . . .

Now, about the donations. I just had a letter from Tom Moore saying that the Walker Centre (Art gallery??) in Minneapolis will take all the water colors I wish to send them. And will evaluate at $250 (the usual size ones) if I send letter from Ankrum Gallery here, showing that I sold at these prices. Too good to believe. I just wrote Tom to make sure that they are bona fide for Treasury De- partment—on gifts. I could work direct and save you this trouble, or, if it is better to have procedure through a lawyer, then turn it over to you, to offer donations and get proper letters of acceptance from them. What do you think? (Am beginning to wonder if Treasury Department will put up a howl about all these donations —since it is so obviously being done to reduce gross income???) Further, I recall last year's letter from my attorneys here when writing U.C.L.A. Library; they mentioned that I was making the donation of MSS etc. because of my high regard for the University and appreciation of all they had done for me. Is this necessary— this line of approach?

As for Night Life books; yes, I can get my ex-wife Eve at Big Sur to mail copies out, but would like to know how many you think you can dispose of—at $250 per. And should I wait and have her mail direct to the various institutions, or just to you?

Now then, if Walker Center can and will accept all I wish to send, if this is legit., maybe I won't send you more just yet. (Unless you get urgent requests for more from your people.) Incidentally, with the Jewish holidays coming on, and having met and become good friends with a charming young Israeli actress—Ziva Rodann— I painted a half dozen big ones with Jewish themes. Two of the best I gave to Jakob Gimpel, the concert pianist, who has become a good friend of mine. (He is from Lvov, Poland, originally—and Jewish, of course.) One night here we had seven very wonderful musicians here, who played all night for us, including Gimpel. Tremendous. And all Jewish. (Amazing what virtuosi the Jews are, eh? Not always so good as composers, though.) You know the joke about the Jewish mother who is always after her son to practise? He is coming home from long tour, worn out, and feeling sick. She meets him and says: "What's the matter son, are you sick? Come straight home—and lie down and practise!" (I hate these Yiddisher mammales!) But they get their boys to the top, what! (Whereas our kids, we Goyim, are just lazy, dispassionate, and prefer TV to homework of any kind.)

This is getting long, but I must continue. . . . The other day, looking for a passage on Sirota (whose wonderful recordings I now have—and if you don't you must!) ⟨and so⟩ I read Nexus all through to find it. I was almost overcome by my own writing. This is a marvelous book, I find, about the Jew in my life, music, art, literature, and the struggle (for a Goy) to become an artist. I almost wept with joy. Now I think it superior to most of the other books I wrote; it's from the center of my being. Mad, a good part of it. Sublime even, sometimes. Enough!

Don't recommend me to read more about censorship, etc. I've had a good bellyful. Did I tell you that Marcuse's book has been accepted by my new English publishers—Mac Gibbon and Kee? And an American publisher is in the offing, I hear. My agent in Paris is handling the book for Marcuse. I suppose you've seen or read about Alec Craig's book on the subject?[3]

Amazed that Satan in Goray is out of print. I am writing the Noonday Press to make sure and to find out if we are to have more of Singer's books soon—in translation. He drives me crazy, this wonderful Yiddish writer.

Another little thing . . . I asked Ziva Rodann to read to me from "Cancer" in Hebrew. Lo and behold, it sounded like the cooing of a dove. All the harsh guttural sounds were eliminated— she does it purposely, she says. She thought the translation very good.

About the Greek "book"; well, it's mostly Anne Poor's drawings. My text is only about 15 typed pages long—that's the whole text. So it's hardly a book. Viking brings it out, at about ten bucks, I believe.

Do give warm greetings to Gladys Fuller whom I remember vividly. When the smoke clears away I shall see what I can do to make her happy. I wish I had a secretary like her. I have been corresponding with a beautiful Chinese woman in Hong Kong (actress, director, etc.) whom I thought might make a secretary—but she'd be better as a concubine, I imagine. Again, enough! now I must think about money—and how it gets that way. Love to Mamie and to all the youngsters. Love all around, as my wife Evie always says.

Whew, what a tirade . . . Forgive me!   Henry

P.S. Have you seen a most interesting pamphlet (about 4 pages or more) on sex problem by the Quakers of England?[4]
Forgot to say I am dealing direct with Bryn Mawr College—may take (6) or more.   HM.[5]

---

1.   Miller had made recordings with Ben Grauer in 1956 and in 1962: "Henry Miller Recalls and Reflects," two 33⅓ R.P.M. long-playing records, ed. Ben Grauer (New York: Riverside Records, 1956); Henry Miller, "Life As I See It," one 33⅓ R.P.M. long-playing record, ed. Ben Grauer (New York: Offbeat Records, 1962). References to these records and to Grauer may be found in Miller's correspondence with J. Rives Childs (Wood, ed., Collector's Quest).
2.   Sentence added by hand at end of paragraph. The Grove edition of Harris's autobiography was edited by John F. Gallagher who, in his prefatory acknowledgements, thanked "Arthur Leonard Rosse, Literary Executor of the Frank Harris Estate, not only for the privilege of editing My Life and Loves, but also for his advice and endless patience." See also Gertz 8/29/62, notes.

3.   Alec Craig, *Suppressed Books* (New York: World Publishing Co., 1963).
4.   Postscript written by hand, vertically in left margin of first page.
5.   Written on envelope flap, by hand.

TL(CC), 2PP., AIR MAIL   October 9, 1963

Dear Henry: I had a conversation last night that will interest you. George Leighton,[1] a famous Negro attorney, and I spoke at Temple Sholom, the largest reform congregation on the North Side of Chicago. Our theme was the civil rights explosion. The audience was a very large one and deeply interested. After the meeting a Mr. William Levine came up to me to chat. It turned out that he has been the head barber of the Covenant Club, a leading Jewish club, for forty years. I suddenly remembered, as he talked to me, that our friend Roger Bloom had mentioned him once or twice. I referred to this fact in my conversation, and Mr. Levine was at first startled and then proceeded to give me a thumbnail sketch of Roger.

It appears that Mr. Levine has always been deeply interested in prisoners, and for many years has visited the different institutions of the state in order to instruct inmates on barbering and to counsel them generally. Thus, he got to know Roger, when Roger was an inmate in Stateville, and he took to him immediately. According to Mr. Levine, he and a Rabbi Irving Melamed (whom I also know) got so absorbed in Roger that they did all that they could to get him released on parole and ultimately succeeded. According to Mr. Levine, Roger behaved beautifully for six months, and the two of them were quite delighted over their role in the matter. Then, Roger got hold of a gun and went down to St. Louis, where he held up a currency exchange and got $3,000. It was so easy a job that he tried another one, and this time he was caught and sent to prison.

I know your viewpoint—you are not interested in a guarantee of any success on the part of Roger. You just feel that he ought to be out of prison, and you will hope that this time he makes it. Still,

I feel that I owe you this story, for whatever use you care to make, or not make, of it.

I received a long and very persuasive letter from Roger yesterday, in response to one I sent to him only a few days ago. When I write to him I will do no preaching. I will try to be as unselfconscious as if I had never talked with Mr. Levine.

Mr. Leighton, with whom I shared the platform last night, has been involved as attorney in several celebrated capital cases. He is one of the very few Negro attorneys of our community who has represented white clients in both criminal and civil matters. At one time he was Paul Crump's attorney. He is now involved in a downstate case, involving a white man sentenced to death for the rape-murder of a child. Mr. Leighton is completely persuaded of the innocence of this man, where he is usually rather cynical about the questions of guilt or innocence. He held us spellbound, when we got together after the session at Temple Sholom and exchanged stories about our cases. I got so absorbed in his story about this particular case that I am going to make it a point to attend the habeas corpus hearing on the matter on November 6, regardless of what else I have to do at that time.

I have finally seen a copy of the book, *Henry Miller and the Critics*, as I suppose you have. I am still perplexed by the question as to whether or not, and how, I might get the book into the hands of at least some members of our Supreme Court, for the reasons I have heretofore discussed with you.

Mamie and the children send their most affectionate greetings to you.   Always yours, ELMER GERTZ

---

1. Leighton, who graduated with honors from Harvard Law School, is now (1977) a United States District Judge in Chicago, and an adjunct professor at the John Marshall Law School. For more about Leighton see Gertz, *A Handful of Clients*, p. 321.

APS, 1S.   10/17/63

Dear Elmer— Have copy of Marcuse's book (German)—do you still want one? Will be pub. in England. Bklyn case postponed till January now. Was up for trial today. *Plexus* out in England and *Cancer* in Brazil (Portuguese). Bryn Mawr has taken 5 W.C's and may take more. Trying to find libraries to take Night Life book. Have you placed any paintings yet? Am in love again.

Henry

TL(CC), 1P., AIR MAIL   October 21, 1963

Dear Henry: I will write to you on other matters very soon, but I though that you would be interested in the enclosed material about *Tropic of Cancer*, which emanates in California but which I picked up here in Chicago at the convention of Citizens for Decent Literature.

Saturday I had an extremely interesting experience. I spent the day with Louis Nizer, the author of *My Life in Court*. During the course of the day we visited Paul Crump at the penitentiary. Perhaps, I will tell you more of this later.

Just be patient with me.

The very best from Mamie and the children.

Always yours, ELMER GERTZ

Encs.

TL(CC), 1P., AIR MAIL, PRIVATE AND CONFIDENTIAL

October 23, 1963

Dear Henry: This little story will amuse you. A lawyer of my acquaintance was in a bar with a member of the Illinois Supreme Court, and they both drank far more than they should have, the only difference between the two being that the lawyer had his wits about him. When the judge was sufficiently plastered, the lawyer asked him, "Why hasn't the court handed down the *Tropic* decision?" At this point the judge should have walked out on him, but, instead, answered, "There are enough *Tropic* decisions throughout the country without our writing another one. We are going to wait until the United States Supreme Court hands down its decision." Then, as an after word, the judge added, "Personally, I think it is a . . . dirty book."

Assuming the lawyer gave me an accurate report, and I have no reason to doubt his word, I would say two things: (1) We won't have a decision in Illinois until we don't require it, by reason of the Supreme Court decision; and (2) If other judges feel as this one does, it is just as well that we wait.

The lawyer argued a bit with the judge, in a pseudo-drunken manner, saying, "Don't you know *Tropic* is available everywhere in the state, including two blocks from the court house?" The judge expressed ignorance of the fact and seemed rather surprised. My informant sayeth nothing further.

I have been feeling rather lousy, largely because of overwork. I am not forgetting my promises to you and they will be redeemed.

Always yours, ELMER GERTZ

ALS, 1P.   10/25/63

Dear Elmer—   Got your recent letters re Cancer, judges, leagues for Purity—etc. Pass on . . .

Bryn Mawr is taking (5) more W.C's—just shipped—and (1) Night Life. The Westwood Art Assoc. here will take (10) W.C's and 15 Night Life books. Colby College, in Waterville, Maine, has taken two. Walker Art Center, in Minneapolis, will take a few.

I still need to raise $10,000 more! Want to remind you or your secretary not to overlook the Art place in Colorado (Aspen?) or the college in Fort Hays, Kansas. My friend there—the Librarian—might possibly be induced to take 5 or 6. I'm working overtime.

Enclose letter from Bowinkel which might be of use. Will have a better typed one shortly.

My friend Seferis, the Greek poet,[1] just got the Nobel Prize, I see.

Down with judges and juries! (Best to Mamie)   Henry

---

1.   Greek poet-diplomat George Seferis (pseud. Giorgos Sefiriades, 1900–1971), Ambassador to the United Nations (1956–57), and Ambassador to Great Britain (1957–62). As revealed in *The Colossus of Maroussi*, Miller became acquainted with Seferis in 1939, through Lawrence Durrell. See also references to Seferis in the Durrell-Miller correspondence for the years 1940–53.

Under cover of a brief note dated October 30, Gertz sent Miller a letter from Roger Bloom.

ALS, 1P.   10/31/63

Dear Elmer—   I just read your text in the Kentucky Law Journal[1]—it's wonderful! How did you ever find time to do it? This piece will be read far and wide, I feel, and not only by the legal gents.

Mr. Batt wrote me he sent the reprint of "obscenity & the Law of R." to all *nine* judges (or is it 7?) on the U. S. Supreme Court. I wonder if that was a good move? Seems to me, if I were one of them, I wouldn't want to be "influenced" in this manner. What do you think? Must stop—am off to the Valley for overnight.   Henry

P.S. Rice University in Houston, Texas, will take (10) of my W. C's *and* a N. L. book—have a good old friend there. A dentist friend may have me donate (10) more to a local art group—plus (15) copies of N. L.—all at my figures.

---

1.   "The 'Tropic of Cancer' Litigation in Illinois," 51 Ky. L. J. 591, 592–93 (Summer 1963).

TLS, 1P.   Nov. 6, 1963

Dear Elmer,   Just a little word to ask how your secretary is doing about the placing of my water colors. I keep thinking of time
always; can't afford to get bogged down at the last minute. Also,
I wonder if she is able to get the appraisers of the various institutions to whom you are making donations to agree to my valuation
of the paintings. As you know, the larger ones, normal size, I expect
to be valued at $250.00 each; I think I also gave you some smaller
ones, and believe when I sent them I suggested they be valued at
$100 or $150, don't remember which now. Am I right?

If there were a serious discrepancy between their figures and
mine I would prefer to have the paintings back, as I believe I can
persuade Bryn Mawr and the Westwood Art group to take still
more, and at my figure. So, do let me know soon, won't you?

I'm giving U.C.L.A. library today a half dozen water colors,
two oil portraits of me (by others) and a batch of MSS and letters,
which I trust will just about cover my requirements.

After I paint another dozen or so water colors I hope to get
back to the one act play, and perhaps send you a rough draft, when
it seems near shape.

Am always busy, always pestered with demands, chores of one
sort and another. No rest for the weary.

Soon I'll send you an enlarged photo of my wall here, which
will interest you, I think. Am waiting for more prints. This is like
my blackboard: if it were horizontal I would also dance on it.

All the best now to you, Mamie and the youngsters. I have
been reading the life of Alexander the Great lately. He is one of
the men I have a great respect for—a fabulous character who
achieved the seemingly impossible. (And who, to my surprise, I
find had excellent ideas about a world state. I prefer him infinitely
to his tutor Aristotle.)   Cheers! Henry

TL(CC), 1P., AIR MAIL   November 7, 1963

Dear Henry: I have been up to my neck in work, complicated by a secret visit of Nathan Leopold. We had managed, somehow, to keep the newspaper people from learning of the visit until yesterday. Now it is out, and it complicates my life somewhat. Keep the matter under your hat for the time being. Later I will tell you more of this fascinating story.

I am told that there is a wonderful picture of Ziva Rodam, the Israeli actress, and yourself. I would love to get a print of it.

The very best from all of us.

Sincerely yours, ELMER GERTZ

Gertz wrote again on November 12, explaining why he had not proceeded in "the matter of the gifts," adding, "If there is any form of letter of gift which you have been sending out to the others to whom you have given books or paintings, I wish you would send me a copy of it."

TLS, 1P.   Nov. 15, 1963

Dear Elmer,   Just a word to say, with regard to the donations, that I write no special form letter—merely ask if they are willing to accept donations (at my valuation).

I am going to send you photos soon—one of Ziva and me, and one of my wall here, which you will find has a special flavor. Simply waiting for more prints from the photographers.

Wait to hear more about Leopold. Sounds intriguing and mysterious.

I'm off to Hollywood now, to be given a special private showing of Greta Garbo and John Gilbert in "Devil and the Flesh." Have been waiting 25 years to see this film.

All the best now—"love all around." Henry

TL(CC), 1P.   December 2, 1963

Dear Henry: Tom Moore has asked me to send you the manuscript of Henry Miller on Writing. I understand you want to double check the galleys.

   With this letter I am sending several others, to make up for lost time.

   The very best from Mamie and me.

                              Always yours, ELMER GERTZ

cc: Mr. Thomas H. Moore

TL(CC), 3PP., AIR MAIL   December 2, 1963

Dear Henry: I have been deeply concerned about the gifts of pictures and books that I undertook to arrange for you. When I thought that I had time for the task, you asked me to withhold the matter for the time being. Then when you wanted me to proceed, I could not do so, and the matter preyed on my mind. I feel better now. The incomparable Mamie is taking this task upon herself and it will be done in the next day or two. We have already purchased all of the wrapping material (of a kind to protect the pictures), and Mamie will do the packaging herself immediately. I will prepare the letters of gift and sign them in your name; sending copies to you and retaining a set for myself. Mamie will then personally deliver those for donees in and around Chicago and the others will be mailed out. As to the pictures that are in our possession, there will be no questions or problems for you. When we run short of pictures, we will tell you how many we need, so that you can send them on to us. As to the books, *Into the Night Life*, we will have to give you instructions.

   Now let me see if there is anything covered in any of your recent letters that I have neglected, because of the pressure of work.

   1. If you can spare a copy of the Marcussi[1] book, please do so.

   2. I don't think that Mr. Batt was wise in sending your essay

on obscenity to the Nine Old Men, good as that essay is. They might resent it. Still, one can never tell how the judiciary reacts and what influences them. This essay may be the very thing to influence them to our way of thinking. I am afraid that we won't know for months. Meanwhile, the Illinois Supreme Court takes it as a reason for delay. Our case has gone over to the January term.

3. I look forward to the photo of Ziva and you, and, if you will pardon a mere numeral to encompass a new love, I am eager to know more about it. Likewise to see the photo of your wall.

4. Of course, Ben Grauer's plans for a stage presentation of your works is exciting and feasible. I think it can be highly successful artistically and financially. I would love to learn more of the details.

There is just no sense in this cataloguing of unfinished matters. You understand my situation. Instead of there being a respite, I get more involved in cases that tear me apart. I am dreadfully self-conscious about all of the pressure to which I have subjected my secretary Gladys. And Mamie takes the brunt of it; besides her worrying about me. In a little while my life will be a more relaxed one, I hope. Then I can do all that needs doing.

Leopold was very eager to visit Chicago, and his surviving brother was equally eager that he stay away, because of his fear of publicity. He had been here for a few hours upon his release from prison in March, 1958, but because of the fact that the press virtually besieged him, he saw virtually nothing of the city. His pretext was that there was to be held a conference of authorities on parasitology and tropical diseases, and he was in charge of such project in Puerto Rico. He did hold private conferences with some of the best informed persons in his field; but for the rest, he spent his time with friends such as myself and relatives. When Mamie and I first picked him up, he expressed the desire to visit the graves of his parents and oldest brother. This had been impossible in 1958. Now he was able to utter lonely prayers (the Aramaic *Kaddish*) and to deposit sprigs of flowers. And he wanted to see our children. Then on his last day in town, he had us take him to all of the homes, schools and other familiar sights of his life prior to his conviction and confinement in 1924. Some were gone and some were seedy in appearance, all of the old glory gone. It was a sentimental journey, particularly impressive because Leopold has an outer surface that is restrained and sometimes cold and even cynical.

We managed to escape the press for the most part, although they tried. After he was gone, several columns appeared in the Chicago *Tribune*, a transcript of a private talk he had delivered to the staff of the Church of the Brethren, the organization that had sponsored his parole position. The *Tribune* got this in the usual fashion, by brow-beating an inexperienced cleric.

In all, new dimensions were given to a story that still interests me profoundly, and not alone because I was so prominently a part of it. The story is told, at least in part, in my forthcoming book, *A Handful of Cases*.

Since Louis Nizer and I last visited Paul Crump, the prison authorities seem to have become more circumspect in their handling of him. Crump's difficulties were very much in my mind when recently I read a book on the imprisonment of Oscar Wilde.[2] (I have written a review of it for the Chicago *Daily News*.) Strange to say, in all these 65 or more years the British Government had never previously permitted the use of the official prison records. They show that the wardens interfered with reading and writing by Wilde in the same senseless fashion as with Crump today. Ultimately, the rules were relaxed, so that Wilde might read some of his favorite writers, and he composed the long apology subsequently published as *De Profundis*.[3] I hope that Crump will be afforded similar opportunities ultimately. Nizer and I are working on the matter.

To revert to matters at home, our daughter-in-law Sue is returning to her classes at the Art Institute and will do more painting. She has been working to build up a nest-egg for furniture, a family, etc. But Ted has prevailed upon her to resume her art work. Mamie, too, is finding that she has some artistic talent, at least enough to impress her teacher and herself.

More later. Affectionate greetings from all of us.

Always yours, ELMER GERTZ

1.   Ludwig Marcuse, *Obszön* (see H. M. 9/7/63, notes).
2.   H. Montgomery Hyde, *Oscar Wilde: The Aftermath* (New York: Farrar, Straus & Company, 1963).
3.   London: Methuen and Co. [1905].

On December 3 Gertz reported: "The water colors referred to in the letters have all been sent out. Mamie packed them with the utmost care and sent them by first class mail, insured, and marked for special handling. It was quite a job!" He also included a list of six libraries to whom Into the Night Life should be mailed.

APS, 1S.   12/3/63

Dear Elmer—   Many thanks for that clipping of I. B. Singer's text. *Very interesting indeed.* How are you making out with the water colors? Time is *getting short.*

I finished my chores in that regard and am back on the play again.   Hurrah! Henry

Another letter about gifts was sent by Gertz on December 4 in which he described how the water colors had been prepared for mailing and offered to send out more donation letters and paintings.

TLS, 1P.   Dec. 5, 1963

Dear Elmer,   Yours of Dec. 3rd, with all the copies of letters written to donees, received. Whew! What a job! I feel guilty.

All I pray now is that there will be no hitch, that the donees won't backslide or quibble about prices, etc.

I am getting the six Night Life books out tomorrow, from here, as I had Eve ship a batch to me recently. By the way, these six books won't have any slip covers—there are no more slip covers left. Do you think I ought to reduce the price of the book therefore to $225.00?

With all that I have out now, in all directions, I doubt if I should send you any more water colors to donate. Or, if it seems important, maybe we can have respective institutions take donations for 1964. I'm a little worried now that I may be overstepping my donation—⟨f⟩ or gift allowance. Reason I am not quite certain yet, is because I am waiting to hear what UCLA will allow me for MSS. and documents submitted to them.

I also trust we will receive acknowledgments before the year is up!

I sent you the Marcuse book "Obszon" yesterday, and today a periodical from Columbia Univ., which Schwartz sent me. Contains an important article on the Church's censorship of books. Note this—that none of my books, thus far, are on the Index Expurgatorius. Strange.

Note what you say about Leopold and Paul Crump. There is this Bill Witherspoon now too.

Meanwhile give Mamie a good hug for me and blessings on your secretary. When I make a new good big water color, may I send her one as a gift—would she like that? or what? A night life book? Sound her out, please.—I mean, your secretary![1]

I'll also pick up framed enlarged color prints tomorrow evening of that wall photo, of which I'll send you one. Don't send me X'mas cards or gifts, please. I don't observe X'mas, even though I'm a Goy. Nor Yom Kippur either, for that matter. X'mas is every day, or not at all, what!

Tonight I see the co-producer of the film "David & Lisa" through a friend. Seems he has come from Philadelphia to talk to me about possibility of making a documentary film on my painting proclivities. We'll see what he proposes.

Marcel Marceau in Paris, approached to do Auguste for film of "The Smile" appeared to be enthusiastic—but wants a lot of money.

Enough now. More soon.   Henry

P.S. Seems there's a film showing called "Take (Me? Her?) She's Mine" in which reference is made to my books—students protest by sit down against their banning. Haven't seen it yet. Stars James Stewart & Sandra Dee.[2]

---

1.   Sentence added to paragraph by hand.
2.   Postscript written by hand, vertically, in left margin.

APS, 2SS.   12/6/63

Dear Elmer Gertz   Just got 12 more Night Life copies from Big Sur AND these HAVE slip covers—so forget what I said in my last about this.

Big ideas (last night) for that doc. film—1¼ hour long project in color—et cetera!   Henry

TL(CC), 3PP., AIR MAIL   December 9, 1963

Dear Henry: I have now disposed of all of the water colors in my possession, since I sent the last two to Northwestern University. I want to remind you that the librarian there is enthusiastic about getting even more of your water colors, as per the copy of his letter that I sent to you. I would suggest that you send an additional supply to him, or forward some to me for delivery to him. Not only is this good from a tax viewpoint, but from the viewpoint of your reputation as a water colorist, writer and personality, it is well that the leading schools and public institutions have samples of your work.

I am sending herewith a copy of a letter dated December 6 from Mrs. Marian Clarke, the Curator of The Watkinson Library at Trinity College, Hartford, Connecticut. I am sure that this letter will give you very great delight. To me, it is significant that the leading schools want your work, despite the efforts of local bigots to stamp your writings as obscene. I would send Mrs. Clarke four water colors and *Into The Night Life*. Re-reading her letter, I am delighted at her description of your work and her comments on your generosity.

As additional letters come in, I will acquaint you with their contents.

Of course, I have your letter of December 5, which delighted us.

My secretary, Gladys Fuller, got tremendous joy out of your suggestion that you send her "a new good big water color." She looks forward to it with enthusiasm. It is generous and thoughtful of you to think of her. I might add that I have delivered a good hug to Mamie for you and blessings to my secretary.

I am looking forward to the Marcuse book and the enlarged color prints that you are sending me. Out of respect for your devout irreligiosity, I will not regard them as either Christmas or Hanukkah presents, but simply as another expression of your friendship.

I have not seen the Jimmy Stewart picture in which you figure, although Eddie Schwartz told me about it. I look forward to seeing it at a rare moment of leisure.

I should feel very badly at this time for a variety of reasons. My friend, Otto Eisenschiml,[1] died yesterday, and the young daughter of the Chicago columnist Kupcinet (Kup) was murdered in Los Angeles a few days ago. For a lot of reasons, I value Kup. He has been one of our staunchest advocates in his column, not only in the fight against so-called obscenity prosecutions, but in the fight against capital punishment.

Bill Witherspoon is a puzzling case. I am afraid that there is very little chance of saving his life, although every effort will be expended by those in charge of the matter.[2] I am sure that your letters have helped ease his torture.

My friend, George Leighton, is doing brilliantly in another capital case, which is, in effect, being retried on a writ of habeas corpus. He has been able to prove, thus far, the fraudulent nature of the confession and other "evidence" which led to the death penalty. I get added joy out of George's success, because it is another major example of the breakdown of the color line. Miller is white and George is colored. He and his firm have represented a number of white clients in recent years. I know few other examples of this.

The casting director of *David and Lisa*, Bob Sickinger, is running the theatre at Hull House and is doing a fantastically good job. One day I would like to suggest either a reading or a stage performance of some of your work at Hull House.

Do tell me more of the negotiations towards the appearance of Marcel Marceau in the film of *The Smile*. He would be perfect for the part. I am sure that *The Smile* is one of your several writings of assured immortality.

More soon.

Affectionate greetings from all of us.

Always yours, ELMER GERTZ

Enc.

---

1. Dr. Otto Eisenschiml, well-known chemist and historian, author of *Why Was Lincoln Murdered?* (Boston: Little, Brown and Company, 1937), and other books. Eisenschiml and Gertz were among the founders of the Civil War Round Table. See Gertz, *A Handful of Clients*, "Litigating the Civil War" (pp. 195–228).
2. On June 3, 1968, in a 5 to 4 decision, the United States Supreme Court set aside Witherspoon's death sentence in a landmark opinion which held that prospective jurors who do not believe in capital punishment cannot be excluded from a jury for that reason alone. See "Ruling Saves Cop Killer From Chair," *Chicago Tribune*, June 4, 1968, pp. 1, 4.

    Gertz filed an *amicus* brief in the Witherspoon case, in behalf of the American Civil Liberties Union, which in part summarized and analyzed data about public opinion polls on capital punishment. The petition for executive clemency that Gertz had filed earlier, as attorney for Witherspoon, was pending at the time of the Supreme Court opinion. This petition thereupon became moot.

Gertz continued to send Miller letters about donations—two on December 10 and one on December 11. In those of the tenth he inquired whether he should write other institutions, and reported that Immaculate Heart College "would be simply delighted" to receive as many of Miller's works as he would care to send. On the eleventh Gertz forwarded letters from the Adult Education Council of Greater Chicago, Northwestern University, and the Philadelphia Museum of Art.

ALS, 1P.   12/11/63

Dear Elmer—   What are we to do about libraries who accept gifts and refuse to mention value of same? (as the Newberry, for ex.) Now a letter of acknowledgment from Univ. of Minn. for Night Life book but no mention of value.

More tomorrow or next day. Am hopping.   Best. Henry

TL(CC), 1P., AIR MAIL   December 12, 1963

Dear Henry: Here is my daily bulletin.

To answer your question about libraries and other institutions which accept gifts and then fail or refuse to mention the values, bear in mind that the value does not depend merely upon an acknowledgment thereof by the donee. For tax purposes, the value can be established in many ways which are open to us—appraisals (and we have enough of these through the acceptance of various gifts at our values), sales, comparable gifts by others, etc. What you will do, or rather your tax accountant will do, is to file a return in which the details of the various gifts are listed (date, name and address of donee, description of gift, fair value). This may be accepted. If questions are raised, there will be a conference of some sort and, in the end, the likelihood is that there will be an agreed valuation. I would say the chances are that the $250 valuation per picture and book will be acceptable because, in all of the circumstances, it is fair. At the proper time you can, if necessary, show the Treasury Agent the copies of letters from various libraries and others who write in such enthusiastic terms about your work. If necessary, too, you can give them copies of the books and articles about your water colors. All of these things would show that you are a legitimate artist giving away works of art having genuine value.

Anything can happen in this irrational world, but I would not be too worried if I were you, Henry.

I know that you will be interested in the enclosed copies of letters, particularly the one from the University of Virginia. Please advise what to do as to these.   Always yours, ELMER GERTZ

Encs. (Dictated but not read by E. G.)

ALS, 1P.   12/13/63

Dear Elmer—   Your letters and the replies to them are flooding in. Now I'm down with a good cold and resting. Doubt if I will bother to send out any more paintings or books this year. After first of year I will recommence. You certainly have done valiant work. Please tell your good secretary that I may hold up sending her the painting promised till after the X'mas rush.

I'm a bit concerned about the acknowledgments which fail to mention valuation of paintings or, like a recent, one which says "which Bowinkel values at $250.00." Doubt if this is Kosher for our Treasury Dep't.

I got the MSS. of Tom's (HM on Writing). Seems good to me—very good.

Have fine offer for documentary film but am not sure yet that I want to accept. Foresee a lot of work and travel—sounds fatiguing. I'd like to go off alone somewhere and just do nothing. Get worn down with all that goes on around and about me. Cheers!

Henry

TL(CC), 1P., AIR MAIL   December 13, 1963

Dear Henry: Now that I have completed the work in connection with the various gifts I arranged for you, I am returning to you my various letters of November and December, 1962, relating to the subject. You may need them for your own files.

One thing more on another subject. I have a couple of unanswered letters from Roger Bloom. I really ought to write to him.
Before doing so, I would like to have a summary of what you know
as to the situation, as it relates to Attorney Eagan or any other part
of the story.   Always yours, ELMER GERTZ

Encs.

ALS, 1P.   12/16/63

Dear Elmer—   Yours of the 12th, regarding valuation of pics,
is reassuring. OK.!

These letters from institutions are most surprising. Suddenly
they are all eager and grateful.

I think I will hold off sending any more W.C.'s or books out
until after first of year. I don't know quite where I stand, until I
hear what U.C.L.A. is accepting. And further, there is too much
risk of loss and damage mailing things now.

I will write these people who want things—and those who
asked for more—shortly, myself. You've done a prodigious amount
of work. How to thank you?

I gave Bowinkel (to send you) a framed colored photo of my
wall. Think you'll like it.

All for now. Best to Mamie.   Henry

ALS, 1P.   12/17/63

Dear Elmer—   About Roger Bloom. He's now transferred to
Moberly, Missouri—Box #7. (same Reg. No.—69529.) It's a sort
of model—on your honor place—he's outdoors, etc.

Eagan never replied to letters. Think I told you that the
Prison Parole Board is against him. I still suspend judgment, myself.

My friend Bob Fink has a lawyer-friend trying to work on the

Federal people—they are the ones who don't want to parole Roger. So there it stands.

This is a sad time of the year for me—worse than Yom Kippur, for some reason. The world seems more than ever crazy to me at X'mas. They've really fucked Jesus up good and proper. I refuse to observe the day any more—or New Year's either. What's "new" about it, eh?   Best! Henry

P.S. I got the letters you returned. And I read about Supreme Court's attitude. Where are we now???[1]

---

1.   Postscript written vertically in left margin.

TL(CC), 2PP., AIR MAIL   December 19, 1963

Dear Henry: I get a tremendous lift out of looking at the picture of you and Ziva Rodam. I cannot reconcile it with some of the gloomy language in your most recent letter.

I hope that you will be singing another tune soon. I hope, also, that your rejection of gladness does not encompass your birthday as well. I remember that on the 26th you are celebrating (Or are you not celebrating?) another birthday. This will convey my very best to you on that occasion; if that occasion is not worth referring to, then just in general.

Thanks much for sending me the Columbia University Forum, containing the article on forbidden books, which I shall read with the utmost interest. The literature in this field grows, and I try to obtain as much of it as possible. Incidentally, the December 23 issue of Newsweek has a sort of literary history of the year, featuring Frank Harris' *My Life and Loves,* John Cleland's *Memoirs of a Woman of Pleasure,* and your *Tropic of Cancer.* It is intriguing to as vain a person as myself to find that I have been involved in all three books. I feel an almost proprietary interest in them.

With this letter, I am sending an editorial from the Chicago

Daily News.[1] From what I can gather, it is, in effect, a pronounce-
ment by the United States Supreme Court that *Tropic of Cancer*
is constitutionally protected. The finding is circumscribed by technical rules of law, which I will not bother to explain to you. Within
the next few days we are going to file a petition in our case pending
before the Illinois Supreme Court and call the court's attention to
the two Supreme Court orders and ask our court to affirm Judge
Epstein's decision. I think that this may happen or, at any rate,
there ought to be an opinion before the end of January. I will, of
course, keep you fully informed. I will, also, try to ascertain how
all of these things affect the Brooklyn prosecution, which now looks
as if it may have to be dropped. For a definitive word, we must, of
course, hear from Cy Rembar.

I have received almost all of the receipts from the donees of
your water colors and books and will send them to you before the
end of the year. It might pay for you to exhibit the material to your
tax accountant and get his opinion, and then pass it on to me. If
you would rather have him communicate with me directly, that is
all right also.

I have told my secretary that you are holding up sending her
the painting until after the Christmas rush, in order to prevent
damage to it. Gladys has the best space on her living room wall
marked for this picture, which excites her increasingly, sight unseen.

I will write to Roger Bloom in the next day or two. I hope that
he will finally be out, and stay out. I have had a regular epidemic of
letters from prisoners everywhere who want me to rescue them.
They have the most exaggerated view of my qualities as a criminal
lawyer, which I ain't.[2]

The kids and Mamie send their love to you.

Always yours, ELMER GERTZ

1.   "Censorship Loses a Round," *Chicago Daily News*, December 18,
      1963, p. 14. The editorial commented on the United States Supreme
      Court's refusal to review a decision by the California Supreme Court,
      in the *Zeitlin v. Arnebergh* case, that *Cancer* was not obscene (see
      Gertz, 7/5/63).

2.   Elmer Gertz has a reputation as a criminal lawyer due to his success
      in the Leopold, Ruby, and similar cases, but regards himself as a gen-
      eral practitioner specializing in First Amendment and civil rights
      litigation.

TL(CC), 1P.   December 23, 1963

Dear Henry: I now have receipts for all of the water colors and
silk screen books that I have presented in your behalf, except those
from Roosevelt University, the Art Institute of Chicago and the
Fort Hays State College. I will write to these to remind them
to send the receipts. Those that I have are all in the forms submitted by us, except in the instances of the Newberry Library and
the White Art Museum of Cornell University. When all of the receipts are in my hands I will send them to you, so that you may turn
them over to your tax accountant.

I am sending with this letter a page from last Saturday's edition of Panorama, the magazine section of the Chicago Daily News.
It contains my review of a new Oscar Wilde book,[1] which you may
find interesting. This is the third review I have written this year for
Panorama.   Always yours, ELMER GERTZ

Enc.

---

1.   "Little Men Ground Out His Soul," *Chicago Daily News*, December
      21, 1963, "Panorama" Section, p. 10, a review of H. Montgomery
      Hyde, *Oscar Wilde: The Aftermath* (New York: Farrar, Straus &
      Company, 1963).

WHAT GREAT GOOD FRIENDS YOU ARE AND HOW
VERY GRATEFUL I AM FOR YOUR NEVER ENDING
FAVORS HAVE A GOOD CHRISTMAS

HENRY MILLER

[*Wire to Elmer and Mamie Gertz at home, 24 Dec. 1963. Pacific Palisades, Cal.*]

TLS, 2PP.   Dec. 26th, 1963

Dear Elmer: Herewith copy of letter to Mr. Blau.[1] The result of reading the new law (Vol. 5—page 81) of what? At bottom it reads "copyright 1963, Callaghan & Co." Anyway, Blau can furnish you this if you don't have it.

As you see, I am asking him to take over for me—and for you, if that seems O.K. It's getting too thick, all this detail work. I have no guts for it. Bad enough making the water colors, a job which certainly did not help with my other work.

The total of seemingly legitimate donations thus far is just about $20,000. Which is what I am allowed, apparently. As you know, there is a 20% and a 30% deduction permitted, the former for educational (and religious) organizations only. About two-thirds of mine are in the 30% category.

I will be writing shortly to those institutions which requested additional material of me. Maybe I can offer them this next year. At the moment I don't feel like doing another thing. I have done nothing all year but worry about "making it" on time, or not making it at all. The amount of thought and effort I have given to earning the above huge deduction is frightful—and destructive. The whole problem seems to me to be how to earn just enough to pay one's living expenses and pay no income tax. But I can't solve it. The best I can hope to do henceforth is to guard the exchequer, not make sentimental gifts, and when I get a dollar remember that most of it goes to the government.

This is my birthday and I am in a little better spirit. Not much. I feel that the past year was completely wasted, and that what I earned (which so many envy) not only brought me no joy but innumerable problems and headaches. I smile when you mention the impression you received on gazing at the photo I sent you. Certainly every day is not a black one. There do come moments of happiness, but they are fleeting. And even where there looks to be happiness, don't be too sure. Nothing is pure and genuine.

If circumstances permit I'll try to take a couple of weeks' vacation in Mexico—late January possibly. It all depends on how I weather Jan. 15th, when I make another huge tax payment. And how the domestic situation is here—I won't go into that now, but only tell you that it couldn't be worse.

Had a letter today from Roger Bloom who writes optimistically about conditions in the new prison at Moberly, Mo. (Box 7). Some times I think he is better off remaining there than getting out and facing the world we live in. Go to the doctor tomorrow for a check up—that stretched muscle is agonizing and getting no better. But that's the least of my worries, to be honest.

As for the Cancer film project, the latest is that Bernie Wolfe (script writer) is suing my corporation (Rellim) as well as Joe Levine and the two producers. I don't blame him at all. In fact, I help him out now and then—he is in a bad way financially. And there seems to be no getting together to settle the quarrel. One result is that I lose my monthly salary (with which I paid my monthly expenses, rent, taxes, alimony, etc.) until the thing becomes alive again. The other film project—"To Paint is to Love Again" is in the negotiating stage. Not so much money in it, but better chance of a good film, including travel abroad (to visit other artist friends and include them in the film—Delaney, Max Ernst, Brassai, DuBuffet, et alia). But lots of work on my part—more headaches. Sometimes I wonder why I ever say Yes. But this time I am thinking it may be nice to leave such a picture for my children in later years.

As for "Harry" (the play) my friend and translator in Paris is showing it to Jean-Louis Barrault for possible production at his theatre, l'Odeon, and hoping to get Belmondo to play ⟨obliterated⟩ Harry. He is also active now in lining up Paris TV for "The Smile" and at my suggestion, hoping to get Azvenour (one of my favorite actors) to play Auguste. Don't know what Patti Hardesty has accomplished definitely with Marcel Marceau.

And that's the top of the news for today. So far I have not heard (congratulations) from the two people I most wanted to hear from. And if I don't, well—fuck it all! I say. Next year I make a desperate effort to enjoy myself in my own way. Sounds bad, putting it that way, doesn't it? I say it only because I seem to be living every body else's life but my own most of the time. And my days are getting shorter and shorter.

I'm having Eddie Schwartz make up letter heads for me—and at the bottom in red ink will be printed: "The time of the hyena is upon us." (A Zulu saying)

Now for a brief nap. "Pass world, I am the dreamer who remains." (Roy Campbell)

But please don't worry if my reports sound pessimistic. I always get by eventually. And not every minute of the day is as grim as I may make it seem.   Cheers. Avanti! Fuck a duck! Henry

---

1. In this one-page, closely-typed letter to Edward Blau, Los Angeles attorney, Miller asked whether he could turn over to Blau "the correspondence which I have relative to donations" for "completion of the necessary data" to support his income tax return. He also made reference among other things to Blau's having said that Gertz's "letters to the institutions were not valid." In writing to Gertz on December 27, Miller explained that he had not quoted Blau accurately.

TL(CC), 2PP., AIR MAIL   December 27, 1963

Dear Henry: Mamie and I were deeply touched by your Christmas Day telegram, more so because we recall your words with respect to that once pagan, now commercial, holiday.

I had occasion to send out a telegram myself on Christmas Day—to my friend George Leighton, who was able to persuade Judge Perry to spare the life of another Miller,[1] this one convicted of the rape-murder of a child. There will be either an appeal or a new trial in the matter. Meanwhile, a second death case in which

Leighton is the attorney comes up for decision before the same judge in a few days. Leighton ought to win this one, also.

Meanwhile, I cannot summon any real hope for Bill Witherspoon. It would be tragic if his gifts were lost because of outmoded practices by society. I know that you are a source of comfort to Witherspoon.

And what a beautiful picture it was that you sent us. It arrived yesterday. It is in a place of honor in our den, and it will serve to remind us of your visit. When will it be repeated?

Opinions seem to differ with respect to the effect of the two orders of the United States Supreme Court in the California cases.[2] I am sending herewith a copy of a letter from Cy Rembar. I am inclined to agree with De Grazia, rather than Rembar, in this matter. In any event, there are likely to be pronouncements from the Illinois courts, including the Supreme Court, within the next few days or weeks. I shall keep you informed.

As the picture says, Viva la Ziva! And, also, Viva le Henri!

The very best from all of us to you.

Always yours, ELMER GERTZ

Enc.

---

1.   By letter dated 12/6/76, Gertz informed F. F. L.: "Lloyd Eldon Miller was ultimately freed. After George Leighton became a judge, another friend, Willard J. Lassers, took over the Miller case and carried it to the U.S. Supreme Court. The Court castigated the State of Illinois for suborning perjury and other misdeeds. Miller's case constitutes a great argument against capital punishment. He was once a few hours away from execution."

2.   See Gertz 7/5/63, notes.

TLS, 1P.   Dec. 27th, 1963

Dear Elmer,   Before I forget it want to remind you to send me the shipping and postage bills for all the mailing you have done— before the end of the year, if possible, so that I can pay you and deduct from my tax bill, yes?

I'm seeing the lawyer this afternoon, with all the correspondence, and trust he'll take over the job. I hope it doesn't seem that I am intruding on your efforts—on the contrary, I wanted to save you further hack work. I made reference in my letter to Blau that your letters to the Universities were not "valid." That wasn't his expression. What he said and meant was that they were too "interested," if I remember right. Something more formal and detached was what he had in mind. I'll let him clear this up when he writes you.

I haven't had a chance to read your critique of the Wilde book yet. Just been through the legal dope you sent me. This sounds promising. I hope for Rosset's sake, the N. Y. decision will be reversed. He must be losing a fortune.

Some of your queries in the batch of letters you sent me I see I never answered. Later, gradually. No I never saw the book catalog of the Fort Lauderdale man.[1] If sale of paintings was listed they might be useful—the prices, I mean.

That's about it for the moment.

Please tell your secretary I haven't forgotten about the painting for her. Just a little more patience. But let me thank her here once again for all she has done.   My best meanwhile. Henry

---

1.   On December 10 Gertz had written: "Did you see the catalog put out by a Fort Lauderdale bookseller? It contains a number of Henry Miller items, including some of your paintings and drawings. As I recall, there are a couple of illustrations of your work."

APS, 2SS.   12/28/63

Dear Elmer—   Rosset seems eager to publish "The World of Sex." I have my doubts about advisability of this. Suggested he have his lawyer read closely pages 53–74 dealing with first wife and her mother.

Hope the receipts from Universities are on way to me. Must begin double-checking soon.

Did I tell you to look up current issue of "Mademoiselle" for
my article on "Love"? I wonder what Judge Epstein would think of
it? Some one just gave me this book—"Jews, God, and History."[1]
Shalom!   Henry

1.   Not identified.

1964:
January 2–June 28

January Miller's "Love and How It Gets that Way" published in *Mademoiselle*.

Gertz speaks before Caxton Club on "Freedom to Read, 1964."

February *Just Wild About Harry* published in Germany.

May Miller tapes television interview with Steve Allen.

June Litigation over *Cancer* film settled out of court.

18 June Illinois Supreme Court, reversing Judge Epstein's *Cancer* decision, rules that book is obscene.

22 June United States Supreme Court summarily reverses Florida *Cancer* conviction.

7 July Illinois Supreme Court withdraws ruling that *Cancer* obscene, and affirms Judge Epstein's decision.

APS, 2SS.   1/2/64

Dear Elmer—   Got the package of letters—receipts 12/31/63
—thank you. Forwarded them to Blau. Checking the postal receipts
I see it comes to only $18.95. Is this correct—or are there more to
follow? Seems too modest. Will send you check when you reply.
As for the effort and the labor you contributed that I can never
pay you for.
        Cheers!   Henry

> On January 17 Miller wrote Gertz's secretary, Mrs. Gladys Fuller,
> expressing concern that he hadn't "heard from Elmer recently."
> He also mentioned that he had not forgotten about the promised
> painting, and that he had been suffering from his stretched muscle:
> "Six weeks of unremitting pain night and day."

ALS, 1P.   Jan. 18th 1964

Dear Elmer—   Since I don't hear from you I'm enclosing check
for what I totaled the postage bill up to. If it isn't right, tell me
what it is exactly. I have an uncomfortable feeling that something's
awry, that perhaps I've offended you in some way, and that that
explains your silence. I pray it's not so, for to offend you or hurt
you in the least way is beyond my thinking.
        We've had more drama, more harassing problems here at
home, if home you can call it. (It's more like a morgue.)[1] But I
won't go into that or into all my aches and pains. I'm alive and
breathing, and that's something. I know you must begin to wonder
if I am turning sour or bitter in my old age. No, I'm not. But sometimes things get a bit too thick, even for me, with my thick skin.
        I'm reading Heinrich Mann's novel about Alexander the Great[2]
and am vastly intrigued with the character of his friend Clitus whom
he killed in a moment of drunken rage. If I had Durrell's talent I

would write a play around this strange, enigmatic relationship. Have cleared my desk once again in order to get back to the play. Let me hear from you. Best always to you and to Mamie.   Henry

---

1.   Living at the Miller residence were his third wife (Janina M. Lepska, mother of Valentin and Tony) and her husband. See H. M. 2/15/64.
2.   Heinrich Mann was Thomas Mann's older brother. The novel referred to has not been identified. *The Blue Angel* was a rendition of Heinrich Mann's *Professor Unrat*.

TL(CC), 3PP., AIR MAIL   January 21, 1964

Dear Henry: It is strange, indeed, that I should neglect you, a person for whom I have such admiration and affection. I am in a very peculiar state of mind. I have had to work at a killing pace and feeling it more than I usually do, both physically and emotionally. I find that when I am in such a state, I lapse into silence. I don't write, telephone or communicate, and I resent cross-examination. I always bounce back and surely will this time.

It is likely that the Illinois *Tropic* case will finally be decided by our Supreme Court tomorrow. It should be a favorable decision and an affirmance of Judge Epstein's decree. But anything is possible in our Supreme Court. For example, the court might transfer the case again to the Appellate Court, or it might even reverse, but how it could do so, I am at a loss to anticipate. At any rate, we should know. If there should be a reversal, then, of course, we would take the case to the United States Supreme Court on a petition for writ of certiorari.

I had an interesting matter before my favorite judge, Hubert Will. The Chicago Transit Authority had issued a list of books, magazines and newspapers which they would not permit to be sold on CTA premises. The list included the newspaper of one of my best clients. Interestingly enough, I was able to persuade the CTA to reverse itself with respect to my client's newspaper, after I had filed suit. Last night, when I talked with the judge on another matter, he kidded me about the quality of my client's newspaper, but felt exactly as I did about any public censorship. I felt certain after his remarks that, if the CTA had battled, instead of yielding, I would have won. The matter on which I appeared before the judge in his chambers related to Dick Gregory, the famous topical comedian, whom I am opposing in the lawsuit. If Gregory is typical of entertainers, they are indeed a bunch of neurotics. (So, you will say, are all of us!)

I am sending an announcement of a talk I am going to make before the Caxton Club here. I hope that in the course of that talk I will comment upon the victory in the *Tropic* case. If not, I will let off some steam.

Of course, I am curious about your home drama, but I feel that when you want to tell me the details you will do so, without my prodding. However bad they are, you have the consolation that one day they will be transfigured creatively in your writings.

In the process of trying to recapture some verve, Mamie and I drove to Madison, Wisconsin, where our younger son is a student. There we saw a preview of a moving picture, *The Man in the Middle,* starring Robert Mitchum. Knowing how much you are absorbed in the problem of justice, I strongly recommend this film to you. It is a largely unsentimental account of an army court-martial.

The letter I sent you the other day from the Library of Congress is a very significant one. I hope you will do something with respect to it. Please advise me as to your intentions. Just what is the situation presently with respect to the gifts? I hope that you will keep me informed.

I read your extremely fine piece in *Mademoiselle* on love. What would interest me is the reaction of the sort of person who reads *Mademoiselle.*

You will remember that I have been recommending to you and Barney Rosset the publication of *The World of Sex.* I still feel that it ought to be published, subject to the legal involvements, and they don't concern simply the question of obscenity. I hesitate to express an opinion, when Barney will have his own lawyer look into the matter. I am going to re-read the passages suggested by you. I apologize for not having done so until now.

I may send you an article that I wrote ⟨in⟩ for an historical publication on the Black Laws of Illinois.[1] It may shock you to know that the allegedly free state of Illinois, Lincoln's state, was almost as bad as any southern state in the pre-Civil War period.

I thought by now that you would be in Mexico. I would love to be there, or, indeed, anywhere.

Is there a chance of your coming our way or anywhere near us?

Of course, I am concerned about the Brooklyn trial. Just where does it stand? I hate hounding Rembar unduly, although he is very accommodating.

I am confused as to the status of the *Cancer* film. Is it going to come out this year? I do hope that you will give me the story. It is too bad that Bernie Wolf has found it necessary to sue. I hope that he is not like my "friend" Meyer Levin, who sues, or is sued, constantly. I have a case pending against him for Nathan Leopold. I don't know whether or not I have discussed it with you.

This letter must sound dull and uninspired, because that is how I feel. I will try to do better either later today or tomorrow.

Affectionate greetings from Mamie and all of us.

Ever yours, ELMER GERTZ

1.   Elmer Gertz, "The Black Laws of Illinois," *Journal of the Illinois Historical Society*, Autumn 1963, pp. 454–73.

TL(CC), 1P., AIR MAIL   January 22, 1964

Dear Henry: Just a word. In The New Republic of January 25, there is an advertisement, reading as follows:
"HENRY MILLER'S *Maurizius Forever* . . . is a grim and grisly story of a prisoner who protests injustice. The theme is not alone the inadequacy of human justice, but the impossibility of ever attaining it. Never has Miller written with greater emotional con-

viction and intellectual penetration. Autographed, limited edition. Orig. $2.50. Price only $1.00 ppd.

KAARE NANSEN, PUBLISHER
Old Moon Rd., Rt. 1, Box 188, Michigan City, Ind."

Did you by any chance turn over the book to the publisher? I suspect that he is Russell Knutson, who published an essay of yours on obscenity some years ago.[1]

Affectionate greetings from all of us.

Ever yours, ELMER GERTZ

---

1.   *Pornography and Obscenity*, two essays by D. H. Lawrence and Henry Miller, Foreward [sic] by Russell F. Knutson, Preface by Florence Arslen-Hasratoff, Introduction by Maurice Parmelee (Michigan City, Ind.: Fridtjof-Karla Publications, 1958).

TLS, 2PP.   Jan. 23, 1964

Dear Elmer: I was indeed relieved to get your letter though somewhat disturbed that you are killing yourself with work. What a pity it is that as we get older, instead of having more leisure we have less. Everything connected with "work" (not creation) is abhorrent to me. I have probably sounded very pessimistic in my recent letters, and it's shameful, I think. (I woke up in the middle of the night obsessed with the idea of writing a crazy article on "The Joys of Melancholia".) Last night I went to bed with Marie Corelli's "Life Everlasting," written in 1911.[1] When I started the Prologue I knew I had something: it was like taking a draught of crystal clear spring water. What wisdom she had, what radiance, what supreme faith and courage! Nobody would believe, I suppose, that yours truly could find a writer like Marie Corelli instructive and inspiring. But she is. I first read her about 40 years ago—and never forgot the experience. About ten years ago, at Big Sur, I read several of her books and was highly impressed. Now once again. But you know how I stumbled on this book? I was looking thru the card file at the local library for a book by Ludwig Wittgenstein called "Tractatus Logico-Philosophicus," which Walter Lowenfels had recommended to me in 1934 or '35.[2] Just getting round to it now! What doggedness, eh?

Enough of all that. Mention it only to say I refuse to get enveloped further in the bogs of despair. Monday I take my boy Tony (now 15½), to "The Army and Navy Academy" in Carlsbad, California—a private school, highly recommended. He's seen it and likes it. I think it will do him good. It will also lift him out of the poisonous atmosphere here. The girl, Valentine,[3] is getting married (at 18) on Feb. 14th, and will then go with her husband to Europe on a tour, six months, economy way, they say. What I shall do then I don't know yet. I think I'll hold on here, in any case.

I gave all the letters from the Universities to Blau, the lawyer, to follow up for more complete data—expect he's doing that now. Feb. 7th I take a deposition in connection with the Cancer film biz. I don't understand the whole mess, but the lawyers do, I hope. At the worst, I will be out $100,000—which I don't have. I am sort of sitting back amused and watching it. The other documentary film project is still in negotiating stage; frankly, I am beginning to wonder if I will do it. Means more work, more rushing about, endless details, queries, interviews, etc. Is it worth it? Certainly not money wise.

Stanley Fleishman read "W. of S." at my request and agrees with me that it is subject to libel and slander—the parts concerning my ex-wife and her mother. Barney is pressing me. I've told him what I think and fear.

(Must clear you up about my friend Bernie Wolfe: he would never dream of suing me, personally; he had to sue my corporation. All with my consent and understanding, and I hope he wins!)

I'll keep an eye open for the Mitchum film. Did you see America, America? The editor of "Mademoiselle" writes that my article was a great success, caused lots of talk, and a sell out of the issue. I have received some fan letters—no different from most.

One woman wrote that she was content to remain alone with Jesus, not having any luck with men. (Sic)

I listened in on TV yesterday hoping to learn about decision of Illinois Supreme Court, but no news. Suppose I'll hear soon.

Yes, I answered letter from Library of Congress. And I am not surprised about the State of Illinois in pre-Civil war days. When or if I will get to Mexico for a brief vacation I don't know. Hope your speech before the Caxton Club is a success.

About my play Harry. It has just been taken by the big theatre in Copenhagen, and is now being read by the National Theatre in Brussels. Renate writes from Berlin that twenty German theatres are begging to read the script now—the book will be out in German (finally) first week in February. Told her to send you a copy—should be a handsome job. As for "The Smile" (film) Patti Hardesty writes that she saw Marcel Marceau and he is enthusiastic to do Auguste, if Jean Renoir will direct the film—for next October. The Opera of it, in Hamburg, is definite for January, 1965. Capricorn comes out in England shortly, followed by Nexus, two different publishers.

I don't know when I will get to Chicago—or anywhere. By the way, Roger Bloom is quite happy in the new prison, a model one, where he is treated quite royally, he says—thanks to all the influential friends now interested in him, which means you as well as me, and others. And he still has a chance for Federal parole—next May.

Now then, don't answer this in usual style. Just a post card now and then, about urgent matters, will do. Conserve your strength. It's useless for me to tell you to take it easy, since I can't do it myself, though I try every day. But remember, we only live once—make the most of it. Work is the least of it.

When I think of Alexander the Great*—I have read several books about him recently—he fires me!—I am completely dumfounded. How could one man do what he did—and in such a short span? I know of nothing like it, do you?

Enough now. Give my love to Mamie and all the youngsters. Please give the enclosed to your noble secretary.[4] I do hope the water colors I am sending now will please her. I'm just about cleaned out now. But am painting again between times.

Cheers! Abi gesundt! Prosit! Henry

*And what I like about A. is the disregard he had for that old spoof —Aristotle![5]

P.S. I mailed Gladys' card separately.[6]

---

1. Marie Corelli [pseud.], The Life Everlasting: A Romance of Reality (Los Angeles: Borden, 1945). See also Henry Miller, "Marie Corelli: A Recommendation," New York Times Book Review, September 12, 1976, p. 55.
2. Ludwig Josef Johann Wittgenstein, Tractatus Logico-philosophicus (New York: Harcourt, Brace & Company, Inc., 1922). For references to Walter Lowenfels by Miller, see Gunther Stuhlmann, ed., Henry Miller Letters to Anaïs Nin (New York: G. P. Putnam's Sons [1965]). A number of letters Miller wrote to Lowenfels in the 1930's were published in The Outsider journal, ed. Jon Edgar Webb, Vol. 1, Nos. 1, 2, and 3 (Fall 1961, pp. 63–66; Summer 1962, pp. 75–80; Spring 1963, pp. 81–85).
3. Miller's daughter was named for his grandfather, Valentin Neiting. However her name is frequently spelled "Valentine," as it is here.
4. Miller wrote Gladys Fuller that he was having two water colors sent to her, adding, "Take good care of Elmer—he SHOULDN'T work so hard!"
5. Written by hand.
6. Written by hand on envelope flap.

TL(CC), 2PP., AIR MAIL   January 30, 1964

Dear Henry: Some while ago, you asked me to send you photographs of the water colors that you gave me. I did not ignore your request, but several persons who promised to make the photographs for me failed to deliver. Finally, our friend Gene Lovitz, who can always be depended upon, took the photographs and they came out excellently. I am sending them to you under separate cover.

In addition to the pictures in my home and office, Midge has one in her home, Jack has one in his apartment at the University of Wisconsin, and Sue and Tel have two in their apartment. I will try to have photographs taken of these, so that your records will be complete.

Some while ago, I sent you a copy of a letter from The Art Institute of Chicago, mentioning about their returning the two water colors that we sent to them. Since then, these have been returned to me. They are now in my possession. I can keep them or return them to you, as you wish. Please bear them in mind.

Gladys is looking forward to the receipt of the water colors that you are sending her with great excitement. I certainly appreciate your interest in her, as she is a real jewel.

It is strange how one's viewpoint changes. Now that I have gotten certain matters out of the way, I am beginning to feel much less pressure and my state of mind is greatly improved. Now all I have to worry about are financial matters, and those, strange to say, are much less annoying than the pressure of deadlines.

One brief I had to prepare related to a case in which I represent a former federal prisoner, who is blinded in one eye through the neglect of the authorities who permitted a psychopathic prisoner to be in an open cell with my client and others. If I did not know of other similar cases, it would pass belief.

Paul Crump's mother telephoned me today about a few relatively minor problems that he has. I spent a good deal of time with him recently and hope to see him again soon. I continue to be disgusted by the utter lack of understanding on the part of those charged with responsibility for the penal system. With any real thought or effort there would be the possibility of a vast improvement in the prisons. Now and then there is a failure, and it cannot be charged to the system.

I got one young man out of prison who had been there on a murder charge. I was extremely fortunate and got him out when he had served less than ten years. I thought that he would never again get into difficulty, as he seemed to be a very fine young man with character and brains. Alas, the other day he was picked up for burglary. The situation is worse than if he had never been released, because he now has a wife and child.

I had a delightful experience last night, when I spoke before the Caxton Club on Freedom To Read, 1964. The audience and I were in a very receptive mood and we enjoyed ourselves very much. The *Tropic* litigation was a principal part of the discussion. I was flattered that some of the men who were my teachers in law school attended the meeting, as did the librarians of several leading universities and public institutions, including the librarian of U.C.L.A.

A dear friend of mine, Dr. Jack Cowen, has just returned from a trip in the Middle East, in which he visited Greece, the Aegean Islands, Turkey, and several of the nations surrounding Israel. Jack is one of the most distinguished ophthalmologists of the Middle West and is a boyhood friend of mine. He is an artist, musician and ornithologist of great ability. I mention him because I was delighted to see in his sketch book a number of scenes connected with Alexander.

If is it not imposing too much, I do hope that, as arrangements are made for the publication of your various books in England and elsewhere, you ask the publishers to send me copies.

Enough for the moment. Love from Mamie, the youngsters, and, to describe her in your words, my noble secretary.

Always yours [*Elmer Gertz*][1]

---

1.   Letter signed but name not, as usual, typed.

ALS, 1P.   2/4/64

Dear Elmer—   Thank you so much for the photos of the WC's! Somehow they don't look so hot to me now. Did these you sent include the two returned by Chicago Institute? If not, please mail me these two *originals* (W.C.'s) will you? I need all I can get— heavy demands.

Hope Gladys got hers by now and finds them to her taste.

About new books—do you mean you would like British and other foreign editions, regardless of language? Did you never get

British "Cancer" or "Plexus"? Expect you will receive German edition of "Harry" very soon.

Glad to hear pressure seems to be letting up.

This is a quickie. Henry

> On February 5 Gertz informed Miller that he was sending the two Art Institute water colors by insured mail. In response to Miller's inquiry about foreign editions he said: "Yes, I would like to get any books of yours as they come out, regardless of language, if it is not too much trouble for you to arrange this. I never got the British Cancer or Plexus."

ALS, 1P.   Feb. 10th '64

Dear Elmer—   Here is a copy (which was enclosed with the original, probably an oversight) of the reply to my letter regarding the edition of "Maurizius" advertised in a N.Y. magazine, which you told me about.

I no longer recall what sort of deal I made with Knutson for these unbound copies. (I don't think I knew there were 1800!) It's quite possible I may have waived royalties.

Here's the strange thing. I never looked inside the copy of "Pornography & Obscenity"[1] which he brought out. It came at one of those busy times. Now I see why he was given jail sentence—because of the photos of nudes. I don't seem to find the list of so-called banned books he says was included—perhaps this was separately thrown in.

Before I make answer I wonder if you know anything about him or the case. All rather strange.   In haste. Henry

P.S. You might return his carbon letter. I have just the one copy of "P. & O." Should I send it to you?[2]

1.   See Gertz 1/22/64, notes.
2.   Postscript written vertically in left margin.

APS, 1S.   2/10/64

Dear Elmer—   About foreign editions of my work—I can't recall what you *have* or if you have any. Could you get one of the
family to list what you do have and then I can begin filling the
gap. It may be easier for me, in some instances, to have books sent
you direct from publishers. Hope W.C's arrived for Gladys Fuller.
I got ones you sent.   Henry

ALS, 1P.   2/11/64

Dear Elmer—   Further pursuant to my letter re "Maurizius
Forever" biz. In my haste yesterday I did not notice that the nude
photos I mentioned were in a separate publication (like a mag.
in format) entitled "The Psychology of Nudism" by John Carl
Flugel—Alethea Pub. Inc. Chicago. The nudes prominently feature
the women's thick rose bushes—both on cover and inside. Now
then, whether this was enclosed with "Pornog. & Obscenity" I don't
remember.   Again—in haste. Henry

TL(CC), 2PP., AIR MAIL   February 12, 1964

Dear Henry: I have your card and letters dated February 10
and 11, and hasten to reply to them before I get tied up in some
way or other.
    Yes, I do know Russell F. Knutson, whose letter to you I am
returning herewith. Knutson is a good-looking and charming person who manages to get into trouble constantly. As far as I know,
his trouble has related only to convictions for the sale of obscenity,
but I am not sure. I got to know him when I was president of The
Shaw Society, a group that staged readings of Shaw's plays and
carried on other activities. Knutson used to be very helpful to us
and sold literature at our meetings, all of it unobjectionable. He
was very eager to have me do some things for him. He was going

to put out a new edition of Bernard Shaw's great essay on the penal system and asked me to write an introduction. This I did and he raved about it. Then he tried to get me to defray some of costs of publication and I refused. Thereupon, he became critical of my essay. He wanted me to edit an anthology of writings by Frank Harris, and this I did. Nothing came of ⟨them⟩ that either. By that time Knutson was in the penitentiary once more. I next heard from him at the time he got out. He bore a message for me from one of the inmates. Incidentally, I ordered a copy of *Maurizius Forever* from him, but have not yet received it. I would be extremely careful, if I were you, in all dealings with him. Since I am on the scene, I would suggest that you communicate with him through me.

Is Joe Levine still involved in the *Tropic of Cancer* movie? I seem to sense that something has gone wrong. Just what is the status of the matter?

I have been in the process of going over contracts in connection with a movie dealing with the rehabilitation of Nathan Leopold. The moving picture people seem to require yards of material. We have already gone through about three or four drafts.

By the way, I have a copy of Knutson's edition of the book, *Pornography and Obscenity*. Incidentally, I was the attorney for Maurice Parmelee in a libel action here. He is the one who wrote the celebrated book on nudism, which was the subject of an obscenity prosecution. That case was won.

You ask about which foreign editions of your work I have. I was sent, through you, the Hebrew edition of *Tropic of Cancer*. When our son Jack was in Mexico, he bought the Argentinian editions of *Cancer* and *Capricorn*. So far as I now recall, those are the only books of yours in any foreign tongue that I have.

I did not write to you to give you my impressions of the particular passages from *The World of Sex*, because my copy seems to have been misplaced. For the life of me, I don't know where it was put. It may even have been swiped. I hope not.

Yes, Gladys has received your two water colors. Apparently your card crossed her letter, because she wrote to you. They are truly beautiful. No wonder you think less of some of your older water colors. Those two of Gladys' will truly enhance her apartment. Thanks again for your thoughtfulness.

I am still working at a killing pace.

Affectionate greetings from all of us.

Sincerely yours, ELMER GERTZ

Enc.

ALS, 2PP. 2/15/64

Dear Elmer—   The B'klyn people are after me again and I am phoning Stanley Fleishman tomorrow (Sunday)—will hold this open to report what he says. They threaten to start extradition if I don't come voluntarily—in a week!

Yes, Joe Levine and producers still fighting. Both he and I make depositions next week—separately—before (3) lawyers. I'll know more later, perhaps. At present, all stymied. I think producers are suing him, he them, and Wolfe, the script writer all of us— one for $75,000.00, the other for $25,000.00.

What I'll do about foreign editions is have publishers send you them direct. I already wrote one, Longanesi in Milan, to send you all he published so far. Will take a little time.

I've decided against publication of "World of Sex" (ditto *Sexus*) and told Rosset so for the first, and an English publisher for the second.

I don't know what to say to Knutson at present. Glad you told me about him. He sent me just *one* copy.

My play may still be taken in N.Y. Good opportunity all around. But they have to raise more money first.

By April I have to find a housekeeper who can also cook and be my secretary. Lepska and new husband getting out then. Should you hear of a good prospect let me know. I have one in mind already, but she is in N.Y. Supposedly just what I'd want. Has *all* the qualifications—*plus*. (!)

Soon I'll send you an etching—one of ten I made in Berlin. Just signed & numbered them. Kept only 5 of each and rest back to Berlin to be sold by my friend Springer there.

Another of my Marini heads was sold recently to Hirschhorn, the great art collector. A Brooklyn boy like myself—I met him once. Reminds me in some ways of Joe Levine.

Hildegard Knef (Neff) wants to do a film (German) portraying (3) women from my books (!). Would be great. I go to dinner Saturday next with Alex. King, Groucho Marx at Steve Allen's home.   Enough! Abi gesundt! Henry[1]

---

1.   "Enough! Abi Gesundt!" and signature written vertically in left margin.

TL(CC), 2PP., AIR MAIL   February 20, 1964

Dear Henry: I stupidly forgot to send the greetings and good wishes of Mamie and myself in connection with Val's marriage. We would love to know more about it. We would love, too, to know what we could send. Put down my thoughtlessness to the fact that I have been tied up beyond endurance.

I am going to New York for a couple of days in connection with a deposition. I will be there from the wee hours Saturday morning to late Monday. If you should want to get in touch with me for any reason, you may address or call me at the Berkshire Hotel, 21 East 52nd Street, New York City (Telephone: PLaza 3-5800).

In your letter of February 15, you said you were going to talk to Stanley Fleishman and then report to me what he says. I have not heard anything as yet. I don't know how you could be extradited, in view of the rulings of the California Supreme Court and what the United States Supreme Court has done. If the Brooklyn people are so eager to proceed, they ought to sever you from the case and ⟨plead⟩ proceed as to the others. What does our friend Cy Rembar say?

I don't suppose any progress will be made on the *Tropic* picture until the pending battles are out of the way. What brought them about anyway?

Thanks much for making arrangements with respect to the foreign editions of your book. I hate to put you to so much trouble, but I hate even more being without the books.

I think you are wise in your decision with respect to *The World of Sex* and *Sexus*, although the former could be published with certain passages excised.

I shall certainly bear in mind what you say with respect to your needs as to a combination secretary, housekeeper and what have you. The lucky person would not die from boredom.

I look forward to the etching that you are sending me.

The Chicago Loop Synagogue has finally printed post cards of Abe Rattner's window. I am sending two of them herewith. If you need any more, I think I can get them.

Do you know that the University of Illinois Press is publishing a magnificent volume about Rattner?[1]

Was the head sold for the same price as the other ones? You might suggest to the Brooklyn authorities that, if they want you so much, they could buy one of your heads, instead of extraditing you.

I would love to see Hildegarde's portrayal of three of your women. It should be memorable.

What an inviting picture is conjured by the dinner with Alexander King, Groucho Marx and Steve Allen. If Shirley MacLaine were also there, it would be even better.

Mamie and I had some extremely interesting experiences in recent days. A group of us spent a week-end with a rabbi, and, believe it or not, it was a very exciting experience. The problems of life and death took on content and meaning. Just when I thought the rabbi was leading a perfect existence, I learned that he is happily married, except that his wife lives in New York and he lives in Cleveland.

Last night I presided at a panel discussion, in which **Harry Mark Petrakis** was one of the participants. He is a Greek-American writer who captures my imagination. Have you read any of his short stories or novels? I think that they will interest you.

Affectionate greetings from all of us.

Always yours, ELMER GERTZ

Encs.

---

1.   Unidentified. However, see Allen Stuart Weller, *Abraham Rattner* (Urbana, Ill.: University of Illinois Press, 1956).

HOPE YOU'LL GET OPPORTUNITY TO TALK TO REMBAR WHILE THERE. ADVISED REMBAR YESTERDAY I WILL NOT APPEAR IN BROOKLYN VOLUNTARILY HIS HOME TELEPHONE NUMBER IS [*omitted*], OFFICE PHONE [*omitted*], YOU MAY BE ABLE TO MAKE VERY USEFUL SUGGESTIONS, ALL THE BEST

HENRY MILLER

[*Wire to Gertz at Berkshire Hotel, New York City, 21 February 1964. Pacific Palisades, California.*]

ALS, 1P.   2/21/64

Dear Elmer—   What a good long letter—yours of the 20th. I telegraphed you at once, urging you to see Rembar if possible. Stanley Fleishman will take care of matters at this end, if they come and get me.

The quarrel (Cancer film) is between Levine and producers and Wolfe (script writer) and Levine. All stupid too—could be settled easily, I think. I make a deposition (as do all the others) on March 10th. Hope to get to Mexico after that.

Would love more Synagogue cards when convenient. Color rather pale, I notice. I only know vaguely about Rattner book— he has had so much trouble getting it done.

Don't know what price was put on head, but imagine the maximum, as Hirshhorn is rich.

I've met Shirley MacLaine several times. Quite a card. But nothing compared to Ava Gardner or Sophia Loren!

No, I never heard of Petrakis. But don't send me anything to read—am swamped.

Why those Brooklyn people are so eager to get me there I can't figure out. They can't hope to win, can they?

Still painting! Lots going on here.   My best! Henry

TL(CC), 1P., AIR MAIL   February 26, 1964

Dear Henry: While in New York I received your telegram. In fact, I received an extra copy of the same telegram. I immediately talked with Cy Rembar and he was very glad to hear from me. He, too, has suggested a severance to the Brooklyn District Attorney. He is in the process of filing, and perhaps has actually filed, a United States District Court proceeding, trying to enjoin prosecution of the Brooklyn case. Cy is eager to have my assistance and, of course, it will be forthcoming. I will give more thought to the matter and communicate with him again. Meanwhile, I suggest that you bring me up to date.

I was simply buried in work while in New York and even more so since my return. Tomorrow I hope to write again in response to your letters and other matters.

Affectionate greetings from all of us.

Always yours, ELMER GERTZ

P.S. I received a package containing the Italian editions of your work. They are truly beautiful. Some of the foreign publishers do a much better job than our American publishers. Even without knowing the language, it is nice to fondle the volumes.

I don't know whether or not you have the enclosed material about the Rattner window. In any event, you could use an extra copy, I am sure. I hope to get to you some more post cards.

ALS, 1P.   2/27/64

Dear Elmer—   Don't know that 1 have any information to offer about the Brooklyn biz. I just signed an affidavit for Rembar. The enclosed came today.[1] Looks to me now (reading the affidavit) that Rembar is really moving ahead.

I write two or three foreign publishers every day or two to send you all they have published of my work. Japanese may be very slow.

Hope you get German version of my play soon—should have it already, from Berlin. I like it very much!

Don't work too hard! Henry

P.S. Sure glad to hear Rembar will accept your assistance. How can we lose then? (Isn't that Cassius Clay a lunatic? "I'm the greatest!")

---

1.   Unidentified.

TL(CC), 2PP., AIR MAIL   March 6, 1964

Dear Henry: Thanks much for the etching that you were good enough to send me. Not even considering that it is your very first effort in that medium, it is surprisingly good. It will have an honored place on one of my walls.

All, all is a weariness of the flesh, as I write. I am dog-tired, and there seems to be no escape from the trap in which I find myself. Surely, it is not through greed, because I can't say that I am making anything. The busier I am, the more I seem to maintain my amateur standing.

Tomorrow I go to Kansas City to discuss a trial I have undertaken for the last part of March.

I have not heard more from Rembar. I am sure that I will. If so, I'll let you know. What is possessing the Brooklyn crowd, I don't know. They can scarcely win.

You will get more of the post cards soon. They don't do justice to the window, but they serve to remind one of it.

I am looking forward to receiving the foreign editions of your works that you are obtaining for me. I hope that these do not represent too much trouble for you.

I took over a seminar in constitutional law at Northwestern University Law School yesterday (it's Ted's *alma mater*). I had a sort of Socratic discussion with advanced students and a couple of professors on so-called obscenity cases, with particular reference to the *Tropic* cases. It was fun while it lasted; then I had to race through all sorts of things at the office.

Are you definitely leaving for Mexico and for how long?

All of our best to you.   Sincerely yours, ELMER GERTZ

APS, 2SS.   3/9/64

Dear Elmer—   Get the post card habit—reduces labor! Can't go to Mexico yet. Had to swear I wouldn't leave country until B'klyn biz. is settled (!) Haven't had word from Rembar recently. Each day or so I write more publishers to send you books. Quite a list!

Don't wait to get ill before you take a rest! I have hopes now of finding a combined sec'y-cook-chauffeur. Would mean a lot to me. Can't make headway as things are now.   Henry

ALS, 1P.   3/12/64

Dear Elmer—   Enclose invoice from Danish publisher (which please return) just to show you that I am on the job.[1] Have over a dozen more publishers to write. I take it you want them regardless of what language.

Note all the copies of letters you sent others.

No further news yet re Brooklyn. Spent 5 or 6 hours the other day making deposition before 3 lawyers—in the *Cancer* film litigation. What an ordeal! No one seems to know what the goal is.

Did you receive copy of play in German yet, I wonder?

This in haste again.   Henry

---

1. Invoice from Hans Reitzel Publishers Ltd., Copenhagen, dated September 3, 1964, giving names and prices of thirteen Miller books sent to Gertz.

TL(CC), 2PP., AIR MAIL   March 17, 1964

Dear Henry: Today I received the English editions of *Cancer* and *Capricorn*, for which my thanks. I deeply appreciate your efforts in getting your books for me. I want them regardless of language. I belong to that very peculiar race of the acquisitive. I hold on to everything except money.

In the end I hope you will let me know how much you pay for the various books, so that I may pay you for them. It is enough that you go to so much trouble in my behalf.

The more I hear from you with respect to the *Cancer* film litigation the more puzzled I am. So far as the film is concerned, where does that leave you? Is there going to be any film? If so, when?

No, I have not received a copy of the play in German yet.

I am interested in your having to agree to stay in the States while the Brooklyn case is pending. I have not heard from Rembar recently, so I don't know how things stand.

I will be curious to see this combination secretary, cook, chauffeur and what have you. I don't want to boast, but Mamie is a combination secretary, masseuse, manicurist, pedicurist, and everything else. I often wonder what I have done to deserve such comfort.

Somehow, the enclosed release by the FHA interested me enormously. Maybe it's a sign of our growing up that even a bureaucracy will permit art to be included in the costs of a public-aided project.

I hope that I will have good news to report to you Thursday, as per the enclosed copy of a letter to Barney.[1]

My daughter-in-law Sue is back to classes at the Art Institute and is doing more painting than in a long while, also, some sculpture. She has not looked better in ages.

Affectionate greetings from all of us.

Sincerely yours, ELMER GERTZ[2]

---

1. Gertz was once more anticipating a ruling from the Illinois Supreme Court on Judge Epstein's *Cancer* decision. On March 20 he sent a letter to attorney Edward de Grazia, with a carbon to Miller, advising that the court had again recessed without acting on the case.
2. Signature typed, but letter not signed.

ALS, 1P.   March 21st '64

Dear Elmer—   No word about Supreme Court decision (Chicago) yet—suppose it was delayed again. Nothing further on Brooklyn yet either.

Wouldn't think of letting you pay for foreign books. I must owe you a fortune by now—in one way and another! ! !

Nobody knows if there will be a film (Cancer) or not. All is obscure, tangled, mystifying. A *pre*-trial comes next month. I hope a settlement will be made—out of court.

I abandoned idea of getting Swedish sec'y (etc) from N.Y. A friend of Val's will help me out—cook one meal a day and clean up—till I find the "ideal." (!)

In a letter from my Swedish publisher (W.&W.)[1] they say the critics there are full of praise for my work and several have mentioned me for the Nobel Prize. (sic)

I've made a few very good, big, new WC's recently. Feeling wonderful now.

My best to Sue—and to *Mamie* toujours—à jamais (*forever*)!

Henry

P.S. Did I tell you that Girodias (Olympia Press) got 1 year in prison, $20,000.00 fine, and is forbidden to publish for 20 years? (Some sentence!) Can't manage to get copies of de luxe illus. edition of *Sexus* (in French). *Rare item.*[2]

---

1.   Wahlström & Widstrand, Stockholm.
2.   Postscript written vertically in left margin.

ALS, 1P.   3/21/64

Dear Elmer—   Thought enclosed might interest you.[1] What news from Illinois Supreme Court? (Please return letter, yes?)

In haste, Henry

---

1.   Letter was the one referred to in Miller's earlier communication of the same date, from his Swedish publisher, Wahlström & Widstrand.

TL(CC), 2PP., AIR MAIL   March 24, 1964

Dear Henry: Thanks much for the Dutch edition of *Tropic of Capricorn* and your amusing inscription.[1] Somehow, in Dutch there is nothing wild or dangerous about the words. Perhaps, the next time that we have an obscenity case involving your writings, we ought to submit some foreign editions, rather than the American or

English edition. In that way, the court cannot properly condemn what you have written.

Thanks, too, for sending me the material about Joe Levine and the other stuff that you sent with the book.

I don't know whether or not I have acknowledged receipt of the English editions of *Cancer* and *Capricorn*. Those I can read.

In an important work used in some of the universities, the Massachusetts *Cancer* case is set forth. The book is entitled, *First Amendment Freedoms—Selected Cases on Freedom of Religion, Speech, Press, Assembly*. It is edited by Milton R. Konvitz and published by Cornell University Press.[2] I know the book because I have been asked to review it.

A group of us met at Noon today to discuss what, if anything, can be done to speed up a decision by the Illinois Supreme Court. We came up with some ideas, none particularly good. We may do something or other to stir up the court in the next couple of weeks. Our problem is not to anger them.

It is very generous of you to insist upon paying for the foreign books. Such generosity is characteristic of you.

What you say about the Swedish reaction to your works is extremely interesting. If you were, in fact, awarded the Nobel Prize, it would make a lot of red faces, here and elsewhere. Mamie and I saw a somewhat amusing film dealing with the Nobel Prize, based upon the novel by Wallace.

What you say about the Girodias conviction and sentence is fantastic. It is much like some recent sentences here. Madame De Gaulle seems to be having a very bad effect on freedom in France.

I have a series of debates on obscenity and the law—one tonight with the former head of the Criminal Division of the United States Attorney's office, one in a couple of weeks with the same person, and then later in the month with Judge Eiger, before whom some of the *Tropic* cases are pending.

I am still commuting back and forth, to and from Kansas City. I will be there again this Thursday and will remain for about a week, until the case is tried and disposed of. If it becomes necessary to communicate with me, I will be at the Muehlebach Hotel.

I have just received the letter from your Swedish publisher. I have made a copy of it and I am returning the original.

Affectionate greetings from all of us.

Sincerely yours, ELMER GERTZ

---

1.   Published by DeSteenbokskeerkring, Amsterdam, 1964. The inscription reads:

> Dear Elmer—
>   This just came!
> (From "the Busy Bee"
>   publisher)
>   Can you read it?
>   Henry 3/20/64

Miller had earlier inscribed a copy of the Grove Press 1962 edition of *Capricorn* as follows:

> For Elmer Gertz—
> And let's hope he does not have to
> defend this one—though he *could*
> defend any thing!
>   Henry Miller Chicago, 11/4/62

2.   Milton R. Konvitz, *First Amendment Freedoms: Selected Cases on Freedom of Religion, Speech, Press, Assembly* (Ithaca, N.Y.: Cornell University Press [1963]).

TL(CC), 2PP., AIR MAIL   April 3, 1964

Dear Henry: I returned yesterday from Kansas City, where I was fortunate enough to win a criminal case in the federal court. Of course, I was associated with a leading firm in the matter. It was more exciting than any drama over television, but we had to work at a killing pace—about 15 hours each day.

While I was in Kansas City, I noticed that the bookshops carried *Tropic of Cancer*, *Tropic of Capricorn* and *Fanny Hill*. There seemed to be no excitement about the matter. I also read of arguments before the United States Supreme Court in a couple of obscenity cases. It appears, therefore, that this subject is very much under consideration and important decisions are likely to be reached.

I received the current report of the Illinois Supreme Court

today and I noticed under the heading of Cases under Advisement for the May Term, 1964 that our case is number 4. This is the highest it has been on the call. At the same time, the case involving Lenny Bruce is also under advisement for the same term of the court. In the Bruce case, the Official Reporter phrased the issue as "Were words used by defendant in nightclub routine merely 'dirty words' or obscene in meaning of statute?"

Finally, I noticed that in a special session of the Illinois Supreme Court, held at the University of Chicago, another obscenity case was argued, this one involving *scienter* (knowledge).[1]

As soon as I had a free moment, I talked with the American Civil Liberties Union attorney about the desirability of proceeding with the inquiry, a copy of which I mailed to you before going to Kansas City. He now feels that a decision in our case is so imminent that it might be unwise to press the court too much. We will talk about it early next week.

When I returned to the office I was delighted to find that I had received a number of your books from Hans Reitzels Forlag and Buchet-Chastel. Thanks much.

Mamie was our mascot in Kansas City. My client, his family, everyone, simply loved her. As always, she was extremely useful to me—taking care of many chores and leaving me free to concentrate on the case.

Affectionate greetings from all of us.

Ever yours, ELMER GERTZ

---

1.   In *Smith v. California*, 361 U.S. 147 (1959), the United States Supreme Court ruled that for an obscenity conviction of a bookseller to be constitutional, there must be some proof of *scienter* (knowledge, or awareness) on the part of the dealer that the material in question was obscene, since the lack of such a requirement might "tend to work a substantial restriction on freedom of speech." "For if the bookseller is criminally liable without knowledge of the contents, and the ordinance fulfills its purpose, he will tend to restrict the books he sells to those he has inspected; and thus the State will have imposed a restriction upon the distribution of constitutionally protected as well as obscene literature: 'Every bookseller would be placed under an obligation to make himself aware of the contents of every book in his shop.

It would be altogether unreasonable to demand so near an approach to omniscience.' And the bookseller's burden would become the public's burden, for by restricting him the public's access to reading matter would be restricted."

ALS, 1P.   4/9/64

Dear Elmer—   Just a word to say I had a good visit a few days ago from Max Eastman (of the "Masses") and Feike Feikema, an author. They told me a new law has been passed which means writers will only pay a flat 25% (capital gains) tax on income, from 1964 on. If true, good news! My tax accountant knows nothing of it as yet.

Rembar wrote me other day—B'klyn still determined. Only concession he could get thus far is that they will notify him when ready to get me so that he can appeal to Gov. Rockefeller. Sometimes I wonder—are they bluffing? We should soon know. Meanwhile I'm a voluntary prisoner here—can't move.

I'm all alone now and looking for a housekeeper. Keeps me dancing. But am quite content—and in fine shape, *I think*.

This in haste.   The best! Henry

In Gertz's letters of April 9 and 14 he spoke principally of the receipt of several foreign editions of works by and about Miller.

TL(CC), 1P., AIR MAIL   April 15, 1964

Dear Henry: I have received more books from your German publishers, including the very beautiful edition of *Just Wild About Harry* (with your intriguing water color); and I have also received several books from your Swedish publishers. These foreign editions are so gay in appearance that they light up my den.

How long does Rembar think that you will be a house prisoner, as it were? I am going to talk with him as soon as I can, in the effort to see if anything can be accomplished.

This has been a very exciting day for me. In addition to the usual business, I celebrated Mamie's birthday and a landmark victory in the *Compulsion* case. In that case I sued Meyer Levin and others in behalf of Nathan Leopold, and the court today decided that I was entitled to summary judgment on the issue of liability. Now I must proceed with the proof of damages. One day soon I will tell you more about the case, as it is an extremely important one. I filed it over five years ago and have been waiting for several years for the court's ruling.[1]

Today I ran into Judge Epstein and he, too, was much concerned about our Supreme Court's delay in the *Tropic of Cancer* case. He no longer even attempts to inhibit his views. There were several appellate and trial court judges around us when he asked me about the case.

In back of my mind has been the dread spectre of what happened six years ago yesterday—the death of my first wife in very tragic circumstances. It is amazing how a happy aftermath can blur even the bitterest memories.

Affectionate greetings to you from Mamie and myself.

Always yours, ELMER GERTZ

---

1.   See Gertz, *A Handful of Clients*, pp. 149–92, for an extended account of litigation involving *Compulsion*, Meyer Levin's novelized version of the Leopold-Loeb murder case. Gertz was finally unable to prevail in his effort to defend Leopold's right to privacy. His plea was rejected by Illinois' highest court. The case remains a notable one, however. In handing down its ruling against Leopold, the Illinois Supreme Court for the first time declared that there is a common law right of privacy in Illinois, but held that Leopold could not benefit from this right on the grounds that he had remained a public figure during the years following his crime.

TL(CC), 1P., AIR MAIL   April 20, 1964

Dear Henry: Today I received from Daphne Fraenkel in London a book, entitled *The Michael Fraenkel-Henry Miller Correspondence called Hamlet, Volume I and Volume II.* This both puzzled and delighted me. It brought to mind the acrimony over the projected new American edition and other things that we have discussed in our correspondence. Is this publication a surprise to you or did you and Mrs. Fraenkel come to terms? I am deeply interested.
        Affectionate greetings from Mamie and all of us.
                              Sincerely yours, ELMER GERTZ

        I also received three volumes from Lausanne—beautiful ones!

ALS, 1P.   4/22/64

Dear Elmer—   About that Hamlet book. I asked Tom Moore to order it for you—gift from me. Daphne has never written me about this edition, nor even sent me *a* copy. Tom communicates with her. Guess she's a sworn enemy of H. M.
        I haven't answered other letters—been so damn busy—especially now that I'm alone.
        Better get in touch with Rembar, yes. Last from him wasn't very cheering. Don't know why they delay serving me warrant.
                              Best to you all! Henry

Gertz commented further on the *Hamlet* situation on April 24, and recommended that Miller look at the April 22 issue of *Variety*, which featured material about Joe Levine, a two-page *Tropic of Cancer* advertisement, and an article about Gertz's *Compulsion* victory.

TL(CC), 1P., AIR MAIL   May 4, 1964

Dear Henry: I received a letter today from Cy Rembar. The
portion of it relating to your situation in Brooklyn reads as follows:
     "In the Brooklyn prosecution, the case against the local dis-
tributors has been dismissed (by agreement). The case against
Henry has been severed (on the District Attorney's motion) and
the case against Grove Press and Barney Rosset is going forward on
a stipulation of facts. There will of course be a conviction and an
appeal."
     Although Cy does not say so, I should think that they would
be content to wait now until the rest of the case is disposed of. To
make assurances double, I have written to him.
     Affectionate greetings from all of us.
                              Always yours, ELMER GERTZ

TL(CC), 1P., AIR MAIL   May 8, 1964

Dear Henry: The other day a prison chaplain who knows Roger
Bloom telephoned me. We tried to get together, but complications
arose and we had to content ourselves with a long telephone conversation. You know the particular chaplain, Reverend Earl Grandstaff. You will remember that you had dinner with him and his
family. They cherish the warmest recollections of you.
     As to Roger, I was told that it is unlikely that he will be re-
leased at an early date and that he is becoming reconciled to this.
The reason is that, one member of the Parole Board, in particular,
feels that Roger's long record and the various federal detainers preclude special consideration for him. The chaplain is very eager that
I visit Roger, and he says that my letters as well as yours help keep
up his morale, and that a visit would do him worlds of good. What
do you think of this idea?
     Affectionate greetings from all of us.
                              Sincerely yours, ELMER GERTZ

ALS, 1P.   5/9/64

Dear Elmer—   Yes, I think it would be a wonderful idea to visit
Roger Bloom—if you can spare the time!

That Brooklyn biz. sure sounds crazy.

Have you heard of this book—"Eros Denied" by Wayland
Young (Grove Press)—just out. It's another breach in the wall.
Don't fail to look it over!   This in haste. Henry

Still alone here but getting by O.K. I did a 2½ hr. interview with
Steve Allen (*here*) last Sunday. Should go on TV in 2 weeks or so.
Will let you know date!

TL(CC), 2PP., AIR MAIL   June 2, 1964

Dear Henry: Following your suggestion, I obtained a copy of
the book, *Eros Denied*. I made the mistake of showing it to Mamie
and have not been able to look at it since. It keeps her spellbound.

I have had to content myself with reading the latest volume in
the *Oxford History of English Literature*, which deals with the eight
authors regarded as the outstanding ones of the past generation.
The list includes Shaw, Lawrence, Joyce, Hardy, James, Conrad,
Yeats and Kipling, which in itself is extraordinary. I have already
read about half of the book. I think that, despite the academic
tone, you will find it very stimulating, particularly the long essay on
Lawrence.

A group of booksellers asked me to meet with them one night
last week. In addition, Hoke Norris of the *Sun-Times* and Robert
Cromie of the *Tribune* were present. The censorship situation in
Chicago continues to be very bad, with the police and other law
enforcement agencies responding to the pressure of the so-called
citizens groups, largely Catholic. The difficulty is compounded by
the withdrawal of the indemnity by publishers. I have been able to
persuade Grove Press and Putnam's to protect booksellers to some
extent in cases in which I will represent them. We are in desperate

need of some new decisions by the United States Supreme Court and these are likely to be handed down some time during this month. I am sending herewith copies of the Hoke Norris and Jack Mabley articles,[1] to which I refer in the enclosed letter to Milton Perlman. These columns indicate the difficulties we have in Chicago.

I hesitate to make any more prophesies about our Supreme Court in connection with the *Tropic* case, except to say that in mid-June it will hand down some more decisions and it is not impossible that one of them will be in our case.

Do let us know when the Steve Allen interview will be released. Allen is a very remarkable person by television standards. How is he by civilized standards?

Are you still enjoying your lonely splendor?

Affectionate greetings from all of us.

Sincerely yours, ELMER GERTZ

---

1.   Hoke Norris, "Critic At-Large: No 'Candy' for Sale," *Chicago Sun-Times*, May 31, 1964, Section 3, p. 2; Jack Mabley, "Suddenly . . . New Attitude on Smut Here," *Chicago's American*, June 2, 1964, p. 3.

APS, 2SS.   6/2/64

Dear Elmer—   Just found a young woman to help me—cook, clean, type letters. Coming today. About time, as I was about ready to break down. My daughter Val (*and husband*) return about end of July and they will stay with me and give all the help I need. So— at last a break.

I will be on Steve Allen's show soon—try to let you know in advance. May give broadcast (already taped *here*) in 3 sections of ½ hour each.

No further news from Brooklyn or on the Levine litigation.

Hope all's well with you good people! !   Henry

APS, 2SS.   6/18/64

Dear Elmer—   A quickie just to say that the film (Cancer) litigation seems to have been settled satisfactorily out of court. Details
later. Rembar writes—"Things seem to have quieted down in
B'klyn so far as you are concerned." (What does *that* mean?) "The
case is going forward against Barney & Grove Press."

        They won a victory (Grove) over seizure of Evergreen Review
recently.[1]   More soon! Love to Mamie. Henry

---

1.   A federal injunction was obtained against the district attorney of Nas-
      sau County, who had seized copies of Grove Press's *Evergreen Review*
      to use as evidence in an obscenity prosecution (*Evergreen v. Cahn*,
      230 F. Supp. 498 [1964]). The complaint cited a chapter from *Eros
      Denied* by Wayland Young, and photographs by Emil J. Cadoo. (See
      Rembar, *End of Obscenity*, pp. 501–2.)

ILLINOIS SUPREME COURT HAS REVERSED JUDGE EP-
STEIN. AFTER CONSULTATION, WE HAVE DECIDED
TO APPLY IMMEDIATELY TO UNITED STATES SU-
PREME COURT FOR CERTIORARI. ROSSET, REMBAR
AND I ARE IN CONSTANT COMMUNICATION. I WILL
BE IN NEW YORK MONDAY. COPY OF OPINION FOL-
LOWS.   ELMER GERTZ

| [Wire to Miller, 18 June 1964.] |

TL(CC), 1P., AIR MAIL   June 19, 1964

Dear Henry: You have no idea as to how busy I have been
since the announcement of the dismal news from the Illinois Supreme Court. I say dismal news, even though Barney Rosset, Cy
Rembar and I have not sulked or become discouraged. As a matter

of fact, we welcome the opportunity to go to the United States Supreme Court.

I am conferring with Cy and Barney in New York this Monday. I don't know how long I will be there, but it will probably be long enough for us to hew out a petition for writ of certiorari. Much is at stake in this case, far more than *Tropic of Cancer* or even you. If we don't prevail, freedom of utterance will be set back for at least a generation. I am sorry that you have to be the guinea pig, but, then, perhaps we are also.

Judge Epstein has been subjected to a lot of abuse, but is bearing up well. I hope that he will like what I have written to him. I have talked with him on innumerable occasions and he is wholeheartedly in our corner.

Most of the time, while I am in New York, I will be in Cy's office [*address and telephone number omitted*]. I will be staying at the Grosvenor Hotel. Keep cheerful and don't worry.

Always yours, ELMER GERTZ

TLS, 1P.   June 20th, 1964

Dear Elmer,   I'm just in receipt of yours of the 19th with more clippings, and telegram of previous day. Believe me, I don't feel either discouraged or depressed by the news. (It's ironic, of course, that two big States like New York and Illinois, supposedly advanced culturally, etc., should be the only ones to adopt this course.) We know it's politics and not the will of the people. And in my opinion it will prove to be a boomerang. With all that's going on now in the way of legislation we are suddenly not going to move backwards.

I was even prepared for this eventuality, I might say. Once again through my astrologer friend in Lausanne.[1] Around March she wrote me that this year would be full of legal troubles, that I would be continuously before the eyes of the public, and that if I won in one instance I'd lose in another—but eventually win out over all. And she didn't mean in a distant future. It's in the stars that Cancer won't fail—I told Barney that when he published it.

Maybe it's good that we have some fireworks occasionally. When the book is fully accepted here in this country that will be the death of it, as I predicted long ago.

Well, soon the film project will be reopened. That may add more fuel to the flames.

One thing I don't quite understand yet—because of that expression "a certiorari," which I can't find in my dictionary, and that is, if the U.S. Supreme Court nullifies the Illinois' court decision, does that mean the book will be free for circulation anywhere and everywhere in the U.S. or just in Illinois?

Judge Epstein. . . . I'm sorry to hear that he has been subjected to continued abuse and criticism. He is certainly a wonderful man and I hope you will give him warm greetings from me.

The Grosvenor, by the way, is the hotel I stay at when I am in N. Y. Did you ever try the Chelsea on 23rd Street—an old hostelry but under good management and has a distinguished clientele— and still reasonable in price. A landmark.

Good luck and all the best meanwhile.

You may be glad to hear that I have cleared the decks and am now going over my one act skit with a view to finishing it soon. I feel I have begun a good, new cycle. By October it will be definitely so, according to "the stars" once again.   Henry

---

1.   Jacqueline Langmann. See H. M. 8/5/63.

TL(CC), 3PP., AIR MAIL   June 24, 1964

Dear Henry: When I arrived at Rembar's office Monday morning, I was delighted to receive your letter of good cheer. The stars were apparently right.

I hope that you know of all of the sensational developments since my telegram to you, telling of the adverse Illinois Supreme Court decision. I don't know if the newspapers out your way carried the story or if Stanley Fleishman called you. At any rate, here is what happened.

There had been a rather poorly handled case in Florida involving *Tropic of Cancer*. The attorneys, in effect, waived the constitutional issue and this, legally speaking, put us out of court, both so far as the Florida Supreme Court is concerned and the United States Supreme Court. Notwithstanding, Ed de Grazia decided to take what he regarded as a hundred-to-one chance and filed a petition for certiorari. This means a petition asking the Supreme Court to consider the case and enter some judgment order with respect to it. At that time, a movie case[1] had been pending in the United States Supreme Court for a considerable period of time, and the court was dragging its feet on it. It should have been decided a year ago last June, but it was put over for the next term of the court ⟨and⟩ which did not, in fact, hold oral argument on the case until a few weeks ago; and, incidentally, Ephraim London, who argued the matter, did not do a good job. He was not his usual brilliant, perceptive self. When I read the transcript of his argument, I was annoyed beyond words. There was also pending at that time in the United States Supreme Court an outrageous case from Kansas,[2] in which the authorities had violated every constitutional safeguard with respect to searches and seizures and had condemned a number of books to be burned. This case was brilliantly argued by Stanley Fleishman before the Supreme Court.

At any rate, Monday the United States Supreme Court reversed the obscenity conviction in the movie case, but the justices split all over the lot as to the reasons for the reversal. Justices Brennan and Goldberg wrote an opinion that sounded as if we had dictated it. It confirmed our view of the law, that nothing can be banned unless it is utterly without any redeeming social importance, including in this definition literary and artistic importance. They also decided that the standard to be applied was not of every locality, but a national standard. In other words, if the book or film were generally acceptable throughout the country, it could not be banned in a particular area. Justice Stewart said obscenity was confined to hard-core pornography, which is, in effect, what Justices Brennan and Goldberg said more effectively. Justices Black and Douglas said that all censorship is unconstitutional. In other words, we have as an absolute minimum, whenever anything of literary value is being considered, five votes. I can discuss the views of the other justices later.

The court that same day set aside the Kansas judgment and laid down some very strict rules with respect to procedure in obscenity cases. The court then went on to accept jurisdiction over another case involving the entire concept of movie censorship. A few years ago they had held that movie censorship *per se* is constitutional, depending on the rulings in the particular cases.[3] Now they are prepared once again to review the entire subject matter, and my guess is that the concept of censorship boards will be thrown out and that movies, like books, will have to be judged through prosecution for obscenity, rather than through submission to censorship boards.

Then, to show the mood in which they were in, the court, by a 5 to 4 vote, granted certiorari (that is, agreed to consider) the Florida *Tropic* case, and summarily (that is, without briefs or argument or loss of time) reversed the Florida decision against the book.[4] This means, as we interpret it, that *Tropic* may be sold anywhere in the United States. But to make absolutely certain of this, Cy and I have been in consultation for days now and are going to take certain steps to see to it that *Tropic* runs into no more trouble anywhere. I will give you the story in detail as soon as I catch my breath.

Affectionate greetings from all of us.

Always yours, ELMER GERTZ

1.   *Jacobellis v. Ohio,* 378 U.S. 184 (1964), involving *The Lovers.*
2.   *A Quantity of Books v. State of Kansas,* 378 U.S. 205 (1964).
3.   *Times Film Corporation v. Chicago,* 365 U.S. 43 (1961).
4.   *Grove Press, Inc. v. Gerstein.* For more about the United States Supreme Court decision, see Gertz 8/30/62, notes.

TLS, 1P.   June 28th, 1964

Dear Elmer,   At last I sit down to say a few words about the
exciting decision of the U.S. Supreme Court and to thank you for
keeping me so well posted with telegrams, clippings, and letters. I
have been going like a top here for days—Tony just off to Europe
with his mother, my elder daughter[1] leaving for Africa, unexpected
visits, household work (despite secretary-cook), and so on. Just incredible. Once again I have cleared the decks, to get down to finishing the play.

But about the decision. . . . I still don't quite see how one
now gets the US. S. C. to make a decision on the Illinois and New
York State judgments.[2] But I assume you and Rembar have worked
out a plan. It will be wonderful if you get the green signal for the
whole U.S.

Looking at a television news broadcast the other day, where
a stiff-necked Southerner was being interviewed about Jacksonville,
Mississippi and other civil rights matters, I heard him say contemp-
tuously—"it's one thing to pass a bill, it's another to enforce it."
He left it very clear that "they" would fight any bill or law tooth
and nail—to hold "the niggers" down or in their place. He never
once said Negro. It was disgraceful, but I hope the whole country
listened in, just to see what mentalities these ignorant white bas-
tards have.

In New York I don't anticipate much trouble, somehow, but
Illinois is a horse of another color, eh? One wonders what "their"
next move will be.

News Week editor here called me up and asked for a few
words on the decision, which I willingly gave this time, mentioning
Rosset and yourself—praise for the valiant fight you put up. I hope
they don't leave that out.

I also told him the book (Cancer) is now printed in twelve
languages, and distributed without trouble even in such Catholic
strongholds as Argentina and Brazil. The only country at present
where the book was suppressed immediately on appearing is Fin-

land. Poland and Jugoslavia are now about to publish some of my
books, not the Tropics yet, of course. In Germany the sale of the
public (unexpurgated) edition of Cancer has reached the 100,000
mark—very big for Germany, where books are expensive. Capricorn
has an *advance* sale there of over 20,000 already. England gives no
trouble on either book—and of course Cancer there has sold well
over 100,000 and next year, I believe, goes into a paperback edition.

So, as always, America ends up last. If the U.S. S. C. had not
given its OK it would indeed have been disgraceful. I wouldn't be
surprised if soon the enemies of progress in this country make an
attempt to impeach the members of the Supreme Court—or isn't
that possible under our Constitution?

Anyway, congratulation, warmest thanks, and good luck to the
end. Curious, eh, that my astrologer was so firmly right? By the
way, have you had a chance yet to peek into "Eros Denied"? You'll
find wonderful ammunition there, I think.

All the best to Mamie and all the family. I await further news.

Henry

P.S. I told you, didn't I, that Levine settled with the producers out
of court?[3]

---

1. Barbara Sylvas Miller, born in 1919, Miller's daughter by his first wife,
    Beatrice Sylvas Wickens, a Brooklyn pianist.
2. By reversing the Florida *Cancer* conviction (*Grove Press v. Gerstein*),
    the United States Supreme Court indicated that to hold *Cancer* ob-
    scene was improper, although the Court offered no opinion in the case.
    On July 7, 1964, the Illinois Supreme Court withdrew its ruling that
    the book was obscene, citing the United States Supreme Court's ac-
    tion in *Gerstein*, and affirmed Judge Samuel B. Epstein's decision of
    February 21, 1962, in the Superior Court of Cook County. The court's
    order read:
       "On June 18, 1964, this court adopted an opinion in this case
    holding that the book, 'Tropic of Cancer' is obscene and that its sale
    could therefore be prohibited without violation of the constitutional
    guarantee of freedom of the press. On June 22, 1964, the Supreme
    Court of the United States in the case of *Grove Press, Inc. v. Ger-
    stein*, by per curiam order, reversed a judgment of the District Court

of Appeal of Florida which had held that the book, 'Tropic of Cancer' was obscene and had restricted its sale and distribution.

"On the court's own motion, acting under the controlling authority of the decision of the Supreme Court of the United States in the Florida case, which involved the identical book that is the subject matter of this case,

"IT IS ORDERED that the opinion heretofore adopted by this court, in this case, is withdrawn and the judgment heretofore entered is vacated.

"IT IS FURTHER ORDERED that the judgment of the Superior Court of Cook County is affirmed."

The courts of other states eventually followed suit, but in some instances litigation continued for another two years (see Hutchison, *Tropic of Cancer on Trial*, pp. 242–43).

3.   Postscript written by hand on second page (reverse of first page).

Afterword

Afterword

The Meaning of Friendship

It is a source of wonder and of joy that I got to know Henry Miller so early and so well. When I became one of the attorneys for his publisher Grove Press and, nominally, for Miller himself, I was told that I was not to communicate with Miller, because he disliked lawyers and litigation. I was supposed to keep him out of the courtroom and away from those who would take his deposition or otherwise bother him. Everything would be handled through me or my professional associates, chiefly Charles Rembar. If we had to go beyond ourselves, then the enterprising Barney Rosset and others at Grove Press would take care of things.

This arrangement did not consider that our opponents could force Miller to submit to questioning and that if we or Miller resisted, the matter could be thrown out of court or Miller subjected to other sanctions. Nor did it consider the sort of attorney and person that I am. When I get into a situation, in or out of court, whether legal or literary, I explore it in depth.

When I was the attorney in a suit involving English earthenware, I learned all that I could about the product, and was able to examine its leading manufacturer with apparent authority. When I represented a yachtsman in a suit over a racing vessel, I learned all about such sailing ships, although I am in mortal fear of the sea. As a result, I was able to cross-examine the most highly regarded nautical architect, the designer of ships that had won the America's Cup on several occasions. That is the nature of the legal craft as practiced by me for forty-seven years. Some of us become experts for the duration of the proceeding, then forget all that we have learned in our crash course and go on to the next subject, which we master briefly.

When I was called upon to represent publisher and author in Illinois in what turned out to be a multiplicity of suits, I had read nothing by Miller and very little about him. Of course, I had to read *Tropic of Cancer* without delay, because that was what it was all about. I had to absorb critical opinion of the book and know something of the man, just as I had learned about English earthenware and American racing ships in other cases. As my correspondence with Henry Miller reveals, I became what readily may be described as a profound student of Miller and his writings almost instantly, not simply because I wanted to succeed in the various cases, but even more because I became intrigued by him. I have never ceased to be interested in him. He is the natural follow-up to my interest in Frank Harris, the protagonist of my first book in 1931. Barney Rosset, as I have said elsewhere, regarded the extent of my preparation as "almost frightening"; Charles Rembar commented with delight; the judge was impressed; Henry Miller, of course, was the most pleased.

I was aware that no litigated author, so far as I could learn, had ever really known his lawyer or exchanged letters with him with any frequency or genuine intimacy. Certainly, James Joyce did not become a close friend of Morris Ernst in connection with the famous *Ulysses* suit, and Ernst was a very articulate person, if not a man of letters, and infinitely curious and persuasive about men and ideas. D. H. Lawrence was dead before lawyers battled in the courts over *Lady Chatterly's Lover*; as he told Frank Harris, he never would make old bones. He was consumed early by tuberculosis and the fires of his genius. Frank Harris, too, had become involved with the police, because of *My Life and Loves*, more through his young selling agents than directly, except, surprisingly enough, with respect to the French gendarmes. When he feared criminal involvement as he planned to visit America again a few years before his death, he persuaded me, a young man, not yet a lawyer, to talk in his behalf with the famous defender of the distressed, Clarence Darrow. It was to me, not to Harris, that Darrow wrote, promising to defend Harris. This never became necessary.

Why, then, did I achieve so unique a role as the correspondent and confident of Henry Miller? In the beginning, as I have said, I had no expectancy of being personally involved with Miller the man any more than the litigant. None of the other lawyers in the many *Tropic of Cancer* obscenity cases across the land had such intimate involvement and some of them were men of considerable parts, like Rembar, Stanley Fleishman and Edward DeGrazia. I did not write to Miller in the first instance. He wrote to me, through the intercession of Edward P. Schwartz, as is told in the very first letters of this collection, and soon became just as concerned about me and mine as I was about him. His concern was touching and inspiring.

The selections in this volume stop in July 1964, when the *Tropic of Cancer* litigation was at an end and the highest court of the land found, in effect, that the book was entitled to constitutional protections. This gives the book a kind of unity. It is the story of the successful struggle to free one controversial work from the bigots. Never afterwards (with a single and temporary exception in Pennsylvania) was *Tropic of Cancer* attacked in the courts by the police and public prosecutors. Indeed, none of Miller's other writings were subsequently the subject of legal attack—not even the highly vulnerable *Sexus* or *The World of Sex* or *Quiet Days in Clichy* or *Tropic of Capricorn*. He was home free, increasingly recognized as a great literary pioneer and unique personality. Educational television found him fit for general viewing. His triumph was the victory of all writers whose works have substantial value. My *Tropic of Cancer* associate, Charles Rembar, may be right when he proclaimed "the end of obscenity" in a book of that name. The obscenity battles now are over shoddy films and other such trash, rather than serious works. Miller gave me credit, probably too much credit, for this result. He was quick to recognize what I had done, more reluctant to recognize the roles of others. That is what friendship sometimes does to the judgment, and I am not complaining.

I was involved in many legal matters with Miller, some dealt with in this book and others belonging to the later phases of our friendship. Miller consulted me constantly about all of the *Tropic* cases, not only the ones in Illinois over which I had direct charge, but the many in other parts of the country, particularly the mischievous Brooklyn effort to charge him with criminal offenses. It may be surprising to some to learn that I never received a penny of compensation on these matters from Miller himself—only from Grove Press in connection with most of the Illinois matters but none of the other cases in which I helped. As many letters show, I advised Miller about the making of gifts for the purpose of obtaining income tax deductions and did much work, some of it tedious, with my wife, Mamie, and secretary, Gladys Fuller, in distributing these gifts, all without compensation. In this period and later I worked in behalf of Miller's prison friend, Roger Bloom, becoming his parole sponsor when he was finally released, this necessitating continuous contact with him and the filing of reports. When Miller, like a conventional parent, worried about the possible drafting of his son, Tony, at the time of the war in Vietnam, he came to me for advice. When it looked as if the young Japanese-born entertainer, Hoki, with whom he was in love, might have to leave the country, he asked me to help keep her here. There may have been other legal problems, too, that I have forgotten for the moment. The nature of our friendship was such that either could call upon the other without embarrassment or compensation other than the joy of helping.

And when Miller was not enlisting my aid, he was asking my talented and devoted wife for assistance, sometimes in unexpected ways, as when he wanted her to trace a provocative criticism of America and Americans attributed to Walt Whitman, who generally sang our praises. She had never done any literary research, but persisted and was fortunate enough to find the source in a most unexpected place, and he was pleased, hardly more so than Mamie.

Our relationship was filled with such reciprocal delights. It was never one-sided or too demanding. The unexpected was the special ingredient of our friendship.

Those who read the correspondence will know that initially Miller was attracted to me because he thought I was what he regarded as a rare bird, an American lawyer who had a degree of culture and could write. He formed this impression partially on the basis of reading my ancient book on Frank Harris, issued three years before Miller had published his first book, *Tropic of Cancer*. This impression was strengthened by my reviews of two of his books in the *Chicago Daily News*, for which I often wrote. But his always present critical sense was apparent, without diminishing our regard, as he read my writings in *The Paper*, a precious little periodical of short life, of which I was the nominal publisher. He observed that I wrote about things, rather than being so absorbed in them that my style and substance would be a natural outpouring of what I felt deeply. I did not choose to argue with him, being too intrigued by his opinions and friendship to bother to disagree. I had spent a lifetime in affectionate relationship with persons who differed from me. Friendship is a very complicated thing. It is sometimes won instantaneously, and can survive all differences.

Later, in the years following the period of the *Tropic* litigation, Miller read my book, *A Handful of Clients*, which dealt, among other things, with the *Tropic* cases and my first warm impressions of Miller himself. He wrote an enthusiastic "blurb" for the jacket of the book. This dealt more with me as a man and lawyer than with the qualities of the book. He thought that I was much like Dr. Kerkhoven, a remarkable character in his favorite trilogy by Jacob Wassermann on the nature of humanity and justice. He thought that there was a danger of my being consumed by the unremitting demands of those who appealed to my intense desire to right the wrongs done to them. Also, he compared me to Clarence Darrow, whom he saw as my idol. Thus he escaped the necessity of discussing the intrinsic qualities of my writing. Apparently, he did not know that Darrow had published several books and many articles and had more ties with writers, such as H. G. Wells, than with his colleagues of the bar, for whom he held no high regard. He readily could have made intriguing comparisons between me and Darrow, for, in a sense, I was a footnote to Darrow's career, having succeeded in 1958 in freeing Nathan Leopold, the man whose life Darrow had saved in 1924. Miller felt that Leopold was a natural subject for a certain kind of book, but I sensed that he had reservations about whether I was the person to do the book, just as he had reservations about Leopold's own book, *Life Plus 99 Years*, which I had sent him. Curiously, Miller had more respect for Leopold than the latter had for him. Those who live amidst the obscenities of the prison world tend to question freedom of expression in the larger world.

Later, when my volume of memoirs, *To Life*, was published, Miller again wrote some words in its praise that could be used in the publisher's publicity, again dealing more with the man than with any literary gifts that I might have. In his letters to me, not included in this volume because they are of a later period, he expressed mixed feelings about my book. He was amazed by the richness of my experiences, but was highly critical of my failure to deal adequately with the writers who had influenced me. Apparently, he wanted me to do the sort of study he had done in *The Books in My Life*. He seemed to feel that if books were really an integral part of my life, as I professed, then my impressions of their creators should be a major ingredient in any autobiography.

Miller and I, at one in our love of books, were worlds apart in our tastes. I thrilled to the music of the great poets—Shakespeare, of course, and Keats, Shelley, Wordsworth, Blake, Browning, Tennyson at his best. But Miller was almost indifferent to them, except for his appreciation of his unexpected blood-brother, Rimbaud. I absorbed virtually the whole body of classical dramatic literature, from the immortal Greeks on to Molière, Shakespeare again, and Ibsen, Wilde, O'Neill and, above all, Shaw. These left Miller cold. He could not understand my passion for the allegedly passionless G. B. S. He, a born story teller, loved the story tellers— the picaresque, adventurous, full-blooded, philosophical, spiritual fictionists—Rabelais, Dostoevsky, Balzac, Hamsun, Wassermann, Powys, Corelli, Singer, a veritable judge of differing creators. His favorite mystics were mostly moonshine to me. We both read incessantly, but our literary paths seldom met.

Miller, who on the surface lived so exigently, was confessing, in effect, that transcripts and transcribers of life meant more to him, sometimes, than the actual living of life. He essentially is a

man of words rather than of deeds, and I, his friend, am a doer of
deeds rather than one existing on the verbal plane, much though
I love and practice the writer's craft. He was amazed and almost
daunted by the extent of my involvement in so many activities.
The mere listing of them seemed to exhaust him. That is why he
constantly urged me to rest more, to relax, to attempt less, advice
I seldom could heed until I reached the age Miller had been when
first our lives crossed. The influence of Miller is a large ingredient
in the decision that a few years ago led me to become less im-
mersed in the daily drudgery of the courtrooms.

When my selection of the short stories of Frank Harris came
out, as a sort of final word in my long study of the man best known
for *My Life and Loves*, Miller wrote letters of comment as he read
into the book. I had called "A Daughter of Eve" a great story of
passion, a masterpiece even, although it lacked the explicitness of
language and scene characteristic of Miller and of Harris in his
autobiography. Miller was unimpressed. He thought the story surprisingly old fashioned and undistinguished. But "A Chinese Story"
and "Montes the Matador" and "A Mad Love" he regarded as sur-
passingly good. He quoted his son, Tony, as being enthralled by
"Montes."

One would be impressed and sometimes annoyed or jarred by
Miller's integrity of judgment in personal as well as literary matters.
I regarded myself as a pretty frank fellow, but I would not knowingly hurt anyone by expressing anything harsh to his face. I would
not plant a thorn in his bosom, as Lincoln phrased it. I have sometimes said that I could never give an unkindly opinion about a child.
I would never dream of telling a mother that her baby was ugly
even if he were exceedingly so. My integrity consists in silence or in
the refusal to flatter. Miller would be inclined to blurt out the bald
truth, even if it hurt. He seems to think that we ought to face up to
all facts. In *A Handful of Clients* I told of Miller's scolding my son-
in-law, Henry Hechtman, because Henry had abandoned the fine
arts for commercial work as a means of earning a livelihood. The
young man spent that night in painting a very good still life, as if
to show Miller and himself that he had not lost his innate creative-

ness. In the same way, when Miller saw our son, Jack, after an
absence of years, and observed his gain in weight and the quantity
of food he ate, he remarked, as if such brutal candor were usual,
"Jack, you *fress* [devour], you do not *ess* [eat]." Only the German
idiom could express his disapproval.

Yet, when George Wickes, who had edited the Miller-Durrell
correspondence, planned to do an anthology of the best writings
about Miller, Miller did not hesitate to urge Wickes to ask me to
do an essay for the collection, and this was very early in our friendship. The chapter, "Henry Miller and the Law," is one of the two
original pieces in the book, the others being previously published
material. Later, when *Synthèses*, the French Belgian literary journal,
projected a tribute to Miller on his seventy-fifth birthday, he suggested to the editor that I contribute. I wrote on "My Client Henry
Miller," and the essay was translated into French and published
with other original contributions by the leading literary lights of
several countries, where Miller was more esteemed at the time
than in his native land. I am sure that if other such collections had
been projected, Miller would not have hesitated to recommend me
for inclusion among recognized writers. At the very least, he did
not dispute my capacity to deal with him. More than once he said
that I knew more about his writings than he did himself.

When I became the attorney in the *Tropic of Cancer* litigation in Illinois, my lovely and wise daughter, Margery Ann (called
by her choice Midge), asked, "How can a prude like you be Henry
Miller's lawyer?" A strange question, indeed, to be addressed to
the first biographer of the shameless Frank Harris and the notorious
defender of complete freedom of expression. Troubled and amused,
I asked Miller if I were, indeed, a prude, and he assured me I was
not. On several occasions thereafter I found that Miller by no
means was as enamoured of the complete verbal freedom professed by his followers. He had little admiration for the literary
practices of Norman Mailer, but liked him as a person, despite
Mailer's having gone to immense lengths to prepare an annotated
anthology of Miller's more explicit works. Miller has little taste for

the writings of others celebrated for their uninhibited styles, which they fancy to resemble his. Sometimes he seems to regret his influence. He admires the more restrained genius of Isaac Bashevis Singer, for one, and considers him the best of the living masters of fiction. Yet, he admires Erica Jong both as a writer and person, perhaps because he is surprised that an attractive young woman can write "like a man" without inhibition.

There must be something in me, as in Miller, that suggests the biblical Joseph, who could not be beguiled by the wiles of Potiphar's wife. I, too, resent at times what I have wrought in the protection of expression. I once phrased it that we all have the right to make pigs of ourselves, but when we act as swine and wallow in garbage we are no longer attractive. To me, as to Miller, writers should have complete freedom, but they should have enough literary integrity to express only what is inherent in their art and in the life they depict, not cavort in dirt for the sake of the coin of the realm or what is in fashion at the moment.

When I first became acquainted with Miller, all of his great pioneering works had been written, but were published in this country for the first time during the course of our friendship, possibly in some degree because of it. Only one major work remains unwritten and unpublished—the second volume of Nexus, the last part of the Rosy Crucifixion trilogy. Miller often talked of finishing the book, and made attempts at it now and then. But generally he was inhibited in what should have been an easy task for one of his facility. He seemed to feel that if Nexus were completed, his life, too, would end. By delaying this last work, he was prolonging his life. There came suddenly the physical difficulties of old age, and Nexus necessarily remained unfinished.

It was sad to contemplate this deterioration of a man of such vitality. Fortunately, there was little evidence of any mental decline. Although he spent much time in bed or in a wheel chair, he was his old vibrant self when he made public appearances, as on several occasions when he was on television talk shows. He could sometimes play his dearly loved game of ping-pong from a wheel chair and beat his opponents, some of them unclad females, as he did my physically active and adept wife on other earlier occasions.

It will not be assumed, I hope, that Miller and I share every area of our respective lives or that we are totally alike in our habits. There are whole areas in which we are worlds apart. I suspect that he hardly knew or was interested in my months-long career in winning a place in a highly contested election as a member of the Illinois Constitutional Convention and serving as chairman of its Civil Rights Committee during the years 1969–70. I do not remember sending him a copy of the book I wrote about the new bill of rights we placed in the state's constitution. Miller has always been almost completely nonpolitical, and I have been deeply absorbed in public affairs. I hardly suppose he has voted in an election or given a thought to party platforms or candidates, although, instinctively, he is for the equal rights of all persons, regardless of race, color, or creed. He believes in the Bill of Rights, although he has not read it. I was rather startled at the time of Watergate when he expressed views, in at least one letter to me, much like my own about the villain of the affair, Richard M. Nixon. All of which proves the pervasiveness of Watergate rather than any change in Miller's attitude.

He could be more charitable to the outcasts, criminals, and wrongdoers than to the respectables. Like the poet Heine, he cast his lot with those rejected by society. As he told me, garbage collectors could be more admirable than some writers and other persons of note. Heine dismissed the kastraten, the emasculated people, who carped at his outspoken verse. While no lyric poet, Miller sings vigorously in his own manner in sympathy for those robust and imperfect souls who are not celebrated by the genteel versifiers or the self-consciously virtuous people. He would do more for Roger Bloom and others convicted by the courts than for those who prosecuted them. He was for the condemned rather than those who condemned them. His verbal outspokenness was never at the expense of those who had suffered, justly or unjustly, at the hands of society.

I, too, worked to correct injustice and to achieve a better world. He was more skeptical than I about the prospects for arriving at Utopia. My methods were more cerebral and planned than his. He spoke and acted out of the unrehearsed commands of his heart. Yet, each of us respected the other's life style.

All of his life Miller has been extremely active in a physical sense, not alone in his amours. He has ridden bicycles, boxed, swam, played ping-pong, danced, kept himself lean and trim, by such exercise and not by games other than ping-pong. I have been his antithesis, regarding such things as vexatious, if not foolish. We have been friends because of our differences, rather than our similarities, proof that opposites often attract in friendship as in love.

It must not be supposed for a moment that friendship is something unique in Miller's life. Perhaps the one unusual quality about my relationship with him is my profession. The outlaw in him was generally not attracted to professional persons, respectables of any stripe. It tells much about him that in his declining years he is writing a series of chapbooks about the friends in his life, from his earliest days to, one hopes, the present. One volume of the series has already appeared, and demonstrates that even in his late eighties, as in his forties, he has almost perfect recall of the scenes, sounds, and smells of long ago and that he gives himself away as completely as he does his friends.

His friendships were built, in part at least, upon correspondence. Emil Schnellock, the first artist in his life, one who taught him his love of water colors, comes to mind; one recalls, too, the recently departed and always luminous Anaïs Nin, who helped make possible the first appearance of Tropic of Cancer, and thereafter immortalized both him and his second wife, June, in many glowing pages in her unique diary; Lawrence Durrell, the ebullient young man who was so taken by the first Tropic volume that he wrote in unforgettable words to his master and then visited him in Paris, induced him to go to Greece, and saw him again and again in America and elsewhere, always laughing, always the ebullient young man even as he added years and wives and masterpieces such

as the Alexandria Quartet; and Michael Fraenkel, one of the top
characters in *Tropic of Cancer*, with whom Miller wrote the too
little known *Hamlet* letters, dealing profoundly with life and death
and all in between them.

There were others, some well known today, some distinguished
in another day, some simply Miller's cronies, creative people most
of them, others watchers of time or wastrels, none dull since Miller
dealt with them in his correspondence and in his books. Letter
writing for him, as for me, was an addiction, a slavery, despite our
protests and promises to indulge in it no longer, so as to gain freedom for our life's work.

One thinks, perhaps first of all, of Alfred Perlès, his companion
at Villa Seurat and in Clichy, a literary roustabout, who wrote the
first book about Miller while the two exchanged long letters that
became little books contemporaneously. There were others, dozens
of them in those fantastic Bohemian days in Paris, immortalized in
Tropic of Cancer and later autobiographies published as fiction, for
Miller proves constantly that all art is self-portrayal in one's various
settings.

Miller clearly had a genius for friendship. He attracted people
who wanted to help him. Sometimes these friendships deteriorated
and died or were interrupted. Even the intense Anaïs Nin relationship was upset for a time through the indiscretion of another friend
and healed, it seems, through Roger Bloom, the prisoner who was
close to both of them.

One might ask what there was in Miller that called for these
attachments, sometimes formed quickly and surviving for long periods, through geographical separations and misadventures. The
friendships were chiefly with men, and were more sustained than
his marriages and love affairs. Did he find his creative calling in-
sufficient, or was it, more likely, nourished on such rich and varied
associations? There must have been something in me, as in the
others, a kind of image or reality that struck some sort of spark, or
an alarm, in a creative spirit who was octopus-like in his grasp of
everything that came near him.

Our friendship endures without the intensity of its first years. We continue to write, to see each other, to think of mutual concerns. We communicate telepathically. I suspect that I have meaning in the life of one of the great original personalities of our age. Certainly, he has meaning in my life, giving a sense of completeness to my sometimes wayward spirit.

Chicago, Illinois   Elmer Gertz
18 August 1977

Index

Abbington School Dist. v.
  Schempp, 235n
Abrams, Harry, 75, 76n2
Absolute Collective, The, 96
Adult Education Council, 143,
  144, 191–92, 193, 212, 267
Air-Conditioned Nightmare, The,
  xii, 76n
Alexander the Great, 257, 280, 286,
  287
Alexandria Quartet, The, 201
Algren, Nelson, 69
Allen, Steve, 128, 186, 279, 294,
  295, 310, 311
Aller Retour New York, xi, 55,
  56n3
American Bar Association, 236
American Civil Liberties Union,
  148, 266n2, 305
American Jewish Congress, 98
American Library Association,
  241–42
American Nazi Party, 22, 27
Aristophanes, 195, 200
Art Institute of Chicago, 227, 229,
  233, 236, 261, 272, 288, 290
Ashkenazi, Max (Usher Cohen),
  207, 209

Baez, Joan, 194
Baldwin, James, 77

Ball, Frank, 16, 18n
Bantam Books, Inc. v. Joseph A.
  Sullivan, 165
Barrault, Jean-Louis, 274
Bates, Herbert Ernest, 203, 203n3
"Ben Reitman's Tale," 35n3, 35n4
Bess, Donovan, 71n1
Big Sur, xii, xiii, xv, 2, 18, 25, 28,
  29, 30, 31, 32n4, 35, 45, 55, 90,
  146, 147, 150, 154, 156, 165, 166,
  167, 212, 218, 264, 284
Birge, Vincent, 35, 36n2, 55
"Bizarre Fellowship," 32, 33
Black, Justice Hugo L., 74, 76, 93,
  94, 96, 98, 106, 108, 115, 316
"Black Laws of Illinois," 283
Blau, Edmund, 275, 277, 280, 285
Bloom, Roger, 42, 71, 72, 73, 75,
  83, 85, 103–15 passim; 119, 122,
  126, 127, 128, 132, 192, 193, 215,
  219, 231, 240, 252, 253, 269, 270,
  271, 274, 309, 326, 332, 334
Booth, Audrey Jane, 81, 85n1, 177
Bradley, Van Allen, 163
Brassai, Halasz, 76, 77n, 126, 270
Breit, Harvey, 77
Brennan, Justice William, 115,
  116n3, 136, 164, 315, 316
Bruce, Lenny, 155, 156, 305
Bryan, Judge Frederick van Pelt,
  29, 29n1